Church Courts and the People in Seventeenth-Century England

Church Courts and the People in Seventeenth-Century England

Ecclesiastical justice in peril at Winchester, Worcester and Wells

Andrew Thomson

First published in 2022 by
UCL Press
University College London
Gower Street
London WC1E 6BT

Available to download free: www.uclpress.co.uk

Text © Author, 2022

The author has asserted their rights under the Copyright, Designs and Patents Act 1988 to be identified as the author of this work.

A CIP catalogue record for this book is available from The British Library.

Any third-party material in this book is not covered by the book's Creative Commons licence. Details of the copyright ownership and permitted use of third-party material is given in the image (or extract) credit lines. If you would like to reuse any third-party material not covered by the book's Creative Commons licence, you will need to obtain permission directly from the copyright owner.

This book is published under a Creative Commons Attribution-Non-Commercial 4.0 International licence (CC BY-NC 4.0), https://creativecommons.org/licenses/by-nc/4.0/. This licence allows you to share and adapt the work for non-commercial use providing attribution is made to the author and publisher (but not in any way that suggests that they endorse you or your use of the work) and any changes are indicated. Attribution should include the following information:

Thomson, A. 2022. *Church Courts and the People in Seventeenth-Century England: Ecclesiastical justice in peril at Winchester, Worcester and Wells*. London: UCL Press. https://doi.org/10.14324/111.9781800083134

Further details about Creative Commons licences are available at
http://creativecommons.org/licenses/

ISBN: 978-1-80008-315-8 (Hbk.)
ISBN: 978-1-80008-314-1 (Pbk.)
ISBN: 978-1-80008-313-4 (ePDF)
ISBN: 978-1-80008-316-5 (epub)
DOI: 10.14324/111.9781800083134

I humbly dedicate this book to Trevor Beeson and to the late James Atwell who have both served, in turn, as Dean of Winchester where I live and work. Both put the Church first, above everything else, both were scholars in their own right and both encouraged my strivings to describe and explain the diocese and cathedral of earlier times. I owe both men an enormous debt for the interest they took in my research: Trevor went so far as to write a compelling Foreword to the book and both could be relied on for support and encouragement in times of stress. If my labours fulfil any promise, to them belongs much of the credit.

Contents

List of abbreviations	viii
Foreword	x
Acknowledgements	xiii
Map	xv
Introduction	1
1 Fundamentals	14
2 The nature of Church discipline	46
3 The extent of Church discipline	84
4 Explaining the decline of the courts	117
5 The case of Worcester	160
6 The failure of reform	179
Appendices	
1 Diocesan chancellors	187
2 The nature of Church discipline	191
3 The extent of Church discipline	200
4 Explaining the decline of the courts	212
5 The case of Worcester	221
Bibliography	230
Index	240

Abbreviations

BCP	Book of Common Prayer
BIHR	*Bulletin of the Institute of Historical Research*
BL	British Library
Bodl	Bodleian Library, Oxford
CQR	*Church Quarterly Review*
CRS	Catholic Record Society
CSPD	*Calendar of State Papers Domestic*
DNB	*Dictionary of National Biography*
DWL	Dr Williams's Library
EHR	*English Historical Review*
ELJ	*Ecclesiastical Law Journal*
HARC	Herefordshire Archive and Records Centre
HMSO	Her Majesty's Stationery Office
HR	*Historical Research*
HRO	Hampshire Record Office
IHR	Institute of Historical Research
JEH	*Journal of Ecclesiastical History*
KHLC	Kent History and Library Centre
LMA	London Metropolitan Archives
LPL	Lambeth Palace Library

MH	*Midland History*
ODNB	*Oxford Dictionary of National Biography*
ORS	Oxford Record Society
P+P	*Past and Present*
SH	*Southern History*
SHLS	Somerset History and Library Service
SLSL	Southwark Local Studies Library
SRS	Somerset Record Society
TBGAS	*Transactions of Bristol and Gloucestershire Archaeological Society*
TBHS	*Transactions of the Baptist Historical Society*
TNA	The National Archives
TRHS	*Transactions of the Royal Historical Society*
VCH	*Victoria County History*
WRO	Worcestershire Record Office

Foreword

The Church's courts are not what they once were, and that must be a matter for gratitude for all who might otherwise have been caught up in their earlier proceedings and others who believe them to be inappropriate for a Christian community.

Although the Church's first theologian, St Paul, insisted that the Christian faith, distinctively, accorded priority of faith and love over law, it was inevitable that, once the Church had developed more than an informal structure, some form of regulation of its life would be required. The so-called Pastoral Epistles in the New Testament are indications of this.

Some of the early bishops produced for their churches handbooks encapsulating custom and tradition as they had received it, and by the third century local synods and councils were being convened to regulate more widely matters related to doctrine and church order. It was not until the early years of the fourth century, however, when the Church was considered significant enough to be embraced (some have always thought disastrously) by the Roman Empire, that its life was integrated with that of the state and its disciplines sustained by civil law.

This symphony of church and state survived, though less formally, after the end of the Roman Empire, and the Church continued to convene Councils to deal with matters of faith and order. At the same time it was developing a body of Canon Law that by the mediaeval period had reached a stage when an army of ecclesiastical jurists was needed for its interpretation.

Meanwhile, William the Conqueror entrusted the eleventh-century English Church with jurisdiction over matters deemed to be of its particular concern, involving faith and internal discipline, obviously, but also more widely in the realms of morality and family life, taking in wills, defamation, witchcraft and so on, hence the consistory courts. This separation of responsibility indicated no divorce between church and state. Indeed, until the early part of the nineteenth century the two remained inextricably linked. Spiritual and temporal combined to serve the needs of communities and individuals, God ruling over all.

The importance of Dr Andrew Thomson's scholarly research into the activities of the consistory courts of the Dioceses of Winchester, Worcester and Wells during the seventeenth century is therefore of more than specialist interest. It takes the reader into the social life of England at a time of radical and sometimes violent change. We are given insight into many aspects of community life in the towns and villages – how closely integrated they were, and how difficult it was to conceal misbehaviour, even of the minor sort. Church and state combined to protect a mutual interest in law and order in troubled times, while not insensitive to human frailty and the technical character of many offences. The use of law to compel reception of the sacraments also proved to be tricky territory.

This could not last. The Church's role, essentially a legacy from the mediaeval past, proved to be unacceptable in a society influenced by the Renaissance and Reformation. The first signs of this, clearly demonstrated in the pages that follow, came as the seventeenth century advanced and without constitutional change. The consistory courts were increasingly ignored by those cited to appear before them and their officials struggled with little success and reduced enthusiasm to enforce the verdicts. The Toleration Act of 1689 also reduced the scope for charges related to church attendance and reception of the sacraments.

It was not until the mid-nineteenth century, however, that constitutional changes in church–state relations brought reform to the consistory courts. This removed social offences from their jurisdiction and left the Church with an unwieldy body of ecclesiastical law which, combined with Canon Law, related to virtually every aspect of its own life (including the appropriate bedtime dress for a clergyman), underpinned by the law of the land.

The Church's resort to this law in an attempt to quell liturgical disorder at the end of the nineteenth century created, however, a widespread distaste for legal intrusion in spiritual matters, and in 1974 Parliament was happy to entrust to the Church responsibility for matters concerning its worship and doctrine.

The diocesan consistory courts survived mainly to handle applications from parishes for faculties to effect changes in church buildings and churchyards. These are normally uncontentious and can be granted without a hearing by the Registrar on behalf of the Chancellor. When there is a dispute, public proceedings before the Chancellor provide a useful opportunity for wider community involvement.

The courts have retained responsibility, however, for matters of clergy discipline involving 'conduct unbecoming in the office and work of a clerk in holy orders' (usually, but not always, alleged sexual misconduct) and pastoral neglect. These are obviously much more difficult to deal with satisfactorily and require the appointment of four assessors, two lay and two clerical, to ascertain the facts, with the Chancellor acting as the judge. They nearly always attract wide publicity unfavourable to the Church and this, together with the astronomical legal costs involved, is a considerable deterrent to action in the courts. Resort to them is rare, and settlement out of court is normal.

This suggests that the reforms foreshadowed by Dr Thomson's invaluable research into what now seems a far-distant world are not yet complete. There remains unfinished business.

Trevor Beeson
Dean Emeritus of Winchester

Acknowledgements

The process of research, analysing and interpreting is bound, in some ways at least, to be a unique operation, and as an ex-schoolmaster, never having been in a university department except as a student, and coming to this kind of work in retirement, it has certainly been so: buried in documents and glued to the computer for much of the time, in my case.

One can only conduct research of this nature, even so, with the help of others, and when I look back over the past 10 years and more spent on and off the book, I have had advice and support from many professionals and scholars – all of whom I count as friends – in generous measure. All the consistory court books are lodged in county record offices – Hampshire Record Office, Worcester Record Office and Somerset History and Library Service. I live in Winchester, within walking distance of Hampshire Record Office, and it has been a pleasure – and quite exciting – to visit, in addition to the record office at Winchester, the other repositories at Worcester, Taunton and elsewhere. Enthusiasm for the past is often plain to see among the inhabitants of such places, visits are usually elating and I remain grateful for the interest and support shown, most of the time, towards a stranger none too sure of the procedures in a new record office.

I have to single out two people from these record offices who have given me outstanding help and gone the extra hundred miles with me on the journey to finish the book. One is Mervyn Richens at Taunton. His support – critical for a speedy and successful operation – was unfailing, never oppressive and always supportive – and he was always ready to supply documents at instant notice, willing to advise on matters such as lighting and patient at all times. I can truly say I have never enjoyed more personal service, and I have been to many record offices. The other is David Rymill. He is an outstanding palaeographer, with an excellent command of Latin, and he and I have spent many hours in Hampshire Record Office and in my house, struggling to decipher the illegible and interpret the laconic.

He undertook, moreover, the challenge of reading the first draft of my text, which can only be a tribute to his powers of endurance.

I never cease to be amazed and grateful for help from other scholars. I turned in despair to my friend David Rollason on one occasion and to Ken Fincham on another and they, like David Rymill, took precious time out of their own pressing research to read early drafts and to suggest improvements. I offer my sincere thanks to Ralph Houlbrooke, a pioneer in the history of consistory courts, to whom I have turned more than once when puzzled or stuck; and to Colin Haydon for coming to my rescue, when COVID-19 reigned, with information about Warwickshire. I owe a huge debt to Martin Ingram, whom I met by chance and who took the time to read an earlier version of the book, advised me on its many failings, set me on a new course and entertained me royally into the bargain. Two friends and scholars, John Hare and Matt Reynolds, have time and time again shown interest and given valuable support and advice. I shall always be grateful to Andrew Foster, who gave so freely of his time and advised so wisely on the final stages of the book and, among other things, drew my attention to some of the most recent and relevant scholarship.

I should add that we did not always agree, these scholars and I, and some of our arguments generated much heat but, fortunately, also some light. Argument is the fun of History; and I, of course, must take the blame for errors of fact and interpretation.

I must also, on the more practical side, thank Ed Rollason for his expertise with cartography and, of course, Chris Penfold and the staff at UCL Press who have seen the book through its tortuous journey to publication.

Last but certainly not least, I have to thank Rosemary, my wife, who has been an ever-present help in trouble. I can say no more than *sine qua non*.

Map 1 The Dioceses of England and Wales 1535–43. Source: Valor Ecclesiasticus 1810–34, with modifications by Ed Rollason 2022.

Introduction

In 1642, the three kingdoms of England, Scotland and Ireland were blown apart for the next 20 years by 'a cyclonic shattering' of war, regicide and military dictatorship. The traditional institutions of government – King, Lords and Commons – were abolished and the Church of England with them in 'a great overturning ... of everything in England'.[1] The upheavals of the 1640s and 1650s had profound consequences for the Church and its courts. The Church had, up to this time, sought to control public morals and religious conformity and it possessed judicial machinery to enable it to attempt to enforce it rules and achieve its goals. Consistory courts were the 'regular' means of enforcement within the dioceses; but the Court of High Commission, a national body with occasional diocesan satellites and 'roving powers' of 'intervention', could override the regular, or ordinary, consistory courts.[2] An Act of 1641 abolished High Commission, and further, by removing oaths and punishments from the powers of bishops, the Act also weakened the consistory courts. An ordinance of 1646 next abolished the office of bishop, and with it went the consistory courts.[3] The latter were restored, but without the reserve support of High Commission and without the *ex officio* oath, in 1661, to operate under a dispensation that was traditional, if more moderate than the preceding regime of the 1630s.[4] Within 30 years the Glorious Revolution of 1688–9 took place, however, dethroning the Catholic James II and producing, together with constitutional changes, the Act of Toleration, which inevitably had very considerable implications for religion, the church courts and the enforceability of uniformity of belief and worship.

The Church was a truly pervasive – omnipresent – force in Early Modern England. It meant far more than worship on Sundays or the occasional baptism, wedding or funeral. As well as its roles in education, welfare and land ownership, it enjoyed spiritual jurisdiction over its flock and, through this, it claimed powers over anything to do with life and death, such as wills, and anything to do with truth and honour, such as libel or breach of promise. Conflicts over these matters were private disputes and were known as 'instance' cases. It was left to an individual to bring a case against another but it had to be through a church, or consistory, court. Other matters were seen as the immediate concern of the Church: moral conduct, from sex before marriage, adultery and fornication to bastardy and incest; religious observance, involving attendance at church, communion, baptism, Catholic recusancy and Protestant dissent; church finance, such as church rate and Easter offerings; and, of course, the obligations of churchwardens and the performance of the clergy themselves. The Church had rules – rubrics and canons – about all these matters. It was the prosecutor, and it used its courts to enforce the rules; these were known as 'office', or *ex officio*, cases. The Church was fully enmeshed in everyday life and its consistory courts lay, thus, at the very intersection of Church and people. It was there that Church and people fought over issues central to conscience and to standards of behaviour.

The consistory court in each of the dioceses dealt with both types of work, instance and office, but in separate sessions. Although instance procedures were more elaborate, officials more numerous and, consequently, business more lengthy, it was the office, or disciplinary, work of the church courts which was of greater importance.[5] This book will concentrate on the *ex officio* work of the church courts of three dioceses – Winchester, Worcester and Wells – in the Southern Province of the Church of England during the seventeenth century. A searchlight will be played on the disciplinary work of the consistory courts to establish how they hoped to shape social and religious behaviour in the communities, how far they achieved success and why they failed. The book is an attempt, ultimately, to assess, in general terms, the wider impact of the Church on society during a century of extreme turbulence.

Important research has been carried out on the church courts over the last 50 years. The studies by Ronald Marchant, Ralph Houlbrooke and Martin Ingram have, between them, examined the courts of York and Norwich, Norwich and Winchester, and also Salisbury in the sixteenth and early seventeenth centuries. Jean Potter has examined the courts of the Diocese of Canterbury in the seventeenth century but largely before 1640. Evan Davies concentrates on those of Chichester and Worcester between the Restoration of 1660 and the Revolution of 1688–9, while Martin Jones compares the performance of the courts of Oxford and Peterborough in the years immediately before and immediately after the Interregnum.

William Marshall, William Jacob, Donald Spaeth, Anne Tarver and Barry Till take the subject into the eighteenth century, Till giving an overview mainly of the northern courts, Marshall examining the courts of Oxford and Hereford, Spaeth those of Wiltshire, Tarver that of Lichfield and Jacob ranging widely from 'Cumberland to Bristol and from Pembrokeshire to Norfolk'.[6] A recent synthesis by Brian Outhwaite outlines the rise and fall of the church courts from the Reformation to the nineteenth century.[7]

A number of sociological studies have, more recently, drawn on church court records to examine a range of seventeenth-century communities – Eric Carlson on Cambridgeshire; Geoffrey Quaife on Somerset; Marjorie McIntosh on Havering; Keith Wrightson and David Levine on Terling; and Faramerz Dabhoiwala, Laura Gowing and Peter Laslett nationally. They have, between them, raised issues of the 'class' status of the people summoned and the value of compurgation for settling guilt or innocence. Their chief import for this study of church discipline has been to stress the complementary role of more informal pressures – of clergy, churchwardens, family and even gossipers – on behaviour in seventeenth-century communities.

There is very little with which this study would wish to take issue among the latter group and, in truth, their real focus is different: surveys of communities in their entirety and not a close inspection of church court activity. Occasionally it has been necessary to disturb the consensus: to question the findings of Laslett and Wrightson about bastardy; to contrast the claims of Quaife about compurgation; and to concur with the critics of Gowing about double standards in the treatment of men and women.

There is general agreement among the 'primary' group about the nature or focus of church discipline in the seventeenth century: prosecutions were mainly about morals and religion, with the balance lying more towards morals than religion before the cataclysm of the 1640s; pursuit of moral cases continued, though accompanied by a surge of religious prosecutions from time to time, in the years after the Restoration; and from the 1690s and into the eighteenth century the case load of the church courts was almost exclusively 'moral'.[8] While the results of this study concur, for the most part, with this pattern, detailed analysis of prosecutions at Winchester, Worcester and Wells, the three consistory courts at the heart of this research, reveals some differences. Before the upheavals of the 1640s, Wells fits the 'template', but there was a greater balance between morals and religion at Worcester, while at Winchester religion was dominant. After the upheavals, the 'charge sheets' diverged more sharply: Wells pursued morals, Winchester religion, while at Worcester there seems to have been a division, with regular sessions of the

INTRODUCTION   3

court concentrating on morals and the more occasional visitation proceedings concentrating on religious conformity.[9] By the 1690s, however, Worcester, the only diocese of the three with apparently complete extant church court records for that time, had 'come into line' with national developments, including religious toleration, to focus mainly on morals.

There is real division among the 'primary' historians about the extent of ecclesiastical control. Potter, Tarver, Jacob and Davies believe, *mutatis mutandis*, that the courts survived and even flourished after the Restoration and into the eighteenth century, while Houlbrooke, Ingram, Jones, Marshall, Outhwaite, Spaeth and Till take the view that the *ex officio* court business suffered contraction and decline in the later seventeenth and early eighteenth centuries. Caseloads of the three dioceses of this study point decisively towards decline, even extinction in the case of Winchester by the 1680s, and while the court at Worcester was still a live instrument in the 1690s, its activities were very much shrunken and curtailed. Numbers summoned to the court, their attendance at court and the completion of business in all three dioceses show a relentless decline and underline the diminishing extent of the Church's control over its flock in disciplinary, or *ex officio*, business.

As for reasons for the decline, the court books of Winchester, Worcester and Wells reveal much about reliance by the courts on defective evidence, the class imbalance and the problems with penance. Many failings of the courts have been described and explained before. There is nothing new about 'class', for example, or the problems of penance; but they cannot be ignored and are in fact essential to the narrative. Other writers on these subjects have, moreover, disagreed among themselves. Christopher Hill was a major critic, wholly condemning the church courts and all their works, while Martin Ingram has struck a more generous and sympathetic note, particularly in the matters of compurgation and penance. The flexibility – and mercy – of the church court officials have been acknowledged in this account, but it has to be said that the courts of Winchester, Worcester and Wells do not emerge, on the whole, from the terse entries in court books as sympathetic, reconciling bodies, and the shortcomings in their operation have been stressed here. This study does more than merely confirm the failings of the courts or pile on further examples: it attempts to give its own assessment of the importance or otherwise of these features.

Explanations for the decline have to range more widely than the legal records of the three consistory courts and here this study has to rely, though critically, on the conclusions and suggestions of others. Major societal issues arise at this point – concerning changes in thinking and practice towards religious divergence or morals in the seventeenth and early eighteenth centuries – and these are very difficult to assess. It is still possible at least to question trends such as the reduction of bastardy in the course of the seventeenth century, and it is necessary to navigate, moreover, contradictory interpretations of changing social attitudes at that time. Christopher Hill and David Cressy posit the introduction of new social freedoms by the explosion of sects in the turmoil of the 1650s. Faramerz Dabhoiwala charts the changes in attitudes more thoroughly but, at the same time, shows that such change was not 'exponential' and that conservative groups, albeit transient, emerged which sought to reverse attitudes and behaviour in moral (and possibly religious) matters in the 1690s and into the early eighteenth century. These subjects require much further investigation, beyond the remit of this survey, but attempts have been made to synthesise recent interpretations.

The seventeenth was an acutely turbulent century, as has already been observed, and 'politics' cannot be left out of the explanation for the decline of the church courts. The English Civil Wars, the Interregnum and the Protectorate in the middle of the century, together with the Glorious Revolution towards the end of the century, were decisive. They were, in turn, the product of profound religious and social changes, and the overriding concern of the politicians – the King, his ministers, and members of Parliament – together with the propertied classes was security. Social discontent and religious conflict were the key sources of trouble and revolt and 'the establishment' turned more and more to the secular courts with their greater powers of punishment. The church courts declined in consequence. This explanation, again not original, is fully developed in the course of this study and is identified as the main reason for the decline of the ecclesiastical legal machine.

This study has other original and distinctive features. No other study runs from the 1610s to the 1690s. It treats clergy, churchwardens and the people separately to reveal more sharply the 'condition' of each group. It distinguishes charges from guilt to overcome apparent confusion of the two by other historians and to establish more exactly the proportions of 'proven' wrongdoers in the communities. It questions apparently prevailing views on the pluralism of chancellors, for example, and the role of compurgation. It is, above all, relentlessly focused throughout on three questions. What was the nature of its control? What was its extent? How best can changes be explained? The real punch of the study must lie in the exposure of a truly malfunctioning disciplinary machine: attendance was appalling, business was contracting and the very existence of the courts and church control were in peril by the end of the century.

Sources

'Strikingly repulsive' is how no less an authority than Geoffrey Elton describes the act books of the church courts.[10] 'Only young scholars ... physically strong and possessed of sound indigestion are advised to tackle these materials', he continued.[11]

This study will rely on the 'challenging' archives of the dioceses of Winchester, Worcester and Wells. All three possess good 'runs' of episcopal *ex officio* court books and it is this which really determined the choice of dioceses and the parameters – in terms of dates – for this study. For Winchester, it is true, hardly anything survives of episcopal consistory court activity in the Archdeaconry of Surrey before or after the Interregnum; for the Archdeaconry of Winchester, however, episcopal *ex officio* court books exist, with breaks, for the late 1610s to the early 1620s. The first surviving court book for the archdeaconry after the Restoration covers 1663 and contains proceedings in apparently voluminous but in fact disappointing detail, largely because of massive absence from court of the accused. The sequence continues through the 1670s and early 1680s, but so did the levels of absence, and the volume of business shrank to nothing by the middle of the 1680s.

Survival at Wells in the early years is much the same as Winchester's. There are detailed records, but with breaks, for the late 1610s and early 1620s, and the causes (or cases) for each of the three archdeaconries (Taunton, Bath and Wells) are in separate books. Wells is unique among the three dioceses for survival of documents from the 1630s, and books for Michaelmas terms 1633, 1637 and 1640 in the Archdeaconry of Taunton have been used to illuminate episcopal activity during the time of Archbishop Laud.[12] Problems emerge at the Restoration. Only fragments of episcopal *ex officio* business survive, with cases from all three archdeaconries mixed together in the records; but enough could be salvaged concerning the Archdeaconry of Taunton, though it meant departing from Michaelmas terms and piecing together loose sheets for Hilary term 1663. There is a return to something resembling order by the 1670s, although activities in all three archdeaconries are combined in the same book – reflecting contraction of business, no doubt – and once again prosecutions of people from the Archdeaconry of Taunton can be identified and analysed.

That leaves Worcester, where the diocese and its one archdeaconry were coterminous and, although no books survive for the archidiaconal court, it probably has the best surviving episcopal consistory court records of the three dioceses. There is a complete run of *ex officio* proceedings covering all eight deaneries from 1610 to 1618; and, after a huge gap, records, though thinner, resume in the early 1660s. The 1670s and early 1680s are more problematic. The *ex officio* court books for most of the 1670s and early 1680s continue to record, rather briefly, routine business, session by session. Confusion arises because of interruptions – 'inhibitions' – of entries concerning routine business in the consistory court books by details of separate triennial visitation proceedings. This is so in the court book of 1676–82 used for this study, which also includes the triennial visitations of 1676, 1679 and 1682. The visitation proceedings take the form of presentments with additional notes to many of them, though by no means all, which clearly indicate subsequent prosecutions of many of the accused in court.[13] None of the visitation records gives the place or places of the visitation and what happened, if anything, at the visitation itself, and the precise relationship of these visitation records with the regular proceedings of the court is not at all clear. The later events recorded in the additional notes must have taken place afterwards in the consistory court but how far they were kept separate from ordinary proceedings and how far they may have reduced the volume of the ordinary proceedings is not clear. The other dioceses, Winchester and Wells, do not have these 'dual' records – and nor does Worcester before or after the 1670s and 1680s. The 'routine' sessions of 1675, 1678 and 1680, years without visitations, have therefore been used to ensure more likely comparability with the other dioceses, but several of the visitations have been analysed as well and reference frequently made to them.

Surviving court books dictate a survey from the 1610s or early 1620s to the late 1670s or early 1680s. After the 1680s *ex officio* court books shrink or disappear at Winchester and Wells. At Winchester the last office book comes to an end in 1684, and while there is evidence of the issue of excommunications, absolutions and penances in the 1690s for matters such as fornication – a staple of office prosecutions – either the original case cannot be traced or a case is clearly marked '*promoto*', which was a private prosecution and one not begun, though pursued in the church court, by the ecclesiastical authorities.[14] A stream of court books continues at Winchester into the nineteenth century but they appear to contain only instance and promoted cases. While it is difficult to accept the sudden and total disappearance of *ex officio* business from the Diocese of Winchester, all documentary evidence has vanished. Matters were less abrupt at Wells, where the books show a gradual contraction of operations: first, by the 1670s, office cases from all three archdeaconries are combined in one book; and next, by the late 1690s, all types of cases (office, promoted and instance) from all three archdeaconries are combined in one book.[15] For Wells and Winchester, a study of the 1610s/1620s and the 1670s/1680s is the only practical course. This does have the advantage, however, of bringing into sharper focus a comparison of the state of the consistory courts 20 or so years before and after the Wars and Interregnum and of measuring the effects of the upheaval on the ecclesiastical legal system.

Worcester is, again, different for having a complete *ex officio* court book covering *ex officio* prosecutions at the end of the century. It covers the 1690s/early 1700s, a total of 15 years, in 238 folios, its counterpart for the 1610s five years in 444 folios. It is certainly thinner but clear and systematic.[16] This makes it possible to compare, for this diocese at least, the state of consistory court operations over the century as a whole.

The chief points arising from this summary of available documentation are the excellent, though not always continuous, series of books for the 1610s and early 1620s in all three dioceses; the existence of good books for the 1630s at Wells but none for Worcester or Winchester; the piecemeal nature of documents for Wells at the Restoration; the usable if shrunken books for the 1670s and 1680s; the overlap of 'regular' and 'visitation' records at Worcester in the 1670s and early 1680s; and the survival, unique among the three dioceses, of a book of *ex officio* proceedings at Worcester for the 1690s.

Methods

Survival of documents determines the basic construct of this study: a comparison of the *ex officio* performance of church courts of the 1610s/1620s with the same courts in the 1670s/1680s forming the bulk of the survey, and a concluding comparison of the consistory court at Worcester over the century as a whole. It would have been particularly desirable – fascinating – to compare the work of the courts in the late 1630s and early 1640s with the 1610s and the 1660s but, of the three dioceses, there are gaps in the records of proceedings at Winchester of 38 years from 1625 to 1663 and at Worcester of 43 years from 1618 to 1661 and only Wells has court books for the 1630s and early 1640s. Church court proceedings ceased, moreover, from 1646 to 1660. There are therefore limits to comparisons of the 1630s and 1640s with either what came before or after; and comparisons of church discipline in the Interregnum with the Restoration are ruled out entirely. The Restoration meant, among other things, restoration of the church courts, but it took some time to legislate their revival and more time to begin operations. 'System' emerged at Worcester by October 1661, but the first surviving disciplinary proceedings for Winchester only begin in 1663, while at Wells documentation is very scrappy until the early 1670s and Hilary term 1663 is the earliest point at which, by piecing fragments together, anything resembling coherence could be achieved.

Analysis of the 1630s and the 1660s is therefore doomed for this study at least. There may be an advantage, however, in concentrating on the 1610s/1620s and the 1670s/1680s. The 1630s, the time of Laud and the Long Parliament, were far from normal years; the same can be said for the political uncertainties of the late 1650s and early 1660s. Such extremes – from the interventionist Archbishop Laud to the rusty and creaking legal machine of the first months and years of the Restoration – could, by themselves, have produced misleading comparisons and even something of an optical illusion.[17] The 1610s and 1670s, 20 or 30 years before and after the turmoil, military and political, when matters were (relatively) more settled, may thus be surer standpoints from which to assess episcopal discipline. The political revolution, the wars, the regicide and the wave of radical sects were, of course, still at the centre: a massive – disruptive and decisive – series of events with wide-ranging effects, not least for church discipline and the fate of the church courts, but its effects are perhaps best seen from a distance. The essence of this study, then, has to be a comparison of the 1610s and 1620s with the 1670s and 1680s. How much had church discipline changed between the 1610s and the 1670s? How much was it the same or different in its nature and extent?

This is a selective study. It relies on sampling. Analysis has been confined, in the first place, to one archdeaconry in each of the three dioceses. Wells had three archdeaconries – Wells, Bath and Taunton – but Worcester had only one archdeaconry and Winchester has viable court documents for only one of its two archdeaconries. Investigation has been confined to the activities of the episcopal consistory court in the archdeaconries of Taunton (Wells), Worcester (coterminous with the diocese) and Winchester (as Surrey has only fragmentary surviving records). It was evident from a cursory check of surviving (episcopal) consistory court records in the archdeaconries of Surrey, Bath and Wells that types of case and trends over time were much the same as in the three archdeaconries chosen for this study. They record the same kind of activity over and over again and the only change would have been, obviously, to the numbers of people summoned or, to give another example, the figures for fornication, but not to typicality or to trends over the century. Populations, though not exactly the same, were not dissimilar and overall a rough comparability has been achieved.[18]

No attempt has been made to trace individual cases from start to finish; indeed, because of gaps in the runs of books, that would not have been possible. The method has been, rather, to rely on 'snapshots' at particular – and sometimes critical – points in the seventeenth century. Proceedings in the Michaelmas term for three separate years in each of the three archdeaconries have been analysed: 1613, 1614 and 1615 for the Archdeaconry of Worcester; 1619, 1621 and 1623 for the Archdeaconry of Winchester; and 1618, 1621 and 1624 for the Archdeaconry of Taunton (Wells). It was not possible, mainly because of gaps, to choose identical years, but all the books used have been drawn from the last dozen years or so of the reign of James I. Michaelmas term 1661 for Worcester and 1663 for Winchester, the earliest court books in both cases after 1660, together with Hilary term 1663 for Wells, have been examined in the same way for 'state of play' at the Restoration. The investigation continues with proceedings during Michaelmas term at Winchester in 1678, 1680 and 1681; at Worcester in 1675, 1678 and 1680; and at Wells in 1671, 1673 and 1675. These are the 'restoration' years of Charles II, before the disastrous but brief reign of James II and the Glorious Revolution of 1688–9 which changed the religious and social landscape of the nation.

Eager critics will find fault with this approach: indeed, Evan Davies explicitly condemns research by sampling.[19] Davies confined his study to two dioceses between 1660 and 1689. This is a survey of three dioceses, over a century of sittings, with entries running into hundreds and thousands.[20] Michaelmas was usually the longest term and concentration on it, if only on grounds of manageability, was therefore felt to be justified. Checks with other terms have been made and, just as with the archdeaconries, the results – different numbers but similarity over types and trends – were much the same.

Use of one term, the same term every time, may raise questions about distortion in one particular way: the incidence of communion prosecutions. The key occasion for receiving was at Easter, and while it would be natural to expect a large increase in prosecutions of absentee communicants during Easter and Trinity terms, much depended on the visitation cycle.[21] Visitations by the bishop, provoking prosecutions, took place in Winchester, for example, mainly in September,[22] and this most likely explains the much larger numbers of communion prosecutions at Michaelmas than during the other terms.[23]

The survival of an excellent court book, covering proceedings at Worcester in the 1690s, makes possible a wider-ranging comparison of consistory operations, extending over the whole century, for this diocese at least. Manageability and the desirability of avoiding unnecessary duplication have meant some selectivity, again, and 'interrogation' has been confined to three of the eight deaneries. Evesham, Pershore and Kidderminster are thoroughly representative and seven whole years, in all four law terms, from 1611 to 1618 and from 1690 to 1697, have been analysed. The results, which broadly concur with trends already established for the 1610s to the 1680s, must surely lay to rest doubts about methodology or about conclusions based only on Michaelmas terms. Toleration in 1689 had, moreover, a major impact thereafter on church discipline. The opportunity was too good to miss and the resulting comparison provides a fitting – and decisive – 'coda' to this enterprise.

The intention behind this study of three consistory courts is to reach some definite conclusions about the impact of the Church on society by the late 1690s and early 1700s after a century of tumult and turmoil. This is an ambitious undertaking and hopes of a complete answer would be far too high for a study of this kind. Newton's remark about standing on the shoulders of giants comes to mind at this point and, though an overworked metaphor, it is highly relevant to this survey. The performance of three consistory courts lies at the heart of the survey but conclusions have to be set in context to assess the effect or impact of the courts on the communities they were supposed to oversee. Providing the statistics – of attendance at court, for example – is one thing; but the state of society, its morals and religion in particular, are much larger questions. The study is not without originality and, for example, exploits the often neglected recusancy rolls; but it relies heavily for context on the work of others: Whiteman's population figures, Lyon Turner's indulgence certificates, Watts's dissenter statistics, Laslett's bastardy projections and McCall and Coleby's borough and quarter session prosecutions of religious 'refuseniks'.

Referring to the activities of magistrates in quarter sessions – and to judges in assizes, for that matter – acts as a reminder that the consistory courts were not the only source of moral and religious discipline in the seventeenth century. The consistory courts were nominally under the control of the bishop but, in addition, every archdeacon had his own court within his archdeaconry, operating side by side with the episcopal court and working in much the same way. There were, in addition to the official spiritual and secular agencies, the much less visible but extremely important influences of constables and churchwardens, not to mention pressures within families and from friends neighbours and people living locally. Most of this was informal, of course, 'off the record' and difficult to substantiate. Examination of parallel archidiaconal and episcopal courts would at least have made possible a much more complete survey of the role of the Church. Loss of records makes this impossible for the archdeaconries of Worcester or Winchester but comparisons have been made, where appropriate, with the one surviving archidiaconal book of the Archdeacon of Taunton and with Brinkworth's examination of the activities of the archdeacon's court in the Diocese of Oxford.[24]

Discussion of the secular courts provides not only 'context' but also the key for identifying the real cause of the decline of the church courts. The secular courts began to 'encroach' more and more on the remit of the church courts. Legislation – parliamentary statutes – increasingly allowed prosecutions for bastardy in the secular courts as well as for failure to attend church, and therein, with the steady transfer of business from spiritual to secular courts, lies the real explanation for the downfall of the entire ecclesiastical disciplinary apparatus.

The primary focus of this study has to be episcopal – what the bishop, his courts and his agents did or did not do – not the activities of alternative jurisdictions or even the archdeacons' courts. It exploits to the full surviving episcopal court books and, while accepting its limitations, it does at least provide a thorough account of the bishop's regime within three dioceses of the Southern Province. It should be seen, as with the studies of boroughs by McCall and Coleby, the evidence furnished by Lyon Turner and Watts and the more sociological studies from Laslett onwards, as a contribution to the ultimate understanding of society in seventeenth-century England.

Notes

1 Haller, *Liberty and Reformation*, p. xiv; Hill, *World Turned Upside Down*, p. 12.

2 See Cross and Livingstone, *Oxford Dictionary of the Christian Church*.

3 17 CI c.11 ('abolition' of the courts, 1641); Firth and Rait, *Acts and Ordinances*, vol. 1, p. 879 (abolition of bishops and 'Episcopal Jurisdiction', 1646); Potter, quoting Shaw, gives 1643 but this was just a bill, and Outhwaite is right to link the courts to the fate of the bishops but wrong to state that bishops were abolished in 1643; both Jones and Outhwaite are imprecise to imply specific abolition of consistory courts in 1646 (Potter, 'Canterbury', p. 174; Shaw, *English Church*, vol. 1, pp. 120–1; Outhwaite, *Ecclesiastical Courts*, p. 78; Jones, 'Oxford and Peterborough', pp. 29–31).

4 13 CII c.12.

5 Manning, *Religion and Society*, p. 20.

6 Jacob, *Lay People*, p. 5.

7 For details and other research referred to in this Introduction, see Bibliography.

8 Only Davies and Jones concentrate exclusively on *ex officio* activity, but the others either have complete sections or much to say about cases of this kind. Two have applied a particular rather than a general focus to their work – Davies on religious conformity, and Ingram on morality or 'sex' – but they, like the others, cover the range of relevant office cases.

9 See the next section, 'Sources'.

10 For details, see the list of sources in the Bibliography.

11 Elton, *England*, pp. 104–5.

12 For Winchester, a court book of rather indeterminate proceedings against churchwardens 1636–8 survives at HRO, C1/36; at Worcester books contain a scatter of *promoto* prosecutions among a host of instance cases, e.g. WRO, 794 011 2513, 16 + 17 (1636–8, 1638–9).

13 The court books in question are WRO, 794 011 2722 1, Book 30 (routine session 1675); 794 011 2722 2, Book 32 (routine sessions 1678, 1680 and the visitations 1676, 1679 and 1682); see Davies, 'Religious Uniformity', pp. 75–6.

14 HRO, C1/45 (the last office cases), C13/1 (excommunications), C14/ 1–2 (absolutions), C12/1 (penance).

15 SHLS, D/D/ca/350 (office cases from all three archdeaconries by 1671–3), D/D/ca/368 (office, promoted, instance cases from all three archdeaconries combined by 1697–8).

16 WRO, 802 2760 (1613–18); 807 093 2724, Book 38 (1690–1705).

17 I owe this thought to Dr Andrew Foster.

18 See the section 'Population' in Chapter 1.

19 Davies, 'Religious Uniformity', p. 9.

20 An example, to give some idea of scale, is the *ex officio* court book for 1613–18 WRO, 802 2760 with 444 folios (nearly 900 pages).

21 Canon 21, 1604, required communion three times a year, of which one had to be Easter (see e.g. Bray, *Anglican Canons*, p. 291).

22 Episcopal visitations at Winchester were mainly in September, according to the records, and occasionally August and October (HRO, 21M65 B1/etc.); at Wells, consignation books imply June or July (SHLS, D/D/vc 79, f. 20r, July 1620; D/D/vc 86, no folios, June 1634); at Worcester references to visitations give either no date, just the year (e.g. '1667', 794 011 2513 20, Book 26, f. 59r) or various months, e.g. October 1676, October 1679, May 1682 (794 011 2722 2, Book 32, ff. 1r, 112r, 209r); and the date of Stillingfleet's charge to his clergy is September 1690 (Stillingfleet, *Bishop of Worcester's Charge*).

23 This issue is explored further in the discussion of religious charges in the section 'Communion' in Chapter 2.

24 SHLS, DD/SAS/C795/TN/26, *ex officio*, 1623–4, also transcribed by Jenkins (*Archdeacon of Taunton*); later surviving archdeacons' *ex officio* books cover the archdeaconry of Wells (D/D/ca/363, 1686–98; D/D/ca/370, 1698–1708); also, for the Diocese of Oxford, Brinkworth, *Archdeacon's Court*.

1
Fundamentals

The dioceses and their courts

A study of the consistory courts of Winchester, Worcester and Wells must begin with an outline of the structure of the three dioceses, their populations and, more specifically, the system of courts within the dioceses, the law they administered, their procedures and their officials. These are the background factors – the essential preliminaries – necessary for an understanding of the context and workings of the episcopal consistory courts in the three dioceses.

Structure of the three dioceses

Winchester, Worcester and Wells were three important dioceses lying in the south-east, the Midlands and the south-west of the Southern Province. The Diocese of Winchester stretched in the seventeenth century from the south bank of the Thames to the Channel Islands, but it mainly comprised the modern counties of Surrey and Hampshire which then took in the Isle of Wight. The diocese was divided into two archdeaconries, Winchester (Hampshire and the Isle of Wight) and Surrey. In the Archdeaconry of Winchester – the part of the diocese relevant to this study – there were 10 deaneries and, in round figures, some 315 parishes across the deaneries. For Worcester, diocese and archdeaconry were coterminous and under them lay eight deaneries and a total of about 250 parishes. The Diocese of Bath and Wells at that time possessed three archdeaconries – Bath, Wells and Taunton – and this examination will concentrate on Taunton, where there were between 140 and 160 parishes.[1]

Populations

'Population' is central when attempting to consider the Church's impact on society. The proportions of people summoned to the consistory court, for example, the proportions responding (and attending) and the proportions found guilty must be critical for assessing the extensiveness and severity – or the laxity – of the disciplinary machinery; and this must, in turn, depend on knowledge of the figures.

There was no official national census until the early nineteenth century and Anne Whiteman's calculations based on the Compton Census appear to offer the most convenient and reliable figures currently available. She offers plenty of cautions about trust in, and interpretation of, the figures but they are currently the best available. The Diocese of Winchester had, according to her estimates, an adult population, in round figures, of 93,700 in 1603 and 151,000 in 1676; Wells, meanwhile, had 84,200 in 1603 and 145,500 in 1676. Populations in those two dioceses rose considerably, on the basis of these estimates, over the course of the seventeenth century: Winchester by some 61 per cent and Wells by nearly 73 per cent. Worcester's population, on the other hand, may have been 56,800 in 1603 but it seems to have fallen by as much as 23 per cent to 43,450 by 1676.[2]

Winchester had the largest population, insofar as we can trust the figures, whether in 1603 or 1676; Wells, just a little smaller than Winchester, was next; and Worcester had the smallest and, what is more, is the only one of the three dioceses which appears to have suffered decline, although Whiteman acknowledges that estimates for this diocese are particularly questionable.[3]

Populations in the three archdeaconries (Winchester, Worcester and Taunton), although even more difficult to be certain about, are the ones of true importance for this survey and therefore some attempt at estimates is necessary. Worcester is the simplest because the diocese and archdeaconry were coterminous and the diocesan estimates – 56,800 in 1603 and 43,450 in 1676 – still apply. Winchester had two archdeaconries, Winchester and Surrey, with, again in round figures, the former possessing some 57,700 inhabitants and the latter 33,600 in 1603. The populations had risen in both archdeaconries by 1676, the Archdeaconry of Winchester's to about 68,200 and Surrey's (which included Southwark) to nearly 75,000, representing an increase of 18 per cent for Winchester and, in the case of Surrey, over 120 per cent.[4] Wells is the most difficult to estimate: of the three archdeaconries, Wells (archdeaconry) had the most parishes, fairly closely followed by Taunton, with Bath very much the smallest. With a diocesan population of some 84,000 in 1603 and 145,500 in 1676, this suggests, by admittedly arbitrary calculations, 35,000 for Wells, 30,000 for Taunton and 19,000 for Bath in 1603, and 60,000, 50,000 and 35,000 respectively in 1676 – a rise of some 66 per cent in Taunton.

The key figures for comparisons of consistory court performance which emerge for all these estimates are, with all due caution, for the Archdeaconry of Winchester 57,700 in 1603 and 68,200 in 1676; for the Archdeaconry of Taunton 30,000 in 1603 and 50,000 in 1676; and for Worcester 56,800 in 1603 and 43,450 in 1676. These represent rises in the course of the seventeenth century for Winchester of some 18 per cent and for Taunton of 66 per cent. Only in the diocese and archdeaconry of Worcester, where in some respects the figures are most questionable, might there have been a fall in population from 56,800 to 43,450 – a decrease of more than 23 per cent, or nearly a quarter.

System of diocesan courts

In both provinces, northern and southern, of the Church of England there were courts to enforce the canons and rubrics of the Church.[5] Every diocese within each of the provinces possessed a court for the bishop – the consistory court – and one for each of his archdeacons. The Court of Arches determined appeals from these courts in the Province of Canterbury, and Chancery performed the same service in the Province of York. Appeals might have arisen from time to time in instance business (private disputes) but it should be said that appeals in *ex officio* cases – the subject of this study – were extremely rare and none has been found among the three consistory courts of this study.

Those were the essentials of the ecclesiastical legal structure in the seventeenth century, but there were inevitably considerable differences of detail within the 26 dioceses and even within the three dioceses at the centre of this account. The system was at its simplest and clearest, again, in the Diocese of Worcester. There would, presumably, have been, with a bishop and one archdeacon, two sets of visitations and two courts.[6] Winchester had the two tiers of discipline, with visitations and courts overseen by its two archdeacons and with parallel machinery under the bishop.[7] The episcopal consistory court itself was divided, its sittings at Winchester concentrating on business from the Winchester Archdeaconry and parallel 'mobile' sittings either at Southwark, Guildford or Ewell for business arising in Surrey. The diocesan chancellor presided over the consistory court at Winchester and one and the same chancellor, now entitled 'commissary', presided over the court in Surrey, though surrogates or deputies usually took his place in both courts.[8] The system at Wells, with three archdeaconries – Taunton, Bath and Wells – was even more complex. Each of the archdeacons of Taunton and Wells held his own visitations, as at Worcester and Winchester, and had his own court.

Cases arising from the episcopal visitations of Wells and Taunton were dealt with by the consistory court but in separate divisions or sessions before the Interregnum, and in combined sessions from the Restoration. Bath was 'unique': the archdeacon had no court and all cases from Bath went to the episcopal court at Wells before and after the Interregnum and were dealt with in the Wells division.[9]

Nor is the 'division of labour' between the two levels of courts (episcopal and archidiaconal) absolutely clear. The importance of the case, or of the people involved, may occasionally have determined the choice of court. The case of Richard Green and his wife of Upton Snodbury (Worcester), for example, was transferred from the archdeacon's court to the bishop's in 1691. Incest (the charge) would probably not, by itself, have caused the switch, but the case also involved another diocese, an attorney at law and his clerk and a large sum of money.[10] Ralph Houlbrooke's distinction – lesser cases to the archdeacon's court, major cases to the episcopal court – probably has some validity in that type of case.[11] There was likely to have been, moreover, a certain amount of rivalry between the two types of court and certainly complaints about delay and expense arose if cases moved from one court to the other.[12] Otherwise, the episcopal consistory court heard cases arising from problems presented by churchwardens at episcopal visitations or reported to it by the apparitors (agents of the court), while those arising at archidiaconal visitations were dealt with by the archdeacon or his representatives in his court.[13] This would be irrespective of 'importance'. Certainly, a comparison of episcopal court books with a surviving archidiaconal book suggests that business, if not 'identical' in the two types of court, was much the same.[14]

This attempt to outline the legal structure in just three dioceses of the Church of England illustrates the complexity of the issues and must serve as a warning against assumptions about uniform practice within the two provinces.

Law

The basis of an *ex officio* court case, on which all proceedings turned, was the charge – an allegation of some deed or activity – which the Church considered to be an offence against its laws and, ultimately, the law of God. The major concerns of the Church are clear from the range of presentments (lists of charges) of churchwardens and from prosecutions in the consistory court. Immoral activities – sex before marriage, fornication, adultery, marriage irregularities (banns, licences and 'clandestine' unions), bastardy, harbouring and incest – were the staple business of the court and formed one clear category of offence. Religious commitment was another. Neglecting to attend church, failure to receive communion, work and play on the Sabbath in time of divine service, irregularities with baptism, dissent and recusancy (refusal to attend church) all fall under this category. A third concern centred on finance and, in particular, refusal to pay church rate. Clerical misdemeanour formed another distinct group of transgressions, shortcomings of churchwardens yet another. Clergy could be pursued over the usual matters ranging from non-residence, failure to wear the surplice, conduct of clandestine marriages, administrative breaches (usually neglect of the registers) and dilapidations, together with occasional sex and drink charges, to the rarer issue of simony. Churchwardens were most likely to face prosecution over repairs to buildings, provision and maintenance of fittings and ornaments, failure to present and more administrative irregularities such as failure to purchase Bibles, prayer books and registers.

These were the main subjects of prosecutions in the dioceses of Winchester, Worcester and Wells in the seventeenth century and, except for clerical cases which the bishop would have dealt with, the court to which cases went would depend on where the complaint, or presentment, was laid, the archdeacon's visitation or the bishop's.

Charges must all have had a basis in law and this can in fact be traced to ecclesiastical documents. Foremost were the canons of the Church, particularly those of 1604,[15] and rubrics in the Book of Common Prayer (1559 and 1662). The greatest digest and ultimate source of law was *Provinciale*, a collection of canons and constitutions of the Church assembled by William Lyndwood, together with his own comments and interpretations, in the fifteenth century.[16] Lyndwood was, incidentally, sometime prebendary of Wells, and Robert Sharrock, his most famous editor, was a rector, a canon and, for a few months in 1684, Archdeacon of Winchester.[17]

Visitation articles – the questionnaires about conditions in the parishes compiled by bishops which churchwardens were supposed to complete and produce in the form of presentments at the time of visitations – sometimes link questions to the source or authority to ensure legal backing. A few of Lake's articles for his triennial visitation of Wells in 1626 mention statutes and canons. Morley's articles for his triennial at Winchester in 1674 include far more comprehensive annotations in the margins which call in aid a wide range of sources. These are most frequently the canons, and to a lesser extent rubrics in the Book of Common Prayer, together with statutes and injunctions from Edward I to Henry VIII, Edward VI, Elizabeth I and Charles II, and, ultimately, Lyndwood.[18] These sources were undoubtedly the *fons et origo* of all *ex officio* prosecutions in the consistory courts. Edward Stillingfleet's charge to his clergy before his primary visitation in 1690, drawing a parallel with the origins of common law (custom and practice hallowed by time), postulates, in a similar vein, the existence of 'a Common Law Ecclesiastical'.[19]

This study is based as closely as possible on practice as it emerges or is presented in surviving consistory court books, and it is interesting to highlight some of the references to law during proceedings. There are references to the legal basis for prosecutions, both general and specific, in court books of all three dioceses before and after the mid-seventeenth-century upheavals. To take the book for Winchester, covering Michaelmas term 1623, the wife of Thomas Barling of Sparsholt was accused of 'keeping company with Richard Symes the elder contrarye to Gods ordinances';[20] Samuel Marshatt (or Marshall), rector of Botley, accused of a gamut of offences to do with the surplice, numbers of services and the condition of the churchyard, was ordered to comply 'according to the Lawes of this Realme'; Thomas Fuller, 'perpetual curate' of Upton Grey, was ordered to wear the surplice 'according to the laws of this land'; and Thomas Wayte of Kings Worthy was required to attend church *'jux(ta) statuta'* (according to the statutes).[21] Thomas Haughton, rector of Ipsley/Feckenham, was taken to task similarly *'juxta exegen(tiam) juris'* (according to the requirements of the law) by the consistory court at Worcester in 1691.[22]

There are frequent references to 'the canons' or 'the canons and constitutions' of the Church. Three offenders were required to attend church under these pronouncements at Winchester in 1663, and the formula is particularly noticeable in the court at Worcester, whether in the case of Bartholomew Smith in 1615 or Thomas Phillips, at the other end of this comparison, in 1682, while in 1695 Henry Prosser was accused, also at Worcester, of serving his cure without a licence 'notwithstanding his Ma(jes)ty's late Injunctions' and, a second entry continues, for teaching without a licence 'against the Laws Canons and Constitutions Ecclesiastical'.[23] At least one specific link was made – to Canon 121 – in a case involving competing archidiaconal and episcopal jurisdictions at Winchester in 1621.[24]

Ex officio procedures

Episcopal visitations, or assemblies of bishop, clergy and churchwardens,[25] were held every year at Winchester, but in other dioceses, including Worcester and Wells, visitations were triennial.[26] The course of business at visitations may have varied as well. The canons of the Church laid down the procedure, to some extent, for visitations. The bishop or chancellor – in practice usually a deputy – was required, according to Canon 119, to issue articles to all churchwardens. These were sets of questions about the state of the buildings, clergy and parishioners (their morals, church attendance and participation in communion, for example, in the case of parishioners). Canon 116 required churchwardens to produce their answers – lists of potential offenders – in the form of presentments at the visitation. These proceedings may at first seem at odds as there would not have been 'time sufficient' for the churchwardens to receive the articles and produce answers at the same visitation. Possibly the bishop's questions were sent to churchwardens beforehand so they could reply at visitation; alternatively they may have received the articles at the visitation and returned their answers afterwards. The canons were probably not conceived to provide comprehensive, step-by-step procedural instructions, however, and can be reconciled if Canon 119 is seen as applying to the new churchwardens and Canon 116 to the preceding year's churchwardens. Both transactions could then have taken place at the same time; but, with 26 or 27 dioceses, over several hundred years, controlled by countless bishops and managed by a swarm of officials, practice was bound to vary from visitation to visitation.[27] The relevant visitation books for Winchester, Worcester and Wells remain, needless to say, silent on the matter.

The court books of Worcester and Wells run continuously (allowing for losses of books) from year to year even though visitations were triennial in those dioceses. It must have been the case, therefore, that apparitors, incumbents and parishioners, as well as churchwardens, were free to bring a charge to the notice of the court officials at any time, not just every third year, and there is evidence of this happening at both Wells and Worcester. John Salkelite, vicar of Wellington (Wells), presented more than one parishioner for moral or religious offences during Michaelmas term 1618; Robert Reason, rector of Otterhampton (Wells), did so in 1621; and there is specific reference to presentments 'by the minister' at the court at Worcester before and after the mid-century upheavals.[28] The phrases '*ex ore Thomae Crosse*' and '*ex ore Maria(e) Morlie*' (at the wish or request of Crosse or Morlie), both at Wells in 1637, strongly imply parishioner 'intervention', while at Worcester in 1617 John Cullumbyne, vicar of Kidderminster, seems to have been brought to book '*per querelam parochianorum*' (through a complaint from the parishioners).[29]

It was the duty of clerks to prepare the books, probably under the scrutiny of a notary public. Much was apparently done in advance. They composed the introduction to each daily session according to a 'formula' which is surprisingly similar in the three dioceses: sometimes even the time of day but usually the date and place ('plenary' sessions usually in the cathedral or the location if *in camera*), together with the name of the judge, his qualifications and position (vicar general, official principal or surrogate) and the name of the notary public responsible for recording proceedings. Then, deanery by deanery, each case was listed: parish, name of the accused person or persons, the charge (not necessarily with complete detail) and a summary of the steps taken so far in the case. These were usually the date of the 'citation' (summons to attend) together with the name of the apparitor (or messenger) who had served it. All this, or some of it, was written in advance and, on the day itself, the notary public or one of his scribes would record events and outcomes. The notes were usually terse and in a mixture of abbreviated Latin and English; if detailed, however, they would sometimes overrun the space allowed and would be squeezed into a convenient space to the side or at the bottom or somewhere else on the page, or, indeed, another page.

A citation was a summons for the accused to attend the consistory court and presumably contained the charge he, she or they had to answer.[30] If the accused could not be found, a further order, called a *viis et modis*, was issued. What exactly was in the order is by no means clear from surviving court books of the three archdeaconries, but presumably apparitors were to search for the accused and, if they could not find him or her, to fix the writ, ordering attendance at court, to the accused person's church or house; '*valvae*', '*foris*' and '*ostium*' (different words for door or entrance) all appear in this connexion. An apparitor fixed a *viis et modis* writ to 'the door of the customary habitation' of Michael Bride at Bretforton (Worcester) in May 1614; at the other end of the timescale, in October 1671, his counterpart at Wells attached an order concerning Frances Goodland to the church at Swell.[31] The Winchester court book of 1663 is full of such writs which were fixed to the house or church of the accused, and it was sometimes said that they had been 'cited in spirit'. Attaching notices to houses and churches remained common practice at Winchester in the 1670s.[32]

If the accused had been found and served with the citation but failed to attend the session, the judge could 'reserve' (adjourn or carry over) the case to a later session. For persistent absence the judge could order excommunication. A distinction was drawn between 'lesser' and 'greater' excommunication: the former was suspension from church and deprived the offender of baptism, communion and burial according to the rites of the Church of England; the latter banned all contact with society, which apparently included employment (taking it or giving it), trade, access to the courts (secular and religious) and even wills.[33]

The court books for the three dioceses of this study record excommunication for the most part without detail in various abbreviated and semi-legible forms, and there is hardly any indication of the two distinct levels (the strictly religious exclusions and the wider secular isolations) which are supposed to have applied. Occasionally the judge ordered a specific suspension from entering church, and several examples can be found in Worcester's early seventeenth-century books.[34] A plain instruction to excommunicate is presumed, otherwise, to have been the 'religious' ban – on attendance, communion and burial – and these were the most frequent excommunication orders by far. 'Aggravation' implies intensification – another turn of the screw – and, in the context of excommunication, that the more severe form, with secular as well as spiritual penalties, was being invoked. The word aggravation appears in court books for Wells in the 1630s,[35] but as an 'intensifier' it is more clearly observed in proceedings at Worcester. In 1615 a husband and wife were summoned 'for standing excommunicate'; they did not appear and matters were 'intensified' by the issue of an *aggravatio*. In 1679–80, likewise, eight men, accused between them of Quakerism, dissent, absence from church and bastardy, failed to attend court and they first suffered excommunication and then 'aggravation'.[36]

Excommunication is variously described, somewhat carelessly, as a 'sanction', a 'censure', a 'penalty' and a 'punishment' and there is clearly overlap with some of these terms.[37] The key ones are sanction and punishment. Both involved infliction of pain or loss, and an excommunication could be issued in some cases as a sanction or in other cases as a punishment. Ralph Houlbrooke and Martin Ingram are clearest that it was both a sanction and a punishment: a sanction to enforce obedience to or compliance with the court, and at other times an automatic punishment for certain convictions.[38]

The commonest use of excommunication was as a sanction to enforce attendance at court or to produce a certificate to prove, for example, attendance at church, participation in communion or performance of penance. Excommunication in either of these circumstances could not have been a punishment: either accused people had not been tried because they had not come to court or they had already been sentenced ('punished') by an order to undergo penance but had failed, so far, to produce a certificate.

Excommunication could also be a punishment. Scattered through Gibson's *Codex* are numerous transgressions which carried automatic application of excommunication. The wearing of armour by a clergyman

CHURCH COURTS AND THE PEOPLE IN SEVENTEENTH-CENTURY ENGLAND

was one of the more 'out of the ordinary' misdemeanours punishable by excommunication. The most common misdeeds seem, from surviving records of the three archdeaconries, to have been associating with an excommunicate, involvement in a clandestine marriage and fighting or brawling in the church or churchyard (for which, according to Gibson, transgressors could have an ear cut off if they used a weapon).[39] Two men were summoned to court for marrying (women) outside the diocese and lacking ready proof of banns or licence; another man was summoned for attending a dubious marriage ceremony; and two couples – one a curate, no less, and his bride – were summoned for being married in the wrong church.[40] Two women on one occasion and three men on another were summoned for fighting and brawling in church; and a couple was summoned for associating with an excommunicate.[41] In all these cases the accused were present in court so absence was not the issue. All suffered excommunication as a punishment, presumably in its more moderate form.

It is not very likely that the Church would have wished such a state – exclusion at either level – to continue indefinitely. The overriding role of the Church was to remedy, reconcile and reunite Church and sinner. Excommunication, even when appearing as a punishment, was most likely seen as an interim measure to allow time for reflection and with the expectation of a 'settlement' at some time in the future.

For accused people who appeared, proceedings were 'summary'. There were no legal figures such as proctors representing the parties, no exchange of lengthy depositions, no assessment of damages and the like. Those usually long and sometimes serpentine proceedings belonged to the instance (private disputes) division of the consistory court. *Ex officio* proceedings before the Wars and Interregnum might have begun with the imposition of an oath, the infamous *ex officio* oath, but this was abolished in the revolution of 1640–1 and its abolition was confirmed at the Restoration.[42] The essence of the business was an interchange between the judge and the accused. Accused people were formally charged by the judge and they would respond, either confessing or denying the misdemeanour and sometimes explaining the background reasons or excuse for the offence. Confession was the main determinant but, where there was doubt, the judge could order compurgation at a future hearing when the accused would have to produce several parishioners, not as witnesses to the 'crime' but to testify, as friend or neighbour, to their character and likelihood of innocence. Compurgation appears to have been abolished when the church courts were revived in 1661 but, whether legal or not, examples of its use after 1660 can be found in the court books of all three archdeaconries.[43] The accused

FUNDAMENTALS   23

occasionally volunteered testimony from their incumbent and the judge could order enquiries through churchwardens or require them to produce a certificate from the incumbent.

People innocent of the charge were 'dismissed', but where guilt was established, the judge might dismiss them with a warning, usually against conduct likely to lead to an offence – often to a man against consorting privately with a particular woman – or, more positively, with an order to do something such as attend church, receive communion or pay church rate. For cases of immorality, where guilt had been established either by confession or by failure of compurgation, the judge would usually impose penance. Details are scant, and often 'according to the schedule' is the only comment in the books, but from the terse phrasing it would seem that the guilty person or persons had to confess in church on one or more Sundays during or after morning service either before the incumbent and churchwardens or before the whole congregation, more occasionally also in the marketplace before the general public, and they might have had to wear a white sheet. The guilty, to avoid such humiliation, would sometimes request commutation to a money payment, usually several pounds, to the cathedral, the local parish church or the poor. Either way, penitents – and indeed those who received an order to comply in some way – were, finally, required to produce a certificate from the local vicar or rector confirming compliance.

High Commission could impose fines and imprisonment, and there are examples of their use nationally and by 'satellite' commissioners locally in Winchester,[44] where there was a prison at Wolvesey (the bishop's palace). The consistory courts did not have either of these weapons in their armoury, however, and penalties such as fines and imprisonment, still more death, were beyond their reach. The bishop could make a formal request to the secular authorities for the imprisonment of a recalcitrant excommunicate. This procedure was known as a *significavit*: the bishop 'signified' his wish to a local official such as the sheriff of the county, who would then arrest and detain the excommunicate.[45] This power was rarely invoked, however. One instance, at least, has been discovered of the extraction of a bond by the Winchester Consistory Court in an attempt to make (Catholic) recusants in the Tichborne household comply with the law.[46]

Officials

The consistory court, whether of Winchester, Worcester or Wells, was run by a number of officers. Little more can be said about the routine officials. A registrar or actuary, usually of notary public status, was responsible for record keeping, preparing the act book for the next session of the court and entering notes of proceedings on the day. Each court would have had several apparitors – agents or messengers of the court – who mostly served citations (a summons to attend) and *viis et modis* orders (a kind of search warrant).

The chief officer or officers supporting the bishop in the administration of his diocese were the chancellor, the vicar general and the official principal. Numerous attempts have been made to disentangle these offices from each other, a 'knot' made all the more difficult to untie by the fact that very often all three posts were occupied by one man.[47]

It would seem that, as far as the beginnings of the office are traceable, the chancellor was originally keeper of the bishop's seal and, from that position, he became the man to whom the bishop would delegate duties within the diocese as he saw fit. When absent – at court, in the House of Lords or abroad, for example – the bishop would appoint a vicar general to manage affairs, often his chancellor: hence, in many dioceses, the two offices were merged. That left the bishop's consistory court, over which the bishop was required to appoint a legal figure, the official principal, to preside and sentence.

The outcome was that the official principal was confined to the work of the court, while the duties of the chancellor and vicar general were interchangeable and wider in range – institutions, visitations, deprivations, dispensations, probate, licences but not, apparently, ordinations and confirmations. All three posts could be held, however, by one and the same man.

The post of commissary also appears from time to time. His work could be judicial (the court) or administrative (conducting visitations). He was the bishop's representative who could reach a remote area or assume direct control of a body within the diocese. He was usually assigned a specific task, in a specific area, for a specific time, for example, presiding over a session of the archdeacon's court or conducting an episcopal visitation in place of the vicar general and the bishop.

The man meant to be in charge of each diocesan judicial system was the official principal, but all three terms – chancellor, vicar general and official principal – appear in the court books. It can be said with some certainty, from a study of the consistory court books and other documents, that in the Diocese of Winchester the title of chancellor was rarely used;[48] the same was true at Wells, with the notable exception of Henry Deane, who was consistently given the title 'chancellor' in Michaelmas term 1671;[49] but it was heavily used at Worcester after the Restoration, where Baldwyn was almost always referred to in this way. Vicar general appears frequently because the vicar general and the official principal were usually the same man and the clerk wrote both titles at the beginning of proceedings. It must be emphasised that there was some flexibility, certainly none too rigid a system, and that hope of finding a uniform scheme throughout the two provinces is probably doomed to disappointment.

Summary

Twenty-six dioceses, of different sizes and with different histories, were not likely to enjoy completely uniform legal structures. Each of the three dioceses of this study had an episcopal consistory court, but only at Worcester were matters straightforward; Winchester had 'mobile outposts' to deal with business heard in Surrey, while at Wells the court held separate sessions for cases from Taunton Archdeaconry on the one hand and from Wells and Bath combined on the other. The number of archidiaconal courts varied as well: one for Worcester, two for Winchester (one for each of its archdeaconries) and two for Wells (the Archdeacon of Bath had no court of his own). Otherwise, and essentially, the three dioceses were much the same: they had a two-tier structure with episcopal courts at the top and archidiaconal courts below them, with the same officialdom – chancellor, surrogates, notary public and apparitors (often the same people) – administering, through the same summary procedures, the same body of law.

Furthermore, despite shifts and developments over the century affecting all three dioceses, at first glance there was little truly striking change. The legal machine looked much the same, with the two tiers of court and the same officialdom, at both ends of the century. Upon closer inspection, however, there was some change. The notorious *ex officio* oath and compurgation were outlawed from 1661 (although examples of the use of the latter can be found as late as the 1690s). All other features – the charge, question and answer, reliance on confession, inquiry and arbitration – stayed the same.

The same is true of the law: canons, rubrics and Lyndwood were its main sources throughout the century in all three dioceses. There were important changes, however, to the other source, the statutes, most noticeably with the 'Clarendon Code' of the 1660s, involving renewed insistence on attendance at church, receiving communion, using the prayer book and wearing the surplice, together with the outlawing of conventicles.[50] This legislation may help to explain a greater emphasis on these matters at Worcester and Winchester, if not Wells, after the

Restoration.[51] It is much more likely, however, that the new laws accelerated the transfer of religious prosecutions from the consistory to the secular courts of magistrates in the 1660s. Both secular and 'spiritual' courts could enforce statute law but the authorities probably preferred the secular courts with their more severe penalties of fines or imprisonment.

The enactment of poor law legislation had much the same import for the church courts. Statutes such as the Acts of 1601 and 1662 threatened their jurisdiction over bastardy and sex outside marriage. These acts gave a boost to prosecutions for such alleged transgressions but most of the business went to the secular courts in the end.[52]

Although the original aim of this section was 'background', this investigation of structures and systems has anticipated some of the key concerns of this book. The transfer of religious and social prosecutions to the secular courts was a major reason for the contraction of ecclesiastical jurisdiction. The *ex officio* oath certainly and compurgation possibly were two reasons for hostility towards consistory court procedures. The church courts, losing business and lacking support, inevitably declined in consequence. All these matters will of course be explored more fully later in this study.

Diocesan chancellors and their deputies

Although the office of chancellor has been considered, this section will attempt to examine more closely the individuals who occupied the post.[53] Qualifications of diocesan chancellors were laid down in Canon 127 (1604): a minimum age of 26; learning in civil and ecclesiastical law at least to MA or LLB level; together with the oaths of supremacy and subscription to the *Thirty Nine Articles*.[54] This section will, first, try to gauge, from an assortment of biographical sources,[55] how far successive seventeenth-century chancellors of Winchester, Worcester and Wells measured up to these requirements. It will proceed to examine other aspects of their appointment, including experience, pluralism, appointments for life and attendance at court, insofar as they can be derived from the same or allied sources.

The suitability of these men, their strengths and weaknesses, will emerge in the course of this analysis, with inevitable implications for an estimate of the effectiveness of the church courts. They held the fate of the church courts in their hands. Their competence, energy and commitment would determine the regard in which the courts were held and ultimately the extent to which the ecclesiastical authorities were able to exercise control over society at large.

Chancellors

Age

All the chancellors of the three dioceses appear to have met canonical requirements. The age of one or two, such as John Baylie, Chancellor of Wells in the 1670s and 1680s, remains uncertain but all whose dates of birth have been established met the age requirement: Charles Morley at Winchester only narrowly – he would have been 26 or 27 when he assumed control in 1679 – while Christopher Helme, taking control of the court at Worcester aged 60, stood at the other extreme; the rest were in their 30s and 40s.

Education

As with age, so with educational qualifications: it was Morley, Chancellor of Winchester in the 1680s and 1690s, who, again, scraped by, though meeting the minimum requirement, with an LLB, while Baylie, Chancellor of Wells, began as LLB but apparently became LLD by February 1678.[56] The post usually involved higher qualifications in practice and certainly in these 'premier' dioceses. Baylie's predecessors at Wells – Duck, Peirce and Deane – were all LLD, and so were the two chancellors of Winchester between the 1590s and the 1670s, Thomas Ridley and Robert Mason, and, likewise, Morley's immediate predecessor after the Restoration, Mondeford Bramston. The chancellors of Worcester – Barnaby Gorche, Christopher Helme and James Littleton before the Interregnum and Timothy Baldwyn, who occupied the post from the Restoration until the 1690s – also possessed LLDs.

Experience

Experience ought to have had critical bearing on suitability for the post of chancellor – and in particular for work as official principal of an episcopal consistory court – yet there appears to be little discoverable information about the experience, if any, of James Littleton of Worcester or Henry Deane and John Baylie of Wells, and inference and suggestion sometimes have to take the place of certainty even with the others. The man with the least experience, on the face it, was, again, Charles Morley. He was raised, in his mid-20s, to the chancellorship of Winchester 'by the favour of his great Uncle, Dr Morley, Bishop thereof'.[57] Robert Mason's background must also remain questionable at the least: his only noteworthy achievement before his appointment as Chancellor of Winchester in 1628 was, apparently, to have been secretary to the Duke of Buckingham during the expedition to the Île de Ré the year before. Such an opportunity, presuming everything went well, ought to have offered insights into business and organisation which might have had wider applicability. Involvement in a calamity on the scale of the Île de Ré would, by the same token, surely have sunk the hopes of ordinary men. It would seem, however, that the duke's patronage still had sufficient hoist to haul Mason to an ecclesiastical chancellorship.

On somewhat surer footing, if we can trust the standard sources, were several other chancellors. Gorche (Worcester), Duck (Wells), Ridley (Winchester) and, possibly, Baldwyn (Worcester) had all had some experience of advocacy at Doctors Commons, Inner Temple and the Court of Arches. Ridley had combined the posts of official principal in the Archdeacon of Surrey's court and commissary (the bishop's representative) in the same archdeaconry for six years before becoming overall diocesan chancellor in 1596.[58] In the wider world, all four had held posts in education – Gorche as Master of Magdalene College Cambridge, Duck as Bursar of All Souls, Ridley as Provost of Eton and Baldwyn as Principal of Hart Hall – all of which may have meant something more than honorific elevation.[59] Ridley had, in addition, been MP for Wycombe in the 1580s, while Baldwyn had, apparently, in the late 1650s, held the rectory at Llandrillo, though whether as rector or impropriator is not clear (the words 'Sine cura' are ominous).[60]

That leaves Christopher Helme of Worcester before the Wars and Mondeford Bramston of Winchester and Edmund Peirce of Wells in the Restoration. Bramston's provenance, birth apart – he was the son of a Chief Justice of King's Bench – shared something with Ridley and the others, having had some legal experience as an advocate at Inner Temple from 1634 and as a Master in Chancery from 1660 before becoming, at the age of 46, Chancellor of the Diocese of Winchester in 1662. Helme arrived by a rather different route. He became Chancellor of Worcester at the age of 60, which may imply he was past his best, and, indeed, his tenure – 10 years – was one of the shortest. He had, however, spent years as a magistrate in Worcestershire, as rector of Bredon (within the diocese) and as Archdeacon of Derby (outside it);[61] thus, on top of his legal training, he may well have brought to the consistory court better insights than most about clergy, people and their parishes and, more directly relevant, he ought to have had detailed legal knowledge from his archidiaconal court. Peirce was, on the face of it, the most impressive candidate of all: he was Commissary to the Archdeacon of Suffolk, Judge at Admiralty and Proctor at Arches in the 1630s, advocate at Doctors Commons and Middle Temple in the 1640s, a Master of Requests and Advocate General in the royal army in the first Civil War. All these posts were directly relevant, if he performed the duties, to his appointment as Chancellor of Wells, among other posts, in the 1660s.[62]

Pluralism

The appointing process did not stop when these men gained one diocesan chancellorship. The accumulation of other posts, inside and outside the diocese, was another characteristic to be found among these diocesan chancellors, with implications for effectiveness in their work. Gorche, Chancellor of Worcester in the 1610s, combined this office with the onerous responsibilities of mastership of a Cambridge college and, for two or three years, the chancellorship of Exeter Diocese.[63] His successor, Christopher Helme, though divesting himself of his archdeaconry, probably retained his parish and the next man, James Littleton, was concurrently a Master in Chancery. There was much more pluralism, particularly before the Wars and Interregnum at Winchester and Wells. The careers of Ridley (Winchester) and Duck (Wells) fit between them much the same template, and Mason's (Winchester) was not too dissimilar. Duck and Ridley were both chancellors in other dioceses, both officials at Chancery, Requests and High Commission and both were MPs for short spells.[64] Mason, who followed Ridley at Winchester, held a clutch of legal posts – commissary (Surrey Archdeaconry), official principal in the archdeaconries of Surrey and Winchester and judge at the Admiralty and Requests, to which he added the chancellorship of Rochester after the Restoration.[65]

Baldwyn, Chancellor of Worcester from the 1660s to the 1690s, gave up the principalship of Hart Hall but continued the pluralist tradition with concurrent posts as a Master in Chancery and Chancellor of Hereford;[66] Peirce, a magistrate in several counties, a judge at Chancery and the Court of Arches and an MP, did so even more at Wells in the 1660s;[67] but his successors, Deane and Bayley, stuck, like good cobblers, to their 'last', though the latter was also 'Official' (principal) in at least one of the archidiaconal courts of Wells.[68] At Winchester, meanwhile, Mondeford Bramston became a Master of Requests and Commissary for Surrey – fairly modest by earlier standards – and Charles Morley, his successor, raised to diocesan heights by his great uncle's 'favour', was similarly content, or failed to add much else beyond some archidiaconal appointments within the diocese.[69]

30   CHURCH COURTS AND THE PEOPLE IN SEVENTEENTH-CENTURY ENGLAND

Appointment for life

Several other features about the officers give rise to comment about their effectiveness. One was the practice of appointment for life. Evidence for this usually lies in patents or similar documents concerning appointments of chancellors. No documentary proof has been found for Wells but appointment for life was certainly the case with two chancellors – Baldwyn and Price – of Worcester,[70] and with several chancellors – Mason, Bramston, Morley and Mews – of Winchester.[71] It seems likely therefore that the remaining chancellors of Winchester and Worcester and all the chancellors of Wells were given patents on the same – life – terms. Appointment for life ought to have meant freedom from threats and bribes and, thus, to have guaranteed judicial independence, but it also brought in its wake temptations at best to neglect business and, at worst, to commit abuse.

Attendance

Evidence of abuse or corruption by chancellors has not been found in any of the three dioceses of this study in spite of comment by Gilbert Burnet that the church courts were 'the most corrupt courts of the nation ... Oppressing the poor ... dilatory ... fraudulent',[72] but there are some spectacular examples in other dioceses.[73] The attendance of chancellors in court – or, rather, the lack of it – was, however, very much a feature of the three courts.

This survey is always at the mercy of document survival and there are gaps in the flow of books, blanks where the name of the judge should be and too many sessions without introductory statements at all. This is particularly so with the *ex officio* books of Worcester where introductions to sessions in the 1610s are strikingly terse, often giving no more than the date, and it has not proved possible therefore to say how frequently Barnaby Gorche, Christopher Helme or James Littleton took personal charge of the court. Timothy Baldwyn appeared in person once or twice most Michaelmas terms over his 35-year reign, even into the early 1690s. He sat more often than not in September, sometimes in October, never in November and December. He missed most of the sessions during these terms and relied on surrogates. He never sat in his last three years in post (1692–5) and his last appearance in court was in October 1692.[74] It was only at the turn of the century that his successor, John Price, brought a new, if conservative, vigour to the court at Worcester.[75]

Matters are much clearer at Wells than at Worcester in the 1610s, 1620s and 1630s. *Ex officio* business at Worcester under Baldwyn may, or may not, have 'run like clockwork',[76] but it really did so at Wells, with a weekly sitting, usually for 13 or 14 weeks of the Michaelmas term, together with additional, *in camera*, sessions from time to time. These show just how occasional were the appearances of Arthur Duck: three in Michaelmas term 1621 – his best year among the samples; one appearance each in 1618 and 1624; and he never appeared in the three specimen terms of the 1630s.[77] Information at the Restoration is too fragmentary for proper analysis, but *ex officio* records return for the early 1670s (apart from 1673) and these show that Henry Deane sat in all 12 sessions in Michaelmas term 1671 and all nine (the record appears to be incomplete) in Michaelmas term 1672.[78] The poor recording of sittings in 1673 may be explained by an interregnum between chancellors Deane and Baylie, but proceedings appear to have returned to 'normal' and, less like Deane and more like some of the other chancellors, Baylie managed six out of 10 appearances in 1674 and four out of 10 in 1675.[79]

Nothing can be said, similarly, in the case of Winchester, for want of books and information, about Robert Mason's attendance in the late 1620s or through the 1630s to the early 1660s. Consistory court books, though with many gaps and incomplete information, can be examined for his predecessor, Thomas Ridley, and his successor, Mondeford Bramston. It has been claimed that Ridley 'performed most of his duties in person'.[80] Surviving *ex officio* books show he was in court for three out of eight plenaries in Michaelmas term 1598, six out of six during Michaelmas term 1607 and five out of the five during Michaelmas term 1611. For over 50 plenary sessions, however, covering nearly 30 months, between October 1618 and July 1624, after his elevation to Canterbury, he never appeared at all.[81] Bramston never appeared once, leaving Thomas Colenett (surrogate) to conduct all 10 plenary sessions in the busy of Michaelmas term 1663, and from 1676 to 1679, his last three years, in all four Michaelmas terms, he spent a total of four days in full court.[82] Charles Morley, chancellor from 1679 to 1696, was just as bad, if not worse. Surviving *ex officio* court books cover, sporadically, 24 plenary sessions over a period of some 30 months between October 1680 and April 1683, and Morley does not seem to have taken his place in court as official principal once during that time. The *ex officio* court books come to an end thereabouts and it would seem that Winchester suffered the disappearance not only of its chancellor but also of the corrective work of the court itself from the mid-1680s.[83]

Ex officio work *in camera* might be thought to have been more complex and to have occupied more of the time of these eminent diocesan chancellors, but there is little justification in the court books for either assumption. For most *in camera* sessions either the presiding officer is not named, as is the case frequently at Worcester in the 1610s, or the sessions were usually left to surrogates, as at Winchester in 1623, Wells in 1624, Winchester in 1663 and Worcester in 1682.[84] Barnaby Gorche of Worcester sat for a case in April 1615 involving vexatious litigation by the rector of Evenlode against several Oxford colleges. How deeply Gorche was involved in the business and how far there was delegation in the preliminary investigating is not clear, and his role in court was confined to receiving the confession and ordering the rector to acknowledge his fault before the Masters and Doctors of the colleges concerned. Arthur Duck (Wells) sat in chambers in September 1621 in the case of Benjamin Pence. The entry does not record his offence and Duck's only actions were to impose the oath requiring the accused to answer faithfully and then to order an inquiry.[85] Mondeford Bramston (Winchester) heard two cases personally *in camera* in September 1663, one of incontinence, the other of bastardy; both turned on confession and the only matter at issue lay in fixing the terms of commutation. With the possible exception of Gorche and his litigious incumbent, there does not appear to have been anything requiring a great legal mind in these cases.

There remains the possibility that these chancellors, laden with responsibilities, chose to spend most time on the more complex – and more lucrative – instance proceedings of the three dioceses; however, examination of instance court books does not bear this out. Arthur Duck seems to have spent as little time on instance as on *ex officio* affairs during his quarter of a century and more as Chancellor of Wells. Court books show that he never took personal charge of instance business for more than half the instance sessions in the Michaelmas terms of the 1610s and early 1620s – most were worse – and by the 1630s, as with *ex officio* affairs, it is difficult to find him conducting any instance business at all.[86] It was rare to see his counterpart at Worcester, Barnaby Gorche, presiding over instance business, and Timothy Baldwyn's role in instance business at Worcester after the Restoration can only be described, at best, as spasmodic. He seems, from samplings of the record, to have followed much the same pattern as with *ex officio* proceedings, sitting once or twice but missing most of the sessions during Michaelmas terms.[87]

The two 'heavyweight' pluralist chancellors of Winchester were also just as sparing of their time for instance as for *ex officio* work. Ridley did preside over a few instance sessions in his earlier years – two out of 11 and one out of nine plenaries in Michaelmas terms of 1599 and 1607 – but none in the corresponding term of 1624,[88] while Bramston seems to have made no attempt to appear from the start (July 1662) and, continuing as he had begun, sat for four out of 93 plenary instance sessions over the last two and a half years of his chancellorship.[89]

It is, perhaps, not surprising, with all this in mind, to find that at least two of the chancellors of the three dioceses, Ridley and Duck, spent much time on scholarly publications, but it is surprising to learn of the existence of far more active chancellors at Chester, Lincoln, Exeter and York. This claim is based on signatures on paperwork arising from excommunications, significations and absolutions in those dioceses in the years of the Restoration.[90] Whether they matched this bureaucratic proclivity with attendance in court is not clear, but if they did, the different practices must serve as a warning that what prevailed in one diocese or archdeaconry did not necessarily prevail elsewhere.

Deputies

Personnel

The widespread practice of devolving day-to-day management of the court to surrogates or deputies follows from the pluralism and absence of officials principal. There can be little doubt that these men – surrogates, registrars, clerks – were 'most important' in the operation of the consistory courts but, as is so often the case with lesser figures, precise details about vital matters such as age, career and experience are, for the most part, 'difficult to trace'.[91]

The names of many of the deputies can at least be identified. This cannot be claimed with certainty for the consistory court of Worcester where, before the Interregnum and immediately after it, most of the entries are too brief to reveal anything but the deanery and the date. Parallel instance records show, however, that John Archbold, Joseph Hall and Ralph Willett were surrogates of Barnaby Gorche; Thomas Warmestry was one of James Littleton; and, if there was delegation in *ex officio* proceedings before the Wars and Interregnum, these men are likely, among others, to have supplied the service.[92] William Hawkins, William Harewell and, again, Thomas Warmestry were prominent surrogates at the beginning of the long reign of Timothy Baldwyn – their names appear in the relevant *ex officio* book[93]– and John Jephcott and Andrew Trebeck performed similarly in the parallel instance and *ex officio* proceedings of Baldwyn's last years in the early 1690s.[94]

The *ex officio* court books of the 1610s and 1620s for the Diocese of Wells show that Anthony Methwin and Robert Withers were regular surrogates of Arthur Duck;[95] and by the 1630s he seems to have relied more and more on a string of underlings – John Egglesfeild, William

Hunt, John Morley, Timothy Rivett and William Woodhouse among them – to take his place in court.[96] Under Peirce in the 1660s, Charles Thirlby and Thomas Holt seem to have been the main surrogates for *ex officio* proceedings, but others – Pottman, Standish and Lanfire, to name three – appear from time to time.[97] Deane appears to have been much more his own man, but with Bayley's succession to the chancellorship, Thirlby returned as a deputy and was joined, among others, by Robert Creighton, Joshua Lasher and Joseph Shallett.[98]

Surviving books show that *ex officio* proceedings of the consistory court at Winchester lay for most of the time in the hands of impressive-appearing surrogates. In the years 1618 to 1625, first Edward Wickham was Ridley's regular deputy, then Nicholas Darrell (who appears to have been willing to undertake a huge case load in his private chambers); and there was also more occasional assistance from Christopher Hearst, William Trussell and Francis Alexander.[99] There follows a break in the books (presumably lost for the 1630s and none, of course, from 1646 to 1660) and, when sessions resumed in the 1660s, Thomas Colenett served as almost the only surrogate to Mondeford Bramston well into the 1670s.[100] In the last years of *ex officio* proceedings, in the 1670s and early 1680s, as the court ran down, a string of deputies – George Bramston, Thomas Cheyny, Joshua Cooke, John Harris, William Payne, Robert Sharrock, David Standish and Peregrine Thistlewaite – took the place of chancellors Mondeford Bramston and Charles Morley.[101]

Qualifications

The surrogates of all three dioceses appear to have met, or even surpassed, the minimum qualifications for the post: an MA or LLB, or 'a grave minister, or a licensed public preacher'.[102] Of Worcester's surrogates, Hawkins and Harewell were MAs, while Hall, Archbold and Warmestry before the Civil Wars, and Jephcott after them, held doctorates (albeit of theology rather than of law).

Most of the surrogates at Wells before and after the Interregnum held MA degrees, but there were BDs (Egglesfeild, Holt and Methwin) and DDs such as Creighton and Rivett in both periods as well, and even a Bachelor of Music (William Hunt) in the 1630s.[103] There were the usual MAs in the Winchester Consistory Court – Trussell in the 1620s, Thistlewaite and Standish in the 1670s and 1680s – but the stalwarts of the early years – Wickham and Darrell – were DD and LLD respectively. Colenett, surrogate for Mondeford Bramston in the early 1660s, was LLB, and of the men of the 1680s, George Bramston was LLB (later LLD), William Payne DD and Robert Sharrock LLD.

Experience and pluralism

A recent scholar has made much of the control over church courts falling into the hands of lay officials.[104] Most surrogates in the three archdeaconries of this study had clerical origins. Many were parish priests. Archbold in the 1610s, Warmestry in the 1630s and Jephcott in the 1690s all served parishes in the Diocese of Worcester. All three also held cathedral prebends, Warmestry (a surrogate in the 1630s) was a dean and Hall (a surrogate in the 1610s) was both dean and archdeacon (and subsequently bishop twice over).[105] At Wells, likewise, from Methwin in the 1610s, Egglesfeild, Rivett and Woodhouse in the 1630s, Holt, Standish and Thirlby in the 1660s, Creighton and Shallett in the 1670s, to Lasher in the 1690s, all are described as 'clerk' in the consistory court books and were or had been parish priests. Wells was endowed with some 50 prebends and at least a dozen prebendaries appeared as surrogates in the consistory court over the century, of whom one, Thomas Holt in the 1660s, was both canon and (cathedral) chancellor, while Creighton was canon and precentor.[106] Two of these men, Thirlby and Rivett, were also archdeacons.[107] In the Winchester Diocese, it was much the same. Dayrell, Trussell and Alexander in the 1620s, Colenett in the 1660s, and Payne, Sharrock and Standish in the 1670s served parishes; several – Wickham, Darrell, Alexander, Sharrock and Payne – had canonries as well; and, in addition, Wickham, Dayrell and Sharrock were archdeacons.[108]

Jens Aklundh concentrates on chancellors and not their deputies. He paints a picture of conflict between bishops and chancellors to the extent of fisticuffs and brings together an impressive summary of some 60 sermons which make plain to their listeners both an animosity to lay administrators and a 'Pauline' vision of ecclesiastical justice in clerical hands.[109] While never doubting this, there is another side to church court operations in the seventeenth century and it must be fair to attempt a more balanced picture by drawing attention to the men – clergymen – who often performed the day-to-day duties in the courts. Their role was both to serve a great institution with rules and regulations about morals and religious observance and to meet the needs of ordinary people in the parishes. This might, in theory at least, have been a happy fusion of the needs – pastoral and disciplinary – of the Church. Few probably lived up to this ideal and high office was no guarantee of suitability, but most were more than workaday parish priests and there was certainly far more to Sharrock than Wood's famous comment, 'very knowing in vegetables',[110] might imply: he was an editor of Lyndwood's *Provinciale* and, as such, a scholar and lawyer of some distinction.

The effectiveness of the officialdom

Some of the preceding matters of discussion, in particular the pluralism and consequential absence of the chancellors, lead inevitably to consideration of the role of official principal and the effectiveness of the people holding the posts. The questions are whether their frequent absence mattered and whether pluralism can be justified.

There does not appear to be much decisive evidence either way and it is possible to present a favourable interpretation of their role. Much of the *ex officio* business was routine, not to say trivial: adultery of a lowly couple from an obscure village, attendance at church the second Sunday after Easter or even, in instance matters, a tithe dispute about sheaves of corn and numbers of piglets. Such cases required some local knowledge of custom and practice, no doubt, but did not turn on esoteric points of law. Deputies would be quite capable of conducting the business of a consistory court: exercising scrutiny of a case and issuing a judgment if and when any of the accused chose to make an appearance; or very often, in view of the massive absence of the summoned, merely to issue a *viis et modis* warrant or order an excommunication. Chancellors, men of distinction and eminence, would have been better employed in the London Courts of High Commission, Chancery and Requests. Their diocesan role may have been conceived as advisory – offering guidance on points of law – or administrative – organising the pattern of sessions and appointing suitable deputies – or even training them in the intricacies of the law or practice in the courts.

Most of the chancellors were men whose education and accumulation of posts were, on any reckoning, impressive. Arthur Duck of Wells in particular was an ecclesiastical lawyer of national distinction. He was a scholar, an author writing on Roman Civil Law and considered to be 'an excellent Civilian', 'one of the foremost civil lawyers of his age' and he was among 'the most active High Commissioners during the period'.[111] Clearly such men had the potential for advising, training and administering. Evan Davies has claimed that Timothy Baldwyn, Chancellor of Worcester, sat 'with clockwork regularity' every August and September and that, during his tenure, he trained 'an impressive cadre' of no less than 15 surrogates and 10 notaries public.[112] It is true that certainly September and possibly August were 'favourite' months for Baldwyn's visits. Baldwyn sat in court, moreover, with the bishop no less, accompanied by one or two other surrogates, on at least three occasions (one *ex officio* and two instance sessions) – a fascinating combination

FUNDAMENTALS **37**

which may well imply Baldwyn 'training' by example or discussion.[113] In general, however, sessions *ex officio* and instance, in August, if not September, were few. They usually amounted to one, occasionally two, quite exceptionally three and sometimes none at all.[114] Baldwyn was not always present, moreover, and there is no evidence in the court books of advice or guidance being given during these sittings.

Notes by clerks in court books are an unlikely source of illumination for that kind of thing and lack of evidence is not to exclude the possibility of training sessions. Notions of private training sessions, still less seminars, may seem somewhat fanciful, however, on the basis of surviving evidence; and, when the routine absence and pluralism of these great men are considered, they are not likely to have offered much practical assistance – other than how to delegate – to their subordinates. Organising sessions and appointing deputies are equally improbable for the same reasons and their role is likely to have been confined to occasional guidance and advice on a difficult point of law. The system ran otherwise on teams of dependable deputies.

The career and impact of Charles Morley at Winchester shows, however, that chancellors could still be important, if only in a negative sense, and pluralism was not always to blame for neglect. Morley was largely absent from court but he had few other appointments and his standing was weakened by his youth, modest qualifications and lack of experience. It was these shortcomings which are more likely to blame for the severe decline of *ex officio* proceedings at Winchester in the 1680s. His case may therefore prove the maxim: good chancellor, good court, bad chancellor, bad court.

In the light of evidence from the court books of Winchester, Worcester and Wells, it must be concluded, on the one hand, that there were some distinguished chancellors; that they had the potential to fulfil an important role; and that some of them may well have done so. On the other hand, it must also be concluded that there was far too much absence and far too little evidence of critical interventions by the chancellors of these dioceses; that their absence deprived the courts of weight and authority; that an inadequate and unsuitable chancellor could be disastrous; and that the wheels of the Church's legal machine only continued to turn through the faithful efforts of surrogates willing to mount the treadmill.

Bishops as presiding officers

A few bishops undertook some involvement in the consistory court.[115] None came anywhere near the involvement of the 'stakhanovite' Bishop Hooper of Gloucester in the 1550s.[116] The great Diocese of Winchester had a succession of famous bishops in the seventeenth century but none of them – Bilson, Andrewes and Morley among them – appears to have sat in the consistory court. Bilson, it is true, was active in the 'satellite' judicial commission which sat in the diocese from 1606–8 and pursued moral offenders and Puritans.[117] Andrewes and Morley were more typical in keeping their distance from the court. Andrewes immersed himself in preaching and writing, while Morley was modest enough to write to Sheldon, Archbishop of Canterbury, during an appeal from Jersey to Winchester, 'I dare not rely upon mine own Judgement … having soe little skill … in the Ecclesiastical Law', which, while commendable for its honesty, serves to underline episcopal shortcomings.[118]

Worcester likewise suffered a series of bishops – Parry in the 1610s, Blandford and Fleetwood in the 1670s – who did not make much of an impression as diocesans and certainly not in the regular sessions of the court. Thornborough, bishop in the 1620s and 1630s, was more 'vigorous' but, again, not in court.[119] It must be said, however, that there are records of extensive triennial visitations held faithfully under both of the two later bishops, Blandford and Fleetwood, whether they played an active part in them or not. Arthur Lake, Bishop of Bath and Wells 1616–26, was apparently 'energetic' and heard disciplinary cases but 'usually' in his palace and they are likely, thus, to have been small in number and concerning mostly errant clergy. Creighton and Mews followed in the 1670s: Creighton assumed office at 77 and only managed two years in post; Mews took a 'belligerent stance' towards dissenters, reflecting his character, no doubt, but whether in court or elsewhere is not made clear and it is likely to have been intermittent as his main interests were political and military.[120]

There were exceptions. William Peirs, Bishop of Bath and Wells 1632–70, took personal charge of *ex officio* cases, both plenary and *in camera*, sometimes with, sometimes without, assistants from time to time in the 1630s.[121] He continued in post for 10 years after the Restoration but only nominally and, by this time, in his 80s, he buried himself in retirement at Walthamstow. The best bishop of all, from the point of view of involvement in consistory courts, came at the end of the century. Edward Stillingfleet, Bishop of Worcester in the 1690s, frequently determined *ex officio* business with one or two surrogates, and 1693,

FUNDAMENTALS **39**

when he sat once a month between January and October, was a particularly 'interventionist' year.[122]

Avoidance of the court, with or without Morley's modesty, was apparently the preference of most of the bishops, together with their chancellors, and their consistory courts seem to have run, in the main, automatically under a series of deputies. At the very end of the seventeenth century, bishops Stillingfleet and Lloyd (Stillingfleet's successor) were of a quite different stamp.[123] Their active presence in court probably explains the court's survival at Worcester, albeit in reduced form, and the above average achievement with attendance and completion of business.

Summary of this section

It would seem, from surviving evidence, that the chancellors of the three dioceses largely conformed to canonical requirements. These were 'minimal' and covered basics such as age and technicalities such as subscription oaths. A more important requirement concerned qualifications, which were impressive in the case of most of the chancellors but which could be undermined, as at Winchester under the Morleys, by nepotism.

Experience was also impressive overall but all these virtues were more than offset by absence from court and therefore actual involvement in the administration of justice. The practice of accumulating posts made full and even regular attendance difficult and the custom of bestowing appointments for life worsened matters. Chancellors who were absent were not able to offer the courts the benefit of their wisdom, while appointments for life, justified as guaranteeing independence, encouraged the risks of ageing in post, of neglect and even of abuse within the profession.

The system was in fact saved and kept running by a bank of surrogates or deputies. Some of these men were less well qualified but they sat in court, applied justice (according to their lights) and ensured the survival of the ecclesiastical judicial system. Many of them were clergymen, at least knowledgeable about their respective dioceses and possibly sympathetic towards the plight of the people; one of them, Robert Sharrock of Winchester, was even more learned in the law than Thomas Ridley, Arthur Duck or Mondeford Bramston.

When the church courts hit truly turbulent waters in the middle years of the seventeenth century, however, the captains were missing and the bridge was manned by deputies who lacked the standing of their superiors. The shortcomings of officialdom were now exposed and were yet another factor which helps to explain the weakness and decline of the church courts in a time of trial.

Notes

1 Sources for calculations about numbers of parishes: for Winchester, Thomson, *Clergy of Winchester*, Appendix A, pp. 181–5; for Worcester, WRO, 802 2951, box 1 (1661), 802 2951, box 2 (1679); for Wells, D/D/vc 79 (1620), 86 (1634), 41 (1662), 48 (1695).

2 Whiteman, *Compton Census*, Appendix D, Table D/3, pp. c–ci; these are her diocesan totals and, while Wells had coterminous diocesan and county boundaries, the Diocese of Worcester took in part of Warwickshire, and Winchester combined Surrey and Hampshire (including the Isle of Wight).

3 Whiteman, *Compton Census*, pp. lxxiv, cii, 74, 171. Michael Watts gives different – higher – figures for the three counties in which the three dioceses lay: 125,000 (Hampshire), 200,000 (Somerset), 100,000 (Worcestershire); but these are some 40 years later in the early eighteenth century and, while the bishops' returns of 1676 concern adults, his estimates include everyone (Watts, *Dissenters*, p. 509).

4 Whiteman, *Compton Census*, pp. 74, 75.

5 There are numerous summaries of the legal structure, e.g. Bray, *Anglican Canons*, pp. xcii–xcvii, 906–10; Chapman, *Ecclesiastical Courts*, pp. 21–38; Houlbrooke, *Church Courts*, pp. 12–37; Ingram, *Church Courts*, pp. 35–41; Marchant, *Puritans and Church Courts*, pp. 8–9; Marchant, *Church under Law*, pp. 12–15, 38; Outhwaite, *Ecclesiastical Courts*, pp. 2–4; Till, *Church Courts*, pp. 9–15.

6 The existence of an archidiaconal court at Worcester is, without documents, an assumption based on practice at Winchester and Wells.

7 Without archidiaconal court books or a diocesan blueprint, the pattern has to be surmised from scattered churchwardens' accounts, e.g. HRO, 3M82W/PW1, f. 76r (St Peter Soke 1635–6) recording visitations of the vicar general and the archdeacon; LMA, P95/ALLI/45, (Wandsworth 1674–5, no pagination), bishops' and archdeacons' visitations. The survival of *ex officio* episcopal court books from the 1520s to the late seventeenth century is sufficient evidence of their existence; no documents survive for the archidiaconal courts but it is clear from surviving patents appointing archidiaconal officials principal that both archdeacons had their own regimes: in the 1630s, Robert Mason, official principal (OP) for both the Surrey and the Winchester archdeaconries (HRO, DC/B5/8, ff. 17r, 33r); in the 1670s, George Bramston OP Surrey and Charles Morley OP Winchester (DC/B5/11, ff. 51v, 69r).

8 These parallel episcopal consistory arrangements, with a commissary for Surrey, are derived from haphazard introductions in the few surviving court proceedings (LMA, DW/VB1, ff. 78r, 84r, 125r).

9 Humphery-Smith, *Phillimore Atlas*, 'Somerset/30'; borne out by surviving court books: before 1640, a series of episcopal court books for Taunton (e.g. SHLS, D/D/ca/207), likewise for Wells (e.g. D/D/ca/191), with Bath usually combined with Wells; after 1640, notable contraction and cases from Taunton, Wells and Bath are all in the same book (e.g. D/D/ca/350); as for archidiaconal recording, there is one surviving book for Taunton before 1640 (SHLS, D/D/SAS/C795/TN/26) and several for Wells after 1660 (e.g. D/D/ca/363).

10 WRO, 807 093 2724, Book 38, f. 111r.

11 Houlbrooke, *Church Courts*, p. 33.

12 Brinkworth, *Archdeacon's Court*, vol. 1, pp. vi–vii.

13 This distinction is implied in Canon 121 of 1604 (see e.g. Bray, *Anglican Canons*).

14 SHLS, D/D/ca/234 (an episcopal book, 1623); D/D/SAS/C795/TN/26, transcribed by Jenkins, *Archdeacon of Taunton*, especially pp. 21–33 (archidiaconal).

15 See Bray, *Anglican Canons*.

16 See Cheney, *Medieval Texts*, pp. 158, 160, 179, 181; *ODNB*.

17 Lyndwood, prebendary of Wells, 1419–33 (Horn, *Fasti 1300–1541*, vol. 8, p. 65); Sharrock, rector of e.g. Bishops Waltham (HRO, A1/33, p. 23), Canon and Archdeacon of Winchester (Horn, *Fasti 1541–1857*, vol. 3, pp. 86, 90, 95).

18 For the articles of Lake and Morley, see Bibliography (Printed Documents); Morley's 'source per article' annotations were apparently forestalled by Heylyn in 1640 (Fincham, *Visitation*, vol. 1, p. xvi).

19 Stillingfleet, *Bishop of Worcester's Charge*, p. 35.

20 HRO, C1/35, f. 10r (Barling).

21 HRO, C1/35, f. 56r (Marshatt); f. 29v (Fuller); f. 8r (Wayte).

22 WRO, 807 093 2724, Book 38, f. 109r (Haughton).
23 HRO, C1/37, 18/11/1663 (no folios); WRO, 802 2760, f. 235r (Smith); 794 011 2722 2, Book 32, f. 228v (Phillips); 807 093 2724, Book 38, ff. 120r, 120v (Prosser).
24 HRO, C1/34, f. 8v (Canon 121).
25 There are numerous summaries, e.g. Bray, *Anglican Canons*, pp. cviii–cxii; Brinkworth, *Archdeacon's Court*, vol. 1, pp. xi–xiii; Chapman, *Ecclesiastical Courts*, pp. 47–51; Hockaday, 'Gloucester', pp. 216–18, 238–46; Houlbrooke, *Church Courts*, pp. 38–54; Ingram, *Church Courts*, pp. 47–8, 51–4, 332–8, 341–5; Marchant, *Puritans and Church Courts*, pp. 5–7, 9; Marchant, *Church under Law*, pp. 4–6, 10, 137–9, 205, 220–31; Outhwaite, *Ecclesiastical Courts*, pp. 9–13; Owen, *Records of the Established Church*, p. 38.
26 At Winchester, visitation books are marked 'annualis' *passim* and some sequences are consecutive; at Worcester, visitation proceedings show a triennial sequence (WRO, 794.011 2722 2; 802 2951), as do 'Consignation Books' at Wells (e.g. D/D/vc/48).
27 Among modern authorities, circulation of articles before the visitation is possibly implied by e.g. Houlbrooke, *Church Courts*, p. 44; distribution at the visitation, e.g. Ingram, *Church Courts*, p. 45, Fincham, *Visitation Articles*, vol. 1, p. xiv; both versions e.g. Marchant, *Church under Law*, pp. 10, 115.
28 SHLS, D/D/ca/207, ff. 255r, 255v (Salkelite); D/D/ca/224, ff. 93r, 93v (Reason); WRO, 802 2760, ff. 112r, 311v; 794 011 2722 2, Book 32, f. 230v; 807 093 2724, Book 38, f. 110r.
29 SHLS, D/D/ca/313, f. 219r (Crosse and Morlie); WRO, 802 2760, f. 209v.
30 None of the standard studies is particularly detailed or precise about citations or *viis et modis*, exact wording or content, in particular: see Brinkworth, *Archdeacon's Court*, p. xi; Chapman, *Ecclesiastical Courts*, p. 49; Ingram, *Church Courts*, p. 47.
31 WRO, 802 2760, f. 225r; SHLS, D/D/ca/350, 10/10/1671 (no folios).
32 HRO, C1/37 (no folios, *passim*); C1/44, 29/10/1674 (no folios).
33 Sources are Thirty Nine Articles, Canons of 1604, BCP rubrics, statutes; see Gibson, *Codex Juris*, vol. 1, p. 194, vol. 2, p. 1049 (lesser), vol. 2, pp. 1049, 1062 (greater), vol. 1, p. 359, vol. 2, p. 1051 (burials); see also e.g. Bray, *Anglican Canons*; Purvis, *Dictionary*.
34 WRO, 802 2884, f. 117v; 802 2760, ff. 219v; f. 240r.
35 Two cases at Wells in the 1630s involved the accused eating, drinking, employing and making bargains with an 'an aggravated person' – showing that the guilty party was banned from 'secular' activities (SHLS, D/D/ca/295, f. 169r; D/D/ca/313, f. 198r).
36 WRO, 802 2760, f. 236v; 794 011 2722 2, Book 32, ff. 114r, 115r.
37 E.g. Chapman, *Ecclesiastical Courts*, p. 54; Marchant, *Church under Law*, pp. 220–1; Marchant, *Puritans and Church Courts*, p. 9; Jenkins, *Archdeacon of Taunton*, pp. 32, 37, 38; McIntosh, *Havering*, p. 249; Tarver, 'Lichfield and Coventry', pp. 49, 61, 116; Till, *Church Courts*, p. 21.
38 Houlbrooke, *Church Courts*, pp. 48–9; Ingram, *Church Courts*, pp. 52–3; I owe the essence of my understanding of excommunication to discussion with Ralph Houlbrooke.
39 Gibson, *Codex Juris*, vol. 1, pp. 161 (armour), 192 (ear and brawling), 429–30 (marriage), vol. 2, 1049, 1062 (association with an excommunicate).
40 WRO, 802 2884, f. 117v; 802 2760, f. 191v; f. 227r; f. 271v; f. 172r.
41 WRO, 802 2760, ff. 219v–220r; f. 240r; f. 256r.
42 17 CI c.11 (abolition); 13 CII c.12 (confirmation).
43 The legality and incidence of the procedure are discussed in the section 'Compurgation' in Chapter 4.
44 Gardiner, *Star Chamber and High Commission*, e.g. pp. 281, 285, 302, 310, 314, 315, 321 (imprisonment), pp. 268, 304, 312 (fines); HRO, C1/28, ff. 1v, 3r (prison), ff. 3v, 5v, 9r+v, 10r (fines); see also Houlbrooke, 'Decline of Ecclesiastical Jurisdiction', p. 250.
45 5 EI c.23; Gibson, *Codex Juris*, vol. 2, p. 1055.
46 HRO, C1/45, 27/1/1683 (no folios); this appears to challenge use of forfeiture of property, see Cavill, 'Heresy, Law, and the State', especially p. 292.
47 Historic commentaries on ecclesiastical law include Gibson, *Codex Juris*, vol. 1, pp. xxii–xxiii, vol. 2, p. 986; Nelson, *Rights of Clergy*, p. 139; Burn, *Ecclesiastical Law*, vol. 2, p. 7; Rogers, *Ecclesiastical Law*, p. 138; modern summaries include Coningsby, 'Chancellor, Vicar General, Official Principal', pp. 273, 279, 280; Chapman, *Ecclesiastical Courts*, pp. 33–5; Hockaday, 'Gloucester', pp. 204–6; Houlbrooke, *Church Courts*, p. 24; Ingram, *Church Courts*, p. 59.
48 Winchester: Charles Morley is described as chancellor once in *ex officio* books (HRO, C1/45, 15/10/1680); Worcester: Baldwyn likewise (e.g. WRO, 794 011 2513 18, Book 20, ff. 26r,

CHURCH COURTS AND THE PEOPLE IN SEVENTEENTH-CENTURY ENGLAND

127r, 9/1661 and 9/1662 respectively; and 794 011 2722, Book 39, no folios, 6/1692); Littleton also (794 011 2513 17, p. 19, 5/1638).

49   SHLS, D/D/ca/350.
50   Clarendon Code: the major statutes were 13 CII c.1 (Corporation Act); 14 CII c.4 (Act of Uniformity); 16 CII c.4 (1st Conventicle Act); 17 CII c.2 (Five Mile Act); 22 CII c.1 (2nd Conventicle Act).
51   See Appendix 2, Table 9.
52   43 EI c.2; 14 CII c.12.
53   For appointments and departures of diocesan chancellors, see Appendix 1, Tables 1–3.
54   See e.g. Bray, *Anglican Canons*, p. 427.
55   Much of this relies on standard biographical sources: Foster, *Alumni Oxonienses*; Venn and Venn, *Alumni Cantabrigienses*; Wood, *Athenae Oxonienses*; *DNB; ODNB*; to avoid 'congestion' by constant quoting, these sources have only been mentioned in the footnotes when a quotation or unusual information arises.
56   SHLS, D/D/ca/360, 11/2/1678 (no folios).
57   Wood, *Athenae Oxonienses*, vol. 2, *Fasti*, col. 205.
58   HRO, DC/B5/6, ff. 54r (commissary), 54v (official principal).
59   LeNeve and Hardy, *Fasti*, vol. 3, p. 695 (Gorche), p. 583 (Baldwyn).
60   Hasler, *House of Commons*, vol. 3 (Ridley); BL, Addit. MS 36792, frontis (Baldwyn).
61   Horn, *Fasti 1541–1857*, vol. 10, p. 11.
62   See, in addition to the 'standard' sources, Henning, *House of Commons*, vol. 3; Levack, *Civil Lawyers*, p. 261; *CSPD 1660–1661*, pp. 11, 12. Concerning the 'provenance' of Peirce, he was 'perhaps ... a kinsman' (*ODNB*; Henning, *House of Commons*, vol. 3) of William Peirs, Bishop of Bath and Wells, who had a son (Wood, *Athenae Oxonienses*, vol. 2, Fasti, col. 1479) but named William.
63   LeNeve and Hardy, *Fasti*, vol. 3, p. 360 (Master of Magdalene College, Cambridge); Exeter Cathedral Library, D+C 3553, ff. 52r, 58v (Chancellor of Exeter).
64   For Duck see *CSPD 1640–1641*, e.g. p. 210 (Chancellor of London); Levack, *Civil Lawyers*, pp. 225, 226 (Requests); *CSPD 1640–1641*, e.g. p. 381 (High Commission); Thrush and Ferris, *House of Commons*, vol. 4 (MP for Minehead 1624, 1640). For Ridley see LPL, Abbot's Register, vol. 1, f. 157r, vol. 2, f. 236v (Vicar General and Official Principal of Canterbury Diocese); Levack, *Civil Lawyers*, p. 265 (Chancellor Canterbury, Chancery, High Commission); Hasler, *House of Commons*, vol. 3.
65   HRO, A1/30, f. 18v (Commissary of Surrey), DC/B5/8, f. 17r (OP, Archdeaconry of Surrey), f. 33r (OP, Archdeaconry of Winchester), f. 51r (OP, Archdeaconry of Surrey); Levack, *Civil Lawyers*, p. 253 (Admiralty, Requests); KHLS, DRb/Ar/1/17, f. 113r (Chancellor of Rochester). His attempt to become an MP proved abortive (Thrush and Ferris, *House of Commons*, vols. 2 and 6).
66   HARC, AA20/57/05/15 (evidence from wills lodged confirming Baldwyn's presence as vicar general in the early 1660s).
67   Levack, *Civil Lawyers*, pp. 261, 262 (Chancery); Henning, *House of Commons*, vol. 3 (MP).
68   SHLS, D/D/ca/363 (court book of the Archdeacon of Wells, no folios), e.g. 5/2/1686 John Bailie LLD 'offile'.
69   HRO, A1/32, f. 37v (Bramston Commissary); DC/B5/11, f. 61v (Morley, Commissary for Surrey), f. 69r (Morley, Official Principal, Winchester Archdeaconry).
70   WRO, 716 093 BA 2648/10 iii, p. 10 (Baldwyn), p. 122 (Price).
71   HRO, DC/B5/8, f. 10r (Mason); A1/32, f. 37r (Bramston); DC/B5/11, f. 60v (Morley); 11M59/A3/1/2, f. 18r (Mews).
72   Foxcroft, *Supplement to Burnet's History*, pp. 331, 503.
73   See Houlbrooke, *Church Courts*, p. 52; Ingram, *Church Courts*, p. 10; Marchant, *Church under Law*, pp. 243–5; Price, 'Thomas Powell', pp. 94–112; Price, 'Excommunication', p. 106; Till, *Church Courts*, pp. 31–2.
74   For 1661-2, WRO, 794 011 2513 18, Book 20, ff. 26r, 37r, 127r; for the 1670s and 1680s, 794 011 2722 1+2 *passim*; for the 1690s, 807 093 2724, Book 38, back of the book.
75   Robertson, *Diary of Francis Evans*, p. xvii.
76   Davies, 'Religious Uniformity', p. 83.
77   SHLS, D/D/ca/224, ff. 92r, 99r, 108r (1621); D/D/ca/207, f. 224r (1618); D/D/ca/243, f. 32r (1624).
78   SHLS, D/D/ca/350 (Michaelmas terms 1671 and 1672).

FUNDAMENTALS   **43**

79 SHLS, D/D/ca/354 (Michaelmas terms 1674 and 1675).
80 Hasler, *House of Commons*, vol. 3 (entry for Ridley).
81 HRO, C1/26, C1/29/1, C1/30; C1/32, C1/33, C1/34, C1/35.
82 HRO, C1/37 (no folios, 10 plenaries, Michaelmas term 1663); C1/44 (5/10/1676, 12/10/1676, 14/12/1676, 18/1/1677).
83 The relevant book, HRO, C1/45, trails to nothing by April 1684 and there are no more *ex officio* records for Winchester Consistory Court.
84 WRO, 802 2884, 802 2760, HRO, C1/35; SHLS, D/D/ca/243, HRO, C1/37; WRO, 794 011 2722 2, Book 32.
85 WRO, 802 2760, f. 230r (Gorche); HRO, C1/37, f. 19r a+v (Bramston); SHLS, D/D/ca/224, f. 96r (Duck).
86 SHLS, D/D/ca/211, 221, 230, 285.
87 Instance proceedings in 1661 and 1663 were exceptions, with four and three appearances apiece, together with a few in November and December (WRO, 794 011 2513 18+19).
88 HRO, C2/30, C2/34, C2/46.
89 HRO, C2/72, C2/83, C2/84.
90 Aklundh, 'Church Courts', pp. 36–7, 66.
91 Green, *Re-establishment*, p. 121.
92 WRO, 794 011 2513 10 (Archbold, Hall, Willett); 790 011 2513 17 (Warmestry).
93 WRO, 794 011 2513 18, Book 20.
94 WRO, 794 011 2722 4, Book 39; 807 093 2724, Book 38, back of the book *(ex officio)*.
95 SHLS, D/D/ca/243.
96 SHLS, D/D/ca/295 (Hunt, Rivett); D/D/ca/313 (Egglesfeild, Hunt, Morley, Rivett); D/D/ca/331 (Woodhouse).
97 SHLS, D/D/ca/338 3 and 4.
98 SHLS, D/D/ca/354.
99 HRO, C1/32 1 (Wickham); C1/33 (Wickham, Trussell, Hearst); C1/34, C1/35 (Darrell, Alexander).
100 HRO, C1/37.
101 HRO, C1/45.
102 Canon 128 (1604); see Bray, *Anglican Canons*; for degrees at Oxford and Cambridge in the sixteenth and seventeenth centuries, see e.g. McConica, *Oxford University*, vol. 3; Tyacke, *Oxford University*, vol. 4; Curtis, *Oxford and Cambridge in Transition*.
103 SHLS, D/D/ca/313 (Hunt).
104 Aklundh, 'Church Courts', *passim*.
105 For Warmestry, see Horn, *Fasti 1541–1857*, vol. 7, p. 11; for Hall, see Horn, *Fasti 1541–1857*, vol. 7, p. 110 (dean), p. 19 (archdeacon), p. 13 (Bishop of Norwich); LeNeve and Hardy, *Fasti*, vol. 1, p. 380 (Bishop of Exeter).
106 For Holt, see Horn, *Fasti 1541–1857*, vol. 5, p. 13 (cathedral chancellor), pp. 30, 73, 111 (canonries); for Creighton, see Horn, *Fasti 1541–1857*, vol. 5, p. 9 (precentor), pp. 82, 111 (canonries).
107 For Thirlby, Horn, *Fasti 1541–1857*, vol. 5, p. 10 (archdeacon), pp. 42, 99 (canonries); for Rivett, Horn, *Fasti 1541–1857*, vol. 5, p. 18 (archdeacon), pp. 57, 75, 109 (canonries).
108 For Wickham, see Horn, *Fasti 1541–1857*, vol. 2, p. 58, vol. 9, p. 50 (canonries); Horn, *Fasti 1541–1857*, vol. 8, p. 19 (archdeaconry); for Dayrell, see Horn, *Fasti 1541–1857*, vol. 3, p. 106 (canonry), p. 86 (archdeaconry); for Alexander, see Horn, *Fasti 1541–1857*, vol. 3, p. 94; for Sharrock, see Horn, *Fasti 1541–1857*, vol. 3, pp. 90, 95 (canonries), p. 86 (archdeaconry); for Payne, see Horn, *Fasti 1541–1857*, vol. 3, p. 103; Horn, *Fasti 1541–1857*, vol. 7, p. 86 (canonries).
109 Aklundh, 'Church Courts', pp. 14, 67, 68, 70, 98 (conflict); pp. 15, 79–89, 91–2, 186–9 (sermons).
110 Wood, *Athenae Oxonienses*, vol. 2, col. 767.
111 Wood, *Athenae Oxonienses*, vol. 2, col. 125; Marchant, *Church under Law*, p. 48; Levack, *Civil Lawyers*, p. 177.
112 Davies, 'Religious Uniformity', p. 83.
113 Two instance sessions: WRO, 794 011 2722 2, Book 32, 13/8/1685, f. 281v; 794 011 2722, Book 39, 1/9/1692, no folios; one ex officio: 807 093 2724, Book 38, 1/9/1692, back of the book. This would seem to be three sessions with two of them on the same day.

114 E.g. WRO, 794 011 2513 20, Book 27, ff. 150r, 154r, 159r (8/1669, three instance sessions); 794 011 2722 1, Book 30 (no *ex officio* sessions 8/1675 therefore no folio); 794 011 2722, Book 39 (no instance sessions 8/1691 therefore no folio).

115 Sykes, *Sheldon to Secker*, p. 21; Whiteman, 'Seth Ward', p. 170.

116 Price, 'Bishop Hooper', pp. 71, 72.

117 HRO, C1/28.

118 Bodl, Tanner 38, ff. 20–1 (no date).

119 For Parry, Thornborough, Blandford, Fleetwood, see *ODNB*; Willis Bund, 'Ecclesiastical History', pp. 58, 60, 79; for triennial visitations, see WRO, 794 011 2722 1+2.

120 See *ODNB* for these bishops: 'energetic' and 'usually' are drawn from Fincham's entry on Lake, 'belligerent stance' from Coleby's on Mews.

121 *ODNB*; SHLS, D/D/ca/313, ff. 33r, 37r, 40r, 48r (plenaries), f. 29r (*camera*); D/D/ca/331, f. 149r.

122 *ODNB*; WRO, 807 093 2724, Book 38, list at the back of the book for Stillingfleet; Till's more detailed numbers for court attendance by Stillingfleet in his *ODNB* entry may include instance as well as *ex officio* business.

123 Robertson, *Diary of Francis Evans*, p. xvi (nil information again about whether *ex officio* or instance cases).

FUNDAMENTALS **45**

2

The nature of Church discipline

Charges, also known as 'citations', were accusations, of an offence or offences, laid in court and concerned prosecution of three groups of people: laymen and women, clergymen and churchwardens.[1] Lay people formed the largest numbers and the first three sections of this chapter will deal with charges against this group, while later sections address the clergy and churchwardens.

Charges brought against lay people in whichever consistory court were, broadly and again, of three types. Moral charges ranged from fornication and adultery to bastardy and incest; religious charges from attendance and communion, work and play on the Sabbath to (Catholic) recusancy and (Protestant) dissent; and, finally, there were financial charges such as failure to pay church rate or other dues to the Church or its clergy.

Charges against the laity: morals

Public morals were a major concern of the Church.[2] Any form of sex outside marriage – fornication, adultery, incest, masturbation – and even any irregularities threatening the validity of the ceremony of marriage were sins in the eyes of the Church, and so were its consequences such as the production of illegitimate children. The legality of marriage and the legitimacy of children were also important to the community as a whole – to both the Church and its flock – in the interests of a properly ordered society. Both affected inheritance, for example. Further concerns of the Church arose over collection of fees (for the marriage ceremony). Many of the victims of proceedings, the accused, whether men or women, may have felt they had reputations to protect, and the wider public was always worried about the costs of providing for unmarried mothers and illegitimate children.[3]

The main 'moral' charges, to judge from the court books, were 'incontinence' and 'bastardy' in the language of the time. Incontinence, as used in the court books, includes fornication (sexual intercourse outside marriage) and adultery (more specifically intercourse between two people, one of whom is married). People who had engaged in sexual intercourse and who had subsequently married were charged not with incontinence (fornication or adultery) but with the separate transgression of sex before marriage. This explains the two types of charge – sex before marriage and incontinence – and the Church's distinction, though it may appear artificial, has been observed in this analysis. 'Harbouring' (giving shelter to a pregnant woman), likewise, arose from bastardy, but a distinction between the two is consistently maintained in the books and, again, in this analysis.

Sex before marriage

Prosecutions for premarital intercourse (sex before marriage) averaged five a term in the 1610s and 1620s in the courts of Worcester and Winchester, and at that time the two archdeaconries had similar populations. Wells (that is, the Archdeaconry of Taunton), perhaps just over half the size of the other two archdeaconries, had between two and three times as many such prosecutions but the total only came to 13. After the Restoration prosecutions of this type continued at the levels of the 1610s at Worcester but fell almost out of sight in the other two archdeaconries.

How the authorities could tell that premarital intercourse had occurred and so decide to bring a charge is an interesting question.[4] Often there is nothing in the entries except a plain statement of the charge itself. The case against Ellis Cole of Kings Worthy (Winchester) in 1619 arose, apparently, from rumour or gossip ('fame' in the language of the time);[5] otherwise the grounds for this kind of charge at Winchester before the Interregnum are not made clear and afterwards, in the three sample terms, there were no charges. This was very largely so at Worcester, but in two cases in 1615 it was claimed that the woman was pregnant before marriage.[6] This was obviously the best proof of sex before marriage and at Wells, before the Wars, the whole business was sometimes dealt with much more precisely. Some cases, such as John Stradling's in 1621, still apparently began with suspicion and fame, but in 1624 it was said of Richard and Martha Hite that 'they laie in one and the same bead togeather the night before they weare married ... being the sygn of the dolphin', though nothing is said about the witness.[7] Matters were much more explicit in several other cases: the Baleers, for example, were married some time close to St John the Baptist's day (24 June) but their child arrived before Michaelmas (29 September); the Nowells were married 'on the first daie of Maie and (the wife) was delivered of a childe about a moneth ago' (October); and the Goddards produced a child 'within halfe a yeere after they weare married'.[8] These last three cases were in 1618, 1621 and 1624 respectively but by the 1670s numbers of such charges and the precision with which they were laid had fallen away even at Wells.

Incontinence

'Incontinence', encompassing a range of sexual activity outside marriage, formed the largest number of 'moral' prosecutions in the three episcopal courts both before and after the Wars and Interregnum. The charge most often was simply 'incontinence', without details, but occasionally the charge was fornication, as with Samuel Curle and Joanna Hastings, or adultery, as with William Poor and Bennetta Snow, both cases at Winchester in 1619 and 1621 respectively.[9] On a few occasions fornication, adultery and incontinence are all mentioned in the same charge, as in the cases of Humphrey Grigg at Wells in 1621, which must imply that, if not definitely interchangeable, they were viewed by seventeenth-century officials as much the same kind of misdemeanour.[10]

Some behaviour was merely verging on rather than the act itself. Several stood accused of incontinence because of association with a member of the opposite sex: for example, in the early 1620s Peter Barley's wife was brought to the court at Winchester for 'keeping company' with Richard Symes the elder 'contrarye to Gods ordinance'; and Richard Bulpane was summoned to Wells because he 'frequenteth her companie earlie and late'.[11] Clearly suspicions of incontinence were aroused when Marie Hunt was discovered as she 'laie under the sd Penny's bed' (Wells 1621), and when James Challicombe and Tomasina Davie apparently indulged in 'uncivill' and 'unseemely' public foreplay as 'he did ... shew his privie members and she tooke them in her hands and measured (?) them' (Wells 1637).[12]

An entry in the court book for Wells in 1624 leaves open the possibility of a 'threesome'.[13] Other incidents are more explicit. In one case in 1640 Richard Berrie (Wells) volunteered boastfully that he had 'pulled awai [sic] as much haire from her private partes as would stuffe a ball'; and in the same court it was 'comonlie reported' that Maria Oake held her smock in her teeth while James Slape had 'Carnall knowledge of her bodie'.[14]

Rape, exhibitionism, masturbation and even bestiality all appear in the court records and, to avoid excessive divisions on the tables, have been included under incontinence. Masturbation – or, at least, prosecution for it – was extremely rare and, in fact, just two cases have been found in all the specimen years, both in the Worcester Diocese and both in 1614. Robert Walker was brought before the court at Worcester for 'abusinge himselfe in the Churchyard', and Thomas Ballie similarly for 'misusing himself' in the church 'with divers maydes'.[15] At Wells in 1618, Walter Byrn was accused of assailing the chastity of Thomas Popham's servant; in 1624 George Stuckie was summoned to the same court because he 'uppon a Saboth daie in the churcheyard ... took out his privie member shewed it to divers maydes ... and made water against them'; and at Winchester in 1619, John Wilkins was charged with 'abusing An howle (an owl) by way of copulacon'.[16]

Most charges of incontinence, as with sex before marriage, were based on rumour and suspicion. The word 'suspicion' and the phrase (in modern language) that the 'rumour mill' was 'on overtime' occur too many times to enumerate, and the case of Nicholas Bright at Wells in 1621 will have to serve as an example of repetitive phraseology of this kind.[17] Other charges were expressed more strongly: Isotta Greene's honour was 'most suspiciouse ... there being but one bedd' (Wells 1621); and the words *'vehementer'* and *'magnopere'* were deployed in the charge against Emanuel Sands of incontinence with a servant (Wells 1618).[18] Some charges were more soundly based: in 1624 at Wells, for example, Broake was apparently caught in the 'Acte' of incontinence – it does not say by whom – and a couple was discovered by the constable of Dulverton 'in naked bed togeather'.[19]

Incontinence accounts for some of the largest numbers and highest proportions of prosecutions against laymen and women in the Michaelmas terms of the 1610s and 1620s. Charges averaged 65 at Wells and formed as many as a third of all prosecutions (moral, religious and rates) over the three Michaelmas terms at that time. There was a dramatic change by the 1670s, however, to minute numbers of such prosecutions at Worcester and Wells and zero at Winchester.

Bastardy

Bastardy ranks second in these ratings. Wells seems, again, with bastardy cases, to have had the largest numbers (40) and percentages (20 per cent of all prosecutions against the laity) in the early years, while Worcester and Winchester, with double the population of Wells, were much the same as each other, with lower figures and much lower percentages than Wells. As with incontinence, the figures had collapsed by the 1670s and 1680s to zero at Winchester and to handfuls of three or four per term in the other two archdeaconries.

Bastardy was bad enough in an age when illegitimacy was a major social stigma but, if there was one offence which provoked more distress among victims and more anger within certain parts of the community, it was 'harbouring', or sheltering, pregnant women. Entries in the court books for the years examined before the Wars and Interregnum are few and provide very little detail. The prosecution of two widows, widow Madeley at Worcester in 1615 and Alice Wells at Winchester in 1623, reveals something, however, of the 'minuteness' of church officialdom and of the emotional tensions at the time of such a birth: minuteness because part of the case against widow Madeley was that she had allowed the woman to leave before churching; and tensions because of the interruption of terse *formulae* with an explanation, or plea, for once, that 'in compassion and at the entreatie of John Batt she (Alice Wells) did take the sd Joan Batt into her house'.[20] William Brooke was prosecuted *'quod fovet in aedibus eius Maria(am) eius filia(m) ilicite impregnat(am)'* (that is, 'because he takes care of his daughter, Mary, in his own house because she is unlawfully pregnant'). Brooke was helping his daughter, no less, and presumably bearing the costs, but it cut no ice with his accusers and shines a light on prevailing attitudes of Church and community towards harbouring even when no cost to the parish was involved.[21] Other women (and children) were even less fortunate and had to give birth in a 'cowhouse' or among 'sheepings'.[22] Little wonder that, according to the court book of Wells for Michaelmas term 1618, Alexander Mitchell had arranged for a similarly distressed woman 'to be convayed away ... to conceal her faulte' (and his part in the sinful activity).[23]

Bastardy was prosecuted with some vigour in the early years, harbouring clearly less so; in fact, prosecutions for the latter offence averaged two per term at Winchester, six at Wells and three at Worcester in the 1610s and 1620s, and they seem to have shrunk to nothing in all three archdeaconries by the 1670s and 1680s. Local people and churchwardens may have begun to show greater pity towards these female outcasts but what brought about such a change of attitude is difficult to say. In the eyes of the Church, any irregular sex and offspring were sins, and in the eyes of many people at large such activities could only mean a charge on the parish and so had to be deterred, by prosecutions, at all costs in one court or another.[24] An outbreak of social conscience among church court bureaucrats or rate payers – meaning more sympathy towards offenders and fewer prosecutions – does not seem very likely; concerns among legislators and the more prosperous about disorder, maintenance and costs are much more likely to have prevailed. The Act of Settlement, passed in 1662 (with further statutes in 1685 and 1692) and building on the Poor Law Act of 1601,[25] was a product of these concerns. It introduced residence requirements in an attempt to control movements and clarify which parish was responsible for a particular claimant of relief. Its enforcement would have increased prosecutions in the secular courts and may go some way to explaining the decline of business in the church courts. If the incidence of bastardy did indeed fall in the middle years of the seventeenth century, the deterrent effect of the Act may well have been a factor.[26]

Clandestine marriage

Irregularities concerning marriage could include separation of man and wife, the one refusing to live with the other.[27] Examples of separation occur at Worcester in 1614 and Winchester in 1619.[28] Much more common was failure to produce, or to obtain in the first place, either banns or a licence. The Framptons, man and wife, were accused of marrying without licence but failed to venture the crossing from Brading (Isle of Wight) to answer the charge at Winchester in December 1623,[29] and there were numerous parallel cases in the other two dioceses. People were also summoned for merely attending and so being complicit in a 'clandestine' ceremony. John Morehall was one such victim of this at Worcester in 1613.[30] The case of John Colinge and his wife is an example, though much rarer, of marriage 'outside the dioc(ese)' brought to the notice of the same court in the same year.[31] There appear to have been no prosecutions in the 1670s and 1680s at Winchester, but the clerk did not usually record the charge if the accused failed to attend court and it is therefore difficult to tell whether there were any such prosecutions or not at that time; there were certainly a few prosecutions to do with marriage irregularities at Worcester and Wells in the 1670s and 1680s.[32]

Incest

A charge of incest was rare. A Table of Kindred and Affinity, 'authorised' in 1563, laid down the prohibited degrees of marriage and this was inserted into the Book of Common Prayer and reinforced in Canon 99 of the corpus of 1604.[33] Incest means sex between blood relations but could, in the seventeenth century, include further degrees of relationship, such as marriage to one's dead wife's sister, which in the twenty-first century are no longer illegal. 'Straightforward' cases arose when a brother and sister were accused at Worcester in 1615; a father and daughter at Winchester in 1619; and an uncle and 'his own brother's daughter' at Wells in 1671.[34] Three cases from Worcester show that seventeenth-century interpretations of incest were somewhat wider than those in Britain today. John Sherman of Kineton and Thomas Baker of Stourbridge were both accused of marrying their wife's sister, the former in 1615, the latter in 1661; and Joyce Hay of Mathon was alleged in 1682 to have had sex with her stepfather.[35] Numbers overall were minuscule and averaged, at most, one or two per Michaelmas term in all three archdeaconries in the earlier period and were even fewer by the 1670s and 1680s.

Charges against the laity: religion

'Religious' offences ranged from failure to attend church or to receive communion, to work or play on the Sabbath, standing excommunicate, outright religious divergence and abusive behaviour of one kind or another in the churchyard.[36]

Church attendance

Numerous examples of failure to attend the local parish church occupied the scrutiny of the consistory courts. Some were said to be 'slack' or 'negligent coming to church' and at least one was 'idle in the Churchyard at the time of divine service'. These cases are all from Winchester in 1623, but the same phrase, 'negligent coming to church', had been used about defendants at Worcester in 1613.[37]

Deserting the local parish church for another was viewed by church officials, in an age of strict demarcation in such matters, as a transgression, which ensnared John Feilde of Alcester (Worcester) and William Hawkins of Alton (Winchester) in 1614 and 1623 respectively, and there was more than one case of the like at Wells in the 1630s.[38] Length of absence was sometimes mentioned as well. In 1623, Thomas Wayte of Kings Worthy (Winchester) was accused of being absent for two years, and he confessed 'he did absent himself ... by reason there was some difference between himself and the Parson'. The next year it was said at Wells of Richard Huish and his parish church that 'hee hath not byn theare above twice these xii monethes last past'.[39]

CHURCH COURTS AND THE PEOPLE IN SEVENTEENTH-CENTURY ENGLAND

Nor did the requirement apply only on Sundays: absence on the main saints' days was also prosecutable, as Robert Haines of Bengeworth (Worcester), among others, found out in 1615 (if he did not know already) when he was summoned to Worcester 'for workeinge hollidayes'. Six years later Richard Searle was hauled before the court at Winchester for 'refusing to come to Church one [sic] holledays', and in 1637 two men from North Petherton (Wells) were alleged to have missed church on St Jude's day.[40]

All this activity should not be blown out of proportion. Before the Wars and Interregnum, infringements, or rather accusations of infringements, of attendance rules were low, averaging 19 per Michaelmas term at Winchester, 11 at Wells and nine at Worcester. There followed, after the Restoration, a steep decline, from admittedly rather low levels, and prosecutions concerning attendance all but disappeared at Winchester and Wells. The issue was not quite dead at Winchester, however, and the case of John and Jane Hall of Calbourne (Isle of Wight), summoned to the consistory court 'for comeing to Sermon but not to Prayers' in 1663, suggests a fine distinction and close invigilation, though too much should not be built on one case.[41]

Worcester also saw a similar drop in prosecutions for failing to attend church, from an average of nine (1613–15) to four (1675, 1678, 1680) during its 'regular' or 'ordinary' sittings in the appropriate Michaelmas terms. It is interesting to note, however, that numbers were much larger in the visitation records for that year. These reached over 100 in Michaelmas term 1682, but such activity was exceptional even for visitation records and should not be allowed to disguise the usually small numbers of prosecutions when set against the 43,000 inhabitants of the diocese-cum-archdeaconry of Worcester.

Work and play

Work and play on the Sabbath would obviously affect attendance and they account for a fair proportion of prosecutions in the three archdeaconries before the Civil Wars and Interregnum, if much less so after them, though context – in particular, size of population – must always be borne in mind. The range of offences catalogued in the court books is probably a sound reflection of seventeenth-century economic activity. Many of the alleged breaches were, hardly surprisingly, agricultural; and, since the focus of this study is on Michaelmas terms, most had to do with harvesting. George Thorne was summoned to the court at Wells in 1618 because 'he made hay upon the Sabbaoth day' and similarly Edward Symond and James Watt received an order to attend proceedings at Winchester in 1623 'for going to harvest on the Saboth day after evening prayer'.[42] Reaping corn, 'leasing' (gleaning?) it, winnowing it, carting it and grinding it all occurred – or were alleged to have occurred – on the Sabbath on various dates in the three archdeaconries during the 1610s and 1620s.[43]

At Worcester and Wells the cloth trade features nearly as prominently as agriculture. The accusation against Hugh Steeven at Wells in 1621 was that he 'did worke cloathe uppon the Soundaie before St James's day last past all the daie longe'. Others were accused of 'raking' it at Worcester in 1615 and of 'cardeing' it at Wells in 1624.[44] Carting goods, not always specified but likely to have been corn, cloth or timber, on the Sabbath was, inevitably, an associated misdemeanour and, in identical phraseology, different men were charged at Winchester in 1621 and 1623 with 'goeing to cart on the Sabaoth day'.[45] A host of other trades appear in the court books of the 1610s and 1620s: butchering, barbering, brewing and selling ale, baking, building, carpentry, even soap manufacture and clock repairing.[46]

People involved in these activities – agricultural and the various trades – continued to face prosecution in the 1630s, to judge from entries in the records at Wells. Ploughing, cobbling, milling, barbering and selling wares are all specified in the court books and, to take one example, there seems to have been Sunday trading of groceries on an industrial scale at Wellington, whence at least seven people were summoned in 1637 for selling 'cabbade [sic] carretts and turnipps and such like uppon Sundaies in time of divine prayer'.[47]

As with work, so with play on the Sabbath: prosecutions were a regular occurrence before the Interregnum, though in fact hardly overwhelming in numbers or proportions and there seem, again, to have been none in the specimen terms of the 1670s and 1680s. Spending part of Sunday playing bowls was common – allegedly – usually involving, by its nature, groups of young men, and there are examples of prosecutions in all three archdeaconries in the 1610s and 1620s.[48] The same was true for drinking: Originale Lee and Mathew Mallard, for example, were both described separately as an 'Alehouse haunter' in court at Winchester in 1623;[49] and in 1624, Thomas Chappell and others at Chard (Wells) were alleged to have taken exception to the parson's sermon against drink and to have risen up from their seats and left the church 'unreverentlie' to resume drinking in the churchyard.[50]

People were charged with playing at cards and various games, 'ffives' [sic], 'kittles' (skittles?) and 'ninepinns' among them;[51] whether these are different names for the same activity or whether there were

54   CHURCH COURTS AND THE PEOPLE IN SEVENTEENTH-CENTURY ENGLAND

subtle differences between them is not clear from the 'evidence'. A troupe of 11 men was charged with attempting the – possibly – somewhat more uplifting activity of staging a play at Pershore in 1613.[52] Thomas Minchin, also from Pershore but in 1615, found diversion, allegedly, by 'playing on his tabor *temp(or)e divinoru(m) (serviciorum)*' – during time of divine service.[53] Yet others spent Sundays hunting: in just one case, for example, Abraham Lawnder of Evesham (Worcester) was accused, with others, of 'leeding his packe' in 1618.[54]

These transgressions – work and play on the Sabbath – virtually disappear from the books of all three archdeaconries after the Restoration. Attendance continued to be a concern and, although it was no longer 'flagged' in the courts, it is difficult to imagine the disappearance of either work or play on the Sabbath. It would seem that the focus of church officials, insofar as there can be said to have been one, was now trained largely on other, more religious, problems. The Commonwealth and Protectorate had seen an explosion of the 'sects' and, with deference and custom overwhelmed, it looks as if the church authorities knew when to retreat and where to focus their attention – hence there were fewer prosecutions over work and play on the Sabbath and more concentration on church attendance in the Restoration.

Communion

Communion was one of the two remaining sacraments in the Church of England after the Reformation and was a central feature of its worship. Prosecutions were rare at Wells in the 1610s and early 1620s but at Worcester, with an average of 14 a year, failure to receive the sacrament formed a more substantial body of prosecutions. Far larger numbers of laymen and women were summoned to Winchester's consistory court, even above prosecutions for incontinence within the archdeaconry, in the 1610s and early 1620s. Communion offences involved no fewer than 114 people during Michaelmas term 1619, averaged 78 a year and formed some 28 per cent of all prosecutions of laymen and women in the three terms in question. More than one hundred in one term might have been an exceptional statistical quirk, but the large numbers over three terms suggest that diocesan policy – of the newly elevated Lancelot Andrewes to the bishopric – was the motor driving the prosecutions.[55]

The canons required participation at least three times a year, one of which had to be at Easter.[56] Prosecutions can be found in all three archdeaconries for failure to receive in the 1610s and early 1620s.[57] It was said in several cases, moreover, that this had been going on for two, three and even four years.[58] Easter was emphasised in numerous prosecutions: several at Worcester in 1613, for example, and a large group of 19 people from All Saints Southampton (Winchester) in 1623, while at Owslebury (also Winchester) in the same year John Smith and his three sons suffered excommunication over the issue.[59]

Another infringement sometimes arose from the way people were supposed to receive. The Book of Common Prayer ordered receiving 'meekly kneeling' and many cases at Worcester in the 1610s turned on whether people had been standing or sitting to communicate. Jane Saunders was accused of standing in 1613, Edward Hale was one of five similarly accused in 1615, and two groups of suspects – one of 11 in June and another of six in October – were summoned in 1614 for sitting or standing 'unreverently' to receive.[60] Seeking communion at the wrong church was also prosecutable and, again at Worcester in 1613, no fewer than eight communicants were accused of decamping to another church.[61]

Surprisingly, there were hardly any communion prosecutions at Taunton (Wells) during the 1630s (the only diocese of the three with records for the period),[62] and whether this reflects effective Laudian control, diocesan policy to avoid trouble or a tradition of obedience on this issue, at least in Somerset, must remain a matter for speculation. There were few prosecutions again at Wells in the 1660s and the other two dioceses appear to have fallen into line. So it remained at Winchester and Wells and, indeed, with 'regular' proceedings of the court at Worcester in the 1670s and 1680s, but there would appear to have been more vigorous prosecuting over the issue in its visitations. There were 12 communion prosecutions in 1679 and, in contrast to all the other types of prosecution, the enormous number of 79 in 1682. The 12 prosecutions of 1679 all came from St Andrew's Droitwich, and among the 79 cases of 1682 was a group of 17 men, headed by Thomas Freeman, all from Bengeworth.[63]

The validity of Michaelmas term for measuring communion prosecutions has been discussed in the Introduction to this study.[64] Essentially Easter infractions did not necessarily mean Easter prosecutions. There could be a mismatch between an alleged offence at Easter and the date of prosecution because visitations, when churchwardens delivered their presentments, often occurred at times of the year other than April. A comparison of Michaelmas terms with Easter and Trinity terms does not show, in the three archdeaconries of this survey, a rise in prosecutions in the latter two terms. All turned on the diocesan cycle of visitations, which very likely explains why, for example, there were 81 cases during Michaelmas term and 16 at most during Easter and Trinity terms combined at the Winchester Consistory Court in the year 1623–4.

Baptism

Baptism performed according to the rites of the Church of England was another potentially contentious issue, but there are in fact not many examples of conflict and none at all at Wells either before or after the mid-century crisis. The wrong officiant – 'a popish priest' or, more vaguely, 'an unlawful minister', both at Winchester in 1621 and 1663 respectively – was one ground for prosecution; rejection of the sign of the cross was the ground for three cases at Worcester in 1614; and several more baptism refusals, without details, were brought to light by the 'visitation' proceedings at Worcester in 1679 and 1682.[65] Information in these and similar cases is too scant, however, to make sound comparisons or to draw safe conclusions in this field other than to state the obvious: that baptism could be – and sometimes was – another point of conflict, similar to communion, with the established Church, whether from Catholics or the 'sects'.

Occasional prosecution for irregularities to do with the practice of churching arise in the records. The case of widow Madeley, accused of failing to ensure the churching of a pregnant woman she had sheltered, has already been discussed. In another case, proceedings were begun against Jethro Bye at Winchester in 1619 for imposture of a clergyman, 'churching women, burying the dead and reading prayers'.[66] There were several prosecutions of women by the visitation authorities at Worcester in the 1670s and 1680s for failing to undergo churching.[67] The ways in which the problem was sometimes expressed – 'purification' in some of the examples before the Interregnum, 'publick thanks for the safe delivery from the perill of Childbearinge' after the Interregnum – may have been no more than the fortuitous choice of words by a particular clerk but may also have been attempts to present churching in a more positive – and tactful – light.[68]

'Recusancy' and 'dissent'

Prosecutions on religious grounds so far have covered church attendance, work and play on the Sabbath, communion and baptism. It is probably safe to say that prosecutions concerning work and play on the Sabbath did not reflect discontent, at least on grounds of conscience, with theology or the established Church. Work and play on the Sabbath would have been out of the question for Puritans and, no doubt, for Catholics as well; and neither Catholics nor Puritans would have wished to risk prosecution and drawing attention to themselves on such grounds. The other issues – attendance at church, communion, baptism (and even churching)

– were of a different order. They raised the possibility that religious divergence – Catholicism and Puritanism – was the underlying reason for the alleged dereliction. Other charges – recusancy, popery and dissent of various kinds – raise the matter of conscience more directly. Specific reference to recusancy (refusing to attend church) and dissent (belonging to a sect or attending a conventicle and resisting oaths of loyalty to the Church of England) brought prosecution within the orbit of belief, worship and conscience.

Even so, the precise reason for recusancy or dissent is not always clarified in the consistory court books and cannot be tied with certainty to a specific faith or a sect. The relevant legislation – the Elizabethan statutes of 1559, 1581 and the two Acts of 1593 – laid stress on attendance, with fines and forfeiture of property levied for refusal to go to church – recusancy – while avoiding anything specific about religious allegiance.[69] The statute of 1581 was key as it was used for more than a century at the assizes explicitly for 'convictions' of 'recusants' (in the language of the recusancy rolls), but there is no such term in the wording of the Act.[70] Title and context do give some indication, however. Parliament passed the Act of 1581 amid Catholic plots and the arrival of the Catholic mission of priests to England and so its enactment implies a Catholic focus. The first Act of 1593 at last identifies, in the title, its victims as 'Popish Recusants'. There would seem to be some justification therefore in concluding that recusants were Catholics. This was probably largely, but not definitely or exclusively, so; the term could have embraced Puritans of one kind or another in the 1590s and apparently Protestant dissenters after the Restoration.[71]

The context to the second of the two Acts of 1593 was the Marprelate Tracts, and its title – Act against Seditious Sectaries – reflects concern about Puritans. The word dissenter is neither deployed nor defined in the Act and, though it grew into common usage, its scope was often ambivalent. When Sheldon drew his three questions in 1676, he was clear about 'recusants' and used the more specific term 'Popish Recusants'. His third question, however, concerned 'other dissenters', which, in view of the earlier question about 'Popish Recusants', must mean 'Protestant dissenters' but implies that 'dissenter' by itself and without 'other' could embrace all 'outsiders', Catholic or Protestant.[72] The replies of bishops such as Morley of Winchester used the term 'dissenters' to mean both Catholics and Protestants and relied on 'Sectary' and 'Separatist' to identify their Protestant targets,[73] and when the clerk at Worcester entered the charge against John Higgins (and 12 others) in 1679, he labelled him 'a popish Recusant and a Dissenter from the Church'.[74]

Legislation in the last phase of religious persecution, the 1660s and 1670s, is more precise about recusancy, and 'popish' usually precedes 'recusant' in the Test Acts of 1673 and 1678. This phrase is used, furthermore, in the Toleration Act of 1689 and, although 'dissenter' appears by itself in the Act, their Protestantism is clearly implied by the separate treatment of popish recusants.[75] Nonetheless, in light of the ambivalence of Morley and Higgins and the warning of Bowler, some caution about the meanings of these terms is advisable.

Some terms are unequivocal in consistory court prosecutions: 'Roman Catholicke', 'popish Recusant' and 'reputed papist' have all been placed under 'Catholics' in the tables , while 'Quaker', 'Anabaptist' and 'Conventicle' have been placed under 'dissent'. Less precise terms such as 'sectary', 'separatist' and 'Hatte' (the last presumably referring to Quaker practice) have also been placed under 'dissent'. One term, 'de conformitate', is particularly perplexing: such a person could fall into either the Protestant or Catholic camp and the term could even refer to failure to comply with a quite different type of court order such as bastardy. These cases have been placed, arbitrarily, under 'dissent'. The clerks make no attempt to define these terms – nor would a 'theological treatise' by them have been appropriate in the circumstance of a court notebook.

Charges involving (Catholic) recusancy and (Protestant) dissent were minuscule in the specimen Michaelmas terms before the Wars and Interregnum: none at all at Wells and one or two per term at Winchester and Worcester. A handful of people from Alton, charged with 'not standing upp for the sayeing of the Creede' at Winchester consistory court in 1619, are likely to have been Protestants.[76] Interestingly, William Jones of Martin Hussingtree (Worcester) was brought to court in 1614 'for sending his Children to a Recusant schole'. Jane Pippen of Owslebury (Winchester) in 1621 was charged as 'a Recusant and for teacheing young children in papist books'.[77] More disconcertingly by twenty-first-century standards, at least, was the charge of recusancy against three children of Thomas More of Ripple (Worcester) in 1613, even if no further action appears to have been taken.[78] The Catholic religion is only clearly identified in the case of Jane Pippen, but Catholicism has been assumed in the other two prosecutions.

To turn to the 1670s and 1680s, Wells continued to lack religious prosecutions, its focus lying, as before, on moral problems, but pursuit of recusants and dissenters, Catholic or Protestant, became more pronounced in the other two archdeaconries. The charge against Richard Heckley at Winchester in 1663 – absence or non-conformity – is not clear but the defendant felt the need to declare that he was 'noe Sectary', which may imply suspicions entertained by the court of Protestant dissenting.[79]

Numbers of apparently religious offenders – 10 in 1678 and another 16 in 1681 – were still small, but large when compared with the 1610s and 1620s. They also formed a much larger proportion of all prosecutions of laymen and women at this later time but, with very few specific charges of any kind against names of the summoned in what was clearly by then a dysfunctional court, it is difficult to be sure about proportions. Matters had become distinctly ambivalent, moreover, concerning religious allegiance by the late 1670s and early 1680s. Twelve of the 16 offenders of 1681 revolving round Lord Tichborne and his household, were almost certainly Catholics, but the critical word in the charge against seven of the 10 offenders of 1678 is 'conformitate', which could mean anything.[80]

Visitation prosecutions, as distinct from regular proceedings in the court, reveal much higher numbers of divergent parishioners at Worcester in 1679 and 1682 and are often more specific about the religion of offenders and sometimes couple it with absence. Among those classified in the tables as recusants in 1679 was William Taylor, a 'Roman Catholick'; among those classified as dissenters were Joan Richards, 'a reputed Anabaptist'; Rebecca Hunt, 'a Separatist'; the Thomas Haywards senior and junior, both 'sitting with his Hatt on his head in time of Sermon'; and John Penne, standing accused of 'atheisticall neglect of God's worship'.[81] This array of divergence – and more – appears again in the visitation records of 1682: for example, there were 14 'papists', 15 Quakers, two Anabaptists and two 'conventiclers', but five are identified only as 'dissenter'.[82]

These are the numbers of charges concerning divergence – recusancy and dissent – over which legal action was taken by the courts during the relevant Michaelmas term. Two or three points – imprecise terminology apart – should be borne in mind regarding these figures. Firstly, numbers of charges and numbers of people are not necessarily the same as some people faced two, and sometimes three, charges and therefore there is only a rough approximation between the two.

Secondly, there is a disjunction between churchwardens' presentments and cases in court, with some large numbers in presentments but much lower numbers in court. Churchwardens' presentments have survived for both Winchester and Worcester in the 1670s and these show that there were 378 'religious' presentments at Worcester in 1679 and, just a little earlier, as many as 848 at Winchester in 1673. Why most of these presentments were not pursued in the episcopal consistory courts is a question which must be left to speculation, but prosecution in the archdeacons' courts or the secular courts is one possibility, settlement in private another,[83] and this may also explain the total absence of proceedings at the consistory court at Wells in both the earlier and later periods.

It has to be remembered, finally, that presentments were only accusations or 'preliminary charges', not formal charges, and still less convictions, and whether any substance lay behind them or not is yet another matter for speculation.

Misbehaviour

Abusive and insulting behaviour, though not necessarily of religious significance, sometimes was so and, when it occurred in the church or churchyard, it fell within the remit of the church court. An altercation took place in the church at Whitestaunton (Wells) in 1624 during which the congregation was treated to 'manie uncivill and unseemlie speeches' when John Slaie dismissed William Loy as 'a turd in the teeth' and Hugh Stone told William Wakelie to 'kisse my arse'.[84] Quarrelling over church seats was common, including disputes at Blockley (Worcester) in 1613, at North Petherton (Wells) in 1621 and at Fareham (Winchester) in 1623, while Elias Northcote tackled John Tutball in the belfry of the parish church at Norton Fitzwarren (Wells) in 1671 about 'trespass of his Master's cattle ... in a brawling and chideing manner'.[85] This could descend into brawling, with eruptions occurring in church during divine service at Bengeworth (Worcester) in 1613, at Binstead (Winchester) in 1619 and at North Petherton (Wells) in 1621, where Elizabeth Rowe 'did fight, chide and brawle ... to the greate disturbance of the congregation'.[86]

Individual ministers were not immune from abuse – there was one such case per year in 1619, 1621 and 1623 in the Winchester Diocese – and a 'colourful' example was put before the court at Wells in 1618 when William Mager was charged for saying he cared 'not a turd for Mr Cottrell the Minister of Wilton in his drunken humors'.[87] No parallels have come to light in any of the samples of the three archdeaconries in the 1670s, but the problem had not entirely disappeared (and there were several cases of assault in the 1690s).

Cacophony must have disturbed the inhabitants of Stogursey (Wells) in 1618 when William Stoddey and 'others of his consorte ... did ring ... the bells ... in verie disorderlie manner' and at Overton (Winchester) in 1663 when the sexton failed to prevent a similar incident 'after Evening Prayer'. A truly astonishing outbreak of hooliganism, verging on desecration, occurred at Crewkerne (Wells) in 1624: John Webb and five others were accused of accidentally locking a dog in the church, returning, chasing the dog round the church 'most rudelie and uncivillie', washing it in the font, vomiting in the chancel, misbehaving themselves 'most beastelie' and 'fowleing the communion table to the noe smale greife of the parishioners'.[88]

More extraordinarily still, two probable 'skimmington' incidents were brought to the attention of the consistory court at Worcester in the years before the Civil Wars. A skimmington was, apparently, a disorderly procession through the parish involving the flaunting of a person, or an effigy dressed as the victim, to publicise and embarrass adulterers, scolds and the like. In 1615 Lancelot Mathews was charged with 'disguising himself the last Saboath daye ... in woemens apparrell and doing other disorders ... whipping one that rode on a Colestaffe'; and the following year John Bissell was similarly charged in almost identical language with 'disguiseing himself in woman's apparel and ... coming into the Church to the greate offence of the Congregation'. It is not made clear in either of the entries in the court book whether the offence was disruption of a church service, performance of the event on a Sunday or simply the event itself.[89]

Standing excommunicate

Standing excommunicate is the remaining transgression to be considered within the category of 'religious' charges. These were people who had been excommunicated for failing to arrive at court or for rejecting its oaths and edicts – for contempt, in effect – and who refused to seek absolution and make their peace with the Church. They could be summoned to court for review but they usually refused to appear and then the case was deferred yet again or, occasionally, the next step – issue of a *significavit* – followed.[90]

Summoning of excommunicates occurs in the courts of all three archdeaconries in the 1610s and 1620s, though more often at Winchester and Worcester than at Wells.[91] Court notes, brief though they often are, reveal one or two long-standing cases of excommunication: one 'these fower yeares' at Winchester in 1619 and another alleged to have 'stode excommunicated and aggravated these six yeares' at Wells in 1618.[92] People were also subject to summons for associating with an excommunicate. In 1613 Edward Latemore of Yardley (Worcester) was accused of 'converseinge with one John Alan an excommunicate' and William Hutchins of Bromsgrove likewise 'for enterteyninge William Bowden on worke beinge an excommunicated person'. Most strikingly, 11 men were summoned from Old Swinford to the court at Worcester in 1617 'for beinge at the burienge of an excommunicate person viz Ellis Cheltnam'.[93] Prosecutions – in minute numbers – continued at Worcester and Wells into the 1670s and 1680s.[94]

Charges against the laity: church rate

The consistory clerks do not attempt to define 'church rate' as, in their eyes, presumably, there was no need.[95] It was in fact a demand for money – a charge, tax or levy – made by the church or its parochial officials to meet its costs, particularly repairs to the structure of the building, as and when the need arose. It may have borne some relationship to means to pay, such as property values.

The payment is usually called 'church rate' in the court books, certainly in Winchester's, but other terms – dues, duties, levies, quartersett, offerings, taxation – appear as well, and to what extent they were identical or in what way they differed is not made clear.[96] 'Offerings', if preceded by 'Easter', would have been a payment separate from and in addition to any 'rate'. How far it was voluntary is also none too clear, but for a court case to arise, there must have been at least an element of compulsion. There could also be special demands to pay for communion bread and wine,[97] though no case involving refusal to pay such a levy has been found in the court books for the specimen terms.

Groups of seven, eight and 11 individuals were summoned to the court at Winchester in 1621, and on one occasion no fewer than 27 were summoned, all from Romsey, in 1623. A parallel group of five from South Petherton was summoned before the court at Wells in 1633.[98] These 'group' prosecutions suggest the possibility of a particularly heavy demand, an emergency, a clash of personalities, the infection of example, local economic difficulties … the speculation is endless and there is no way of deriving the true explanation from the court books.

Winchester seems to have had, within the constraints of this study, the largest numbers overall: 69 charges in Michaelmas term 1623 and an average of 42 for the three terms between 1619 and 1623, which represents 17 per cent of all prosecutions against the laity at that time. Perspective is again necessary and these numbers – the highest in the three archdeaconries – barely register against an adult population of some 50,000 or 60,000. Numbers at Winchester shrink almost out of sight after 1660, while this seems to have been the case at Worcester and Wells before as well as after the upheavals in the middle of the century.

There is very little information about the actual amounts of money involved in these rate demands. Sums owed are occasionally specified, usually in the region of shillings, and ranged from 10 shillings demanded of Stephen King at Winchester in 1621 down to '2 rates', amounting to a total of six pence, for which officials at Wells pursued John Moore, 'the

Weaver', in 1633.[99] Larger figures – bills for 13 shillings and 4 pence faced by John Colebard (Wells 1637), 15 shillings by Thomas Knight (Winchester 1623) and 24 shillings by Thomas Blake (Winchester 1619) – were quite exceptional.[100]

Demands for money would, nonetheless, have been potentially explosive in an age when a labourer's day wage might have been a shilling or less.[101] The fact that conflict with the consistory courts, as reflected in these numbers, was apparently so minimal is both a surprise and a mystery. It is difficult to imagine a world without money problems and, in fact, contemporary churchwardens' accounts show considerable need for expenditure on both structure and fittings. The persistence of religious divergence in the 1670s and 1680s must have increased potential for resistance, but there are only occasional 'linkages' in the books between the sects and refusal to pay church rate. William Dicks of Tufton was charged with both attendance and rate resistance at Winchester in 1680, while George Robertson of Halesowen, a Quaker and rate refuser who appears on the visitation court lists of Worcester for 1679 and 1682, seems to have been a persistent offender.[102] Researchers are left to imagine that parishioners were generally compliant; otherwise, protest and prosecutions may have been averted by reliance on wealthier benefactors, neglect of repairs and the reluctance of the church, from bishops to churchwardens, to provoke trouble.

Charges against churchwardens

The Church relied for its 'army' on the parish clergy and their churchwardens. They were the links between the ecclesiastical hierarchy and its people. They were the captains and the foot soldiers who kept the Church alive in English society. This section will examine the ways in which the authorities maintained their forces – essentially how it disciplined them – to make sure they were 'fit for purpose' as effective instruments for protecting and advancing the hold of the Church on its flock. This revolves round prosecutions in the consistory courts of Winchester, Worcester and Wells. These show the kinds of charges brought against them and are the best evidence of the concerns and standards of the Church.

An array of duties lay with the churchwardens to keep the parishes in order, many of which can be found in the canons of 1604.[103] The church courts were necessary to expose neglect of these duties, to punish where appropriate, to correct omission and wrongdoing and to encourage compliance among all remaining churchwardens – all this, ultimately, to further and strengthen the interests of the Church and its dominant role in communities. Much depended on the performance of the churchwardens. Good churchwardens who performed their duties efficiently and in full would strengthen the Church in society, while bad churchwardens would greatly damage the standing of the Church and its hold over the people.

Churchwardens from the archdeaconries of Winchester, Worcester and Wells faced a wide array of charges in their respective consistory courts. Some parishes attracted a host of complaints. The churchwardens of Chaddesley Corbett (Worcester) were summoned in 1614 'for want of a sufficient bible and for not providinge bread and wyne for the communion according to the Canon and for want of a Communion pott' as well as for other problems to do with chancel, porch, door and windows. These complaints are echoed at Fivehead (Wells) 60 years later, when their counterparts were summoned 'for things defective … in and about the Church and Churchyard': pews, pulpit, windows, a book for the parish Clerke, pavement, 'wales' (walls) and door are all mentioned.[104] Such a volume of complaints against the churchwardens of a single parish was exceptional, but it illustrates the main charges against churchwardens both before and after the upheavals of the middle years of the seventeenth century.

More modestly, in the scale of things, the churchwarden from Bretforton was summoned to the court at Worcester in 1615 for failing, among other matters, to take the oath of office, and the churchwardens of Holy Rood Southampton were summoned to Winchester in 1621 for irregularities in their accounts.[105] Even more exceptional were failure to perambulate the parish bounds, failure 'to keepe' their organists, failure to ensure the bells were rung when the bishop passed through the parish, offering work to an excommunicate, and even allowing 200 horses to graze in the churchyard, causing damage to graves, 'uppon a fayre day'.[106] These examples indicate some of the more unusual charges. It can thus be seen that any attempt to 'categorise' such a spread of disparate charges presents difficulties. Offences such as these are too few in an inquiry spread over three archdeaconries, covering a large part of the seventeenth century, for the purpose of statistics. These 'isolated' or 'unique' charges have therefore been left on one side and the most frequent charges have been grouped into five categories for the tables: repairs to the fabric or structure of the church; repairs, replacements and improvements to fittings and ornaments; delivery of presentments (lists of alleged failings of their parishioners) at visitations; failure to take the oath of office; and administrative shortcomings to do with accounts, for example, or provision of registers for baptisms, marriages and burials.

These charges – and, indeed, the more unusual charges – brought against churchwardens in the consistory courts are all about the orderly management of the church (its fabric and fittings or the accounts) and the behaviour and conformity of the parishioners (which they drew to the attention of the episcopal authorities through their annual or triennial presentments). Analysis should reveal much about the nature of the Church's control over churchwardens and, more particularly, which of their duties it thought most important.

Issues about structure and fittings do not feature, rather surprisingly, in prosecutions of churchwardens from the Archdeaconry of Taunton (Wells) or, at least, not in the specimen Michaelmas terms before the Wars and Interregnum. Such complaints were (relatively) common, however, as has already been made clear, among the corresponding charges at Worcester and Winchester. Repairs to fabric were concerns at Kings Norton (Worcester) in 1613, for example, where 'the pavement' was said to be deficient, and at Brading (Winchester) in 1623, where the steeple was said to be 'in decay'.[107] Twenty-four churchwardens faced charges of this kind at Worcester in 1615 and 17 at Winchester in 1619. Fittings caused constant problems in the same two archdeaconries: the organ at All Saints Evesham and the bells and pulpit at Martin Hussingtree are just two examples at Worcester in 1613, while there was a host of complaints at Winchester in 1623 – a 'wormeaten' communion table at Havant and missing flagons at more than one church in the archdeaconry will have to serve as illustrations.[108] The highest numbers of complaints about fittings were 13 at Worcester in 1613 and 17 at Winchester in 1619.

There were problems with presentments in all three archdeaconries. Presentments were missing from Sparsholt and were apparently too brief at Twyford, both in the Archdeaconry of Winchester, in 1621 and 1623 respectively.[109] They were missing also from Upton on Severn and Kings Norton, both Worcester, both in 1615.[110] The churchwardens of Wellington (Wells), meanwhile, faced prosecution in 1618 because of a complaint by the vicar for not presenting the names of people failing to receive communion at Easter.[111] Eighteen churchwardens were summoned to the consistory courts at Worcester in 1615 for this kind of offence, six at Winchester in 1621 and four at Wells in 1618. The remaining issues, such as failure to take the oath of office or questions about accounts, were even rarer.

Prosecutions against churchwardens fell sharply in all three archdeaconries after the Restoration. Court books for the Winchester Archdeaconry include two or three complaints about administration during Michaelmas term 1663 but none in the 1670s and 1680s.

66   CHURCH COURTS AND THE PEOPLE IN SEVENTEENTH-CENTURY ENGLAND

Proceedings were a little more active at Wells: reflecting damage in the Wars and subsequent upheavals of the 1650s, no doubt, nine churchwardens faced charges about fabric and 16 about fittings in 1663, but cases dwindled and the highest number – four – concerned presentments in 1671. Matters were much the same in the regular sessions of the court at Worcester: there were half a dozen, mainly about oaths of office, in 1661, and minute numbers in the 1670s and 1680s, with failure to produce presentments just reaching double figures in 1675. It should be said, however, that there were somewhat larger numbers of prosecutions arising from 'visitation' activity in the diocese – 37 charges in 1679, for example – and alleged offences can be found in all five categories during those proceedings: the need for repairs to the steeple of the church at Hanley Castle (1676); for 'the new casting of the fowerth bell ... crackt and ... uselesse' at Upton on Severn (1679); and problems with oaths at Wixford (1682), presentments at Naunton Beauchamp (1679) and administration (a terrier) at Dodderhill (1679).[112]

Only in one category – fittings at Winchester in 1619 – did complaints against churchwardens exceed 30 in any of the Michaelmas terms surveyed in this study. Only twice before the Interregnum were there between 20 and 30 complaints in any one category per term – over fittings again at Winchester in 1623 and over structure at Worcester in 1615. The remainder, whether before or after the upheavals of the 1640s and 1650s, lie between 10 and 20 complaints or else are in single figures, with the exception of 24 charges about presentments at Wells in Michaelmas term 1633 (and 22 about structure in the visitation proceedings at Worcester in 1682).

The crucial issue is the order of importance of the five most numerous categories. The numbers of charges against the churchwardens of Taunton are too small, whether in the later 1610s and early 1620s or in the 1670s, to make any difference to the calculation. At Winchester, charges regarding fittings and fabric (or structure) were the most numerous in the 1610s and 1620s, with proportions of just above and just below 50 per cent respectively. Presentments and administrative failings were next, albeit a long way behind, and there were no charges concerning oaths. Matters were slightly different, meanwhile, at Worcester: there were more problems with fabric than fittings, presentments were rising in number and oaths and administration were either minute or non-existent. The numbers of charges against churchwardens had suffered a steep decline by the 1670s. There were no charges against the churchwardens of Winchester or at Wells, while at Worcester, among the small number of charges brought, those concerning presentments prevailed, followed by fittings and then equal numbers of charges about oaths and administrative failings.

There is, of course, nothing in the books to explain why the ecclesiastical authorities appear to have intervened on such a small, and declining, scale – why, in other words, there were so few charges against churchwardens even before the Interregnum – nor why decline prevailed afterwards. It would be tempting to conclude, from the small and declining numbers of charges, that all was well – and getting better – at parish level. This would chime well with the all too frequent 'omnia bene' assertions in churchwardens' presentments. Other possible explanations range from recording of derelictions in different, but long since lost, books, to lax supervision of their activities. The eclipse of prosecutions of churchwardens at Winchester and Wells by the 1670s and 1680s may lie in the dysfunctionality of their courts by that time. The explanation for the exceptional survival of prosecutions at Worcester, albeit at minute levels, after the Restoration may lie in the keener surveillance of the then chancellors and bishops of the diocese.

Charges, however, are charges. They are not convictions and so assessment of the state of churchwardens and parishes must await analysis of verdicts in the next part of this book. Charges indicate what the concerns of the Church may have been and whom and what it aimed to keep in order. Interest must lie, at this point, in the small scale of intervention by the Church in all categories of offences alleged against churchwardens in the later seventeenth century. The order of concern appears to have been fittings, structure and presentments before the Interregnum, and presentments, then fittings, on the basis of one archdeaconry and on slender evidence, after the Restoration.

Charges against the clergy

The duties and standards required of the parish clergy are, again, set out in the canons of 1604. Behaviour, residence, preaching, vestments, prayer book, conduct of services, baptism, communion, catechising – all these and more are in the canons,[113] and prosecution turned on alleged derelictions. This inquiry asks several critical questions. Which misdemeanours of the clergy most concerned the church authorities? How thorough was the pursuit of clerical wrongdoing before the Wars and Interregnum? Did the scrutiny increase or decrease after the Restoration? Ultimately, did the Church maintain an effective hold on its chief agents for the advancement of its interests?

In 1619, 23 clergymen – rectors, vicars and 'perpetual curates' – serving in the Archdeaconry of Winchester were charged with an array of offences. These form the largest number in any of the specimen Michaelmas terms in all three archdeaconries. The next highest number – 12 clergymen – were also charged at Winchester, in 1623. Numbers, otherwise, at Winchester and Wells never rose above seven in the 1610s and early 1620s. Numbers of those orders continued at Wells in the 1630s, and no clergy appear to have been summoned at all in the 1670s and 1680s in either archdeaconry. Numbers were even more minute at Worcester before the Wars but, contrasting with Winchester and Wells, there were a few in the 1670s and 1680s. The numbers of accused clergy at Winchester before the Wars were exceptional and most of the time, in all three archdeaconries, in the specimen terms at least, numbers were small – and declining.

These clergy faced a long list of charges. This is particularly so at Winchester, again, where the court books show the largest array of alleged clergy offences in any of the three archdeaconries in the late 1610s and early 1620s. The highest number of clergy (18 over the three Michaelmas terms) were accused of failing to ensure proper services. Among them was Ambrose Webb, 'perpetual curate' of Basing in 1623, 'for reading prayers at unseasonable houres', which, if true, may reflect over-commitment because, as a pluralist, he was responsible for Basingstoke as well as Basing.[114] Another 11 were charged over the same period with chancel neglect, one of whom was Robert Pistor, for failing to repair the chancel at Havant.[115] Much smaller numbers fall into the other categories. Samuel Marshatt of Botley was one of five summoned for a surplice offence; John Wharton of St Maurice, Winchester, one of four for administrative irregularities; Thomas Lake of Lyndhurst one of three for pluralism; 'Hill of Bishops Waltham' one of three for licence problems; which leaves Thomas Charlock of Newport (Isle of Wight), the sole defender against a charge of conducting a clandestine marriage.[116]

All these cases are drawn from the Winchester Consistory Court in the late 1610s and early 1620s and concern parish clergy within the Archdeaconry of Winchester. Most of their prosecutions can be paralleled at this time in the other archdeaconries. Indictment for failing to take the oath to perform the office of rural dean seems to have been unique to Wells but missing licences, conduct of clandestine marriages and neglect of services all occur either there or at Worcester.[117] Indeed, the catalogue of indictments against Thomas Lake, rector of Minstead and curate of Lyndhurst (Winchester), in 1619 – chancel decay, preaching licence problems, neglect of the registers, failing to catechise, pluralism – had already been foreshadowed in 1615 by the pluralism of '*m(a)g(istru)m*' Balamy of St Lawrence Evesham (Worcester), to which charge were added refusing to wear the surplice, condoning sitting for communion, ignoring holy days and neglecting to perambulate. These are two further cases, moreover, where pluralism may have lain at the root of many of the other alleged shortcomings.[118]

There were even fewer cases in any of the three courts after the Restoration, though, again, there were more which do not 'make' the tables because of their 'exceptionality'. Christopher Cosyer, rector of Catherington, faced a dilapidations charge, and Timothy Goodaker, curate of Timsbury, a 'conformity' charge, both at Winchester in 1680, but neither has been entered on the tables because of their rarity.[119] Among alleged offences on the tables failure to celebrate communion arose at Wells and clandestine marriage at Worcester, both in the early 1660s,[120] and, perhaps inevitably, there were a few chancel, licence and clandestine marriage issues, all at Worcester, in the 1670s and 1680s.[121]

Averages hide extremes, such as the 15 clergymen accused of neglect of services at Winchester in 1619 or the two in 1623, but they are more reliable for ranking clerical transgressions in terms of occurrence or frequency. Combining the averages for the three archdeaconries suggests conduct of services, chancel repairs, oaths and surplice wearing were the main charges – in that order – in the 1610s and 1620s; licences, services and administrative oversights prevailed in the 1670s and early 1680s.

Those charges and their order may have been driven by the behaviour of the clergy but they also reflect the concerns of the ecclesiastical authorities. What thinking lay behind their charges must remain in doubt for want of evidence but is fairly certain. When the ecclesiastical authorities brought charges about oaths of rural deans,[122] or about licences for curates and preaching, they sought certainty about authentication of the clergy. When they pursued clergy over the maintenance of registers (typical of administrative charges), they simply sought proper record keeping. When they brought charges about chancels, they were concerned about upkeep of the physical plant. Shortcomings over oaths, licences and registers seem to be the result of carelessness and incompetence, chancel problems are likely to have arisen because of expense, and even failing to conduct services may have arisen purely from laziness. Failing to wear the surplice, meanwhile, may reflect religious principle, conscience and scruple, and this would, no doubt, have been the major concern to the authorities.

Several 'cautionary' points should be made. Firstly, there was always the likelihood, in an age when discretion reigned over 'transparency', that cases involving clergymen would be transferred to private hearings at the bishop's palace. The instruction '*Consule dominum Episcopum*' (consult the lord bishop), in the case of George Newton, Vicar of Taunton Magdalen (Wells) in 1633, appears to imply this, as does '*in adventu Dom(ini) Episcopi*' (literally on the arrival of the lord bishop and, possibly, in the presence of the bishop in court or in his palace) in the cases of Benjamin Herbert and Edward Phillipps, rectors of Suckley and Oddingly (both Worcester) respectively in 1680 (and there were more examples at Worcester in the 1690s).[123] It is not always clear whether the accused went to court or to the palace. If discretion was the aim, public listing of the cases would seem to defeat the object of the exercise and, as Peirs and Stillingfleet did sit in their courts from time to time, these cases, the only examples found, may not in fact have been withdrawn to private sessions but heard in open court. Cases may also have been transferred to the bishop's palace before details 'escaped', while others may have bypassed the courts completely and the nature of the charges thereby concealed from public – and later researchers' – gaze.

Nor, secondly, should low numbers and entries omitted from tables be allowed to leave the impression that offences – or, at least, allegations of offences – were always minor or trivial. In 1619 James Goodlad, rector of Binstead (Isle of Wight, Winchester), was cited 'for fiting (fighting) in the chancel' and, as his wife was facing a similar charge, it looks as if they were persisting with a 'domestic' in a public arena. In 1621 Richard Cole, rector of Michelmersh (Winchester), was alleged to have 'gott his said parsonage by Symonie'. In 1633 Robert Mills, curate of Kilton (Wells), faced a charge of threatening the chastity of Mary Proctor.[124] One of these incidents, the fighting at Binstead, does not appear on the tables again for reasons of space and because there were so few charges of this kind. Its seriousness, however, is not in doubt, and although immorality and simony appear only once in the tables, such charges were regarded with similar horror. Exhortation of the parish clergy to 'moral integrity and purity of life' was stressed in the canons, while the 'persistent vice' of simony was denounced in the same corpus as 'execrable', 'detestable sin', 'covetousness' and 'idolatry'.[125]

Such incidents were rare and it is difficult to gauge their effect on the people at large. Some of the cases – even as allegations and still awaiting a verdict – must have caused a stir and by their very nature – brawling, rape and simony – are obviously 'arresting', and it probably only took a few of them to do immense harm to the image of the Church. A total of 23 cases may look small – and even smaller when expressed as a percentage of total bodies of clergy or of all accused people – but the thought of 23 men of God 'in the dock' – 9 per cent of the clergy and 6 per cent of all accused – in the space of one Michaelmas term, even if the transgressions were only allegations, may have seemed shocking and disgraceful then as now. Charges concerning Goodlad's commotion at Binstead in 1619 and Goodaker's conflicts with orthodox belief and practice (if such they were) in 1680 would have been graphic, newsworthy and damaging. Public confidence may well have been shaken even at this early stage in proceedings, before a verdict, by these more spectacular cases of clerical dereliction.

The balance of charges

Most charges against churchwardens at Winchester and Worcester before the Wars and Interregnum concerned fabric and fittings and these were joined by charges about shortcomings over presentments at Worcester in the 1670s and 1680s.[126] The greatest number of charges against the parish clergy before the Wars concerned conduct of services, insofar as it is possible to generalise, together with chancels and surplices, while after the Wars services, again, and licences and administrative matters dominated. Charges, then, against churchwardens and parish clergy remained much the same, *mutatis mutandis*, from the 1620s to the 1680s in the three archdeaconries.

Prosecutions, or citations, against laymen and women did change from archdeaconry to archdeaconry and from time to time over the course of the century. 'Moral' and 'religious' charges were running neck and neck, in terms of balance, at Worcester before the Wars and Interregnum. Imbalance reigned – in opposite directions – in the other two archdeaconries: there were nearly twice as many moral prosecutions as religious ones at Wells, while at Winchester it was the other way round and religious charges outnumbered moral ones. These different emphases became even more pronounced by the 1670s and 1680s, when religious prosecutions continued to dominate at Winchester and moral prosecutions at Wells. Worcester is more problematic to assess at this later date: prosecutions in 'regular' sessions suggest a shift, though not as large as at Wells, from religious to moral prosecutions, but 'visitation' prosecutions imply the opposite, with an extreme imbalance – 5 per cent moral to 75 per cent religious – in the triennial visitation of 1682.

This raises questions about the typicality of the balance of charges and their trends in the nation as a whole. To begin with Elizabethan times, it would seem, when comparing balance in the three archdeaconries with other research, that moral charges were predominant in Norwich, Salisbury, London, Essex and Cambridgeshire, and that this was the emphasis in the Elizabethan Diocese of Winchester as well.[127] This remained the balance in the 1620s and 1630s, though less clearly, in Essex and London,[128] but more so at Chester, Norwich, York, Oxford, Peterborough and Canterbury.[129] Wells, if not Worcester or Winchester, before the Wars and Interregnum would fit this 'template', and Quaife's study of Somerset suggests substantial proportions of prosecutions were moral at Wells.[130] The research of Martin Jones and Margaret Potter, together with comment by Martin Ingram and Anne Whiteman, suggests greater emphasis on religious prosecutions after the Restoration. Kit Mercer has drawn attention, moreover, to a 'brief flowering of persecution' of dissenters in the wake of Exclusion, though, in his study, this was temporary, confined to three peculiars of Canterbury and driven, apparently, by a 'pugnacious' chancellor.[131] This emphasis on religious prosecutions is borne out by the findings of this survey of court activity at Winchester and in the visitation proceedings at Worcester, but not in the regular proceedings at Worcester and not at Wells.

It should be said that the different emphases within the three archdeaconries and elsewhere caution against dogmatic generalisation. While it is quite possible that two of the three archdeaconries, Winchester and Worcester, with an increasing stress on religious prosecutions between the 1610s and the 1670s, were more typical of trends over the seventeenth century, Wells may serve as a warning that what happened in one diocese did not always happen in all the others.

Explaining the shifting balance of charges

Control of morals was probably uppermost in the minds of the ecclesiastical authorities in the early years of the seventeenth century. Rates of illegitimacy increased from the 1590s to peak in the 1610s at 2.5 per cent a year of all births and, possibly, in terms of numbers, two hundred per diocese.[132] The authorities of the seventeenth century would not have had Laslett's figures but even without them, this growing problem may have been too obvious for both Church and state to ignore.

Bastardy, fornication and adultery formed the largest group of prosecutions in the Archdeaconry of Taunton, were equal with religious prosecutions at Worcester and, though surpassed by religion, still involved significant numbers at Winchester before the Wars and Interregnum. To the Church, fornication, adultery and bastardy were moral issues. With their links to vagrancy, they raised concerns about law, order and discipline in the minds of king, Parliament, merchants and gentry, and they provoked apprehensions among rate and taxpayers about the costs to the community for housing, clothing and feeding vagrants, bastard bearers and their children. The Poor Law of 1610 was a reflection of these concerns.[133] The emphasis placed on morality and the prosecution of fornicators, adulterers and bastardy bearers by the ecclesiastical authorities in the consistory courts at Worcester and even more so at Wells in the 1610s may be another reflection of these concerns. They were, moreover, far from alone in the 1610s, to judge from the emphasis on morals in so many other dioceses at this time.

The relative peace of the 1620s and 1630s was shattered by a train of events in the 1640s – the Long Parliament, Civil Wars, the execution of the King – and in the 1650s by an explosion of sects with revolutionary political, religious and social ideas. Besides the more moderate Presbyterians, Congregationalists and Independents, a Pandora's box of extremist sects – Anabaptists, Ranters, Seekers, Fifth Monarchy Men and Quakers – emerged and flourished, rejecting authority, whether government, the courts, the family, or especially the Church and its ceremonies (baptism, marriage and burial). The rise of radicalism in the 1640s, under conditions of war, is not in doubt, nor is the explosion of extremist sects in the 1650s, but their size is questionable. Christopher Hill considers there was 'a great overturning ... of everything in England', and David Cressy writes of 'a decade and a half of freedom, experiment and confused recrimination'.[134] While giving the impression of massive numbers, they have both found precise figures too 'hard to gauge'.[135] Bernard Capp estimates radicals at some 5 per cent of adults in a population of several million. This is a substantial but not overwhelming number, though even a small band of Seekers, Ranters or Fifth Monarchy Men wandering through the streets and lanes, living strange lifestyles and expressing weird – revolutionary – religious and social ideas would have appeared alarming and threatening to usually peaceful communities.

The emergence of these groups, large or small, brought to the fore the two issues central to this study – religious observance and morals – and the enactment of new laws followed. An Act of 1650 'for suppressing the Detestable Sins of Incest, Adultery and Fornication' prescribed prison for fornication and the death penalty for adultery and incest.[136] This was clearly a policy of outright suppression far more severe, even savage, than Elizabethan and early Stuart legislation. Another Act of 1650 for 'Relief of the Religious' is more complex to assess, however. The Act repealed the Elizabethan penal statutes of 1559, 1581 and 1593,[137] but although the penalties – the fines and forfeitures – for failing to attend church had gone, the new Act still required regular church attendance. Both the Instrument of Government of 1653 and the Humble Petition and Advice of 1657 authorised, in almost identical words, a measure of religious toleration but within limits, and this did not extend to supporters of 'popery' (Catholics) and 'prelacy' (Anglicans) nor to 'the licentious'.[138] 'Anglicans' and 'Puritans' (or Presbyterians) had changed places and it was the turn of the former to suffer persecution while the latter, joined by some of the less extremist sects, now enjoyed freedom.

These Acts and constitutions show a rising concern about religion and morals under the Commonwealth and Protectorate but numbers of respective prosecutions may form a better guide to the question of balance. Andrew Coleby shows that there was action in Hampshire with 'a steady stream of presentments, indictments and imprisonments' for bastardy and formication and 'vigorous enforcement' of the law against Catholics and Quakers.[139] It has been left to Fiona McCall, however, to conduct a more thorough analysis. From 2,500 records of assize and quarter session proceedings in a dozen or more English counties and parts of Wales in the 1640s and 1650s she lists 173 potential adulterers, 68 Quakers, 176 Catholics and (one of the largest groups) 316 charged with working, drinking and playing on the Sabbath. Executions for adultery, it would seem, were rare, and likewise restraint was shown towards most Anglicans and Catholics.[140] Her survey has its limits, firstly in numbers of counties and secondly in the exclusion from her lists of sexual or moral charges unless they were linked to religion. Furthermore, it must be remembered, above all, that prosecutions are not the same thing as guilt. Nor, crucially, can any truly certain conclusions be drawn about the balance between moral and religious concerns. If not 'definitive', however, the figures must be 'indicative' and certainly show the continuing pursuit of moral and religious behaviour by those in power 'according to their lights'. The explosions of the 1650s had heightened the ruling classes' awareness of both problems and alerted them to the need for action.

This was the legacy which the authorities – king, chancellor, Parliament – had to deal with at the Restoration. The world had been turned upside down in a whirl of social, religious and political upheavals in the 1650s which left a residue of potential trouble in the 1660s. Hill implies, but does not discuss, the survival of an underclass of difference and discontent, and Cressy's more graphic account about extremist sects forming 'a cultural matrix … aflame with enormities and enmities … which had lost the habit of church attendance, had abandoned the regime of episcopal discipline, or fallen prey to apathy and cynicism' is probably an exaggeration. As for numbers in the 1660s, neither again attempts an estimate, Cressy mentioning 'an unknown proportion of the population' and Hill commenting that 'what went on underground we can only guess'.[141]

The truth of the matter – the scale of the problems – is far from certain. Laslett's research shows a decline in the levels of bastardy from 2.5 per cent for the decade of the 1610s to 1.2 or 1.3 per cent for the 1670s, but in Cressy's view parish registers under-represent the scale of the problem.[142] Whoever is right, even 1.2 per cent could have meant a hundred or more illegitimate births a year in every diocese (if spread, notionally, in an even way) and bishops and politicians would have been aware of and concerned about the social problems of bastardy and vagrancy because of their visibility. They would certainly have had figures (however accurate or otherwise) for the scale of religious divergence. The famous Census of 1676, commanded by Sheldon and conducted by Compton, claimed that, among the adult population overall, some 5 per cent lay outside the Church of England and were either Catholic recusants or Protestant dissenters of one kind or another. Five per cent is, in itself, a significant proportion. Questions have been raised, moreover, about the accuracy – and the honesty – of the Compton Census. Miller and Kenyon, while disagreeing with each other on many points, both estimate the existence of much larger numbers of Catholics, and this may also have been true of Protestant dissenting groups as well.[143]

Of greater importance, however, is 'perception' – what contemporaries knew or thought they knew. The key people were the men of property – the merchants and landed gentry. They saw costs arising from the presence of pregnant women and bastard babies. They saw danger in roaming beggars, travelling ministers, camps in the fields and meetings in barns and outbuildings. Potential turned into reality from Penruddock and Venner in the 1650s, Lambert, Ludlow and Venner again, together with the Yorkshire revolt, in the 1660s, to the Popish and Rye House plots of the 1670s and 1680s.[144] Vagrancy and dissent were major concerns but their ultimate fear – their 'obsession' – was security.[145] The men of property sought 'assurance' about order and control above all else.[146] Their views were shared by governments whether republican or monarchical. These were the overriding concerns of the Rump and Protectorate Parliaments; of Cromwell and the major generals in the 1650s; of Charles, Clarendon and the Cavalier Parliament in the 1660s; and ultimately of the merchant and landed gentry classes at all times.

This legacy of the 1650s governed inevitably the legislation of the 1660s. The politicians of the Restoration took more steps on both fronts. The Act of 1650 concerning adultery and fornication was automatically nullified by the restoration of the monarchy but the Act of Settlement, passed in 1662, built on earlier legislation and increased controls over vagrants, including 'putative fathers and lewd mothers of bastard children', as part of the 'strategy' to achieve an orderly society.[147] It was also the end of the religious policies of the Instrument and the Humble Petition. The emphasis was again on the enforcement of an Anglican monopoly, the exclusion of Catholics and the suppression of Protestant dissenters. Anglicans were once more on top, Catholics remained outlawed and Presbyterians and the sects became considerably circumscribed outsiders. Attendance at church and receiving communion were required for public office and heavy controls were placed on travelling ministers and on the assemblies – conventicles – of dissenters in the 1660s, while Catholics were specifically denied seats in Parliament and political appointments in the 1670s.[148] Security was the consistent and dominant theme which underlay this legislation. The presence of 'rogues, vagabonds and sturdy beggars' is a recurrent theme of the Act of Settlement, and 'schism … rebellion' and 'insurrection' likewise of the Conventicle and Five Mile Acts.

It was in this new, uncertain and unsettling, world, disturbing bishops as much as the secular establishment, no doubt, that the consistory courts were revived in 1661. These courts, including those at Winchester, Worcester and Wells, were expected to play their part in maintaining social order, and most of the bishops, infused with much the same sentiments as the politicians who sat in the Cavalier Parliament, are likely, insofar as they set the agenda, to have been willing agents in the cause. Of course the emphasis differed from diocese to diocese and from bishop to bishop, but their common ground was the maintenance of order and the suppression of any threats to it.

'Local factors' no doubt determined the balance of cases, religious or social, in the years following the Restoration.[149] The personalities of bishops, chancellors and even apparitors and churchwardens may well have played a part in all these developments. In general terms, an earnest bishop here, a diligent chancellor there – or their opposites – could make all the difference. Bishops could speak in different ways on different occasions, maximising the problems at one time, minimising them at another. Bishop Morley of Winchester is a 'spectacular' example of someone changing his tune – with the best of intentions in his case – to suit the mood: orating in urgent terms and demanding action against the 'sectaries' on the national stage, in the House of Lords or when writing to Sheldon and Danby but, ever mindful of the need for peace 'at home', apparently exercising restraint in his own diocesan court.[150]

More specifically, 26 or 27 individual bishops, enjoying extensive power and prestige, were bound to have their own views and the opportunity to impose them. They could, therefore, insofar as they took any interest in their diocese, have turned the machinery at their disposal in any direction they chose, and their articles – the lists of questions – they drew up for their visitations ought to reflect their respective preferences – and prejudices.[151] Surviving articles for the bishops in post at the critical moments of this study – Andrewes and Morley of Winchester, Thornborough and Fleetwood of Worcester, and Lake and Mews of Wells – laid a consistent and heavy stress on religion. Andrewes produced 18 on religion and four on morals in 1619 and Lake 25 and seven in 1626, while Thornborough devised nine on morals but no fewer than 37 on religion for his visitation also of 1626. Their successors' articles were smaller in number but the imbalance remained: Morley's questionnaire (1674) comprised 10 religious and two moral items, those of Mews (1673) and Fleetwood (1679) 11 to two.[152]

Fleetwood's articles and the churchwardens' lists of presentments applied at his subsequent visitation in 1679 are, of course, two separate documents but both show considerable emphasis on religion, and it could be claimed that the tilting balance towards religion in consistory court prosecutions under Andrewes and Morley mirrors their articles, but otherwise there exists a mismatch between bishops' concerns and prosecution categories in their courts. This is particularly so at Wells and to a lesser extent at Worcester in its regular, as distinct from the triennial, visitations. Several factors may explain the discrepancies. There are large gaps in surviving collections of articles for one thing. Categorisation is another issue, particularly so with moral issues where several 'crimes' – for example adultery, fornication, incest, sex before marriage – are combined in one article by most bishops but placed in separate lists in the tables for this study. Some of the sets of articles, finally, are so similar – for example those of Mews and Fleetwood – that they awaken suspicions that some of the bishops took 'short cuts' and borrowed from their colleagues. They would probably have agreed with the general tenor and balance of the articles but, no doubt, with differing degrees of enthusiasm. Wholesale copying implies little time or thought spent on the matter and such articles did not necessarily reflect priorities.

The strongest factor, however, would, no doubt, have been the difference between what concerned the bishop and what his officials, from chancellor to apparitor and churchwarden, found 'on the ground'. Prosecutions are more likely to have mirrored conditions and 'crime rates' in the diocese. The prevalence of Catholic recusancy in one particular area or Protestant dissent in another would dictate the balance of prosecutions, as would the incidence of bastardy. A 'craze' for playing a particular game or sport on the Sabbath or the 'magnetism' of a dissenting lecturer at a conventicle could, by themselves, for example, increase the focus of the courts, secular and spiritual, on prosecutions concerning church attendance. A local flood could bring poverty to a settlement, producing widows and orphans, for example, which in turn could raise concerns about vagrancy and the poor rate in the secular courts and suspicions of cohabitation and prostitution in the church courts. It is difficult to be certain how far the initiative and consequent emphasis arose from general policy decisions of the authorities, lay or ecclesiastical, or how far they were merely responding to particular problems in their areas. This is a conundrum impossible to resolve, but conditions in the localities rather than the sometimes notional perspectives of the bishops are more likely to have determined the balance of cases.

To sum up: the charges throw light on the nature of the Church's attempts to control society – the issues which concerned it and which it wished to prosecute – but this was not at all the same in all three archdeaconries, nor were the trends uniform. Before the Civil Wars and Interregnum moral prosecutions were dominant at Wells, religious prosecutions were dominant at Winchester, while there was a balance between the two at Worcester. By the 1670s and 1680s Winchester and Wells had continued to diverge: Winchester towards religious cases, Wells towards moral ones, while at Worcester the emphasis in regular sessions was moral but during episcopal visitations religious. Factors dictating policy and prosecutions may have been a general, if imprecise, awareness of illegitimacy rates, for example, or the more concrete – visible – evidence of rising dissent. Security was undoubtedly a growing issue underlying political and probably episcopal motivation. The emphasis on one type of prosecution may have been entirely accidental, however, depending on the hazard of local circumstance from the personality of the bishop to the craze for a particular sport.

Notes

1 Churchwardens were laymen, of course, but their duties and any charges against them form a distinct group and will therefore be dealt with separately.
2 See Appendix 2, Tables 1–3.
3 There is disagreement about 'reputation': it was more the concern of women (Gowing, *Domestic Dangers*, e.g. p. 109); it concerned men as much as women (Capp, 'Double Standard Revisited', p. 71; Ingram, *Carnal Knowledge*, p. 31); and the scale of debt proceedings in the sixteenth and seventeenth centuries – 'hundreds of law suits in borough courts' – revealed by Muldrew may have been as much about reputation as about money (Muldrew, 'Rural Credit', p. 177); defamation and debt appear much more in instance business, the key source of their work but not the subject of this study.

4 Quaife suggests six 'categories' of evidence in cases of sexual irregularity (Quaife, *Wanton Wenches*, p. 48).

5 HRO, C1/33, 2/12/1619 (no folios).

6 WRO, 802 2760, ff. 24v, 235v.

7 SHLS, D/D/ca/224, f. 153v; D/D/ca/243, f. 33v.

8 SHLS, D/D/ca/207, f. 271r (Baleer), D/D/ca/224, f. 144r (Nowell), D/D/ca/243, f. 25r (Goddard).

9 HRO, C1/33, 3/12/1619 (no folios); C1/34, f. 14v.

10 SHLS, D/D/ca/224, f. 123v; Martin Ingram, among others, takes the same view (Ingram, *Carnal Knowledge*, pp. 93–4).

11 HRO, C1/35, f. 10r; SHLS, D/D/ca/224, f. 94v.

12 SHLS, D/D/ca/224, f. 126v; D/D/ca/313, f. 191r.

13 SHLS, D/D/ca/243, f. 70v.

14 SHLS, D/D/ca/331, ff. 164v, 166v.

15 WRO, 802 2760, ff. 329r, 14v.

16 SHLS, D/D/ca/207, f. 244r; D/D/ca/243, f. 27v; HRO, C1/33, 3/12/1619 (no folios).

17 SHLS, D/D/ca/224, f. 109v: *'suspicat(ur) de incontinen(tia)... q(uo)d de super laborat pub(li) ca vox et fama'* – i.e. 'he is suspected of incontinence ... because the rumour mill is busy'; translation is problematic and 'rumour mill' may seem a little 'free' but it is difficult to know exactly what the clerk and his contemporaries had in mind – rumour, gossip, damage to reputation(?); an entry on the next folio, in English, runs 'there hath bine and is a com(m)on fame thereof'; see also Carlson, *Marriage*, p. 144.

18 SHLS, D/D/ca/224, f. 253r; D/D/ca/207, f. 261r.

19 SHLS, D/D/ca/243, ff. 64r, 98r.

20 WRO, 802 2760, f. 419v; HRO, C1/35, f. 3v.

21 WRO, 802 2760, f. 339r.

22 WRO, 802 2760, f. 308r ('cowhouse'), f. 320v ('sheepings'); see also Gowing, *Common Bodies*, pp. 151, 153, 157–60.

23 SHLS, D/D/ca/207, f. 240v.

24 See e.g. Dabhoiwala, *Origins of Sex*, pp. 22, 29; Gowing, *Common Bodies*, pp. 157–60, 161–2, 165–6; Wrightson and Levine, *Terling*, p. 127.

25 43 EI c.2; 14 CII c.12.

26 See, for fuller discussion of these points, the sections 'Church and people: the impact of its courts on society' in Chapter 3 and 'Wider reasons for decline by the 1670s' in Chapter 4.

27 Prosecutions of officiating clergymen for this 'crime' will be dealt with in a later section.

28 WRO, 802 2760, f. 393r; HRO, C1/33, 11/11/1619 (no folios).

29 HRO, C1/35, f. 57v.

30 WRO, 802 2760, f. 55v.

31 WRO, 802 2760, f. 5v.

32 E.g. WRO, 794 011 2722 2, Book 32, f. 158r (9/1680, clandestine marriage); SHLS, D/D/ca/350, 6/12/1671 (no folios, no banns or licence).

33 Canon 99 (1604); see Bray, *Anglican Canons*, p. 890.

34 WRO, 802 2760, f. 80r; HRO, C1/33, 3/12/1619 (no folios); SHLS, D/D/ca/350, 30/10/1671 (no folios); these relationships are still illegal in the UK (Sexual Offences Act 2003).

35 WRO, 802 2760, f. 23v; 794 011 2513 18, Book 20, f. 38v; 794 011 2722 2, Book 32, f. 258r; in the last case, step relations aged 21 or more can marry in England, Wales and Scotland (Marriage Act 1986); the age of the woman is not clear in the court book and my comment presumes she was over 21.

36 See Appendix 2, Tables 4–6.

37 HRO, C/135, ff. 14r, 55v, 15r; WRO, 802 2760, ff. 374r.

38 HRO, C1/35, f. 6r; WRO, 802 2760, f. 66r; SHLS, D/D/ca/295, f. 162v.

39 HRO, C1/35, f. 8r; SHLS, D/D/ca/243, f. 98v.

40 WRO, 802 2760, f. 236r; HRO, C1/34, f. 4r; SHLS, D/D/ca 313, f. 232v.

41 HRO, C1/37, 27/10/1663 (no folios).

42 SHLS, D/D/ca/207, f. 246v; HRO, C1/35, f. 24v.

43 HRO, C1/34, f. 17r (reaping); WRO, 802 2760, ff. 330r (leasing); 52v (winnowing), 15r (carting); HRO, C1/35, f. 23v (grinding).

44 SHLS, D/D/ca/224, ff. 141r (Steeven); WRO, 802 2760, f. 237v ('raking'); D/D/ca 243, f. 71r ('cardeing').

45 HRO, C1/34, f. 7r; C1/35, f. 55r.
46 HRO, C1/34, f. 13r, C1/35, f. 14v (butcher); SHLS, D/D/ca/207, f. 279v; HRO, C1/35, f. 20v (barber); SHLS, D/D/ca/207, f. 218r; HRO, C1/34, f. 34r; WRO, 802 2760, f. 51r (brewer); SHLS, D/D/ca/243, f. 98r (baker); WRO, 802 2760, ff. 283r (carpentry), 416v (builder); SHLS, D/D/ca/243, f. 98r (soap); WRO, 802 2760, f. 21v (clock).
47 SHLS, D/D/ca/295, f. 115r (ploughing); D/D/ca/331, f. 196r (ploughing); D/D/ca/295, f. 90v (cobbling); D/D/ca/331, f. 200r (milling); D/D/ca/295, f. 90v (barbering); D/D/ca/313, f. 219r (groceries).
48 HRO, C1/35, f. 13v; WRO, 802, 2760, f. 183v; SHLS, D/D/ca/207, f. 251r.
49 HRO, C1/35, ff. 20v, 21r.
50 SHLS, D/D/ca/243, f. 44v.
51 WRO, 802 2760, f. 133r; SHLS, D/D/ca/224, ff. 144r, 157v; D/D/ca/243, ff. 47r, 76v.
52 WRO, 802 2760, f. 279r.
53 WRO, 802 2760, f. 283v.
54 WRO, 802 2760, f. 253v.
55 Horn, *Fasti 1541–1857*, vol. 3, p. 81; visitation books HRO, C1/33 (1619), C1/34 (1621), C1/35 (1623).
56 Canon 21 1603 (e.g. Bray, *Anglican Canons*, p. 291).
57 WRO, 802 2760, f. 256r; HRO, C1/35, f. 7r; SHLS, D/D/ca/243, f. 40r.
58 HRO, C1/35, ff. 9r, 16r, 19v.
59 WRO, 802 2760, f. 123v; HRO, C1/35, ff. 15v (Southampton), 33v (Smith).
60 WRO, 802 2760, ff. 54r; 61r–65r, 237r.
61 WRO, 802 2760, f. 238r.
62 E.g. D/D/ca/295, f. 106v.
63 WRO, 794 011 2722 2, Book 32, ff. 115v (Droitwich), 241v (Bengeworth).
64 See Introduction; see also Appendix 2, Table 7.
65 HRO, C1/34, f. 25r; C1/37, 2/10/1663 (no folios); WRO, 802 2760, f. 136r; 794 011 2760, f. 230v.
66 WRO, 802 2760, f. 419v; HRO, C/133, 12/11/1619 (no folios).
67 WRO, 794 011 2722 2, Book 32, ff. 112r, 116r, 230v.
68 E.g. WRO, 802 2760, f. 14v; 794 011 2722, Book 2, f. 230v.
69 1 EI c.2; 23 EI c.1; 35 EI c.1; 35 EI c.2.
70 See TNA, E 377 *passim* for citations of the Act of 1581 and use of terms such as recusant and conviction.
71 Bowler, *Recusant Roll*, p. xxxvii.
72 Sheldon's Three Questions e.g. BL, Harley MS 7377, f. 61v.
73 E.g. Morley, Bishop of Winchester, LPL, MS 639, f. 270r; BL, Egerton MS 3329, f. 121r.
74 WRO, 794 011 2722 2, Book 32, f. 113v.
75 25 CII c.2; 30 CII c.1; 1W+M c.18.
76 HRO, C1/33, 12/11/1619; WRO, 802 2760, f. 125v (both 'Recusant'), 11/11/1619 (dissenters?).
77 WRO, 802 2760, f. 132r; HRO, C1/34, f. 7r.
78 WRO, 802 2760, f. 285v.
79 HRO, C1/37, 6/11/1663 (no folios).
80 HRO, C1/45, 8/11/1678, 22/11/1678, 7/10/1681, 22/11/1681 (no folios); even fuller treatment of Tichborne mentions *conformitate*, church attendance and the sacrament but is not specific about his Catholicism (e.g. C1/45, 27/1/1683).
81 WRO, 794 011 2722 2, Book 32, ff. 112v ('Roman Catholicke'), 117r ('Anabaptist'), 117v ('Hatt'), 135v ('Separatist'), 114v ('atheist').
82 WRO, 794 011 2722 2, Book 32, e.g. ff. 226v (papist); 253v (Quaker), 217v (Anabaptist), 253r (conventicler), 211v (dissenter).
83 See Thomson, 'Dissenters and Recusants', 2014, pp. 100–5.
84 SHLS, D/D/ca/243, f. 69r.
85 WRO, 802 2760, f. 216v; SHLS, D/D/ca/224, f. 97v; HRO, C1/35, f. 46r; SHLS, D/D/ca/350, 3/10/1671 (no folios).
86 WRO, 802 2760, f. 219v (Bengeworth) ; HRO, C1/33, 3/12/1619 (no folios) (Binstead); SHLS, D/D/ca/224, f. 97v (North Petherton).
87 HRO, C1/33, 12/11/1619 (no folios); C1/34, f. 13v; C1/35, f. 13v; SHLS, D/D/ca/207, f. 278v.
88 SHLS, D/D/ca/207, f. 284r; HRO, C1/37, 4/12/1663 (no folios); SHLS, D/D/ca/243, f. 103r.

THE NATURE OF CHURCH DISCIPLINE   **81**

89 WRO, 802 2760, ff. 81v; 204r; skimmingtons are more fully discussed in the section 'Penance' in Chapter 4; and see Ingram, 'Juridical Folklore', pp. 62, 68–74.

90 See, for discussion of these steps, the section '*Ex officio* procedures' in Chapter 1.

91 HRO, C1/35, f. 23v; WRO, 802 2760, f. 144r; SHLS, D/D/ca/207, f. 283r.

92 HRO, C1/33, 12/11/1619 (no folios); SHLS, D/D/ca/207, f. 283 r.

93 WRO, 802 2760, ff. 173r, 123r, 212v–215r.

94 E.g. SHLS, D/D/ca/350, no folios, 17/10/1671; WRO, 794 011 2722 2, Book 32, f. 229v.

95 See Appendix 2, Table 8.

96 E.g. HRO, C1/35, f. 8v, C1/45, 1/10/1680, SHLS, D/D/ca/224, f. 108v (rate); WRO, 794 011 2722 2, Book 32, f. 113r (dues); HRO, C1/34, f. 17r, WRO, 802 2760, f. 132v ('dewties'/'dueties'); WRO, 802 2760, f. 21v, 794 011 2722 2, Book 32, f. 224r ('lewens'/'levy'); HRO, C1/35, f. 24r (quartersett); HRO, C1/34, 15/12/1619, WRO, 794 011 2722 2, Book 32, f. 114v ('offering'); HRO, C1/35, f. 53v ('taxacon').

97 E.g. HRO, 75M72/PW1, Churchwardens' Accounts, North Waltham, e.g. p. 72, 1613–14; PW2 (no pagination) 1699–1700.

98 HRO, C1/34, ff. 23v, 17r, 9r (7, 8, 11); C1/35, ff. 11–14 (27); SHLS, D/D/ca/313, f. 233r (5).

99 HRO, C1/34, f. 13v; SHLS, D/D/ca/295, f. 108v.

100 SLHS, D/D/ca/313, f. 233r (Colebard); HRO, C1/35, f. 7r (Knight); C1/33, 12/11/1619 (Blake, no folios).

101 Bowden, *Economic Change*, pp. 19, 29, 166, 192, 193, 369.

102 HRO, C1/33, 1/10/1619 (no folios); WRO, 794 011 2722 2, Book 32, ff. 113r, 229v.

103 E.g. canons 20 (communion bread), 81, 82, 83 (fittings), 85 (repairs), 89 (accounts), 109–12, 116 (presentments); see Bray, *Anglican Canons*.

104 WRO, 802 2760, f. 184r (Chaddesley Corbett); SHLS, D/D/ca/354, 16/11/1675 (Fivehead, no folios).

105 WRO, 802 2760, f. 231v (Bretforton); HRO, C1/34, f. 10r (Holy Rood Southampton).

106 HRO, C1/33, 11/11/19, no folios (perambulation); SHLS, D/D/ca/313, f. 191v (organist); D/D/ca 295, f. 156v (bells), f. 155v (horses); WRO, 802 2760, f. 121r (excommunicate).

107 WRO, 802 2760, f. 120r (pavement); HRO, C1/35, f. 54r (steeple).

108 WRO, 802 2760, f. 218v (organ); f. 120v (bells and pulpit); HRO, C1/35, f. 22r (table); f. 18v (flagon).

109 HRO, C1/33, 2/12/1619, no folios (Sparsholt); C1/34, f. 39r (Twyford).

110 WRO, 802 2760, f. 324v (Upton on Severn); f. 142v (Kings Norton).

111 SHLS, D/D/ca/207, f. 256v (Wellington).

112 WRO, 794 011 2722 2, Book 32, f. 9r (steeple); f. 131v (bell); f. 250r (oaths); f. 138r (presentments); f. 116v (terrier).

113 E.g. canons 75 (behaviour), 41 (residence), 45 (preaching), 58 (vestments), 14 (prayer book), 56 (conduct of services and baptism), 21 (communion), 61 (catechising).

114 HRO, C1/35, f. 5v; Webb was vicar of Basingstoke 1593–1648 and curate of Basing (dates unknown) – see Thomson, *Clergy of Winchester*, pp. 194, 224.

115 HRO, C1/35, f. 22r.

116 HRO, C1/35, f. 56r (Marshatt); C1/33 (no folios) 11/11/1619 (Wharton), 15/12/1619, (Lake); C1/35, ff. 20r (Hill), 57r (Charlock); Hill of Bishops Waltham is in inverted commas in the text because it has proved difficult to identify him and the one reference so far discovered does not give his first name.

117 SHLS, D/D/ca/224, f. 130r (oath); WRO, 802 2760, ff. 5v (licence), 375r (marriage), 16r (service); D/D/ca/207, f. 221v (licence).

118 HRO, C1/33, 15/12/1619 (Lake); WRO, 802 2760, f. 236v (Balamy – designation 'mrm', and no first name in the court book).

119 HRO, C1/45 (no folios) 15/10/1680 (Cosyer and Goodaker); 'conformity' is ambiguous and could mean either failure to conform to the belief and worship of the Church of England or failure to produce the necessary certificate confirming compliance; or, because not specified, the crime may not have been about religion at all but some secular crime.

120 SHLS, D/D/ca/338 2, no folios, 27/1/1663 (communion); WRO, 794 011 2513 18, Book 20, f. 40r (marriage).

121 WRO, 794 011 2722 1, Book 30, f. 250v (chancel); f. 258r (licence); 794 011 2722 2, Book 32, ff. 160r, 170r (clandestine marriage).

122 Prosecution for failure to take the oath for the post of rural dean e.g. Edward Cheepewrighte, rector of Norton Fitzwarren, 17/12/1618 (SHLS, D/D/ca/207, f. 267v); these were all cases

occurring at Wells in the 1610s and 1620s, not subsequently and not in the other archdeaconries but, though not representative, too many to ignore.

123 SHLS, D/D/ca/295, f. 163v (Newton); WRO, 794 011 2722 2, Book 32, f. 166r (Herbert and Phillipps); 807 093 2724, Book 38, ff. 109r, 120r, 120v (1690s).

124 HRO, C1/33 (no folios), 3/12/1619 (Goodlad); C1/34, f. 42v (Cole); SHLS, D/D/ca/295. f. 150v (Mills).

125 Canons 5 (1556), 9 (1556), 40 (1604); see Bray, *Anglican Canons*.

126 See Appendix 2, Table 9.

127 Houlbrooke, *Church Courts*, pp. 278–81; Ingram, *Church Courts*, pp. 17, 68, 238; Dabhoiwala, *Origins of Sex*, p. 16; McIntosh, *Havering*, pp. 242, 244–7; Carlson, *Marriage*, p. 143; the usual questions of exact comparability arise with many of these authorities.

128 For Essex: Wrightson and Levine, *Terling*, pp. 119, 125, 126; for London there appears to be some difference between Dabhoiwala, *Origins of Sex*, p. 16 and Gowing, *Domestic Dangers*, p. 31; vagueness and disagreements must serve as a reminder of the hazards of generalisation and the eternal truth that what happened in one diocese may not have applied elsewhere.

129 Marchant, *Church under Law*, p. 217; Jones, 'Oxford and Peterborough', pp. 17–20; Potter, 'Canterbury', p. 54.

130 Quaife's work needs clarification concerning both the areas covered by his courts and his percentages; for example, did sex before marriage form a third of all charges or of lay charges alone? (Quaife, *Wanton Wenches*, pp. 38, 58, 187).

131 Ingram, *Church Courts*, p. 372; Whiteman, 'Re-establishment', p. 125; Jones, 'Oxford and Peterborough', pp. 48, 63, 64; Potter, 'Canterbury', pp. 193–4 (she persists with the word 'presentments'); Mercer, 'Ecclesiastical Discipline', pp. 352, 358.

132 Laslett, 'Comparing Illegitimacy', p. 14.

133 7 JI c.3.

134 Cressy, *Birth, Marriage, Death*, p. 174; Hill, *World Turned Upside Down*, p. 12.

135 Cressy, *Birth, Marriage, Death*, p. 180.

136 Firth and Rait, *Acts and Ordinances*, vol. 2, p. 387.

137 Firth and Rait, *Acts and Ordinances*, vol. 2, p. 423.

138 Firth and Rait, *Acts and Ordinances*, vol. 2, pp. 831, 1048.

139 Coleby, *Central Government and the Localities*, p. 54 (bastardy, etc.); pp. 61, 62–3 (Catholics, Quakers); TNA, E 337/63.

140 McCall, 'Breaking the Law of God and Man', p. 140 (number of records); p. 143 (table of offences); pp. 155–6 (adulterers); pp. 165–7 (Catholics and Quakers); p. 156 (executions).

141 Hill, *World Turned Upside Down*, pp. 281–91, 311; Cressy, *Birth, Marriage, Death*, p. 12, and see also pp. 181, 182, 183, 316, 334, 418.

142 Laslett, 'Comparing Illegitimacy', p. 14; Cressy, *Birth, Marriage, Death*, pp. 73–4.

143 Whiteman, *Compton Census*, p. xxiv; Thomson, *Bishop Morley*, pp. 56–8; Miller, *Popery and Politics*, p. 9; Kenyon, *Popish Plot*, p. 14.

144 Hutton, *Restoration*, pp. 150–2; Greaves, *Deliver Us from Evil*, preface, where he lists a large number of rebellions and conspiracies 1660–3.

145 Coleby, *Central Government and the Localities*, p. 52; Hindle, *State and Social Change*, p. 178.

146 Brooks, 'Law and Revolution', p. 306.

147 14 CII c.12.

148 13 CII c.1 (Corporation Act); 14 CII c.4 (Act of Uniformity); 16 CII c.4 (first Conventicle Act); 17 CII c.2 (Five Mile Act); 22 CII c.1 (second Conventicle Act); 25 CII c.2 (first Test Act); 30 CII St II c.1 (second Test Act).

149 Outhwaite, *Ecclesiastical Courts*, p. 62.

150 For his severity, see Bodl, Carte MS 80, ff. 757–9 (Lords); Bodl, Tanner 42, f. 5 (Sheldon); BL, Egerton MS 3329, f. 119 (Danby); for restraint, see e.g. Appendix 2, Tables 1, 4, 8; for wider discussion see Thomson, *Bishop Morley*, pp. 41–51, 54–6 (attempts at unity); pp. 50, 51, 60, 99 (tough stance); pp. 98–9 (restraint of the court).

151 For wider discussion, see Fincham, *Visitation*, vol. 1, p. xix, vol. 2, pp. xvi, xvii.

152 See Bibliography (Printed Documents) for all these sets of articles; some of the issues appear more than once in the articles of a particular bishop, while others are combined in one article, so arbitrary decisions have been necessary and comparison among the various sets is not truly rigorous, likewise correlation of the sets with the lists of charges drawn up in the tables for this study.

3
The extent of Church discipline

Inquiry now moves to the extent of the Church's disciplinary powers. This part of the study will attempt to measure the impact of the Church and, in particular, its judicial machinery on the people in the communities. To do this it will first establish the pattern of sessions, or sittings, of the consistory courts in the three archdeaconries in the 1610s and the 1670s. It will then deal in the same way with the numbers summoned to answer charges in consistory courts, the numbers responding and attending the judicial proceedings and the success, or otherwise, of progress towards completion of business. The outcome (or verdict) was the climax of the whole process and the numbers found guilty of particular offences will offer further, if not decisive, evidence of the impact of the church courts – or, rather, their limits – and hence the extent of ecclesiastical authority over society by the end of the seventeenth century.

Nor will this be the end of the inquiry. Context is critical. Numbers summoned and numbers found guilty will be compared with the populations of the three dioceses to bring some proportionality to the discussion. Comparisons of these and other aspects mentioned earlier – attendance and completion of business – will be made with other dioceses where research has been carried out to show how typical, or otherwise, were the three archdeaconries of this study. Comparisons will also be made of the three consistory courts with other 'controls' which will range from the secular courts to gossip. These checks will go a long way to ensure perspective and to assess the impact of the church courts of Winchester, Worcester and Wells on the communities of the seventeenth century.

Sessions of the consistory courts

Even the relatively simple exercise of scrutinising the daily sittings or sessions of the consistory courts of the dioceses of Winchester, Worcester and Wells can act as an indicative dashboard for the condition of the ecclesiastical judicial system in those places.[1] Numbers of sessions of the respective consistory courts and, more particularly, comparison of the numbers before and after the revolutionary years of the 1640s and 1650s can reveal much about the state of the church courts and their impact on the people. Figures will serve as preliminary indicators of the health of the judicial arm and trends over the course of the century. Such an inquiry will serve as the first step towards resolving the issue at the heart of this investigation: the extent of the 'reach' of the Church into society.

Conduct of business in the consistory courts of all three dioceses was mainly in full, or 'plenary', sessions, together with a few further sessions 'in camera'. The largest number of plenary sessions held in Michaelmas terms before the Civil Wars would appear, at first glance, to have been in the Archdeaconry of Worcester. Sessions occupied 26 days in 1613 and averaged 21 days per term over the three Michaelmas terms of 1613, 1614 and 1615. The Archdeaconry of Taunton comes next with an average of 13 days and the Archdeaconry of Winchester, with an average of seven days, third.

Winchester and Worcester both had populations of some 50,000 to 60,000 in the late 1610s and the numbers of sessions in the archdeaconries ought to have been much closer than in fact they were. The explanation for this difference, in spite of similar populations, must lie, firstly, in the possible loss of court books for Winchester, and secondly, in recording practice at Worcester. Winchester's three court books – for 1619, 1621 and 1623 – only cover sessions from October to December and may, thus, without September, be far from complete records of the respective Michaelmas terms. With complete records covering September, Winchester's sessions might well have equalled Worcester's. Recording practice at Worcester may further accentuate sessional difference from Winchester. The clerks of Worcester rarely listed the events of each session under a proper heading and the larger number of days, averaging 21 for the three Michaelmas terms of 1613–15, is derived from their extra notes, which clearly show further activity on numerous occasions. If only the headings are used, as at Winchester, the average number of court days at Worcester falls from 21 to eight or nine. This would bring numbers of sessions at Worcester and Winchester more closely into line and reflect their similar populations.

That would still leave the Archdeaconry of Taunton with the smallest population (*c.* 30,000) and the largest number of sessions (13). There is no documentary explanation for this discrepancy and speculation is therefore necessary: for example, management of caseloads to spread work over a larger number of sessions may be one, more likely, possibility.

Whatever the problems with numbers of sessions in the mid-1620s and early 1630s – and similar difficulties arise with the later figures – there can be no doubt of the steep drop by the 1670s and 1680s. Average numbers of court days for Michaelmas terms fell from seven to three at Winchester and from 13 to eight at Wells. Developments at Worcester are, again, less clear: the average for three Michaelmas terms in the 1670s and 1680s was seven – a very steep fall if the average was 21 in the 1610s – but hardly changing if the average for the 1610s was only nine. One set of debatable figures (those from Worcester) does not derail the whole argument, however, and it is abundantly clear from the documents used in this comparison (and parallel documents have been examined as well) that in two of the three dioceses there was a noticeable contraction of court sittings.

The documents show that the plenary sittings invariably took place in the cathedral in all three dioceses but there were other sessions in private – '*in aedibus*' – or, as might be said today, *in camera*. These were usually held in the chambers of the judge but more occasionally in a college, a castle, a guest room, the bishop's palace and even an inn. William Hunt and John Morley, two of Arthur Duck's surrogates at Wells, spent three days during Michaelmas term 1637 hearing the cases of 17 people at 'the three cuppes in Taunton'. Examples of the irregular locations can be found in the court books, and some locations, such as the bishop's palace, were used both before and after the Interregnum.[2] Why this was so, whether problems of travelling or wish for privacy, for example, is again not explicit in the documents. These occasions were likely, by their nature, to have been far more haphazard in their incidence than the regular or plenary sessions and certainly fewer, which makes grounds for conclusions none too sure. Average numbers of sessions *in aedibus* fell at Wells from three in the 1610s to one in the 1670s, and at Winchester from four to none, while at Worcester it remained at one a term.

It would have been fascinating to have had evidence of performance of the episcopal consistory courts in the 1630s – the time of William Laud at Canterbury – but records of daily practice at Worcester and Winchester do not appear to have survived. The court books for Wells in the 1630s, including those for the Archdeaconry of Taunton, do exist, however. They show that the court continued to sit throughout the 1630s to deal with cases from the Archdeaconry of Taunton with the same regularity – no more, no less – as in the 1610s and 1620s. This may well have been so with the courts of Winchester and Worcester but without proper records it is difficult to say with certainty.[3]

Problems with records also make it difficult to comment on recovery of the courts at the Restoration. The first usable paperwork for Wells (Archdeaconry of Taunton) is fragmentary, but the six plenary and the two sessions *in aedibus* discovered, together with the poor condition of the documents, suggest a 'rocky' start and probably that decline had begun by the early 1660s. Surviving documentation for the first year or so after the Restoration at Worcester implies a similar hesitancy in the first year of the Restoration. It would seem that both bishops, Peirs of Bath and Wells before and after the Interregnum and Morley, newly raised to Worcester in 1660, faced much the same problem – lack of system and coherence – at that time. Coherence, if on a reduced scale compared with the 1610s, returned to Worcester with the arrival of Morley in person in September 1661 and likewise to Wells in the 1670s with the appointment of a new chancellor, Henry Deane, in 1668. Winchester at first glance was the exception. The first surviving court book lists 10 plenary and no fewer than 14 sessions *in aedibus*, but this was in Michaelmas term 1663. This may reflect the presence of Morley again as he had been translated from Worcester to Winchester in May 1662, and possibly also the genuine enthusiasm of officials for the restored regime or, at least, their attempt to demonstrate loyalty, whether sincerely or otherwise, to a newly arrived bishop. The silence of the record under the ageing Duppa, Morley's predecessor from 1660 to 1662, is ominous, however, and when numbers of sessions in the 1670s and 1680s are examined and other – critical – tests, such as completion of business, are applied, it is clear that recovery, if ever there was one, was extremely brief. Furthermore, numbers of sessions soon sank nearly to nothing and seem to have died altogether by the mid-1680s at Winchester.[4]

Although not strictly relevant to the argument about decline, it is interesting to note one feature of consistory operations at Worcester – proceedings on Sundays – during Michaelmas terms 1613, 1614 and 1615. The notes of the clerks are, as usual, extremely terse and it is difficult to be sure of events themselves or their sequence. None appears to have been a 'proper' – or formal – session. Business was confined to excommunications (three at least on one exceptional Sunday) and absolutions; while 'proceedings' were probably no more than announcements during divine service.[5] There is a further record of business on Sunday, 1 October 1676, with a formal heading, a long list of some 750 names and action against 45 of them during Michaelmas term 1676. This is potentially consistory court activity on a huge scale, but no action, other than writing the heading and presumably listing the names, appears to have taken place on that or any other Sunday.[6]

Observance of saints' days was also 'endangered' by the court – some of them clearly regular proceedings – at Worcester: St Luke's day (18 October) in 1613 and 1614; St Simon and St Jude's day (28 October) in 1615; and St Andrew's day (30 November) in 1682. The court at Wells breached, likewise, St Andrew's day *in aedibus* in 1624 and in full session in 1675.[7]

It seems extraordinary that any action at all, even if merely the issue of an excommunication or a clerk making a list, took place on a Sunday, colliding flagrantly, as it did, with the fifth commandment; and it is the more astonishing since one of the main categories of prosecutions in these courts was working on saints' days and Sundays. Robert Peters, however, remarks on exactly the same thing and at much the same time in the Archdeaconry of St Albans.[8] Court activity – much of it apparently 'routine' – may have been seen as the Lord's work on the Lord's day, or else as an astonishing disregard of its own rules, wherein may have lain one of the seeds of its downfall.

It would seem that secular court activity could also occur on the Sabbath. Richard Dewes was summoned to Worcester in 1613 for 'striking the minister … in time of divine Service by serving a process and misdemeanour in the Church'.[9] Thomas Dowdinge was summoned, likewise, to Wells in 1633 for trying to serve a magistrate's warrant 'att prayer time' on a Sunday, in the course of which he caused some disturbance to minister and congregation.[10] Both accounts are none too clear – legibility apart – about whether, in Dewes's case, he was a secular or spiritual official and whether, in Dowdinge's, it was the disturbance or the serving of the writ which provoked the summons. What these incidents reveal about the relations of the ecclesiastical and the secular courts is interesting in itself: they represent two examples of conflict, either contradicting Geoffrey Quaife's picture of 'harmony' between the two jurisdictions or, since such incidents were rare, confirming his claim.[11] Common to both and more relevantly here, it would seem that court action on the Sabbath was attempted and prosecuted by the Church, which would appear, on the face of it, to be a truly astonishing act of 'double-think'.

To conclude: the number of daily sessions of the consistory courts is a simple but clear way to measure and compare the activity of the consistory courts and, more importantly, to establish a trend. The trend, on these readings, was downwards, certainly at Winchester and Wells, if not at Worcester. The numbers serve as a barometer of the health of the ecclesiastical judicial system, and they were lower at the end than at the beginning of the century. They suggest – only suggest at this preliminary stage – a contraction of church court activity and a reduction in the extent of the Church's control over its seventeenth-century flock. It is always possible in theory that, while numbers of sessions went down, items or volume of business increased. This should be settled in the course of the next two sections.

Summoning of laymen and women

What were the numbers of those summoned to the respective consistory courts?[12] This question will be addressed in this section. Numbers of sessions were contracting in all three archdeaconries over the course of the seventeenth century and strongly imply decline of the church courts. The numbers of accused, or summoned, at particular dates in the seventeenth century should provide a more certain reading of the rising, or falling, trajectory of consistory court activity and act as a surer indication of the life and health, or otherwise, of the ecclesiastical judicial system. This section will deal with the numbers of those summoned to court as a whole – laymen and women, churchwardens and clergy – comparing the three archdeaconries and trends over the century. A separate section will then give more specific attention to the summoning of clergy and churchwardens.

The total numbers of people summoned – lay, churchwarden or clerical – to the Winchester Consistory Court averaged 350 or so for each of the three Michaelmas terms 1619, 1621 and 1623; at Worcester at nearly the same time, about 300; and at Wells about 260. It is interesting to note some differences between the three archdeaconries in the numbers summoned. At Winchester and Worcester, with some 57,000 to 58,000 adults apiece, the numbers summoned (350 and 300) were somewhat different, while at Taunton, with only half the population, the numbers (260) were, in that light, surprisingly high for its size.[13] Explanation is as difficult as ever but possibilities include a higher offending rate or a more vigorous prosecution policy. More important is the minuteness of the proportion summoned in all three archdeaconries.

The Restoration marked a return of the courts after an absence of nearly 20 years and, not surprisingly, there are problems with the records. Systematic recording of *ex officio* business at Worcester begins at Michaelmas term 1661, at Winchester even later, at Easter term 1663, while at Wells, Hilary term 1663 is the first for which anything approaching coherence, by assembling fragments, is achievable.[14] Wells ought, perhaps, to be discounted but, for what it is worth, the number of people summoned from the Archdeaconry of Taunton during Michaelmas terms fell from an average of 260 a term in the 1610s to a mere 47 in Hilary term 1663. The evidence for Winchester and Worcester points in different directions. Numbers summoned to the court at Winchester in Michaelmas term 1663 rose to more than 680 – the highest figure for any year in this survey – in line with its record number of sessions at that time and reflecting, no doubt, renewed vigour, for whatever reasons, at the Restoration. At Worcester, just a little earlier (Michaelmas term 1661), the figure of 86 marks the first evidence of decline in numbers summoned but from which there was some recovery by the 1670s and 1680s, albeit to nothing like the levels of the 1610s.

Average numbers summoned all fell in the comparable Michaelmas terms of the 1670s and 1680s. At Worcester, where the population may have declined over the century by nearly a quarter, the fall of accused people from 300 to 40 was greater than 85 per cent, although it should be said that there were larger numbers – 198 in Michaelmas term 1682, for example – during some of the triennial visitations.[15] At Winchester and Wells decline was even more dramatic. Numbers of accused people plunged from 350 to 35 at Winchester and from 260 to 16 at Wells – some 90 per cent of more in both archdeaconries – while, over the same timescale, their populations were moving in the opposite direction and, in fact, were rising by 18 and 66 per cent respectively.

It is interesting to note that the same bishop – George Morley – was in charge at Worcester in 1661 and at Winchester in 1663. He may have had more sinners among his flock at Winchester or had more vigorous officials than at Worcester. It may be a reflection of the politics of the time: 1660 would have been a moment for caution in the early months of the Restoration, while 1663 saw a more confident assertion of discipline now that Church and King were back in power.

As there is hardly any other research of consistory activity in the seventeenth century, it is difficult to provide context and to be sure how far Winchester, Worcester and Wells were in or out of step with developments elsewhere. The study by Martin Jones of Oxford and Peterborough is the only one, so far, to do so. It is not entirely clear whether he is discussing numbers of cases or numbers of people, but there was certainly a contraction of business and this could only mean a contraction of people. Trends at Oxford and Peterborough provide some evidence that decreasing numbers of people summoned to the courts of Winchester, Worcester and Wells were part of a wider pattern of decline.[16]

One further consideration may imply that the decline was even steeper over the seventeenth century as a whole. The Court of High Commission and its more occasional diocesan 'satellites' were operating before 1640. There may or may not have been diocesan satellite commissions in the 1610s or 1620s, but such a body sat four times, hearing 45 *ex officio* cases involving 32 people from the Diocese of Winchester, in Michaelmas term 1606.[17] Nationally, meanwhile, 80 to 100 cases, *ex officio* and instance, 'went through some stage' at High Commission in London on a typical day; and in October–November 1631 (part of Michaelmas term) it heard *ex officio* cases involving some 16 people (including three 'Romish recusantes' from Wells).[18] It is difficult to measure, with such incomplete evidence, the effect in a typical year of this activity on legal business – in particular, numbers of people summoned – in the dioceses, but without the commissions there would probably have been at least some more business at the consistory courts of Winchester, Worcester and Wells (and other dioceses) before the Wars. The abolition of High Commission (and its satellites) in 1641 was confirmed at the Restoration,[19] and from that time there was no competition from that source to reduce diocesan consistory court activity. Without the distorting effect of High Commission, encroaching on church court operations up to the 1640s but ceasing to do so from the 1660s, the decline of diocesan consistory court business would have appeared all the steeper.

Summoning of clergy and churchwardens

Although churchwarden and clergy numbers have been included with lay statistics to give an overall assessment of attendance at the respective courts, both groups are worth brief but specific attention to highlight their proportions of the whole body summoned and changes over time.

Average numbers of churchwardens summoned over three Michaelmas terms both before and after the Interregnum appear to have been low at Wells. They were somewhat higher at Winchester and Worcester, with 32 a piece and proportions of the whole body of churchwardens of 5 to 7 per cent. Numbers summoned in all three archdeaconries were minute by the 1670s and 1680s – the highest number was at Worcester, with an average of fewer than 10 per term – and proportions were negligible. These proportions sit well in the main with findings for Peterborough, if not Oxford, in the 1630s but diverge from both, being much lower, in the 1670s.[20]

Twenty-three clergymen were summoned to court at Winchester in 1619, nearly 10 per cent of the total number of incumbents in the archdeaconry, but this was exceptional. Corresponding numbers and percentages of clergy were much lower in the other years at Winchester and in the other two archdeaconries before the turmoil of the 1640s. Worcester, with an average of five suspect clergy per term, was the exception in the 1670s and 1680s; otherwise, prosecutions of clergy drop nearly out of sight. Proportions of clergy appear at first glance to have been much higher elsewhere: 26 per cent of Oxford's clergy and 38 per cent of Peterborough's summoned to account for themselves in court in the 1630s; and after the upheavals of the Wars and Interregnum 17 per cent of Oxford's incumbents, 30 per cent of Peterborough's and 20 per cent of Leicestershire's faced the same plight; but different timescales are involved and Leicestershire's 20 per cent, for example, extends over 50 years and amounts to about two clergymen per annum.[21] It is likely that numbers and proportions of clergy facing prosecution were small and declining whether in the archdeaconries of Winchester, Worcester and Wells or elsewhere in the southern province.

One or two factors may conceal figures which would, if known, have increased the numbers and proportions of clergy summoned. Diversion of cases to the bishop's palace has already been discussed.[22] It is not always clear, furthermore, whether rectors were lay impropriators. Use of the title 'mrm' (*magistrum* or master) could apply to a lay man or to an ordained person. Two cases at Winchester in 1619 illustrate the point. At Wield the impropriator was alleged to have failed to appoint a curate, and at St Mary Bourne both its rector and its vicar were summoned on different charges.[23] The impropriator and the rector are likely to have been lay people and numbers of clergy have been reduced accordingly, but there is no certainty in these or other cases.

It will be abundantly clear, nonetheless, that the numbers of clergy summoned to the church courts from the archdeaconries of Winchester, Worcester and Wells before the pivotal upheavals of the seventeenth century were few – very few – and even fewer afterwards. Either all was well and there was no need to prosecute, or the authorities were ignorant of the state of their clergy, or they were reluctant for whatever reason – embarrassment, avoidance of publicity, protection of the standing of the institution – to bring formal charges.

Response: attendance at court

After sessions were scheduled and the accused were summoned, the next step in this inquiry is their response.[24] Attendance was essential for the functioning of the consistory courts. If the accused did not arrive, business could not proceed. This often meant that details of the charge were not entered and, as the trial could not proceed, information about other aspects – methods of determining guilt or innocence, the verdict itself and details of warnings or penance – is completely missing from the record.[25]

This is not only a blow for historians who want to know as much as possible about these matters; it has consequences, in turn, for the questions at the heart of this inquiry. Good attendance, on the one hand, would imply that all was well from the point of view of the Church. The writs of the courts would be running. They would be able to enforce attendance. They would be able to try cases. They would be able to determine guilt or innocence. They would be able to sentence or dismiss. Bad attendance would, on the other hand, obstruct progress and would strongly imply that the Church was enfeebled and unable to exercise effective control in the communities. If attendance grew increasingly worse over the century, moreover, this could only mean that the church courts – and control by the Church over its people – were suffering decline. Ultimately attendance decided whether the Church was controlling the communities and imposing its rubrics and canons upon its flock – or not.

The most striking feature about attendance at court, whether of clergy, churchwardens or the public at large, is how low it was. Attendance in all three archdeaconries, whether before or after the Civil Wars and Interregnum, never passed 40 per cent and the courts suffered absence on a truly massive scale. The trend, moreover, appears relentlessly downward in two of the archdeaconries between the 1610s and the 1670s–80s. Average attendance rates at Worcester and Winchester, of close to 30 and 40 per cent in the early decades of the seventeenth century, were hardly impressive. Attendance at Worcester continued to hover round about 37 or 38 per cent for Michaelmas term 1661, but at Winchester in Michaelmas term 1663 the massive numbers summoned and the prodigious activity of clerks and apparitors proved a truly thankless task, with fewer than 4 per cent stirring themselves to attend. The labours of the mountain had indeed produced a mouse. An absence level of more than 90 per cent can only be described as catastrophic and was a sign of things to come.

Wells (or, rather, the Archdeaconry of Taunton) does not fit these trends so neatly. Attendance of 96 per cent at the Restoration can be discounted in view of shaky state of the records and only 20 per cent of the summoned arrived in court in the late 1610s and early 1620s. Amazingly, and in spite of the presence of Bishop William Peirs, who took some interest in the court and sat in person on several occasions,[26] together with the overall direction of the Southern Province by William Laud from 1633,[27] attendance at Wells, certainly concerning cases in the Archdeaconry of Taunton, sank to 12 per cent for the three specimen Michaelmas terms of the 1630s. This is an average and, in view of the importance of the decade, it is interesting to note that attendance in the three sample years of the decade fell from the 'heights' of 14 per cent in Michaelmas term 1637 to 9 per cent by Michaelmas term 1640. It looks very much as if the flock had gone astray – or on strike – certainly by the time of the Short and Long Parliaments.

Whether there was anything to the promise, or not, of high attendance at Wells at the Restoration, it was not sustained. Attendance averaging 27 per cent in the 1670s was, nonetheless, an improvement on its performance (20 per cent) in the 1610s, and better than Worcester's and Winchester's in the 1670s (10–12 per cent). This may reflect the stewardship of Henry Deane and possibly John Baylie, two officials principal in succession, who appear to have given more personal direction to the consistory court at Wells in the early 1670s.

Overall attendance was bad and absence massive in all three consistory courts in the seventeenth century. Other research, though there is little enough of it, appears to support this assessment of attendance in the three archdeaconries. Martin Ingram, it is true, highlights attendance of 70 per cent for an archdeacon's court – not the bishop's – in the Diocese of Salisbury. Ronald Marchant shows, however, for episcopal courts in eight archdeaconries within the dioceses of York and Norwich, attendance ranging from 20 to 46 per cent, more in line with Winchester, Worcester and Wells, in the 1620s and 1630s.[28] Even Evan Davies confirms lacklustre attendance at Worcester in the 1670s, while Martin Jones shows a complete turnaround at the courts of Oxford and Peterborough from attendance of 60 per cent in the 1630s to absence of 60 per cent in the 1660s.[29]

Attendance at sessions held *in aedibus* (or *in camera*), meanwhile, was excellent at Winchester, Worcester and Wells and, no doubt, elsewhere. This should not be surprising since the regular plenary sessions, particularly those of the 1670s and 1680s, were hardly overwhelmed with work and requests for private meetings in chambers are likely to have come from the accused, in most cases probably to save embarrassment. In the case of a clandestine marriage which was heard at

Winchester in December 1623, it is not made clear in the court at whose initiative – the bogus clergyman's, the two marriage parties or the ecclesiastical authorities themselves – the hearing took place *in camera*.[30] The two marriage parties appear to have failed to make the crossing from the Isle of Wight, possibly overcome with shame or reluctant to bear the cost, and their 'trial' was consequently adjourned. The 'clergyman' had to face painful music – exposure and banishment – and, while he may have requested the session, it is surprising that he was willing to attend such hostile proceedings.

Completion of business

The preceding section on attendance has already shown that completion of business by the courts was endangered.[31] The next stage in the inquiry will therefore be a thorough investigation of completion rates in three archdeaconries to establish how much business was or was not completed in both the 1610s and the 1670s. It will then be possible to gauge more precisely the 'bite' of the consistory courts and their trajectory – stable? rising? or declining? – by the end of the century and, ultimately, whether or not the Church was maintaining its hold over society.

There were three possible outcomes by the end of Michaelmas – or any other – term in the archdeaconries of Winchester, Worcester and Wells: either the accused was cleared and regarded as innocent, or he or she was found guilty or the case remained unresolved. Only about 5 per cent of the accused were cleared of charges during the specimen Michaelmas terms in the three archdeaconries before the Wars and Interregnum. It is possible, moreover, to infer different levels of enthusiasm – or reluctance – from some of the verdicts, though admittedly without too much certainty in view of the vagaries arising from hasty clerking. Denial under oath by George Bangse of a charge of Sabbath hedging met with a curt '*d(i)miss(us est)*' (case dismissed) at Worcester in 1615. In further cases at Worcester between 1615 and 1617, John Heming and Anthony Yacron are two examples of people who left the same court with the rather unsettling '*donec*' (unless or until) hanging over their heads, although they were apparently cleared, for the time being, respectively of bastardy and incontinence; while John Belling, who took an oath against a charge of incontinence, was dismissed but the judge then struck an inconclusive note by setting the apparitor on further inquiries.[32] Similarly at Wells in 1624 the judge (or clerk) closed a case involving the incontinence of Elinor Bulford with the hardly ringing endorsement 'nil contra eam agend(um) fore' (no action).[33] Several people at Winchester in 1623 – Collins, Searle, Stevens and Maunder are four examples – underwent successful compurgation over charges of incontinence only to be dismissed with a warning against consorting with the female involved in the case except in public places.[34] Collins received an assurance, however, that his 'pristine standing' would be restored. So too did Searle and Stevens, and for them the judge ordered a 'statement in writing' to confirm it, though it is not made clear where these statements were to go or what was in them.

Innocence was an even rarer conclusion after the Restoration. George Aldridge, accused of incontinence, offered to take an oath and to undergo compurgation at Winchester in 1663 but the judge appears to have taken his word for it and, as with some of his fellow accused of 40 years earlier, he was dismissed without a stain on his character and sent off with a supporting statement.[35] Elizabeth Owsley was able, at the same time, to produce a statement at Wells from her rector explaining that, at the time of the presentment, she was living at West Buckland where 'she did constantly frequent the Church'. The judge dismissed her forthwith and, at least in this case, the basis of the judgment was clear and the outcome decisive.[36] By the 1670s and 1680s, however, barely 1 per cent of accused people on average left court free of charges.

Measuring guilt is by no means an easy or accurate exercise either. Some guilty verdicts – as distinct from accuracy or truth – are beyond question. Thomas Brunsdon of Wonston was found guilty of failing to attend church; John Bennett of Wherwell of working on the Sabbath; Joanna Gosse of Houghton of committing bastardy; John Harding of Liss of conducting an irregular burial; William Elms, 'cl(er)icu(s)' of St Mary Bourne, of omitting to read prayers at evensong; and the churchwardens of Highclere of neglecting repairs of their church.[37] These all lived within the Archdeaconry of Winchester and are examples of people found guilty in the consistory court sitting at the cathedral during Michaelmas term 1621. Its counterpart at Wells, dealing with the Archdeaconry of Taunton a few years later, in 1624, produced verdicts of guilty on Alexander Burrow of Crewkerne and Thomas Criddle of Aisholt, both for working on the Sabbath;[38] while at Worcester in 1675, a guilty verdict was pronounced on Francis Gough and Ralph Knight for fighting in the church at Peopleton.[39]

In all these examples, conviction is absolutely certain. The indicators are confession and punishment. Six of the seven (two of them churchwardens at Highclere) found guilty at Winchester in 1621 had all confessed, as had the two workers on the Sabbath at Wells in 1624 and the two fighters at Worcester in 1675. Penance followed for the guilty parties at Worcester and Wells but at Winchester, although penances were frequently issued, this was not so with the seven people itemised: Brunsdon was issued with an order to attend services; the churchwardens received instructions to arrange repairs within a given time frame; Elmes and Bennett were dismissed with warnings; and Gosse and Harding, who both pleaded ignorance of the law (about churchings and funeral arrangements respectively), were merely dismissed.

Confessions and punishments show beyond doubt that verdicts of guilt must have been pronounced. Entries in the court books in many other cases lack details and guilt has to be surmised. Thomas Balchilde of Wonston and Thomas Brixey of Kings Somborne were probably found guilty of failure to pay church rate at Winchester in 1621, together with Edward Sherier of Hayling Southwood for incontinence, John Davies of Titchfield for drunken abuse, Joanna Cooke of Ovington for communion neglect and the Butlers, man and wife, of St John's Soke, Winchester, over attendance at church.[40] At Wells in 1624, similarly, verdicts of guilt against Susan Rendell of Creech St Michael and John St Alban of Bicknoller in two quite separate cases of incontinence are highly probable; likewise the Allercotts, John and William, of Withycombe for playing on the Sabbath; likewise also Mary Traske of Chard for charges of incontinence, neglect of communion and keeping 'a disorderly house att unseasonable times'.[41] Finally, it is very likely that at Worcester in 1682 'the minister' of Church Lench, the churchwardens of Hanley Castle and John Patricke of Ombersley were pronounced guilty, respectively, of neglecting the chancel, ignoring building repairs and adopting (religious) dissent.[42]

In these cases guilt is strongly implied but a 'definitive' statement of the verdict is missing from the record and there is no mention of anything as conclusive as a confession to show how the verdict was reached. Brixey's payment of church rate only after an inquiry and Sherier's failure to produce compurgators or to perform penance fall into this category. The necessity for a court case, concluding with an order to pay the rate (Balchilde), to attend services (the Butlers), to receive communion (Cooke) or to perform penance (Davies), comes within the same category. Vital information, such as a confession, showing how the verdict was reached may be missing but a guilty outcome is almost certain in all these cases before the court at Winchester in 1621. Matters are slightly less certain at Wells in 1624. The cases of Rendell and Traske both end with declarations of deficiency in compurgation and, while penance ought to have followed, there is nothing other than an uncommunicative 'non' (non appearance?). The other example at Wells, John St Alban's case, also ends inconclusively but he was ordered – and failed – to perform penance. Worcester, certainly in the visitation of 1682, is the least informative. Anne Taylor's is the only confession among 52 cases ending in guilt during Michaelmas term and, hence, the only definite conviction. In all the remaining cases – the minister of Church Lench, the churchwardens of Hanley Castle, Patricke of Ombersley and the other 47 cases (or people) – 'clerking convention' of the court appears to have precluded statements showing a definite verdict. While nothing specific is indicated, guilt can usually be safely inferred from orders to repair or attend, for example, or, better still, the issuing of penance, all of which occur in the three cases (Church Lench, Hanley Castle and Ombersley) discussed and in many more.

It looks as if, in light of all these comments and cautions, the total number of convictions for all offences (religious, moral and church rate) in the three archdeaconries combined during Michaelmas terms of the 1610s and early 1620s averaged about 90 per term and that they had shrunk to seven or so per term by the 1670s and 1680s. While numbers were collapsing dramatically, proportions of accused people found guilty in the three archdeaconries remained very much the same, whether in the 1610s or 1670s, at between a fifth and a quarter of accused people. Worcester before the Civil Wars and Wells after them saw higher conviction rates; otherwise only small proportions were found guilty within the three archdeaconries.

There are cases where it is not possible to determine the outcome, guilt or innocence, from the entries in the consistory court books. A few come to an end abruptly, without explanation, both before and after the upheavals of the 1640s and 1650s.[43] Far more numerous are prosecutions which reach a clear full stop – 'dimiss' – though, again, without explanation. There are examples of this in all the specimen Michaelmas terms at Winchester, as well as in the other archdeaconries, in the 1610s and early 1620s;[44] and there was more of it, certainly at Worcester and Winchester, in the 1670s.[45] Quite striking is the case of John Gate of Thruxton, 'an old man of the age of 88 yeares', brought before the court 'because he did but onlie dig up a Turnippe' on the Sabbath. The case was cut short with 'dimiss' and in strict forensic terms there is nothing explicit about his guilt or innocence.[46]

Gnomic or opaque phrasing concludes some of the proceedings. At Wells in 1621 the clerk of the court closed his notes with 'ordinat(um) est negot(iu)m' (the matter is settled); at Winchester his counterpart of 1623 just wrote 'p(ar)ticipavit' – he has participated (in communion); while at Worcester in 1680 the scribe placed it on record that the offending clergyman would be dealt with 'coram D(omi)no Ep(iscop)o et satisfecit ei etc.' (in the presence of the bishop and satisfied him/reached a satisfactory settlement with him).[47] In all these examples there is no statement either of guilt or 'acquittal' – no outcome or 'verdict' – just silence at this critical point.

Other cases are ambivalent and, again, leave the outcome – guilt or innocence – open to interpretation. Samuel Butler and William Hall are two such examples at Winchester in 1619.[48] Butler was alleged to have failed to stand for the creed, and there were doubts about the validity of Hall's marriage. Both produced certificates but it is not clear whether these merely confirmed that all had been well from the beginning or whether the certificates were issued after matters had been put right – innocence with the first possibility, guilt with the second. Similarly in the same court four years later, Richard Johnson of Shalfleet and William Chartrain of Alverstoke both faced a charge of failing to pay church rate and the apparitor informed the court in each case that the accused had paid, but questions linger.[49] In 1621, meanwhile, two pairs of churchwardens, from Kings Somborne and Upper Clatford, were summoned to expand upon their presentments; they could be viewed as guilty of slovenly surveillance of their parishioners or as helpfully assisting the court with extra detail – it depends on the extent of the shortcomings of the presentments, which is not made clear in the court books.[50]

Parallel examples occur at Worcester at this time concerning individuals such as Jane Saunders of Rowington, Jane Cowp of Bengeworth, Richard Sneade of Bredicot and the Fitters, man and wife, of Evesham.[51] The churchwardens of Broom, summoned over repairs, certified at the 'fourth time of asking'. The time it took to arrive is suspicious but the court case may have been occasioned as much by sluggishness in exhibiting the document proving innocence as by neglect of the repairs themselves.[52] Missing Bibles at Dudley, Halesowen and Belbroughton, meanwhile, provoked prosecutions of their churchwardens, the latter pairs being 'dismissed' when certificates – either confirming that all had been well from the beginning or that omissions had been resolved – were supplied.[53] Replication of some of this followed, albeit on a smaller scale, in the 1670s and 1680s.[54]

Suspicions of guilt surround some of these cases but terse notes and, crucially, missing detail in the court books allow doubts to persist about guilt or innocence. The accused, churchwardens or an individual, might have produced – or have been required to produce – a certificate that all was well, but it is often not clear whether matters had been satisfactory all along, the 'paperwork' merely confirming this, or whether something had been amiss and had now been put to rights. The first circumstance meant innocence, the second guilt, and usually it is not clear which was the case.

THE EXTENT OF CHURCH DISCIPLINE

With 'innocence' at 5 per cent and 1 per cent for the respective periods and 'guilt' between 20 and 25 per cent for the same periods, unresolved cases take the lion's share of outcomes. Unresolved cases, on average, never comprised fewer than two-thirds of the cases in all three archdeaconries in the 1610s and early 1620s. They formed nearly four-fifths at Wells at that time and, astonishingly, rose above four-fifths during the 1630s – so much for the efficiency and discipline of Laud and Peirs.[55] The state of play was more varied in the immediate aftermath of the Restoration, with rates soaring to 95 per cent at Winchester, remaining at two-thirds at Worcester and improving considerably at Wells. By the 1670s and 1680s, unresolved cases amounted to 63 per cent at Wells and 83 per cent at Winchester and Worcester. Wells, at 63 per cent, represents an improvement on earlier performance, but at Worcester and Winchester the trend of unfinished business, increasing from two-thirds in the 1610s and 1620s to four-fifths in the 1670s and 1680s, clearly signalled a relentless rise in unfinished business and the consequent decay of both courts.

Failure to complete business on a substantial scale is confirmed by Evan Davies, no less, and by Martin Jones. Inspection of the statistics offered by Evan Davies shows a consistent failure to bring prosecutions to a conclusion (though it should be said that, by conjecturing private settlements, this does not stop him from claiming an 80 per cent completion rate). To take the sample years of this study (1675, 1678 and 1680), even on his figures, 25 per cent of cases remained unresolved at Worcester in 1680 – the best year of the three – and 1675 was the worst year, when 45 per cent of business remained incomplete. This was so, furthermore, with 75 per cent of business arising from the visitation of 1679. Calculations by Jones show, likewise, shortfalls of 50–60 per cent at Oxford and Peterborough in the 1630s and, although matters remained much the same at Peterborough in the 1660s and 1670s, unresolved case rates reached 80 per cent at Oxford in the late 1660s.[56]

So much for what statistical analysis appears to show. The largest numbers of outcomes by far, within the three archdeaconries, both before and after the upheavals, were prosecutions without resolution. It is quite possible that more cases were resolved than silence in the court books implies. The judge at Winchester probably thought the prosecution of Gate over a turnip offence too minute for the court, or he may have felt the need to show mercy towards a poor, ageing and possibly befuddled old man. The ultimate guiding principle was – or ought to have been – to reconcile offenders with the Church, and no doubt issues were often settled informally in private and out of court. Both types of case – the trivial and those with potential for quick and informal resolution – would change the balance considerably. The trouble with the statistics is their likely failure to present a complete picture; the trouble with speculation is its lack of certainty.

Guilt

Pronouncement of a verdict was the climax of proceedings in the consistory or any other court. The purpose of the consistory courts – and, indeed, of courts in any other legal system – was (and is) to determine guilt or innocence. Churchwardens' presentments and charges in court are not the answers to this. Too many historians give the impression that presentments and charges reveal, for example, the state of morals or the degree of absence from church in the communities at some particular time. Charges are indeed a revelation but of the Church's 'agenda' – what it hoped to achieve or how it hoped to shape society. Charges are fine therefore for understanding the concerns – the nature – of Church controls, but they remain accusations (or allegations). They do not tell us anything about guilt: how many people had refused to attend church, for example, or had indulged in fornication.

The central question of this part of the study is 'extent': the extent to which the Church and, in particular, its consistory courts controlled society in the seventeenth century. To establish how effective the church courts were, it is essential to determine the numbers found guilty of particular offences and then to compare these with conditions in society.

Charges show what the ecclesiastical authorities strove to achieve; verdicts show what their courts actually achieved. What were the numbers in each category of offence? How do these numbers compare with conditions in the parishes? What was the state of morals in the communities? What was the state of religion? Was the Church really achieving effective policing of the communities? Was the Church shaping morals? Did it have an impact on religion? Or was it having very little or no effect?

Those are the questions which require answers in order to measure the impact of the Church on society in seventeenth-century England. This section will therefore focus on guilt. It will seek to establish numbers found guilty of the main types of offence – in other words, how many people were convicted of moral offences, how many of religious offences, how many of church rate offences – and which convictions occurred in numbers of any significance. These will then be compared, in a subsequent section, with conditions in the communities, and in this way it may be possible to estimate something of the impact of the ecclesiastical machinery on society.

Lay guilt

The most important moral misdemeanours in all three archdeaconries, in terms of numbers of convictions, were bastardy, sex before marriage, incontinence (fornication and adultery) and clandestine marriage.[57] This was the case in the 1610s and 1620s and also in the 1670s and 1680s. The most important religious convictions at both times were work and play on the Sabbath, neglecting to attend church, failure to receive communion and misbehaviour in church or churchyard.

Bastardy was the most common of convictions for moral misdeeds, with 11 per term when averaged over three Michaelmas terms. This was at Worcester between 1613 and 1615. Bastardy was still the most frequent conviction in the other two archdeaconries but came to barely half of Worcester's record, and numbers of convictions for the other moral misdemeanours were even lower. Bastardy was outnumbered, however, by one type of religious offence, working on the Sabbath, again at Worcester, where there were 21 convictions on average in the three terms used for sampling. While there were convictions for other problems in the three archdeaconries, in particular attendance at church, communion, abusive behaviour and play on the Lord's Day, none averaged more than half the deeds classed as work.

Convictions changed considerably after the Wars and Interregnum. In the specimen terms of the 1670s there were hardly any moral convictions: none at all at Winchester and just one or two per term for bastardy at Wells, together with similarly minute numbers for clandestine marriage at Worcester and Wells. The same is true of religious convictions. There were no convictions at Wells in the three terms of the 1670s. Gone were the convictions for work and play on Sundays at Worcester, and nearly so for abusive behaviour. There were still no convictions for (Catholic) recusancy in any of the archdeaconries, although the average for (Protestant) dissent was three per term at Winchester and one per term at Worcester, and another three per term for failure to attend church at Winchester. It should be said, however, that there were more religious convictions in surviving triennial visitation proceedings of the 1670s and early 1680s at Worcester and attendance, communion and dissent all feature strongly in those proceedings.

Nothing has been said about church rate. Lay convictions were few, with the exception, this time, of Winchester, where rate convictions overtook moral, if not religious, convictions and averaged slightly more than a dozen in the three terms of the late 1610s and early 1620s. This arose, exceptionally, however, from a mass prosecution of 28 offenders from Romsey in 1623. There were convictions concerning church rate in the other archdeaconries before the Interregnum but numbers were, again, extremely small, and there were no convictions at all in the three archdeaconries in the specimen terms of the 1670s and 1680s.

Insofar as any pattern can be discerned, it would seem that numbers of religious convictions outweighed moral ones in the 1610s and 1620s and there was little to choose between the two categories after the Restoration. It is possible to detect a shift in stress among religious convictions from such matters as work and play on the Sabbath in the 1610s to church attendance, communion and dissent in the 1670s. There are some grounds for this in convictions in the court at Winchester and in the visitation proceedings at Worcester in the 1670s and early 1680s.

The development of real importance, however, was the steep decline of convictions in the courts of all three archdeaconries from relatively small numbers before the Interregnum to very nearly nothing during the Restoration. Averages of 11 per term for bastardy at Worcester, of 13 for church rate at Winchester and of 21 (the highest) for working on the Sabbath, again at Worcester, in the 1610s were decidedly small. With numbers all below three per term in the 1670s, and often zero, they were infinitesimal when set against archdeaconries with populations of 30,000 (Taunton), 43,000 (Worcester) and 68,000 (Winchester). Improvements in morality and conformity can be ruled out, an issue that will be examined in a subsequent section of this survey;[58] otherwise, the blame must be placed on the feebleness of the courts, which apparently lacked instruments to compel attendance or to complete business, together with imperfect standards of proof.

Guilt of churchwardens

Repairs to the structure or fabric of buildings, together with fittings, furnishings and ornaments, formed the bulk of churchwardens' shortcomings. This is strikingly so at Worcester and Winchester in the 1610s and early 1620s and, insofar as small numbers allow definite conclusions, convictions concerning oaths, presentments and administrative matters are barely visible. Among 'structure' and 'fittings' offenders at the Winchester Consistory Court in 1623 were the churchwardens of Chilbolton, found guilty of 'wanting a surplace' and neglecting the church wall; those of Droxford, where the communion table was 'at fault'; and those of Brading, where the steeple was 'in decay'.[59] At Worcester, the other diocese with relatively large fabric and fittings convictions, their counterparts at All Saints Evesham fell foul of

THE EXTENT OF CHURCH DISCIPLINE 103

the judge in 1613 because of damage to the vestry and the 'organs'.[60] Rarer among convictions of churchwardens was failure to report working on forbidden days but, in one of the few such convictions at Wells in the 1610s and early 1620s, the churchwardens of Stogursey were judged guilty in 1618 of failing to present people working on the fifth of November, it 'being the king's ma(jes)ties holyeday'.[61]

The vagueness and terseness of the 'regular' entries in the court books of the 1670s make it difficult to be certain of any convictions of churchwardens at Worcester, but 'visitation' activity indicates convictions mainly to do with fabric and fittings and for little or nothing else. The failings of the churchwardens of Great Malvern in 1676, for example, included the need for 'a booke of Homilies and a Terrier and ... amendment of the Roofe of the west end of their church'.[62] At Wells, meanwhile, convictions of churchwardens dropped nearly out of sight and at Winchester totally.

If numbers are averaged for the three Michaelmas terms in the 1610s and early 1620s, 20 churchwardens were found guilty per term at Winchester, 16 at Worcester and one at Wells; hardly any were convicted in all three archdeaconries in the 1670s and early 1680s (although the visitation books record some prosecutions in the Worcester Consistory Court at that time).

Clerical guilt

If convictions of churchwardens for their shortcomings were important, convictions of parochial incumbents – rectors, vicars, 'perpetual curates' – were even more so. They were the men 'at the front', 'the captains' of the Church. They did the day-to-day work, conducting the services, ministering to the needs of their parishioners, setting an example of a wholesome way of life – at least that was the theory; and the image of the Church – the regard in which it was held and the support it would therefore receive – depended on effective ministry by the clergy in the parishes.

There were always clergy accused of wrongdoing of one kind or another – 23, quite exceptionally, at Winchester in 1619 – and, while a few were cleared, most cases remained unresolved at the end of term, usually because of absence, but possibly because of transfer out of 'the public gaze' to private audience before the bishop. Outcomes from subsequent proceedings, if there were any, including those in the bishop's palace, could have increased the numbers of the guilty – a little. It should be borne in mind, however, that even the revelation of wrongdoing by just one or two clergymen would have done immense harm to the standing of the Church.

Although numbers of guilty verdicts, or convictions, were minute – so much so that averaging them or providing percentages is pointless – the offending incumbents managed between them to commit an array of at least a dozen transgressions. Categories with the largest – if that is the right word – numbers of convictions over the three Michaelmas terms at Winchester in the late 1610s and early 1620s concerned neglect of the services, or 'offices', of the Church and problems over chancel repairs. Richard Underhill, rector of Whitchurch (Worcester 1614) and Samuel Marshatt of Botley (Winchester 1623) are examples of the former, while Robert Pistor, rector of Havant (Winchester 1623), represents the latter.[63] These convictions may raise questions of religious divergence but neglect of services probably arose from nothing more than laziness – sloth – and chancel problems from the prospect of expense.

Cost or sloth may explain the failure of Edward Rood, apparently a visiting preacher at Upton Grey (Winchester 1623), to secure a curate's licence, and the reluctance of Edward Cheepewrighte, rector of Norton Fitzwarren (Wells 1618), to take the oath of rural dean; greed may account for the pluralism of 'm(a)g(istru)m Balamy' of St Lawrence, Evesham (Worcester 1615); and apathy may have caused the absenteeism of 'mrm Phelps' of Badsey (Worcester 1615).[64] It is more difficult to identify the motivation of Thomas Charlock – perhaps a sense of importance, even the thrill of imposture but, most likely, fees – who was found guilty at Winchester in 1623 of conducting two clandestine marriages, one in the tower of Newport Church, the other in the belfry of Brading Church, both on the Isle of Wight, both at six o'clock in the morning.[65] Questions about conformity to the canons of the Church of England arise in several cases: Thomas Fuller, 'perpetual curate' at Upton Grey (Winchester 1623), was convicted of failing to wear the surplice; this, together with condoning sitting for communion, was another of Balamy's transgressions at Evesham (Worcester 1615) and of Samuel Marshatt's at Botley (Winchester 1623).[66] There is no reference in any of these cases to Puritanism or the sects, but derelictions involving the surplice and sitting for communion must raise suspicions of such sympathies.

These cases arose across the three archdeaconries, but mainly at Winchester, and all in the 1610s and 1620s. After the Restoration there was a fall in clerical convictions, from a very low 'height' to zero at Wells, but there were still a few at Winchester and Worcester. Interestingly, at Worcester in 1680 Edward Cookes, presumably rector of Tardebigge, was pronounced guilty of 'serial' clandestine marriage offences, suffered excommunication and subsequently sought absolution. Intriguingly, at Winchester, also in 1680, the case of Timothy (Goodaker), 'perpetual curate' of Timsbury, turned on '*conformitate*' – failure to conform in some way with the Church of England – and he was ordered to 'certify' compliance through his churchwardens.[67]

If there were accusations and charges, there were, within the strict Michaelmas term samples of this study, no definite convictions concerning moral behaviour. Robert Milles, curate of Kilton (Wells), accused of attempting the chastity of Mary Proctor, appears to have failed to attend sessions twice during Michaelmas term 1633 and was suspended, but there was no specific pronouncement of guilt and suspension would have been a temporary measure awaiting proper resolution.[68]

The main clerical convictions before the Civil Wars and Interregnum concerned services, chancels, surplices, clandestine marriage and the related problems of pluralism and absenteeism. After the upheavals there were convictions for clandestine marriage, curates' licences and possibly religious divergence, but few convictions otherwise. The six found guilty of an offence at Winchester in both 1619 and 1623 were the largest numbers in any of the specimen Michaelmas terms before the Civil Wars and Interregnum, and in the other archdeaconries the numbers of the guilty never rose above two. By the 1670s and 1680s, numbers shrank to one or two per term at Worcester and Winchester and to zero at Wells.

Church and people: the impact of its courts on society

The question still to be tackled is the condition of religion and social issues in the three archdeaconries and in England at large. An assessment of these phenomena should provide context and make possible some assessment of the part played by the consistory courts in shaping them and, hence, the extent of their control over society.

Inquiry into the condition of society raises huge issues. The seventeenth was one of England's most turbulent centuries. The nation suffered a 'cyclonic shattering'. The issues were complex and the statistics are imperfect but there can be no doubt that the cyclone triggered 'a great overturning of everything in England' and unleashed major social, religious and political problems in the nation.[69] The upheavals, including the overthrow of censorship and the church courts, left a legacy of religious and social dissent nationwide in the years after the Restoration. Parliaments and Cromwell under the Commonwealth and Protectorate had failed to contain or suppress the sects and a turbulent underside, 'a cultural matrix … aflame with enormities and enmities … which had lost the habit of church attendance, had abandoned the regime of episcopal discipline, or fallen prey to apathy and cynicism', survived into the Restoration.[70]

There were groups, both Protestant and Catholic, outside the Church of England throughout the seventeenth century but it is not easy to discover definitive statistics to show the scale of religious divergence before the Civil Wars and Interregnum. The consistory courts themselves turn out to be of very little use for such estimates. Catholic recusants and Protestant dissenters leave surprisingly little trace in consistory court books and few explicit citations of such suspects can be found. It is possible that other transgressors brought before these courts were religious malcontents. Prosecutions for work and play on the Sabbath are less likely to indicate rejection of the Church on grounds of conscience or belief. Such behaviour was certainly offensive to Puritans and therefore unlikely to be committed by them, and neither Puritans nor Catholics would have wished to draw attention to themselves unnecessarily. Other infractions – failure to attend church, to receive communion, to arrange baptisms, for example – could well indicate discontent and divergence. There are some striking numbers of communion citations at Winchester in 1619–20: 15 from All Saints Southampton, 58 from Alton and no fewer than 80 from Romsey.[71] This mass resistance was very different from the picture drawn 16 years earlier by Archbishop Whitgift for Queen Elizabeth: 30, admittedly, failing to receive communion at Romsey but none at Alton or All Saints Southampton.[72] A certain amount of caution is necessary, however, when dealing with consistory prosecutions. Illness, laziness or emergencies could just as well explain absence from communion. Furthermore, while the two are often confused, charges are not convictions and guilt was by no means established until the sentence was pronounced. Two of the 80 from Romsey and two dozen of the 58 from Alton were dismissed (presumably innocent) and substantial numbers – almost all the accused from Romsey – were adjourned or vanish from the record. Convictions were rare, and even the ever willing resort to excommunication suffered by all 15 from All Saints Southampton and 18 of the 58 from Alton should not be seen as guilt. Excommunication in this type of case was not so much a punishment, since the accused had not been tried, but was applied as a sanction to attempt to enforce attendance at court to settle the issue. Some of them might well have been guilty but, again, other factors, such as the expense of a journey to Winchester, rather than religious belief, might have been a consideration.[73]

Consistory court evidence for religious divergence may be weak but there were certainly sizeable groups, both Catholics and Protestants, outside the established Church. Families such as the Throckmortons, the

Talbots and the Blounts, some of them much involved in the Gunpowder Plot of 1605, were all substantial Catholic landowners in Worcestershire. The Catholic Tichbornes of Hampshire underwent extraordinarily contrasting fates at the hands of Elizabeth I and James I, from execution to holding office and even gaining knighthoods. The Puritans were, at the same time, actively capturing both lectureships and the magistracy. Puritan magistrates controlled the quarter sessions at Bridgwater (Wells), for example, as early as the 1590s and at Worcester by the early seventeenth century. The same city authorities set up a lectureship, usually occupied by Puritans, in 1614, and others followed: by the 1630s there were similar appointments at Evesham, Dudley and Kidderminster, the last occupied by Richard Baxter, no less.[74]

Powerful Catholic families continued to reign in Worcestershire after the Restoration, together with the Bishops, Cannings and Sheldons of Warwickshire (parts of which were in the Worcester Diocese), and the Tichbornes of Winchester were still important estate owners in Hampshire.[75] Evidence from Worcester is, again, most detailed for Protestant dissenting activity. George Fox made five visits to the county in the 1650s, 1660s and 1670s. Three hundred Quakers assembled at Inkberrow in 1669 and two years earlier, in 1667, a meeting of Fifth Monarchy Men, reputedly as many as 2,000, at Oldbury had to be broken up by the militia and subsequently dealt with by magistrates in the quarter sessions.[76]

Stronger statistical evidence for the existence of Protestant dissenters comes from the Declaration of Indulgence of 1672.[77] Licensing of ministers and meeting places, each with a congregation, under the terms of the 'amnesty' brought numbers out into the open for the period 1672–3. At Winchester and Taunton licences were issued to or received by nearly 40 dissenting ministers, together with licences for just short of 60 meeting houses, in both archdeaconries, while at Worcester at least 16 ministers and nearly 30 houses qualified.[78] Three years later, in 1676, Henry Compton (Bishop of London), under instruction from Sheldon (Archbishop of Canterbury) and Danby (Charles II's minister), launched his national inquiry into the scale of divergence, Catholic and Protestant, from the Church of England. Bishop Morley's statistical return acknowledged the existence of some 1,000 Catholic recusants and 8,000 Protestant dissenters, which came to 6 per cent of his flock, at Winchester. Bishop Creighton's return, at 4 per cent (180 or so recusants and 5,800 dissenters), was somewhat lower for Wells, while Bishop Fleetwood's return, at 5 per cent for Worcester (720 recusants and 1,325 dissenters), was exactly the same as the overall average for the Southern Province.[79]

Other precise – statistical – evidence ought to have come from the recusancy rolls. These run, unbroken, for almost a hundred years from the end of the reign of Elizabeth I to the first years of William of Orange and comprise lists of forfeitures of property and fines for refusing to 'enter church, chapel or usual place of common prayer'.[80] They show some fairly sizeable groups of church absentees facing the assizes in the early 1620s: 20 from Hanley Castle and ten or more in several other places in Worcestershire on one occasion; a dozen from St Cuthbert, Wells, on another; and, at about the same time, three dozen from Twyford and 20 or more from Christchurch, Titchfield and Otterbourne in the Winchester Archdeaconry. Total numbers of 'convictions' at the assizes are even more striking. While a total of only 38 absentees were fined £60 at Wells in August 1625, 152 were fined £80 at Worcester in March 1622, and 282 were fined £100 apiece on one particularly busy day at Winchester in July 1621. Nor did conviction rates change much over time, if the Winchester assize is anything to go by. Long lists of fines in 1676 – 216 on one day in February and another 267 at a sitting in July, including groups of 16 at Twyford, 17 at Bedhampton, 19 at Brown Candover and 20 at Basing – suggest that absence was as bad as ever at Winchester. Fines, at £20 each, were, however, much lower than in the 1620s. It is difficult to draw definite conclusions about the other counties, Somerset and Worcestershire, at this time: the disappearance of recusants – church refusers – from these counties (or archdeaconries) is less likely and the loss of documents more so.[81]

The one thing the rolls show beyond dispute is a persistent degree of 'recusancy', by which the rolls apparently mean absence from Sunday worship in the established church, stretching over the entire seventeenth century. More expansive statements in the rolls about the convictions or, even better, details of the proceedings – what was said in court – would have clarified the reasons for absence from church and, in particular, whether the recusants were Catholic or Protestant; but these are missing from the rolls. The penal statute of 1581 is sometimes mentioned in the rolls and it would seem that prosecutions were always brought under this Act. The Act of 1581 highlights 'the Romish Religion' but, when the Act identifies the offence as failure to attend church, it is not specific and does not discuss the grounds, acceptable or otherwise, for absence and anything, old age or sickness, for example, could have been the cause. The lists in the rolls are explicitly of convictions, however, involving huge fines and implying steadfast consciences of offenders. An ageing woman or a sick man would have been unlikely to refuse to attend church on principle and they would have escaped conviction. The critical question

THE EXTENT OF CHURCH DISCIPLINE **109**

is whether the absentees, so carefully listed in the rolls, were Catholic or Protestant, to which there is no conclusive answer.[82]

To turn from evidence of religious divergence in the 'localities' – Winchester, Worcester and Wells – to the nation as a whole, estimates of the number of Catholics or Protestants differ considerably and are almost impossible to establish with certainty. According to Whitgift's survey of the 26 dioceses of the two provinces, 'recusants' – people, Catholic or Protestant, refusing to attend church – numbered between 8,500 and 8,700 in 1603.[83] Surviving returns for Compton's Census in 1676, covering 24 dioceses, provide totals of 12,550 Catholics and 93,100 Protestant dissenters – altogether 105,680 'outsiders', or 5 per cent of the population of England and Wales.[84] All these figures are suspect, those for Catholics of the 1660s and 1670s in particular. While two modern writers agree that the numbers were considerably higher than those dispatched to Compton by Morley, Creighton, Fleetwood and the others in 1676, they differ widely – from 60,000 to 250,000 – in their estimates.[85] When it is recalled that numbers of Protestant dissenters were much larger, although still played down either consciously or unconsciously by the bishops, it becomes clear that allegiance to the Church of England was far from universal, that there were substantial bodies of religious opinion outside its remit and that persecution in the courts, whether spiritual or secular, was a lost cause.

Figures for social problems are also problematic. It is difficult to find any figures for vagrancy and, while work has been done on bastardy, it rests on somewhat slender foundations. The 'apprehension' of 25,000 vagrants over 37 counties during the 1630s may indicate something of the scale of the problem.[86] Other research, based on 98 parishes in England and Wales, suggests that bastardy fell from 2.5 per cent of births in the 1610s to 1.2 or 1.3 per cent in the 1670s.[87] Even so, in terms of figures, these percentages could represent substantial numbers of illegitimate births: perhaps two hundred a year on average in every diocese in the 1610s and one hundred a year in the 1670s, if spread evenly, but differing considerably from diocese to diocese, no doubt, if only because of the varying size of diocesan populations.

Some of these statistics, whether for religious divergence or for bastardy, can at least be questioned. The calculations are subject to all sorts of objections: the small size of the samples (37 counties, 98 parishes) for bastardy; suspicions of bias, however conscious or unconscious, if not deliberate attempts to deceive, among bishops conducting their own surveys about religious allegiance; together with gaps and disorder in the recusancy rolls. It is, therefore, very difficult to determine with much precision the condition of society in either respect (religious or social) in the seventeenth century. It leaves scope, moreover, for speculation. The figures could be wrong and there could have been considerably more – or less – bastardy, recusancy and dissent than available statistics suggest. Even if taken at face value, religious divergence at 5 per cent and bastardy at 1.2 or 1.3 per cent may be seen by some as high and by others as quite low.

With only the deficient recusancy rolls for the century and suspect bishops' surveys for the 1670s, it is difficult, moreover, to establish trends for religious divergence. The figures for Catholic recusancy may well have remained fairly stable between the 1610s and the 1670s but, after the wave of fanatical sects under Commonwealth and Protectorate, numbers of Protestant dissenters were probably higher by the 1670s.[88] Statistics for bastardy, meanwhile, cover the whole century and imply a downward trend between the 1610s and the 1670s.

The consistory courts were certainly failing to suppress both Catholic recusancy and Protestant dissent, but the figures suggest they were enjoying more success with bastardy. Doubts must remain, however, about linking the church courts with the downward trend of bastardy. They were feeble, toothless bodies which proved unable to summon people or to complete business and, if the Church enjoyed any success at all, it may have been through its other agencies.

Consistory courts were not the only engines of ecclesiastical control. One alternative agency was activity at episcopal visitations, where informal correction and settlement of a charge may have occurred. The visitation books for Winchester and Wells do not record, for the large part, discussions or decisions, formal or informal. A rare instance of what appears to be informal discipline survives in the book recording the episcopal visitation of Winchester Archdeaconry in September 1691. A note at the back of the book shows that William Hilary, rector of Minstead and curate of Lyndhurst, received careful and detailed orders about preaching and prayers, during winter and summer, in both places.[89] The court books for the four triennial visitations of Worcester in the 1670s and early 1680s – apparently the only surviving books recording triennial proceedings in the diocese – are also relevant to this kind of discipline, as the lists of presentments or charges – standard content of visitation books – have marginal notes by many of the cases. These would seem to indicate subsequent action, though this is not specifically confirmed, back at the cathedral in the consistory court.[90] There are no notes by other names and action (or not) is entirely missing. Possibly the problem was resolved in these cases there and then, informally, 'on the spot'. Practice at Worcester with presentments – whether they were sent in advance or brought to the visitation – is not clear but, if the churchwardens brought their presentments on the day of the visitation, the clerk could only have arranged the lists after the event and, while this does not rule out informal decisions 'on the spot', they did not record them at Worcester. These informal proceedings would, moreover, have required the accused to have been present and, again, there is no evidence for this. While it is possible that problems with fabric or fittings may have been resolved informally between officials and churchwardens, 'discussions' with wider numbers of laymen and women would not have been practical in terms of either time or attendance. The claims of Evan Davies that some prosecutions either began or were continued at visitation and were sometimes finished later in court have proved too fanciful for Worcester.[91] Such proceedings may have occurred at other times or elsewhere but the records for Worcester simply do not bear this out.[92]

The archdeacons' courts (as distinct from the episcopal consistory courts which are the subject of this study) may have been another agency taking business away from the consistory courts but they were still church courts and part of the ecclesiastical machinery of control.[93] Peculiar jurisdictions within the three archdeaconries (dioceses), each with its own court, would have had the same effect.[94] There were, in addition, the 'oversight' of churchwardens, the 'counselling' roles of parish priests and the private sessions by bishops. Archdeacons' records are largely missing for the three dioceses and conversations of parishioners with churchwardens in the street, with clergy in their vestries or with bishops in their palaces would, by their nature, have been discreet, even informal, leaving no record. The Church may therefore have enjoyed greater direct power than a study confined to its consistory courts would otherwise imply.

Other 'weapons' of social control lay beyond the powers of the Church, in particular self-regulating or self-arbitrating mechanisms in the communities, and secular prosecutions at assizes and in magistrates' courts. Keith Wrightson and David Levine describe 'a constellation of legal institutions' circling the village of Terling (Essex) in the seventeenth century.[95] Eric Carlson examines 'internal' social control within a range of parishes in Cambridgeshire in the sixteenth century, and David Underdown in his study of Dorchester (Diocese of Salisbury) lays stress on the corrective roles of neighbours and families, and even the power of gossip and rumour.[96] Questions arise, again, about some of these enquiries. The claims are important but, no doubt inevitably, lack statistics. It is therefore difficult to establish sound and clear conclusions about the extent of these activities or to determine trends over time.

Consistory court controls over society, its religion and its morals, were declining but it is difficult to gauge the extent or effectiveness of alternative regulating agencies in the communities, and, indeed, at root, to be sure what was the state of religion or morals at any particular time.

Such figures as there are for illegitimate births suggest numbers shrinking over the century but still in their hundreds in the dioceses in the 1670s and 1680s. They suggest numbers of recusants, probably mainly Catholic, in their hundreds, similarly in the dioceses, but probably static over the century; and numbers in the thousands for Protestant dissenters and rising after the upheavals of the 1640s and 1650s. These figures contrast starkly with consistory operations. The highest numbers of those summoned for bastardy in this study are at Worcester: 50 in Michaelmas term 1615 and, after the Restoration, seven in the corresponding term in 1675. The highest numbers of those summoned for religious divergence were five dissenters at Winchester in 1619 and 16 recusants, again at Winchester, in 1681. Convictions are the decisive issue, however, and these were even fewer: for bastardy, 14 at Worcester in 1615, shrinking to one at Worcester in 1675 and one at Wells in 1671 and, again, in 1675; for religion, one recusant at Worcester in 1613 and another in 1614, together with three dissenters at Worcester in 1680 and a total of 10 at Winchester in 1678 and 1680.[97]

The church courts were clearly in retreat. They were in endangered territory in the 1610s: their business was shrinking, their orders were defied and their punishments were ignored. Figures for summonses and convictions in crucial fields were minuscule by the end of the 1670s and there could be no plainer advertisements than those of the moribund state of consistory jurisdiction as the century drew towards its close.

Notes

1 See Appendix 3, Tables 1–3.
2 Some of the more unusual are: cathedral itself, HRO, C1/35, f. 57r, 23/12/1623, C1/45 (no folios), 19/5/1680; guest room, C1/37 (no folios), 7/9/1663, C1/45 (no folios) 27/1/1683; castle C1/35, f. 118r, 4/6/1624; college, C1/44 (no folios), 27/1/1677; inn, SHLS, D/D/ca/313, f. 189v, 6/10/1637; bishop's palace or registry, D/D/ca/295, f. 163v, 3/12/1633, D/D/ca/331, f. 194v, 2/12/1640, WRO, 802 2760, f. 135v, 20/10/1614, 794 011 2722 2, Book 32, f. 158v, 2/9/1680, 807 093 2724, Book 38, f. 109r, 8/2/1694.
3 Consistory courts reached their 'apogee' under Laud (Marchant, *Church under Law*, p. 230) but were marked by opposition and futility (Potter, 'Canterbury', pp. 125–30).
4 HRO, C1/45 – the last surviving *ex officio* court book for Winchester stutters to a halt with three cases in May 1684, involving four people, all of whom were absent.
5 WRO, 804 2760, f. 219r (3/10/1613), f. 258r (14/11/1613), f. 268v (9/10/1614), f. 21v (22/10/1615), f. 280r (5/11/1615).
6 WRO, 794 011 2722 2, Book 32, f. 1r.

7 WRO, 802 2760, ff. 50r, 131v, 145r, 418r; 794 011 2722 2, Book 32, f. 222r; SHLS, D/D/ca/243, f. 96v; D/D/ca/354, 30/11/1675 (no folios).

8 Peters, *Oculus Episcopi*, p. 52; I remain enormously grateful to Ralph Houlbrooke for this reference and for his very helpful advice about the phenomenon.

9 WRO, 802 2760, f. 377v.

10 SHLS, D/D/ca/295, f. 114v.

11 Quaife, *Wanton Wenches*, p. 221.

12 For numbers summoned see Appendix 3, Tables 4–6.

13 See chapter 1 for fuller discussion of populations; also Whiteman, Compton Census, Appendix D, Table D/3, p. ci.

14 HRO, C1/37 (Winchester); SHLS, D/D/ca/388 2 and 4 (Wells).

15 For discussion of triennial visitation prosecutions see Introduction.

16 Jones, 'Oxford and Peterborough', pp. 20, 48, 63, 64.

17 HRO, C1/28.

18 Usher, *High Commission*, pp. 260, 281; Gardiner, *Star Chamber and High Commission*, pp. 181–260 (it is not always clear which were *ex officio*, *ad instantiam* or *promoto* cases).

19 16 CI c.11; 13 CII c.12.

20 Jones, 'Oxford and Peterborough', p. 228; the usual cautions with comparisons apply; it should also be said that numbers and proportions were somewhat higher at Worcester for the three visitations.

21 Jones, 'Oxford and Peterborough', p. 228; Pruett, *Parish Clergy*, p. 128; allowances must again be made for different methodologies as well as for different timescales.

22 See the section 'Charges against the clergy' in Chapter 2.

23 HRO, C1/33 (no folios), 11/11/1619 (Wield), 12/11/1619 (St Mary Bourne).

24 See Appendix 3, Tables 7–9.

25 See e.g. Ingram, *Church Courts*, p. 22.

26 *ODNB*; SHLS, D/D/ca/313, ff. 33r, 37r, 40r, 48r (plenaries), f. 29r (*camera*); D/D/ca/315, ff. 140r, 154r; D/D/ca/319, ff. 44v, 51r; D/D/ca/331, f. 149r.

27 Archbishop of Canterbury 1633–45, Horn, *Fasti 1541–1857*, vol. 3, p. 9; Quaife's view that Laudian 'surveillance' at this time was 'thorough' remains an assertion, at least as far as the court at Wells is concerned (Quaife, *Wanton Wenches*, preface, unnumbered).

28 Ingram, *Church Courts*, p. 347; Marchant, *Church under Law*, p. 205; reviewing other research illustrates, again, the hazards in attempting true comparisons, e.g. whether courts were archidiaconal or episcopal, whether cases were *ex officio* or *ad instantiam*, or whether counting was of causes or people.

29 Davies, 'Religious Uniformity', Appendix 2, p. 359 (attendance at Worcester for the same sample years 1675, 1678 and 1680 was 50, 59 and 71 per cent respectively); Jones, 'Oxford and Peterborough', pp. 91, 92–8.

30 HRO, C1/35, f. 57v.

31 See Appendix 3, Tables 10–12.

32 WRO, 802 2760, f. 283r (Bangse); f. 79r (Heming); f. 453v (Yacron); f. 315r (Belling).

33 SHLS, D/D/ca/243, ff. 93r, 103v.

34 HRO, C1/35, f. 14v (Maunder); f. 26v (Collins); f. 51v (Stevens); f. 52v (Searle).

35 HRO, C1/37 (no folios), 5/10/1663 – *D(omi)nus ... eumq(ue) fam(a)e su(a)e pristin(a)e restituit* (literally, 'and the judge restored him to his former standing').

36 SHLS, D/D/ca/338 2 (no folios), 13/3/1663.

37 HRO, C1/34, f. 9r (Brunsden); f. 13r (Bennett); f. 9r (Gosse); f. 7v (Harding); f. 14r (Elmes, in fact 'perpetual curate' of St Mary Bourne); f. 12v (churchwardens of Highclere).

38 SHLS, D/D/ca/243, f. 71v (Burrow); ff. 28v, 42r, 56v, 71r (Criddle).

39 WRO, 794 011 2722 1, Book 30, f. 259r (Gough and Knight).

40 HRO, C1/34, ff. 23v, 40v (Balchilde); ff. 9v, 24v (Brixey); ff. 17r, 31r, 37r (Sherier); f. 17v (Davies); ff. 6r, 22r, 41v (Cooke); ff. 5v, 22r, 41v (Butler).

41 SHLS, D/D/ca/243, ff. 79r, 89r, 99r (Rendell); ff. 87r, 99r, 104r (St Alban); ff. 88v, 99v, (Allercotts); ff. 40r, 45r, 55r, 67r, 80v (Traske if the same person).

42 WRO, 794 011 2722 2, Book 32, f. 236v (minister), f. 220v (churchwardens), f. 210v (Patricke).

43 SHLS, D/D/ca/207 (1618), f. 248v (Vyncombe); HRO, C1/33 (1619, no folios), 12/11/ 1619 (Cornellis); SHLS, D/D/ca/350 (1671, no folios), 28/11/1671 (Blache).

44 HRO, C1/33 (1619, no folios), 3/12/1619 (Ray); C1/34 (1621), f. 29r (Elderwell), f. 21r (Newbolt); C1/35 (1623), f. 19r (Andrewes), f. 7r (Dawes), f. 19 r (Downes), f. 54r (Gouge);

f. 27r (Willyer); WRO, 802 2760, f. 186r (Cooke), f. 66r (Feilde), f. 271r (Henley); SHLS, D/D/ca/207, f. 252r (Stuckie).

45 WRO, 794 011 2722 2, Book 32, f. 260v (Norris); HRO, C1/45 (no folios), 22/10/1680 (Kelsey); outside the limits of this part of the survey (Michaelmas terms 1610s to the 1680s), 11 men were dismissed for attending 'a burieinge of an excommunicate person' in June 1617 (WRO, 802 2760, ff. 212v–215r) – 'dimiss' – and no statement of guilt or innocence – but probably showing mercy by the judge.

46 HRO, C1/34, f. 12v (Gate).

47 SHLS, D/D/ca/224, f. 143r (Gove); HRO, C1/35, f. 5v (Steevens); WRO, 794 011 2722 2, Book 32, f. 158v (Wolmore).

48 HRO, C1/33 (no folios), 2/12/1619 (Butler); 11/11/1619 (Hall).

49 HRO, C1/35, f. 24r (Johnson); f. 1v (Chartrain).

50 HRO, C1/34, f. 24r (Kings Somborne); f. 27v (Upper Clatford).

51 WRO, 802 2760, f. 54r (Saunders); f. 219v (Cowp); f. 417v (Sneade); f. 227r (Fitters).

52 WRO, 802 2760, f. 181v.

53 WRO, 802 2760, ff. 184v, 185r.

54 WRO, 794 011 2722 1, Book 30 (1675), f. 257v (churchwardens of Bedwardine St John); HRO, C1/45 (no folios), 8/11/1678 (the Rayners).

55 For a different assertion, see Quaife, Wanton Wenches, preface (unnumbered).

56 Davies, 'Religious Uniformity', Abstract 1, p. 1; Appendix 2, p. 359; Jones, 'Oxford and Peterborough', pp. 81, 83–4, Tables 4.5, 4.6 (differences – types of court, gaps in the record, dates, for example – underline, again, the need for caution with these comparisons).

57 See Appendix 3, Tables 13–16.

58 See the section 'Church and people: the impact of its courts on society' in this chapter.

59 HRO, C1/35, f. 2v (Chilbolton); f. 19r (Droxford); f. 54r (Brading).

60 WRO, 802 2760, f. 218v.

61 SHLS, D/D/ca/207, f. 272r.

62 WRO, 794 011 2722 2, Book 32, f. 9v.

63 WRO, 802 2760, f. 16r (Underhill); HRO, C1/35, f. 56r (Marshatt); f. 22r (Pistor).

64 HRO, C1/35, ff. 6r, 29v (Rood); SHLS, D/D/ca/207, f. 267v (Cheepewrighte); WRO, 802 2760, f. 236v (Balamy), f. 234v (Phelps); the last two both lack a first name in the relevant book.

65 HRO, C1/35, f. 57r.

66 HRO, C1/35, f. 29v (Fuller); WRO, 802 2760, f. 236v (Balamy); HRO, C1/35, f. 56r (Marshatt).

67 WRO, 794 011 2722 2, Book 32, ff. 160v, 170r; HRO, C1/45 (no folios), 15/10/1680; in the latter case (Goodaker), 'conformitate' is ambiguous and the case could have involved either failure to conform to the doctrines and worship of the Church of England or that he had failed to supply a certificate to do with some other kind of offence.

68 SHLS, D/D/ca/295, ff. 150v, 175r; possibly also 'Setle' of Coughton (Worcester) in 1661, accused of bastardy, which he denied, and the case was adjourned to a session beyond December 1661 (the limit of this sample); John Humphrey is listed as vicar of Coughton in 1661 (WRO, 802 295, box 1, no folios) so there are problems of identity, and 'mrm' Setle could be read as 'wm Sete', which means Setle could have been a layman (WRO, 794 011 2722 2, Book 32, f. 33v).

69 Haller, Liberty and Reformation, p. xiv; Hill, World Turned Upside Down, p. 12.

70 Cressy, Birth, Marriage, Death, e.g. pp. 12 (cultural matrix), 182, 185 (baptism), 332, 334 (marriage), 418 (burial); Hill, World Turned Upside Down, passim and, in particular, pp. 12, 308–10, 312.

71 HRO, C1/33 (no folios).

72 BL, Harley MS 595, ff. 220, 231, 235.

73 For a discussion of excommunication see the section 'Ex officio procedures' in Chapter 1; for the importance of guilt see the section 'Guilt' in this chapter.

74 Willis Bund, 'Ecclesiastical History', pp. 51, 53, 54–5 (Catholics), 56–7, 60–1, 66–7 (Puritans) in Worcestershire; Cox, 'Ecclesiastical History', pp. 84–5 (Tichbornes/Hampshire); Scott Holmes, 'Ecclesiastical History', p. 42 (Puritans/Somerset); Bradford, 'Social and Economic History', p. 314 (Puritans/Somerset); Richard Baxter was a leading figure among the Presbyterians, a preacher and a writer who produced numerous abortive schemes in the 1660s and 1670s to unite Presbyterians and Anglicans.

75 For Warwickshire see Haydon, 'Kineton', p. 167; Haydon, 'Mouth of Hell', pp. 23, 24; for Winchester (Tichbornes), e.g. HRO C1/45 (no folios).

THE EXTENT OF CHURCH DISCIPLINE 115

76 Willis Bund, 'Ecclesiastical History', pp. 73, 74, 75; '2,000' appears to be a wild exaggeration; George Fox was founder and leader of Quakerism in the seventeenth century.

77 E.g. Browning, *English Historical Documents*, p. 387.

78 Lyon Turner, *Original Records*, vol. 2, pp. 781–7 (Worcestershire), 788–804 (Warwickshire), 1035–52 (Hampshire), 1079–126 (Somerset); the lists show larger numbers but with question marks; my figures are based on issue or receipt of licences, without question marks, and are therefore the definite, though minimum, numbers; see also Haydon, 'Kineton', pp. 167–8.

79 Whiteman, *Compton Census*, pp. 69–70, 169–70, 553; together with, for Morley, LPL, MS 639, f. 270r and BL, Egerton MS 3329; Compton's figures appear again in *CSPD 1693*, pp. 448–9, and were apparently still being relied on for recruitment of soldiers 17 years after they were first compiled.

80 The phrase can be found in e.g. 23 EI c.1 (1581), 35 EI c.1, 35 EI c.2 (both 1593), and is sometimes quoted in the rolls.

81 TNA, E 377/28, E 377/29 (the 1620s), E 377/70, E 377/71 (the 1670s).

82 It is 'probable' that 'separatists' or 'sectarians' formed 'only a small fraction' of convictions before 1660: Bowler, *Recusant Roll*, p. xxxvii.

83 BL, Harley MS 280, f. 157r/v; f. 172v: figures are given twice and there is a discrepancy of *c*. 200 for the Southern Province.

84 Whiteman, *Compton Census*, Appendix F, pp. cxxiii–cxxiv; these are round figures, after screening by Whiteman, of adults (16+) in 24 dioceses.

85 Miller, *Popery and Politics*, p. 9; Kenyon, *Popish Plot*, p. 14.

86 Hindle, *State and Social Change*, p. 169.

87 Laslett, 'Comparing Illegitimacy', p. 14, Table 1.1 (a); Cressy, *Birth, Marriage, Death*, pp. 73–6; Wrightson and Levine, *Terling*, pp. 126–34.

88 'Protestant dissenters' is a term of 'convenience': they were by no means a cohesive unit, ranging from Presbyterians to Fifth Monarchy Men and Quakers, who probably hated each other as much as they hated 'Anglicans' and Catholics.

89 HRO, B1/53 (back of the book).

90 WRO, 794 011 2722 1 + 2.

91 Davies, 'Religious Uniformity', pp. 75–6.

92 Houlbrooke, *Church Courts*, p. 45; Ingram, *Church Courts*, p. 45.

93 Only three books of archidiaconal *ex officio* activity have been traced so far, all for Wells: SHLS, DD/SAS/C795/TN/26 (Taunton 1623–4); D/D/ca/363 (Wells 1686–98); D/D/ca/370 (Wells 1698–1708); for bishops' private sessions see e.g. SHLS, D/D/ca/295, f. 163v (12/1633), D/D/ca/331, f. 194v (12/1640); WRO, 802 2760, f. 135v (10/1614), 794 011 2722 2, Book 32, f. 158v (9/1680), f. 166r (11/1680); 807 093 2724, Book 38, f. 109r (2/1694), f. 120r (9/1695), f. 120v (6/1696).

94 I owe this point to Dr Robert Bearman and, in particular, the existence of a court in the peculiar of Stratford on Avon (in Worcester Diocese).

95 Wrightson and Levine, *Terling*, p. 112.

96 Underdown, *Fire from Heaven*, pp. 100–1.

97 The figures for Winchester are somewhat suspect and 'conformity' could mean an order to obey such laws as the Act of Uniformity (i.e. they were dissenters) or it could mean simply to obey a court order (which could cover a multiplicity of crimes).

4
Explaining the decline of the courts

The consistory courts of Winchester, Worcester and Wells were clearly in decline by the end of the seventeenth century and this chapter will attempt to explain it. Explanations will rest in the first place on examination of surviving court books to expose what they reveal about the reasons for the decline of the courts before wider issues are considered.

The examination will offer a full account of the main consistory procedures and punishments, with examples of their enforcement, to show how they damaged support for the courts. Particularly problematic procedures revealed by the court books were excommunication, the *ex officio* oath and compurgation; the main punishment was penance; and each of these will be considered in turn in order to establish their strengths and weaknesses. The court books also reveal much about the type of people summoned and punished by the ecclesiastical authorities, in particular their class and occupations; and this study will weigh the effects of these findings on attitudes towards the church courts. If the church courts were treating all people in the same way and if, to do so, they were using reliable procedures and effective punishments, then the general public – and even the accused – might have viewed ecclesiastical discipline in a more favourable light and the judicial machinery of the Church, if not flourishing, might have survived. Distrust of the methods and of the purview of the courts meant loss of supporters and defenders and, at the very least, when ecclesiastical justice was in need of friends, it found they were too few.

A final section will move away from the court books and consider wider issues. This will set the 'internal' problems in context and attempt to conclude how far they were to blame for the decline of the courts and how far other factors came into play.

Excommunication

Excommunication was essentially a sanction of the court to try to force people to comply: to attend its sessions, to respect its orders, to perform its punishments and to pay its fees.[1] It was occasionally a punishment in itself but mostly it was a means to enforce the will of the court.[2] It was hoped that by depriving people of the sacrament or, in the more extreme version, by excluding them from courts (secular as well as spiritual) and trade, they would be forced to surrender to the court, attend its sessions and accept its judgments.

The first problem was usually attendance, and the first response of the court was to issue a ways and means writ (*viis et modis*). These were issued when the accused person could not be found and a citation (or a summons to answer a charge) was therefore undeliverable in person. About 18 or 19 ways and means orders were issued per term at Worcester and Wells in the 1610s and 1620s. No *viis et modis* orders appear to have been issued by the courts at Winchester in the three sample terms of 1619, 1621 and 1623; but since attendance was hardly any better there than in the other dioceses, compliance with a court summons was not the reason. Detection of the accused may have been more efficient or the court officials may have preferred other weapons, but the fact that so many entries state that the citations were announced in church may suggest that the accused could not be found and a *viis et modis* order had been issued but not entered in the book.

There appears to have been greater use of the orders in all three archdeaconries after the Restoration. Over 880 *viis et modis* orders were issued by the court at Winchester in 1663 – an amazing explosion – and while numbers fell sharply, the orders continued to be relied upon in the 1670s and 1680s. Comparisons of the 1670s and 1680s with the 1610s and 1620s cannot be made for Winchester, but numbers of *viis* orders were down at Wells and, if they were up at Worcester, this was because of a shift in the balance between *viis* and excommunications orders while overall numbers, whether of those summoned or absentees, were down in all three archdeaconries as the business of the courts declined.

If the accused failed to respond either to the original citation or to a ways and means order, progress in the case was stalled. Ways and means orders were renewed (and renewed) against the 'missing persons' and, presumably when the citation had been served but the accused failed to attend, cases were 'reserved' (and reserved), that is, adjourned, until the accused arrived in court or he or she was excommunicated.

CHURCH COURTS AND THE PEOPLE IN SEVENTEENTH-CENTURY ENGLAND

Adjournments rose at Wells to well over two-thirds of actions against absentees in the 1630s. Wells is the only one of the three archdeaconries with records for that time, and the evident resistance to the court is an interesting insight into the limits of Laudian rigour.[3] Adjournments in all three archdeaconries were sharply down by the 1670s, and this was again a reflection of the lower numbers summoned and, at root, the contraction of the judicial process.

It was at this stage that the court usually ordered excommunication. A hundred and more excommunications during one term must, on any reckoning, be considered high, but there were, for example, 104 at Worcester in Michaelmas term 1614, 126 at Wells in 1621, 127 at Winchester in 1623 and no fewer than 131 in Wells in 1633. Numbers of 129 and 138 were still possible after the Restoration at Winchester in 1663 and at Worcester in 1682; otherwise, numbers were much lower in all three archdeaconries in the later period if only, again, because of the contraction of business. Declining trends in the volume of business and excommunication rates between the 1630s and the 1670s in the two dioceses of Oxford and Peterborough confirm the collapse, in both respects, at Winchester, Worcester and Wells.[4]

Estimates of 'cumulative' numbers of excommunicates – total numbers of excommunicates in a diocese at any one time – must be a hazardous exercise. Ronald Marchant calculates that 5 per cent of the populations of York, Norwich and Chester were excommunicate and postulates the existence of 'a seam of irreligious people' in the Northern Province.[5] Such may – or may not – have been the case in Winchester, Worcester and Wells. No lists of all excommunicates at any particular time have come to light, overall population sizes are debatable, especially the figures for Worcester, and both of these problems frustrate attempts to estimate proportions of underclasses of 'irreligious people' in the three dioceses.

Absolution brought an end to excommunication and restored the victim to life within the church, including baptism, communion and burial rites,[6] and, if there had been a 'secular' ban (exclusion from courts and trade) as well, to a regular existence in the community. Rates of absolutions would show a wish among victims of excommunication to be rid of the sentence, or not, as the case may have been, and thus, by implication, the regard in which excommunication was held in the seventeenth century. Recording of absolutions is unfortunately far from satisfactory. If there were separate absolution books they appear to be missing. These may have shown a regular stream of absolutions but this is just speculation. Absolutions do appear in the relevant court books but not in a systematic way. There is, consequently, much missing, or 'vestigial', about the recording process in all three archdeaconries. References to absolution in the court books either lack a date, are abbreviated beyond confident recognition, or refer only to the fee or some other subsequent action and not to the grant of absolution itself. Examples of all these can be found at Worcester and Wells before the Wars and Interregnum,[7] and there are several at Worcester, again, after the Restoration.[8] Statistics for Worcester are the fullest, it must be said, since – an advantage for this kind of purpose – the clerks recorded all the actions having to do with the accused in one place in the book, whereas at Winchester and Wells events were recorded session by session and breaks in the sequence of the books make it very difficult to trace absolutions beyond the Michaelmas term in question.

Surviving evidence in the court books suggests that, before the 1640s, there were a few absolutions in all three archdeaconries – some of the highest numbers were at Worcester in 1613 – and this continued to be the case in Wells in the 1630s. After the Restoration they disappear from the corresponding court books of Winchester and Wells. Worcester was somewhat different, with a few in 1661 and the 1670s in the regular sessions and a quite exceptional 27 in the visitations of 1682. If these books are at all reliable, it would seem that overall absolutions were relatively few and declining, whether at Winchester, Worcester or Wells, which fits with developments over the century at Oxford and Peterborough.[9]

Activation of the *significavit* procedure was the ultimate weapon in the episcopal armoury.[10] At least two prosecutions of excommunicates for exceeding the 40-day limit can be found in the consistory court book of Worcester for 1614,[11] and after the Restoration there are several examples of its use at Wells in the 1670s and a few more at Worcester in the 1670s and 1680s. One or two of the cases at Worcester state that the contempt in question 'should be signified' to the Crown, while entries in some of the cases at Wells record that the offender had been in a state of excommunication for 40 days.[12] Whether the offenders were apprehended and how long they spent in gaol remains a mystery for want of evidence in the books of the three archdeaconries.

The effectiveness of these sanctions – excommunication and signification – is the crucial issue, and it remains to be tackled. Several recent attempts have been made to defend excommunication. There ought, undoubtedly, to have been strong motives for avoiding the censures of excommunication and, drawing on contemporary correspondence, Jens Aklundh, in particular, makes a brave stab at defending its potency in the seventeenth century: from concerns about spiritual deprivation – losing rights to baptism, marriage and burial by the Church – to worries about social standing, loss of business, disbarment from the courts, denial of voting rights and the prospect of prison.[13] It is true, furthermore, that absence may not automatically have meant rejection of the Church, its discipline and its courts. Cost, illness and departure from the parish would, no doubt, have been other factors causing absence on numerous occasions. Nor did adjournments, ways and means orders and excommunications always fail to produce results. Absentees did appear in court – sometimes – after one or more ways and means orders, either during the Michaelmas term in question or subsequently. Excommunicates – some of them – did seek absolution. Once reconciled, these cases were able to proceed through the court to conclusion.

Aklundh has brought to light some very real concerns but, while he does not overstate the deterrence of excommunication, he points to 'archival silences' in the records and comes close to equating 'voicelessness' with apprehensions about its effects. A degree of caution with arguments from silence must surely be advisable. His apparent disdain for 'quantitative assessment' has encouraged him, moreover, to ignore, rather than to challenge, hard facts.[14] The contrast between a scatter of apprehensive statements about the legal sanctions of the church courts, on the one hand, and the statistics, on the other, is striking. A thorough scrutiny of church court operations in three archdeaconries over the course of the seventeenth century shows high numbers of excommunications and low numbers of absolutions, resulting in poor attendance and failure to complete business on a huge scale – in spite of the 'potency' of excommunication.

The weight of evidence must assuredly cast considerable doubt on the sanctions of the church courts and on their effects on the communities they sought to regulate. Figures so high seem to indicate an 'off with his head' mentality which could only drive the Church into 'wonderland' and discredit. It is difficult to gainsay the failings of excommunication. It was grossly overused and ran the risk of meaninglessness, by dilution, to both victims and the wider public. Victims found comfort in numbers while the public found it impossible to 'ostracise so large a body of people'. Its shock effect or value dwindled and a routine sanction engendered a routine response.[15] The impotence of the courts was meanwhile advertised for all to see. Something of these failings can be caught in the comments of contemporaries in the later seventeenth century, such as Jenkins, the judge, and Sheldon, the archbishop, who expressed concerns in an identical phrase about the use of excommunication 'upon slight matters'; but no action followed.[16]

It would be absurd to expect modern conciliation and arbitration procedures in the seventeenth century but it would not be entirely anachronistic to expect some action over a problem with a long history of failure, nor some recognition of the roles of counselling and repentance. Criticisms of overuse, on the one hand, and of the loss of spiritual and 'civil rights', on the other, were acknowledged, somewhat, at the time and stand against a Church which in its prayers and sermons put so much stress – in the seventeenth century – on mercy and forgiveness.

The *ex officio* oath

Oaths played a key part in the procedures of the church courts. Most oaths were 'routine': apparitors swearing to have delivered a citation; compurgators swearing to the credibility of an accused neighbour; churchwardens swearing that all was well with the fabric and fittings in their parish; offenders seeking absolution and restitution after excommunication swearing their support for the Church and its laws. All these occurred all the time and can be found over and over again in the court books of the three archdeaconries.[17]

More contentious was the *ex officio* oath, by which accused people swore to answer faithfully all questions put to them while in the dock. Not much else is revealed in the court books about the workings of the oath, for example, or the attitudes of officials and accused towards it. The phrase *eund(em) iuram(en)t(o) on(era)vit ... de fidel(ite)r r(esp)ondend(o)* (he charged him with the/an oath to reply faithfully) appears in the 1610s and 1620s occasionally at Winchester but was administered liberally at Wells.[18] The oath was applied in case after case in Michaelmas term 1624 at Wells after the judge had read the charge and before any further proceedings. A year earlier at Winchester, however, in December 1623, when Thomas Charlock was summoned to the consistory court,[19] the judge imposed an oath – *juramentum* – at the outset of proceedings and then read the charge – conduct of a clandestine marriage between Richard North and Nichola Sweete in the porch of the church at Newport (on the Isle of Wight). Charlock confessed and apparently volunteered his 'solemnization' of another clandestine marriage between Peter Frampton and Sara Voxe in the belfry of the neighbouring church at Brading. Both marriages had taken place at six o'clock in the morning, without a licence and with 'the church doore being shutte'. The judge duly pronounced sentence – suspension of Charlock from office for three years – and then proceeded to challenge Charlock's credentials as minister and schoolmaster. Charlock claimed deacon status and said he had a teaching licence, both of which the judge declared invalid. That seems to have been the end of Charlock, and the judge then turned to the other people – the bride and groom and four witnesses from the first marriage – in the drama. The judge issued excommunication orders against the two leading figures, North (groom) and Bushe (witness) – nothing seems to have been said about the bride – but the two men pleaded ignorance of the law and the judge relaxed the excommunication. To receive a sentence of any kind these last two must have been in court, but the three remaining witnesses were apparently absent because their sentence was adjourned. Frampton and Voxe (the other couple whom Charlock had married) also failed to make the crossing from Brading to Winchester and their case too was adjourned.

These – Charlock at Winchester and the other cases at Wells – would all appear to be examples of the use of the *ex officio* oath. This oath was chief among the long list of complaints against the Church and its discipline. Administration of the oath provoked fierce criticism. It was outlawed in the 'revolution' of 1640–1 and, although the grievance was still being raked over in the debates about *The Agreement of the People* in 1649,[20] its abolition was confirmed by statute at the Restoration in 1661.[21]

Most of the 'noise' had come from Puritans such as William Prynne and common lawyers such as the redoubtable Edward Coke.[22] This was essentially a fight between canon and common law. The stand of both Puritans and common lawyers was for the suppression of consistory courts.[23] They were, of course, interested parties. Puritans preferred fraternal admonition on principle but their attitude to church court discipline was coloured, no doubt, by their sufferings at the hands of those courts.[24] For common lawyer practitioners such as Edward Coke, meanwhile, abolition meant more work and greater status for the secular courts, and he and his colleagues probably trained their sights less on the disciplinary side of consistory court procedures and more on the potentially profitable instance business of the courts together with the major cases at High Commission. Both lawyers and preachers saw in the *ex officio* oath, no doubt, a useful weapon, whether justifiable or not, to discredit the church courts.

Much play was made of Magna Carta by Coke and his fellow lawyers, including Beal, Morice and Ashley.[25] Essentially, and disregarding the evident self-interest of common lawyers and, indeed, the Puritans, complaints against the oath with some substance were that accused persons did not know the charge until they had sworn the oath; that questioning could be broadened to cover a wider range of issues which could surprise the accused and catch them without a defence; and that the accused either had to tell the truth, remain silent or lie. Lying raised questions, among the more scrupulous, of conscience; silence could provoke proceedings for contempt, huge fines and indefinite imprisonment; and by telling the truth the accused could incriminate themselves.[26]

There are several reasons for thinking that the impact – or effect – of the oath may not have been so severe, at least at diocesan consistory court level. The charges seem to have come before the oath in the spate of cases at Wells in 1624 so the accused ought to have been aware of their nature. Even if this were not so, the accused could always have asked at the beginning of proceedings.[27] The accused ought, in any case, to have known the contents of the original charge or charges from churchwardens' presentments or from the citations (summonses to attend) which apparitors were forever delivering; and, if compurgation was invoked, the charge would certainly have been clear when the accused and their friends and neighbours took their oaths.

Wider questioning was the issue, and indeed it did occur, for example, in the case of the bogus cleric and clandestine marriage at Winchester in 1623, mentioned previously, where the judge took advantage of preliminary administration of the oath to inquire further about the credentials of the clergyman. Wider inquiry is clearly what happened in that case. It might be said, in its defence, that the judge was surely justified, in the interests of the Church and of individuals, to pursue his inquiries in that case and it was, moreover, an extremely rare occurrence, to judge from the court books, in the three archdeaconries of this study. It might be said, at the same time, against the *ex officio* oath, that the offending cleric should have been charged with any new offences in the usual way and with proper notice.

Where oaths were involved, lying was likely and a charge of perjury a possibility. Ronald Marchant considers that accused persons who denied the charge and were subsequently found guilty exposed themselves to a charge of perjury,[28] but no such proceedings came to light in his investigations nor in this survey of Winchester, Worcester and Wells. The same risk – perjury – presumably arose in certain compurgation proceedings as well. The accused might deny the offence under oath but their compurgators might refuse to swear to their integrity (and therefore innocence). Such an occurrence was rare because the accused chose the participants and, hardly surprisingly, no such examples of disagreement between the accused and their compurgators appear in the court books of the three archdeaconries. In one or two cases, however, a contradictory outcome – where two people were charged with the same misdemeanour and one confessed but the other denied it – does appear in the records and, again, perjury could have been the next step. Two cases at Winchester illustrate the point: in November 1621, Bennetta Snow confessed and

124   CHURCH COURTS AND THE PEOPLE IN SEVENTEENTH-CENTURY ENGLAND

performed penance for incontinence but William Poor, the other party, used compurgation to escape.[29] In December 1623, in (nearly) a mirror image, the wife of Thomas Compton denied incontinence, underwent compurgation and was cleared; her paramour, Henry White, had, meanwhile, confessed and had received a penance order which he, perhaps not surprisingly, refused to perform, and the case came to an end, for the moment, anyway, with his excommunication.[30] Several cases at Worcester in the 1610s make it clear that such a contradictory outcome was a far from unusual occurrence.[31]

In all these cases, one of the parties was likely to have been lying. Confession was sure to end in the dreaded penance and therefore, knowing this, the persons confessing (Bennetta Snow and Henry White) were less likely to be lying (though it is always possible that the person confessing may have been confused, bullied or mistaken in some way). In all the cases the party who chose compurgation had sworn under oath but was more likely to have been lying. How the authorities 'squared' the verdicts and why they did not instigate perjury proceedings is baffling. Reluctance by the consistory courts to pursue matters further may, to their credit, imply a merciful judicial system but, at the same time, their standing was undone, for all to see on occasion, by *reductio ad absurdum* of its own making.

It should be said, in conclusion to this section, that harsher sanctions such as fines and imprisonment could only be imposed by High Commission and that the ordinary consistory courts, if they had chosen to pursue charges of perjury, would not have possessed such powers directly. Their course might have been to excommunicate and then to activate the *significavit* procedure (that is, resort to the secular authorities for an order to arrest the offender) but this latter power – *significavit* – was, like the power to widen the questioning, rarely invoked.[32]

Compurgation

Arriving at the truth – or at least a verdict – was the critical function of the courts.[33] Confessions, denials, documents, inquiry and even 'arbitration' were all deployed in pursuit of justice (as they saw it). Resort to compurgation averaged 11 or 12 occasions for the Michaelmas terms at Winchester and Worcester in the 1610s and five at Wells. It came second as a method of settling a verdict at Worcester (12 compared with an average of 63 confessions) and more like fourth or fifth at Winchester and Worcester, but it still played a substantial part in the legal process before the Wars and Interregnum.

It should be said that in the overwhelming majority of cases, there is no indication of method of any kind in the court books of the three archdeaconries. Sometimes the way in which the verdict was reached is just not described, but in most cases the accused did not arrive in court on the day and the case could not proceed to the 'evidence' stage. Information about evidence is missing from the records for three-quarters of the accused at Wells before the upheavals of the middle of the century, and matters were only marginally better at Worcester and Winchester. By the 1670s and 1680s, proportions were much the same at Wells but had grown to 86 per cent at Worcester and 99 per cent at Winchester. Such figures are yet more graphic indicators of the dysfunctionality of the courts in all three dioceses.

Compurgation relied on friends and neighbours, people with local knowledge, who would testify under oath to the good character of the accused and this was usually decisive when the judge came to pronounce sentence. They were not witnesses of the offence and they were quite different from modern jurors who have no personal acquaintance with the accused, who consider the facts of a case and who deliver their verdict. Numbers of compurgators – or 'hands' – ranged from three to six in the proceedings during Michaelmas term 1623 at Winchester. The number of hands could rise to nine, 10 and even 12, according to other historians of the consistory courts.[34]

Two quite separate but strikingly similar examples from Winchester during Michaelmas term 1623 highlight very clearly the problems with the compurgation procedure. Christopher Maunder and John Searle both stood accused of incontinence and the judge ordered compurgation by three 'hands' for Maunder and six for Searle. Each claimed to be 'a poore man'; Maunder said he had two willing 'neighbours' with him in court and Searle said he could supply four of the six. The judge agreed to both requests, and it must have been no surprise that both were then cleared of the charge.[35] Cases involving compurgation also arose in the other two archdeaconries: at Worcester in 1613, for example, when Richard Shrieve was only able to produce three of the four compurgators; and at Wells in 1618, when Michael Devonsheere could only produce two of the requisite three. Again the smaller numbers were accepted and, after swearing, the accused were acquitted.[36]

In other cases – Roger Bauke, for example, at Worcester in 1615 or John St Albans at Wells in 1624 – both the accused and the compurgators failed to arrive at all. In these two cases the accused were pronounced deficient in compurgation and required to perform penance, which neither of them appears to have done by the end of term.[37] Suspicions of guilt and evasion inevitably arose when people failed to appear in court but disruption and costs were just as likely explanations. Costs were an explicit consideration for Maunder and Searle at Winchester and were, no doubt, a factor in the other cases. When compurgators testified, they did so – invariably – in favour of the accused.

Far worse were the absurd outcomes in prosecutions at Winchester in 1621 and 1623 discussed in the preceding section. Both cases turned on the testimony of friends and neighbours. William Poor relied on four neighbours in 1621, 'the wife of Thomas Compton' on two in 1623. Both ended in 'acquittal'. The other party in both cases had confessed. Intimidation is possible for both confessions – the awesomeness of the occasion if not the sternness of the judge – but much greater suspicion must fall on the integrity of compurgation. Either way, one of the parties in each case was lying and the contradictory outcomes were a mockery of justice.

The church courts came under fire in the political revolution of 1641. The statute of 1641 shot down the rigging – the *ex officio* oath – but the vessel limped on to sink with the bishops in 1646.[38] Furthermore, when it was relaunched at the Restoration, the statute of 1661 was quite specific about oaths and, this time, referred to compurgation as well: 'it shall not be lawfull' for the church courts 'to administer ... the oath Ex Officio or any other Oath ... to purge him or her selfe'.[39] Several historians have claimed that compurgation was abolished at the same time as the use of oaths by the legislation of 1641 and 1661.[40] Compurgation itself may not have been explicitly declared illegal in either of those statutes but oaths were critical for the process and their use 'to purge him or her selfe' was specifically outlawed, though nothing was said, either way, about voluntary swearing.

Compurgations occurred, nonetheless, at Winchester in the 1660s, at Wells in the 1670s and at Worcester in the 1680s (and there are more occurrences at Worcester in the 1690s).[41] The terse notes of the clerk do not allow background or explanation and it is mostly far from clear whether compurgation in these times was imposed by the judge (compulsory) or at the request of the accused (voluntary). Two compurgations at Wells in the 1670s were ordered by the judge but on the matter of voluntariness the record is silent.[42] George Aldridge volunteered at the Winchester Consistory Court in October 1663 to take an oath that he was innocent of adultery and to provide supporting compurgators, but the judge seems, at that point, to have dispensed with the business and dismissed the case.[43] The most specific example of volunteering appears to have occurred at Worcester in October and November 1680. John Francklin sought canonical purgation and the judge obliged. Francklin arrived on the day with his compurgators. He seems to have done no more, but his three supporters swore to his innocence and the judge concurred and issued letters attesting to Francklin's good character.[44]

Questions – critical questions – remain: were the compurgations carried out after 1660 voluntary, and were voluntary compurgations legal? On the first point – whether the occurrences were voluntary – the occasions are too few and the notes too brief for any truly confident assertions. On the second point – the lawfulness of voluntary compurgations – the law looks *prima facie* clear – no more compurgations using an oath so no more compurgations, but voluntary use is not explicitly banned. From the Restoration the bishops and their numerous agents, lay and clerical, were either exploiting a loophole in the legislation or simply ignoring it and no one appears to have been bothered enough to challenge them.

Compurgation was not unique to Winchester, Worcester or Wells, not unique to office cases and not unique to ecclesiastical causes. Both ecclesiastical and secular courts had relied upon compurgation; the system was common to both jurisdictions and, in its defence, if it had so many failings, it should have caused the decline of the secular as well as the ecclesiastical courts. Furthermore, a more positive case can be made for the role of compurgation. Evidence in the form of documents would have been non-existent in most cases such as fornication, modern 'forensics' were certainly non-existent and, in the absence of anything else, compurgation would seem to have been 'a reasonable test'. It 'made sense' to check context and background and to take into account the character and behaviour of the accused from local people who were likely to possess knowledge of the person in question.[45]

Against this, compurgation had undoubted failings.[46] Compurgation provoked complaint for a number of reasons. The first was, very simply, the nuisance factor: the disturbance to routines and the costs of travel and 'subsistence' involved in producing friends and neighbours in a court a distance away and at the day and time of the court's choosing. Corruption and bias, arising from the use of testimony – sworn or otherwise – from friends and neighbours, was another undermining factor. Reliance on such blatantly defective testimony could only heap discredit on the authority of the church courts.

The jury system had, moreover, largely replaced compurgation in the secular courts. Its 'embryonic' beginnings can be traced in secular criminal cases to the Constitutions of Clarendon (1164) and Magna Carta (1215), and although compurgation continued in civil actions such as debt, its use had all but disappeared by the late seventeenth century. This has been ascribed to the growth of a greater degree of professionalism and the adoption of a number of features, juries among them, in place of voluntary community activity.[47] The introduction of juries may seem, at first sight, rather elaborate machinery, involving more people and consuming a great deal of time; but there did not have to be 12 jurors – three or five would have been enough – and a more reliable system might have deterred and reduced the caseload. If matters of church attendance and fornication were of such importance, the Church should, perhaps, have been prepared to consider an improvement of this kind. As it was, the position by the seventeenth century was that the church courts were tied to a system long since abandoned by the secular courts. The comparison was there and, at least potentially, clear for all to see.

Compurgation certainly had not disappeared by 1661, but it was clearly deficient in 'higher standards of proof'[48] (those of 1215), its legality was under question and its use was clearly much reduced. If it was thought to be such a good procedure – an expression of community involvement at its best – why was it declared 'unlawfull' and why was it allowed to decline?

This discussion of two of the methods used by the courts to arrive at a judgment has exposed the failings in the system and, consequently, suggests reasons for the decline of the whole apparatus: the faith placed by the ecclesiastical authorities in compurgations and the *ex officio* oath. Arguments can be made for both compurgation and the oath: the need for both in the absence of more modern methods of establishing the truth; and the restraint, even mercy, shown by the courts over prosecutions for perjury arising from defective compurgations and patent oath breaking. Much of the criticism, particularly of the oath, came, moreover, from 'interested' common lawyers. Other methods used by the church courts, involving documents, inquiry and arbitration, were sound, in principle at least; and the more sparing use of compurgation by the 1670s and 1680s may imply responsiveness of church authorities to the hostility towards and even acknowledgement of the defectiveness of the method. Whether this retreat had come in time to save them or merely signalled a weakness in the system and encouraged the opposition must remain open questions.

The activities of the Long Parliament in 1640–1 showed that the *ex officio* oath was the object of hatred of more than a cartel of common lawyers or a band of Puritan fanatics and should have served as a warning of the disdain for the system of ecclesiastical justice as a whole. Compurgation had been brought into question in the legislation of 1661 and it was a mistake to allow the subsequent revival of the procedure. Its failings – bias, expense and contradictory outcomes – were plain for all to see and its use sent a signal – refusal to modernise – which may have been enough to provoke suspicion, if not alarm and dismay. It was true also that the church courts had suffered from these failing for centuries but had not collapsed. It was certainly the case that in terms of delay and expense the secular courts were just as bad, but they did not use *ex officio* oaths, and compurgations were much reduced and largely replaced by juries. Only the church courts clung to these archaic methods. The death blows – religious toleration and social change – arose from other factors, but they struck a house with weak foundations and few defenders.

Penance

At the end of many cases, the accused person was 'dismissed'.[49] Dismissal marked the conclusion of a case. This could involve two kinds of outcome: those cleared of charges – the innocent – could be dismissed; but so could those who had been found guilty – those who had, for example, received a penance and who had certified its performance; or, to take another example, those who had paid the court fee. The word 'dismissed' simply marked the conclusion of a case. In this study, as far as possible with terse entries and ambiguous language, only those who were cleared of a charge or charges have been classified as 'dismissed' and the guilty, who may subsequently have been dismissed, have been classified according to their sentence.

Penance was a key feature in the sentencing process. To give the complete picture and to set penance in context, the other types of sentencing were warnings and orders. Warnings may be described as the more negative instruction (by the judge) not to do something, orders the more positive instruction to carry out a particular action. The distinction is a fine one; decisions about categories were sometimes arbitrary, and they have been considered together here. Average numbers for Michaelmas terms of 44 or 45 warnings and orders combined are remarkably similar in the 1610s and early 1620s at Worcester and Winchester, but numbers in both dioceses declined drastically by the 1670s and 1680s. Figures for warnings and orders at Wells, meanwhile, were negligible from start to finish.

Fifty penances were issued at Worcester in Michaelmas term 1613 and 53 at Wells in 1624. These were the highest numbers in any one term in the early years of this study. 1624 must have seen exceptional activity at Wells, however, and when numbers are averaged for the three terms, the positions are reversed – 27 per term at Wells and 39 at Worcester. Numbers declined a little at Wells in the 1630s and there were savage drops in all three archdeaconries by the early 1660s. Average numbers shrank to two at Worcester and Wells and zero at Winchester in the 1670s and 1680s.

This section will take a thorough and comprehensive look at sentencing. It will deal with each group – laymen and women, churchwardens and clergy – separately. It will link offences to sentences and strive to demonstrate, thereby, which offences attracted particular sentences. These enquiries should establish the context and, thus, the relative importance of penance. The concluding part of this section will discuss how penance was viewed and whether or not it undermined the Church's disciplinary machinery.

Sentencing of laymen and women: morals

Six people were found guilty of moral offences by the court at Wells in 1618, 14 at Winchester in 1623 and two at Worcester in 1680, for which penance was the usual sentence.[50] The offences ranged predictably from premarital intercourse, sexual incontinence and bastardy to clandestine marriage and harbouring pregnant women. Penance was the fate of Richard Andrewes of Amport and his wife at the proceedings at Winchester in 1623 for sex before marriage; the fate of Joanna Batt, also of Amport, for bastardy; and of Richard Symes of Sparsholt for 'companie keeping with Elizabeth the wife of William Barling'.[51] Penance was the fate of two men at Wells, Robert Carpenter and John Tomkins, both of Taunton, in 1618 for their involvement in a clandestine marriage, as well as the fate of the Beauchampes, husband and wife, at Worcester in 1680.[52]

Judges could show flexibility – a touch of mercy – in their judgments. Alice Hawkins of West Buckland was found guilty at Wells in 1618 of incontinence but her partner, George Campe, was allowed to take it upon himself to act as proxy over the performance of her penance. Alice Wells, yet another inhabitant of Amport, accused at Winchester in 1623 of harbouring, confessed the misdeed 'in compassion and at the entreatie of John Batt'. The judge showed compassion, in turn – or at least one step towards it – and dismissed her with a warning, though she still had to pay the court fee.[53]

Sentencing of laymen and women: religion

Winchester's 39 sentences in 1623 and Wells's 14 in 1618 are typical numbers of sentences of one kind or another for religious infractions during the specimen Michaelmas terms before the Interregnum.[54] Worcester's three sentences in 1680 illustrate the decline after the

Restoration in the regular sessions of the court (though there were more than 20 religious sentences in the visitation of 1682).

The range of sentences was wider for religious than for moral infractions. Warnings, orders and penance were all deployed. Play of one kind or another on the Sabbath usually meant penance; this was the fate of John Morse and Thomas Dible of Taunton (Wells) in 1618 for 'tipling' and the fate of Robert Hayes of Kings Somborne (Winchester) in 1623 for playing quoits and bowls, all these on the Sabbath.[55] Sunday working was sometimes met with penance, sometimes with a warning. The judge imposed penance on Thomas Aishe of Minehead (Wells 1618) and James Watt of Shalfleet (Isle of Wight, Winchester 1623) for working on Sunday, but Thomas Marshall of South Warnborough (Winchester 1623) escaped with a warning after pleading that he tended his cattle out of necessity 'as a deed of pietye'.[56]

In cases of failure to attend church or to receive communion, the response of the judge was usually to issue an order to comply. James Farthing of Luxborough (Wells 1618) and John Wayte of Kings Worthy (Winchester 1623) were both ordered to attend church; William Cawte of Upham (Winchester 1623), having missed communion at Easter, was ordered, likewise, to receive at Christmas.[57] In one of the rare communion prosecutions at Wells at this time John Wardall was found guilty in 1624 of failing to receive the sacrament and, no doubt because this was one of a bundle of crimes, the judge prescribed penance.[58] Penances were also issued for abusive behaviour, for example, at Wells in 1618 against William Stoddey of Stogursey and at Winchester in 1623 against Gilbert Brickleton of St Lawrence and St John, Southampton.[59]

Sentencing for religious infractions remained much the same after the Restoration. In 1680, several members of the Turton family fell into trouble: John Turton senior and his wife of Rowley (Worcester) were ordered to cease involving themselves in conventicles, to attend their parish church instead and to receive communion; in addition, William Turton was ordered in a private session to stop preaching 'contrary to the Lawes of this Kingdome' unless he had a licence from the bishop. To give two examples from the 'visitation' proceedings of Worcester, Mary Gray of Severn Stoke was ordered to attend services and William Peale of Hanley Castle to receive communion in 1682. Prosecutions for dissent reflect the greater emphasis on religious conformity after the Restoration. John Patrick of Ombersley was one such: he was ordered to attend and, when he failed to certify, he was excommunicated.[60]

Sentencing of laymen and women: rate

Only at Winchester in 1623, among the three specimen terms of the three archdeaconries, were any church rate offenders found guilty and sentenced.[61] Twenty-eight altogether suffered this fate at that time. The standard treatment, it would seem, was an order to pay, and examples among the 13 who received orders were Thomas Cooper of Brown Candover, Richard Lipscomb of Ropley and Richard Dastyn of Durley.[62] Unfortunately outcomes are clouded for the other 15, either because of the turn of events or the laconic way of recording them, and it is not clear whether they were issued with an order to pay. Simon Harding of St Michael's Winchester paid and, although dismissed without sentence, the probability is that he complied only under the duress of court proceedings.[63] The other 14, Thomas Smith among them,[64] seem, from notes at the side of each case, to have paid, but there is no indication of the date when they did so and their cases were all adjourned at the end of term. It is possible that they had paid all the time, that they were victims of a misunderstanding, that the court caught up with the fact and a note was made of the payment; it is more likely, however, that they were guilty of delay or even refusal to pay, that the case was adjourned at the end of term and that they paid, under threat of protracted court proceedings, sometime afterwards.

Treatment of guilty churchwardens

Numbers of guilty churchwardens, averaging 18 or so per term over the three terms of the 1610s and 1620s at Winchester – the highest number among the three archdeaconries – were small by any measure and especially in the context of total numbers of churchwardens (600, 450 and 300 or thereabouts respectively within the three archdeaconries). The trends, reflecting those of earlier sections, are not so clear. Prosecutions, and thus convictions, of churchwardens disappear from the court books for Winchester by the 1670s and 1680s, but Wells saw a slight rise in such cases. Worcester, with no definite convictions in the regular session of the court, looks, at first sight, similar to Winchester, but there were prosecutions, and the seemingly incessant transferring of cases from one session to another in the regular proceedings of 1675 must raise suspicions, if not conclusively, of guilt. Churchwardens were convicted, moreover, of no fewer than 18 derelictions of one kind or another in the visitation proceedings of 1679.

Orders to do something – to repair, to present, to take an oath or the like – were the most frequent actions taken by the courts against churchwardens. This was the case when the churchwardens of Evesham St Lawrence (Worcester) were ordered to repair both vestry and organ in 1613. At Chilworth (Winchester) in 1621 'paveing and Belfrie' were in 'decay', and at Hambledon (Winchester) in 1623 the communion table and churchyard rails were in a state of disrepair, over which, in the latter case, the churchwardens were given detailed instructions to provide a new table and, for the rails, either to find out who among the parishioners was responsible or to impose a rate to pay for the work. At the other end of the century (1675) and in a different diocese (Wells) the churchwardens of Fivehead were ordered to tackle a catalogue of shortcomings, from pews and the pulpit to windows, pavements, walls and door of the church and even the clerk's book.[65]

Oaths and presentments offer illustrations of yet more orders and also of the 'baldness' of the entries and the need to infer or surmise. The churchwardens of Chard (Wells) were required to take the oath of office but there is no evidence in the court book that they had done so by the end of Michaelmas term 1673, and the assumption made here is that they were guilty and that the case remained unresolved.[66] The proceedings against the churchwardens of Hanley Castle (Worcester), arising from the visitation of 1679, turned on corrections to their presentments, and there follows just a note that the presentments had been improved and the churchwardens 'dismissed'. The most likely reading is that the presentments had fallen below standards and an order had been issued – hence the inference of guilt.[67] Another case, further showing how guilt could end in dismissal rather than an order or punishment of any kind, arose at Ovington (Winchester 1623), where the churchwardens claimed in court that they had not been told of the celebration of communion at Pentecost so had not bought the wine and the judge, presumably sympathising, merely dismissed them.[68] In these ways classification of sentences frequently lies at the mercy of interpretation in view of the terseness of many of the entries in the court books.

The ecclesiastical authorities were surely right to intervene in order to uphold standards in the parishes, but inevitably churchwardens would have felt harassed by the summonses, embarrassed by the criticisms, worried by the expense and would, no doubt, have seen it as irritating interference by the ecclesiastical authorities.

Treatment of guilty clergy

In the three Michaelmas terms of the late 1610s and early 1620s, 14 clergymen (rectors, vicars or curates) were pronounced guilty of 19 transgressions in the consistory court at Winchester; four clergy of eight offences at Worcester; and four clergy of four offences at Wells. In the corresponding three terms apiece in the 1670s and 1680s, one clergyman was pronounced guilty of one offence at Winchester; four were declared guilty of four offences at Worcester; and none at all were found guilty at Wells. The presence of 'serial' offenders is the reason that the number of offences is larger than the number of individual clergymen. Several were found guilty of two or three offences, while Balamy, curate of St Lawrence, Evesham, ran up a list of five – neglect of services, failure to wear the surplice, condoning sitting for communion, pluralism and oversight concerning 'perambulation' – at Worcester in 1615.

The treatment of guilty clergy can be summarised briefly. The clergy of Worcester and Winchester were guilty mainly of neglect – of the chancel, of the services and, to a much lesser extent, of preaching licences and surplices – and for these the court's usual response was to issue an order or a warning, whether in the earlier or later period. A graver charge of non-conformity was possibly laid against Timothy Goodaker, curate of Timsbury, at Winchester in 1680, for which he too received an order to comply.[69]

Dismissals (closing the case at the court or in the bishop's palace) are none too satisfactory. They do not mean that the clergy in question had never committed the offence and had been cleared of charges. The minister of Tangley was summoned to the court at Winchester in 1619 'for not sayeing service in due time' and promised to reform his ways; nothing was said about a warning or an order (though one or the other was most likely) and the book merely records his dismissal (from the court).[70] At about the same time four incumbents from Wells had apparently failed to take the oath of rural dean, whether through oversight or reluctance to assume the office. There are no details of what actually happened in court – no statement about the issue of an order, for example – just 'dimiss', with the implication that that they had failed to take the oath up till that point and that it had then been administered before their 'dismissal'; but it is possible that, in court, they confirmed that they had already taken the oath and that was why they were dismissed.[71] In the one case post-1660, at Worcester, Philip Rocke, curate of Offenham, confessed to neglect, resigned on the spot and was then presumably dismissed from the bishop's presence.[72]

The sternest action for clerical transgression in the relevant court books, however, was suspension. This was the fate of Thomas Fuller, curate of Upton Grey (Winchester), in 1623 for surplice and drinking problems, and of two curates, William Whittall of Rowley at Worcester in 1613 and Thomas Charlock of Newport, Isle of Wight, again at Winchester in 1623, for conducting clandestine marriages.[73] It was also the fate of Henry Bennett, rector of Aisholt (Wells), in 1640.[74] He seems to have been the only rector among all the clergy of these samples to have received a penance order but his misdemeanour is not specified and, because he did not comply, he suffered suspension. It should be said that suspension, unlike defrocking, was not strictly a punishment which closed the matter but more a temporary step before final resolution of the case; but there the record usually falls silent and when such matters were resolved, if ever, appears impossible to determine.

The problem of penance

Warnings were warnings, orders were orders and little more can be said about either, but penance took many different forms. Penitents had, essentially, to acknowledge their fault in public and suffer, as a consequence, humiliating treatment. The 'choreography of penance' in the Middle Ages involved processions of the penitent and officials (clergy, churchwardens and apparitors), a wand, a white sheet, and beatings or whippings, on one or several occasions, in church, the marketplace or both.[75] Whipping and the marketplace had largely disappeared by the sixteenth century and, though there was a temporary revival from the 1560s to the 1580s, such severe features then fell back into disuse and ordinary clothes and semi-private sessions with clergy and churchwardens were allowed.[76] Winchester followed this trend in the main but there was a particularly egregious case in 1568 and something similar in 1623. In 1568 Robert Ayling was sentenced to suffer four separate days in the market for impregnating his servant.[77] In 1623 Richard Symes, charged with 'companie keeping with Elizabeth the wife of William Barling', confessed that 'he had interest and had consent to have had the carnal knowledge of the body of the said Elizabeth' but '(God be thanked) he was prevented from his purpose'. The judge still pronounced penance: that Symes was 'to stand upon the High Cross of Winchester on Saterday next for the space of two houres and two Sundayes in his owne parish church of Sparsholt'. Symes sought commutation at this point and reached a settlement with the judge.[78]

The initial severity of that sentence may have been a deliberate ploy – a savage penance to force a wealthy man to commutation – and was far from typical, to judge from the seventeenth-century court books used in this study.[79] The judge at Winchester was routinely ordering penance 'according to the schedule' in the sessions of Michaelmas term 1623 – the case of the Holbrookes, husband and wife, is an example – and his counterpart at Worcester chose 'according to the form' for the sentencing in 1615 of Richard Bane.[80] Such standard but opaque wording reveals little about the specifics of the procedure but the main features emerge from a study of other parts of the relevant court books.

The number of Sundays on which penance was to be performed ranged from one for Mary Orchard of Longstock, to two for Joanna Batt of Amport and to three for Henry White of Ringwood. These were all issued by the judge at Winchester during Michaelmas term 1623.[81] The size of the 'audience' differed considerably as well and there were 'degrees of publicity'. Quite often penitents were allowed to appear before the minister and churchwardens, as with a group of four men (Gillam, Hayes, Russell and Thornton) from Kings Somborne (Winchester), again in 1623.[82] Francis Bowden, Joanna Ward and Welch Tucker were ordered by the court at Wells in 1618 to appear one Sunday after evening prayer in the chancel of their church before the minister and churchwardens, together with inquisitors (number not specified), six parishioners and 12 parishioners respectively.[83] Yet others, such as Matthew Mallard of Petersfield (Winchester 1623), were required to perform in front of the whole congregation.[84] Penance for all these people was in church but could still take place in the open market. This was the fate, for example, of at least two men at Worcester: in 1613 Richard White was required to perform penance three times over – at Daylesford parish church, at Blockley church and at Pershore market; and in 1614 John Marten had to suffer likewise at Shrawley (twice) and Little Witley (Withy Parva) parish churches and in the marketplace at Worcester.[85]

Clothing and *accoutrements* were specified only occasionally. Penitents commonly had to wear a white sheet and carry a wand or stick of some kind. This was so for Mary Orchard of Longstock (Winchester) in 1623 and Francis Jellett of Curry Rivel (Wells) in 1618, to name two. Apparel is sometimes less clear as in the case of Joanna Ward of Withypool (Wells) in 1618. She was required to wear customary vestments (*'vestibus consuet(i)s'*) but there is no possessive adjective in this entry and it is not clear whether she was being allowed to wear her own clothes or required to don the usual penance apparel. The use of *'vestibus suis consuet(i)s'* in the cases of William Stoddey of Stogursey in 1618 and Arthur Mondai of Chard in 1624 (both in the Archdeaconry of Taunton) strongly implies that they could wear their own clothes.[86]

Procedures which involved public confession and 'distinctive' clothing were designed to ensure improvement to behaviour, no doubt, but were also designed to humiliate sinners, the more so if they had to suffer on a succession of occasions and if in the marketplace as well as in church. Several cases, hardly surprisingly, can be found in the court books of people seeking adjustments to their sentence. Gilbert Brickleton, accused of abusing the minister in church, was sentenced at Winchester in 1623 to acknowledging his fault before the full congregation during morning service at All Saints Southampton, but at his petition the sentence was reduced to acknowledgement before minister and churchwardens only.[87] No money is mentioned in Brickleton's case, but richer people often sought commutation. The case of Richard Symes, mentioned earlier, provides a good example from the same time and in the same court. The judge had ordered him to stand at the cross at Winchester for two hours one Saturday and likewise on two Sundays in his parish church. The apparently desperate Symes offered £5 to yield a yearly sum for the poor of Sparsholt, £2 and 10 shillings for immediate distribution by the vicar and churchwardens to the poor of the parish and £5 for repair of the nave and chancel of the church at Sparsholt. The judge accepted the payment but insisted on some form of penance, which he reduced to acknowledgement according to the custom, 'penitentially', before the minister and churchwardens any Sunday before the feast of All Saints. It is not clear whether or not Symes had complied by the end of term.[88]

Penances continued after the Restoration but inevitably, in view of the relentless downward trend shown throughout this study, there were fewer of them. Proceedings in all three archdeaconries show the persistence, nonetheless, of some of the former features of penance well into the 1680s. Anne Taylor's is an example of an 'uninformative' instruction, issued at Worcester in 1682, 'according to the schedule', while the entry concerning the Beauchampes, who were ordered to acknowledge their fault in the traditional way, before the minister and churchwardens of Kidderminster (Worcester), in the church, one Sunday, 'in vestis solitis' (in the usual clothes), lacks, again, a possessive adjective. Two cases at Wells, Joanna Cox's of 1663 and John Bagg's of 1671, mention linen, wand and two Sundays; and the proceedings against George Wither at Winchester in 1663 again raise the issues of embarrassment and commutation when he sought, as had Symes 40 years earlier, to avoid 'a great scandall' by reaching a deal with the judge by which he paid £5 'for good and charitable uses' – repair of the cathedral, in fact.[89]

Whether or how far orders of penance were carried out is yet another matter. Penance was entered in the court book and there was usually an instruction to certify performance. Consistory court clerks' notes, whether before or after the upheavals of the 1640s and 1650s, do not seem to have been systematic enough for tabulation in this regard except at Wells in the Michaelmas terms of the late 1610s and early 1620s. There the court appears to have made a greater issue out of the pursuit of people failing to

CHURCH COURTS AND THE PEOPLE IN SEVENTEENTH-CENTURY ENGLAND

perform penance. Offenders are listed for the respective Michaelmas terms: 39 in 1618, 55 in 1621 and 42 in 1624. Such high numbers would suggest, at the very least, considerable dereliction.[90]

The final issue arising from this discussion of penance is the extent to which its enforcement was a factor encouraging hostility to the consistory courts. Penance was guaranteed to generate hostility from one group – the victims – in the communities. It was undoubtedly degrading for the sinners themselves when they had to wear penance clothing, more so when they had to appear before the whole congregation and even more so if they had to expose themselves to the anger and contempt of the public in the marketplace.[91] Small wonder that they failed to perform it or tried to commute it.

The real question for this study is the attitude of the public at large to penance and therefore to consistory discipline. Penance cannot be said to have been particularly harsh or barbaric by seventeenth-century standards. Assignment to the marketplace remained occasionally, but whipping seems to have gone and ordinary clothes and private sessions were allowed from time to time. Furthermore, the church courts possessed none of the fearsome punishments – fines, stocks, prison and the death penalty – available to the secular courts.

The evidence about public attitudes to penance, such as it is, seems to point to support for the practice. Many people at the time appear to have thought the courts, whether secular or ecclesiastical, were too weak. Resort, outside the church courts, to particularly degrading treatment of moral offenders provides a vivid signal of discontent with ecclesiastical justice and the feeling that the usual punishment – penance – for bastardy and adultery was not severe enough. Penance, however humiliating, was seen as lacking severity and commutation as a soft option and an easy escape for the offender. In the fifteenth, sixteenth and early seventeenth centuries, city and borough courts, Star Chamber and Parliament ordered parades of prostitutes and riding backwards on a horse, tail in hand, for a range of offenders. At the same time the skimmington or charivari developed: apparently spontaneous explosions of public contempt in which the sinner or an effigy was pursued by the local people, mocking, smearing and pelting her, him or it, to the accompaniment of a cacophony of pots and pans.[92] Two incidents, which have the appearance of skimmingtons, seem to have occurred in different parts of the Diocese of Worcester within a year of each other and are the only such cases in the court books used for this survey. In December 1615 Lancelot Mathewes of Studley was summoned 'for disguising himself … in woeman's apparell and doing other disorders to the great discontent of the parishioners whipping one that rode on a colestaffe' (cowlstaff?). In October 1616 John Bissell of Rowley Regis was charged with 'disguiseing him selfe in womans' [sic] apparell and cominge ... into the Church to the great offence of the Congregation assembled'. Neither appeared in court in person during the Michaelmas term in question: Mathewes was dismissed in January 1616 'donec', presumably a kind of stay of execution during good behaviour; and Bissell, having failed to appear three times, suffered excommunication in November 1616.[93]

Skimmingtons indicate the popularity of public shaming, at least among certain members of the public, but in some numbers, and, by implication, support for penance insofar as it achieved the same object. There would always be feelings of disgust and outrage among the public towards offenders, however synthetic and hypocritical, however driven by fears for the poor rate, coupled with glee and embroidered by schadenfreude at the discomfiture of others. These people were not against shaming; they approved of it and felt it did not go far enough.

The prosecutions also imply that church authorities, while condemning immorality – the most frequent occasion for skimmingtons – opposed activity of that kind. Their immediate concern would have been disruption of worship in church during a Sunday service but their wider concern was likely to have been the risk to public order. Social order, particularly after the upheavals of the Protectorate and the insecurities of the Restoration, was probably the most powerful consideration causing both secular and church authorities to discourage 'charivari-esque' behaviour.[94] Skimmingtons meant disorder and could be hijacked by troublemakers or turn of their own accord into riots, entailing threats to life and property.

Skimmington prosecutions disappeared, at least from the consistory courts of Winchester, Worcester and Wells, in the later seventeenth century and ecclesiastical penance declined, certainly in volume and possibly in nature, by the 1670s and 1680s. These developments may simply reflect the shrivelling of church court activity in the course of the century, but it is possible that 'social values' were changing and, as barbaric treatment of offenders became less and less acceptable, there may have been 'a long term trend towards more lenient penances'.[95] The trends, insofar as they can be gauged, may therefore have been moving against penance, skimmingtons and, indeed, the stocks. These trends are difficult to identify and need further research beyond the scope of this study. Certainly the world had been turned upside down in the 1640s and 1650s and, though much was restored at the Restoration, the time of revolution had opened a Pandora's box – with lasting consequences.[96] This may have meant greater concerns about law and order in the years of the Restoration but, in the longer term, it also led to the spread of new attitudes to social issues and to religious conformity, fired, no doubt, by a disgust with puritanical intrusiveness in both respects. The harshest forms of punishment may have been becoming less and less acceptable and a minority may even have begun to take to heart the Christian message that penance was a humiliation where there should have been forgiveness.

Class and occupation

Information about social class, for whichever diocese and whether before or after the Civil Wars and Interregnum, can only be described as scant. Eighteen people were identified by class – 14 members of the gentry, three esquires (or armigers) and one knight – among the accused summoned to the consistory court at Winchester during the three Michaelmas terms of 1619, 1621 and 1623 – that is, 18 out of more than a thousand who were summoned altogether. The numbers are even smaller for the other two courts at that time or thereabouts: at Wells seven gentry, at Worcester five from the knight or gentry classes, when total numbers summoned approached 800 for the former court and 900 for the latter.

A handful of knights, gentry and armiger – 13 altogether – were summoned from Taunton to the consistory court at Wells in the 1630s. After the Restoration, the names of 13 of the armiger or gentry classes appear in the lists of the court at Winchester during Michaelmas term 1663, but that was among record total numbers of more than 680 people summoned altogether. Among much lower total numbers (86 at Worcester and 47 at Wells) there was one member of the gentry class apiece in the early years of the Restoration.

Scrappier note taking in the court books and scantier detail and information about such matters as class could only grow worse with the system in decay. No one of any class or rank appears to have been summoned to the consistory court of Wells in the three Michaelmas terms of the 1670s and 1680s. The two people of 'standing', both churchwardens, one an armiger, the other from the gentry class,[97] brought before the court at Worcester in 1675 were quite exceptional among all the samples from the records of the 1670s and 1680s, while in the corresponding terms at Winchester, Lord and Lady Tichborne stand out as the only people whose class is identified among the total of 105 accused during the three relevant terms; indeed, they are the only members of the peerage found in all the years and terms examined, whether before or after the Interregnum, in the three archdeaconries.

The social status of the remainder is not identified in any of these years in any of the three archdeaconries. There are sometimes notes of occupations, however, and although there are not many of these either, working on the Sabbath or without a licence in the case of the professions were considered important transgressions, and a little more can be deduced about status from the lists of charges. Prosecutions among the professions seem to have been rare in all three archdeaconries. Three schoolmasters were summoned to Winchester in Michaelmas term 1619, two to Worcester in 1615 and one to Wells in 1624, while in the corresponding terms in the 1670s and 1680s, only one schoolmaster was charged at Wells and another at Worcester. Nine midwives and surgeons faced prosecution at Worcester in the 1610s but none from the medical professions has been found in any of the samples of the 1670s and early 1680s.

The remainder about whom anything can be said with certainty, at least according to surviving records, all came from 'serving' occupations and hence the lower orders of seventeenth-century society. Agriculture and an array of trades formed the largest groups identified in, or surmised from, the court books, but these are still minute as proportions of all accused people before the Wars and Interregnum. Barbers, bakers, blacksmiths, brewers, butchers, carpenters, carters, clothiers, cobblers, fishmongers, joiners, millers, saddlers, tailors and weavers are tradesmen who can all be found in the court books, albeit in relatively small numbers among the totals summoned, and, perhaps more unusually, a clock repairer and a pewterer. Numbers of tradesmen summoned before the Interregnum were larger at Winchester and Worcester than at Wells, where agriculture was still dominant, and tradesmen numbering 35 and 113 respectively can be identified in the court books of the two archdeaconries. Numbers of tradesmen among the accused fell dramatically to three at Winchester, two at Worcester and none at Wells in the early 1660s. With the exception of one tradesman at Worcester in 1682, none – or, at least, none recorded – appears at all in any of the samples from the three archdeaconries in the 1670s and 1680s.

Agriculture – mainly labourers but with a possible sprinkling of owners – was the other 'large' occupation before the Wars and Interregnum. Only seven were so identified at Winchester but 31 at Wells and no fewer than 54 at Worcester. Fourteen were summoned from Taunton to the court at Wells in the three relevant years of the 1630s but this shrank to three at Worcester in 1661 and none from any of the three archdeaconries in any of the sample years of the 1670s and 1680s.

A few servants can be found among the records of consistory proceedings. Quite exceptionally, ten were required to appear before the court at Winchester in 1681. They all came from one household and were either servants or tenants of the Catholic Lord and Lady Tichborne.

It follows that most of the accused were drawn from among the lower, humbler members of the communities. The clerks entered nothing about class or occupation in most cases. Their careless clerking may explain their omission of class. Clerks may have failed to add, for example, 'armiger' or 'gent' systematically in the court books and many more of the accused could have possessed titles or enjoyed a higher social status than the court books appear to suggest. Omission of title and status is not likely, however, in an age of deference, nor is the absence of sin among the middle and upper circles of society very likely either. 'Likelihood' must serve as the guiding factor here and it looks as if few from the upper classes were summoned to the church courts. As for missing occupations, the clerks had no reason to include them except occasionally to distinguish two people with the same name, as happened with the two Peter Bayleys, both from Alton but one a clothier, the other a carpenter, who were summoned at the same time to the court at Winchester.[98] The offence, not the class of the perpetrator, was the point and, even in cases of 'Sunday trading', the occupation is not always 'labelled' and has to be inferred from the charge. The likelihood is, therefore, that the overwhelming majority of people summoned to the consistory courts were 'ordinary' working people and their relations and dependants, while the court books occasionally acknowledge the poverty of others.[99]

There is nothing new in this account of imbalance: it was true also of earlier times and other dioceses. Christopher Hill and Martin Ingram allude to class imbalance and, more particularly, Ronald Marchant identifies it in sixteenth- and seventeenth-century York and Norwich; Ralph Houlbrooke in sixteenth-century Winchester; Margaret Stieg in early seventeenth-century Wells; and Marjorie McIntosh, Keith Wrightson and David Levine do so in their studies of sixteenth- and seventeenth-century communities in Essex. It was also apparently the case at Oxford, Peterborough, London and elsewhere before and after the Interregnum.[100] Only Margaret Potter claims that prosecutions of the good and the great can be found 'in every year' at Canterbury.[101] The comment of the Archdeacon of Salisbury in 1639 – that he 'never knew any rich men cited to this court though they ... commit ... offences'[102] – would seem to encapsulate strikingly the majority view: that there was class 'imbalance' and that the behaviour of lords and gentry went largely unpoliced and unpunished. It would seem that most of the upper classes escaped legal censure or, at least, escaped public legal censure, while the Church trained its firepower on the lower – and weaker – orders of society.

It remains highly probable, then, that within the upper classes many sinned but few were summoned to court. It is likely that churchwardens were at least in part responsible for this. Churchwardens are likely to have been cautious about naming 'equals' and neighbours in their presentments, especially if some of the latter were contemplating taking the office of churchwarden the following year. Churchwardens may have been even more overawed by the prospect of challenging men of rank and status who gave them custom, work and wages.[103] Churchwardens also may have relied on the upper classes to police themselves or, rather, their drinking and gaming sons and their errant daughters, or at least to pay the costs of consequences such as dowries and illegitimate children. Such outcomes would have left them free to concentrate on the lower orders and poorer people.[104]

Circumspection may also have been the rule for bishops. Bishops' freedom to appoint to clergy livings was heavily circumscribed, being confined to 15 per cent at Winchester where at least 50 per cent of parochial appointments were in the hands of private patrons. Matters were even more constrained at Worcester (8 per cent) and Wells (10 per cent) and private patrons were likely, in consequence, to have been at least as prominent as at Winchester.[105] Bishops could have made a stand against gentry, merchants and even peers but conflict, if they could avoid it, was probably not their first choice, especially as these were the very groups which so often held the keys to parochial patronage.

It is also possible to find ecclesiastical blessing in the late seventeenth and early eighteenth centuries for the disparity on the grounds that punishment of the poor would shame the rich and deter them from sin. Faramerz Dabhoiwala quotes a clergyman in 1697 and a bishop, no less, in 1731, who both expressed such a view quite openly, whether out of naivete or more deliberate dishonesty.[106] The poor had to suffer, apparently, while the rich man was left in his castle to wrestle privately with his conscience. This may seem thoroughly discreditable and reprehensible but there was an ever present concern for security among clergy and laymen alike in the century of plots, revolts and, of course, the Civil Wars themselves. Proceedings against and punishments of nobles and gentry would risk discrediting or antagonising upholders of the social order while at the same time emboldening the lower orders and weakening respect for authority. Security as much as fear or snobbery informed these attitudes.[107]

Such convolutions lead, inevitably, to a more sinister implication: corruption or, at least, 'interested' interference in prosecutions. Ronald

Marchant gives more than one example of influential personages putting pressure on the courts in favour of their clients.[108] While such activity has been difficult to detect and expose in the courts of Winchester, Worcester and Wells, by its very nature, no doubt, the case of Mr ('*m(agist)r(um)*'?) Thomas Baldwyn, in the dock at Worcester in 1682 'for speaking att Conventicles', has a suspicious appearance. The only proceeding or action is the instruction '*Stet p(er) mandatu(m) Dom(ini) Cancellarii*' (stop, or stopped, on the orders of the Lord Chancellor), who was none other than (Chancellor) Timothy Baldwyn.[109]

So far from a 'non-result', then, the missing occupations and, even more, the missing titles speak loudly about the types of persons summoned, or not summoned, as the case may be; about the likely attitudes and policies of the church authorities; and about wholesale avoidance of prosecutions against the 'mighty' and occasional corruption in the operation of the seventeenth-century consistory courts of Winchester, Worcester, Wells and elsewhere.

It was not all bad news, however, and the ecclesiastical judicial authorities did occasionally turn the searchlight on themselves. Parish clergy, the rectors, vicars and curates, the men who took the Church to the people, were summoned to court but in relatively small numbers. Twenty-three summoned to the court at Winchester in 1619 represented the highest number in any of the Michaelmas terms in this survey, after which numbers steadily fell in all three dioceses, most noticeably at Wells where a fairly even downward trajectory can be traced through the 1630s to the 1660s and 1670s. Total numbers of churchwardens charged with wrongdoing rose conversely at Wells – albeit from six to nine – for the three specimen terms between the 1610s and the 1670s but fell decisively – from 97 to 22 and from 93 to three – at Worcester and Winchester. The structure of parishes remained largely static in all three dioceses during the seventeenth century and therefore so too did the numbers of clergy and churchwardens in the dioceses; thus, changes in population, whether rising, as at Winchester and Wells, or falling, as at Worcester, cannot have had much bearing on numbers or proportions of accused clergy or churchwardens. Improvement in standards, accounting for the decline in prosecutions among these groups, is a possibility but not very likely. Laxer controls or a different focus – more on church attendance than the performance of churchwardens – are more likely. There is also the possibility of more private sessions in the bishop's palace to avoid publicity and discredit of the clerical profession, but by its discreet – secret – nature, the evidence is often veiled.[110]

Even rarer was citation of the 'hierarchy'. The case of the Dean and Chapter of Worcester, accused of chancel neglect in the 1610s, is the sole example, within the confines of this study, of any of the more exalted dignitaries of the Church facing the legal music and, interestingly, the record of proceedings in that case is blank.[111] It is somewhat surprising, nonetheless, that the case was brought at all. Almost as rare were prosecutions of church court officials, but these did occur. Chancellors were not immune from corruption and, again, their exposure is to the credit of the church authorities. There are apparently some spectacular examples at Norwich, Gloucester and York, but the suspicious behaviour of Baldwyn apart, nothing on this scale has come to light at Winchester, Worcester or Wells.[112] A few rungs down, Nicholas Bennett, Notary Public and Registrar of the Archdeacon of Taunton, was hauled before the episcopal consistory court at Wells in November 1633 for failing to supply a return of the names of the new rural deans; the case was brought to an abrupt and opaque end with the word 'stet' (stop).[113]

The Church did sometimes appear to accept shame and embarrassment by putting its own officials – clergymen, churchwardens, a Dean and Chapter and even a notary public – on trial; but very few of the upper classes – handfuls of gentry and one peer and his wife – from the three archdeaconries of the Southern Province were summoned to court in the relevant Michaelmas terms from the 1610s to the 1680s. The sights of church court artillery were trained otherwise and overwhelmingly on the poorer and weaker members of society. The parable of the Good Samaritan, the singing of the Magnificat and the chanting of the Litany turned on sacrifice, concern for other people and the triumph of the underdog. Unless these words – sixteenth- and seventeenth-century words found, for example, in the Book of Common Prayer and the Authorised Version of the Bible – are meaningless, there was a striking disjunction between the Christian message and church practice, which must have been obvious to the people of the time. This is likely to have done immense harm to the Church and may help to explain resentment and resistance to its disciplinary machinery. Why should they suffer the expense of judicial proceedings and the humiliation of its punishments, some must have wondered, while others, equal or greater sinners, escaped censure? An explosion of sects and ideas, social, religious and political, had free rein for a decade and more in the middle of the century, and one of the first victims of the parliamentary revolution of 1640–1 was the regime of consistory courts. These courts were revived with the Restoration of 1660, the sects were crushed and their extreme programmes were savagely dashed, but there may well have remained an underground legacy of discontent and resentment. Such a condition certainly would not have helped and may well have contributed to the continuing decline of the ecclesiastical judicial system in the second half of the seventeenth century.

Fees and corruption

Fees were, inevitably, a source of complaint.[114] These were usually reckoned in shillings in whichever of the three dioceses and bore heavily on the poor – the most likely victims of church discipline – when a typical wage was likely to have been no more than a shilling a day.[115] Money led to corruption, another inevitability, and where corruption flourished, it was particularly damaging to the authority of the church courts. Houlbrooke and Ingram both mention, with the same phrase, 'much petty corruption', though Marchant is less insistent and Brinkworth dismisses its existence.[116]

The system of proxies, whereby apparitors stood in for the accused at court, offered scope for corruption. The role of apparitor was as messenger: to deliver writs and excommunications in the parishes and to return certificates of compliance to court. The most spectacular appearance was at Winchester, where Francis Robinson struck a deal with the judge on behalf of Lord Tichborne, involving a bond as surety for attending church and receiving communion, in January 1683. Representation of the accused by apparitor occurred at Worcester in October 1616 and at least six similar arrangements took place at Wells during Michaelmas term 1624.[117] Both 'crime' and punishment are not always made clear nor even the status of the intermediary. He is identified as apparitor in one or two cases but often with just a name and no status, and Francis Robinson is labelled 'servant'. These transactions may have been entirely innocent but opportunities for corruption were there: for the accused to avoid shame and achieve a lighter sentence and for the apparitor or other official to take a bribe.

One or two chancellors certainly suffered spectacular falls from grace in the sixteenth and seventeenth centuries: in 1569 the chancellor of Norwich complained to the bishop about corruption of his underlings only to find himself caught up in such allegations; in 1578–9 Norwich's counterpart at Gloucester, whose reign was characterised by 'laxity' and 'corruption … on a remarkable scale', apparently died while on trial before High Commission; and in 1684 a 'bent' official principal at York committed 'the ultimate treason' of trading his office to others to allow 'farming', or exploitation, of its opportunities.[118] No examples of financial corruption by chancellors have come to light in the seventeenth-century court books, beyond the suspicious involvement of Timothy Baldwyn in the case of a possible relation, for the three archdeaconries of this study.

Wider reasons for decline by the 1670s

Seven problematic aspects of church court procedures and punishments emerge from an examination of surviving court books for the three archdeaconries, all of which played a part in the decline of ecclesiastical justice: excommunication, the *ex officio* oath, compurgation, penance, class, fees and corruption.

No case can be made for corruption but it is possible to put up a defence for each of the other procedures and features of ecclesiastical justice. The church courts had few enough powers, some sanctions were necessary and excommunication did sometimes lead to absolution and did bring people back into the fold. The *ex officio* oath was rarely invoked in the consistory courts and opposition to it came mainly from those who stood to gain. It would probably be too far a stretch to claim for compurgation and penance that they were expressions of community involvement in justice at its best, but compurgation was necessary in an age when there was little or no 'forensic' evidence. Penance enjoyed public support, some of it sincerely driven by moral outrage, and secular court punishments were just as bad (the stocks) or more severe (the death penalty). Complaints about costs were inevitable and church court fees were probably no heavier than fees in the secular courts. Even punishing the poor while leaving the rich to conscience could be seen as sensible in an age when peace was fragile. Law, order and discipline were essential, and the power and standing of the ruling classes had to be maintained, if only to keep potential troublemakers under control.

Nonetheless, excommunications which failed to reconcile church and sinner, compurgation which displaced juries and penance which imposed humiliation were becoming outmoded and outdated procedures by the end of the seventeenth century. If they did not destroy the church courts, they certainly weakened them. Church discipline was really undermined, however, by a number of 'external' factors: political upheavals driven ultimately by social, religious and political forces. The nation suffered over 150 years, from the 1530s to the 1680s and 1690s, a series of events of 'cyclonic' proportions: the Reformation of the 1530s, the English Civil Wars of the 1640s, the Protectorate of the 1650s, the Restoration of 1660 and the Revolution of 1688–9. These were primarily political and religious upheavals provoking questions of power and conscience. At the same time there arose issues of physical survival: recurring harvest failures triggering issues of poverty and suffering and provoking class conflict and civil unrest. Religious divisions meant crises of conscience; economic collapse meant poverty and starvation; both meant conflict and revolt.

The primary concern of the authorities – from the king to the landed gentry and the merchants – was security and, essentially, law and order. The clergy and pulpit were fine for preaching and propaganda, but the church courts lacked the powers to ensure meaningful enforcement of discipline. Excommunication and penance were not 'fit for purpose'. Secular, rather than 'spiritual', instruments had more bite and became the preferred weapons of control. Statutes laid down the law on such matters as religious observance and vagrancy and empowered the secular courts to impose fines, imprisonment and the death penalty on offenders. Retreat and decline of the consistory courts inevitably followed.

The stream of parliamentary legislation makes the point. Statutes of 1559, 1581, 1587 and 1593, for example, gave powers over church attendance to the secular courts. Statutes of 1576, 1598, 1601 and 1610 allowed secular courts, likewise, to deal with vagrancy and bastardy and, most pointedly, the Act of 1610 specifically obliged magistrates to commit single mothers to Bridewell.[119] Parliament, moreover, apparently considered 35 poor law bills altogether between the statutes of 1576 and 1610, nine of them on bastardy, which would have given more powers over morals to magistrates.[120] None of the statutes denied the remit of the church courts and in fact a clause in the Act of 1581 specifically sought to safeguard the role of the church courts in the prosecution of absentees. The stress, however, in all these Acts, whether about recusancy or the poor law, lay on enforcement by assizes, quarter sessions and magistrates (*mutatis mutandis*), and clearly the secular courts were becoming the main engines of control in religious and social matters.

Secular courts of boroughs and counties began, thus, to intrude more and more from the sixteenth century on the traditional work of the church courts. Somerset magistrates were occupied in enforcement of a multiplicity of laws and regulations from that time.[121] Magistrates from a number of counties ordered whipping or the workhouse for more than 200 women, Somerset and Warwickshire among them, for bastardy between 1590 and 1610.[122] The magistrates of Warwick (which was within the Diocese of Worcester) went so far as to appoint an official to prevent outsiders – vagrants and doubtless including bastard bearers – settling in the town in the 1620s.[123] The Worcester quarter sessions of the 1610s were fully occupied with prosecutions for immorality, recusancy, consumption of meat during Lent, sport and play on the Sabbath – all staple business of the consistory courts.[124]

This activity may appear rather piecemeal, but surviving recusancy rolls present a picture of consistent encroachment by the secular legal system on the jurisdiction of the church courts. They show prosecutions – secular prosecutions – on a scale quite different from the church courts: a century and more of victims running into hundreds at a time and suffering fines and forfeitures of property for failure to attend church. The rolls are frequently deficient in critical information but references to the assizes, together with the Lord Chief Justice, Chief Justice at Common Pleas and Justices of King's Bench, leave no doubt that the secular courts were playing a substantial – and permanent – role in religious prosecutions.[125]

The political revolution of 1640–1 had profound consequences for both the clergy and the legal system of the established Church. The laws which governed religious observance and morals were revised and the church courts were diminished and reduced ultimately to zero. An Act of the Long Parliament abolished High Commission, the chief religious court of the Church in Elizabethan, Jacobean and Caroline times, and, further, by removing the power of bishops to impose oaths and order punishment, the Act considerably weakened the (episcopal) consistory courts as well.[126] An ordinance of 1646 next abolished the office of bishop itself and with the bishops went their courts.[127] After the removal of the consistory courts, all ecclesiastical jurisdiction – its *ex officio* (disciplinary) and instance (or private dispute) business – either disappeared or was moved instead to the secular courts. Wills, raising concerns about property and inheritance, were a different matter. People continued to die, property and possessions had to be dispersed and some machinery for their disposal was necessary. It would seem that during the Wars, when even the quarter sessions at Winchester ceased to operate for a time, consistory courts, run by the same officials, chancellors and surrogates, continued to deal, as in the past, with the smaller estates, proving wills, administrations and inventories. This was apparently so at Oxford, London, Worcester, Peterborough, York and Winchester.[128] The Prerogative Court of Canterbury, the ecclesiastical body which had traditionally dealt with larger estates worth more than £5 and straddling more than one diocese, still sat in London, meanwhile, under its presiding officers, Nathaniel Brent and his deputies, until 1653. The Rump at last made secular provision, at that point, in an 'Act for Probate of Wills', with five separate renewals of the 'tribunal', between 1653 and 1659, and all probates and administrations appear to have been settled there for the remainder of the Cromwellian regime.[129]

The 'Act Touching Marriage and the Registering thereof', passed by the same parliament in the same year (1653), was also in effect an assault on the province of the church courts.[130] These had enjoyed a monopoly of matrimonial cases before the 1640s: clandestine marriage (most often when no banns had been called or no licence sought) would give rise, before the 1640s, to a prosecution in the *ex officio* division of the court, while breach of promise, though still about marriage, was more complex and would be referred to instance proceedings. By the Act of 1653 marriages became civil matters and lawyers such as John Selden were quick to justify the new arrangement: if magistrates were entitled to marry people, magistrates should also settle legal issues arising from a marriage. Edward Hyde and Matthew Hale were two lawyers who began to suggest at this time that ecclesiastical justice should be confined to disciplining the clergy only and not laymen and women.[131]

Ecclesiastical justice was, in any case, now dead, but this did not mean the end of attempts to order society. All business which would have been *ex officio*, whether bastardy, fornication or failing to attend church, for example, and all instance cases (such as tithes and defamation) were now left respectively to the criminal and civil divisions of the secular courts, with help, no doubt, from local parish clergy, however informal, and from the major generals, however brutal, for a short time in the mid-1650s.[132] Central concerns of the authorities continued to be moral issues of vagrancy and bastardy, together with religion and the spread of extremist sects. The two Acts of 1650, discussed earlier, were reflections of these issues and emphasised the central concerns of the authorities.[133] The 'Act for the Relief of the Religious' required regular church attendance though without penalties; more severely, the Act 'for suppressing the Detestable Sins of Incest, Adultery and Fornication' prescribed prison for fornication and the death penalty for adultery and incest. Both the Instrument of Government (1653) and the Humble Petition (1657) contained, moreover, sections which condemned 'popery' and 'prelacy' and 'the licentious'. The caseload of the secular courts was, thus, increased and business which had been the monopoly of the church courts was now being settled by magistrates at borough or county levels in the quarter sessions and by judges at the assizes in the 1650s.[134]

The monarch returned in 1660 but with an inheritance from the republican years of the 1650s – a double legacy in fact. The first, in Cressy's inimitable words, was a 'cultural matrix ... aflame with enormities and enmities ... the population had lost the habit of church attendance, had abandoned the regime of episcopal discipline, or fallen prey to apathy and cynicism'.[135] Hill, Cressy and Brooks all claim that abolition of the church courts had been liberating in the 1640s and 1650s and it was therefore much harder to restore respect for church discipline in the 1660s.[136] 'Liberating' is at least questionable: it would depend on how thoroughly the legislation of 1650 was enforced and it is likely that many clandestine Catholics, disruptive sectaries, wandering vagrants and miserable bastard bearers had found themselves in a worse predicament in the 1650s; likely, again, that they would be deadly opposed to a return to the conditions which then prevailed and, indeed, opposed to any disciplinary machinery – church or state – in the 1660s.

The first legacy of the 1650s, then, was hostility of many radical groups to any attempt to regulate religious or social behaviour. For the men of power and property there was a quite different legacy. Their 'obsession' was security,[137] and rebellions and conspiracies from Venner to the Popish and Rye House plots gave them justification. Their answer was expansion of the secular legal arm of justice. The 1650s had shown that, even in revolutionary times, the authorities could manage just as well, if not better, with secular courts alone. It would seem that the politicians of the 1660s saw the advantages and continued on the same course. Magistrates, key to enforcement in the 1650s, thus retained their expanding role in the 1660s.[138] The Act of Settlement of 1662 increased the powers of magistrates to deal with vagrants (including women with bastard children) and return them to their original parish.[139] This was a continuation of poor law history which can be traced through the Commonwealth and Protectorate to the reigns of Elizabeth I and James I. Religious law was now focused on uniformity, preservation of the Anglican monopoly and suppression of Catholic recusants and Protestant dissenters. Two statutes of the Clarendon Code in particular, the Five Mile Act (1665) and the Conventicle Act (1670), targeted itinerant ministers and dissenters' meeting houses and specifically gave magistrates powers to fine and arrest offenders.[140]

Members of the Cavalier Parliament revived the church courts in the 1660s,[141] and nothing was meant deliberately to detract from their authority. They were, nonetheless, weaker bodies. They had been undermined by the alternative probate and marriage developments and the enhancement of the role of magistrates in the vital matters of vagrancy and religious dissent during the Commonwealth and Protectorate. They were now, in 1660, more critically, shorn of the *ex officio* oath and (officially at least) compurgations. They simply lacked the means of effective enforcement. The tools for the job – powers to move vagrants from parish to parish, for example, or to arrest dissenters – lay not in the gift of consistory courts but in the hands of magistrates. Though armed with penance and excommunication and not exactly powerless, the church courts could not imprison or even fine anyone and were in effect marginalised.

Theirs became a secondary role in the regulation of society. At county and diocesan levels the magistrates of Somerset continued to be found in a wide range of prosecutions.[142] Their counterparts at Worcester can be found bailing out Quakers and Anabaptists in 1661, binding over Fifth Monarchy Men in 1667 and being kept busy tackling vagrancy throughout the reign of Charles II, while prosecutions of religious offenders were proceeding at the same time in the quarter sessions at Warwick.[143] There were, meanwhile, parallel developments in Hampshire's secular courts (Winchester Diocese) in the 1670s and 1680s. Wilfred Mildon has plundered the quarter session records of Newport (Isle of Wight), Portsmouth, Andover and Southampton to reveal the vigorous pursuit of Protestant dissenters in the 1670s and 1680s – the magistrates of Andover apparently excelled at fines against preachers, hearers, owners of meeting houses, churchwardens and even constables reluctant to bring charges – and Andrew Coleby's more balanced survey attests to the prosecution of Catholics as well as an array of Protestants – dissenting ministers and schoolmasters, Baptists, Quakers, Independents – before the assizes or quarter sessions of the county.[144] There can be no doubt that secular officials and their courts were consuming the lion's share of religious prosecutions. The activities of magistrates at borough and county levels, together with judges at the assizes, are proof enough of the dominant role of the secular courts in the drive for religious conformity.[145]

Most bishops, moreover, while not abandoning their own courts, helped, no doubt accidentally, to undermine them. There seems to be no evidence of personal involvement – presiding day to day over *ex officio* cases in the consistory court – by any of the bishops of the three dioceses in question during the 1610s or 1670s. It appears, from surviving consistory court books, that Bilson and Andrewes at Winchester, Parry and Thornborough at Worcester and Lake at Wells – the relevant bishops before the Wars – remained aloof from *ex officio* proceedings; in the 1670s, the same was true of Morley (Winchester), Blandford and Fleetwood (Worcester) and Creighton and Mews (Wells).[146] Peirs of Wells, who sat in several *ex officio* cases in the 1630s, is the honourable exception.[147] Yet bishops appear, at the same time, to have involved themselves in the secular magistracy. Babington and Thornborough, bishops of Worcester before the upheavals of the 1640s and 1650s, were magistrates, and Bilson may have served as a magistrate while at Winchester in the early years of the seventeenth century.[148] In one of his letters to Sheldon (archbishop), Morley (Winchester) mentions his discussions with the local magistrates of Surrey (part of the Diocese of Winchester), stressing their confusion about the state of the law concerning prosecutions of

'Sectaries' at the time of the Declaration of Indulgence (1672–3) and urging Sheldon to issue 'a Proclamation' or 'some such authoritative notice' to strengthen the resolve of magistrates in the 'Execution' of the statutes against 'the Sectaries'.[149] David Underdown, writing about the parish level in the seventeenth century, argues that the demarcation between secular constables on the one hand and churchwardens and clergy on the other was by no means hard and fast and both pursued religious and moral cases in their respective courts.[150] This is borne out by evidence from the Winchester Diocese. A vestry meeting at Clapham in January 1661, for example, ominously ordered both churchwardens and constables 'to take special care for prosecuting the Law against idle people that harbour in and about the Parish', and occasional notes in other parish records imply that churchwardens were enforcing the poor law, to the extent of whipping vagrants, in conjunction with secular constables before and after the Interregnum.[151]

How to interpret the relationship of church and secular courts towards the end of the seventeenth century remains far from certain. At best church and state saw themselves less as rivals and more as partners, albeit in varying degrees, in the drive for moral standards and religious uniformity. If so, in spite of the hostile campaign of Edward Coke and in spite of a century and more of encroaching laws, the ecclesiastical authorities do not appear to have foreseen the danger to their judicial system. The bishops were concerned about the enforcement of law and order, as they saw it, in society as much as the rest of the 'establishment' and sought to reduce friction and promote harmony between the spiritual and secular engines of justice – all commendable – but they were at the same time encouraging, unwittingly or otherwise, the transfer of business from church to state courts. They may well have viewed the secular takeover as a 'welcome supplement' to ecclesiastical discipline but, in truth, it was the church courts which had become an adjunct, welcome or otherwise, to the secular arm of justice.[152]

The truth was that the secular magistracy had overtaken the spiritual courts. The upheavals of the 1640s and 1650s had removed the church courts and strengthened the secular courts. To the politicians of the 1660s, the lesson of the 1650s was reliance on the secular courts, and the bishops seem to have concurred. The church courts, certainly of Winchester, Worcester and Wells, were not dead by the 1670s but, encumbered with the outdated procedure of compurgation and the increasingly unacceptable sanction of penance, they were the more easily bypassed by the secular courts. Left with a residue of cases – bastardy, fornication, adultery and incest or Sabbath breaking, recusancy and dissent – which the secular courts had not reached first, their relegation to secondary status was clear for all to see when the Glorious Revolution, with its decisive implications for ecclesiastical justice, overtook them.

Notes

1 See Appendix 4, Tables 1–3.
2 See the section '*Ex officio* procedures' in Chapter 1.
3 See Quaife, *Wanton Wenches*, preface (unnumbered); Marchant, *Church under Law*, p. 230; but also Potter, 'Canterbury', pp. 125–30.
4 Jones, 'Oxford and Peterborough', pp. 20, 63, 118.
5 Marchant, *Church under Law*, p. 227.
6 Only the first two – baptism and communion – are sacraments of the Church of England according to Article 25 of the 39 (see e.g. Bray, *Anglican Canons*).
7 Before the Interregnum: SHLS, D/D/ca/243, f. 23r (excessive abbreviation); D/D/ca/313, f. 197r (reference to the fee only); D/D/ca/295, f. 167v (the case progressed after excommunication so absolution presumed); WRO, 802 2760, ff. 120r, 120v (two more cases where proceedings continued although excommunication had occurred and no absolution was recorded).
8 After the Restoration: WRO, 794 011 2722 2, Book 32, ff. 216v, 222r (no reference to absolution but the case was resumed); f. 224r (reference to the fee only).
9 Jones, 'Oxford and Peterborough', p. 118.
10 See the section '*Ex officio* procedures' in Chapter 1.
11 WRO, 802 2760, f. 279v.
12 WRO, 794 011 2722 2, Book 32, ff. 217v, 230v, 241r, 256v; SHLS, D/D/ca/350, 24/10/1671, 30/10/1671 (no folios).
13 Aklundh, 'Church Courts', pp. 13, 123–5, 127, 177; others proclaiming the potency of excommunication are Davies, 'Religious Uniformity', Abstract 1, p. 1; and Mercer, 'Ecclesiastical Discipline', p. 357. Ingram stresses the redemptive intention of excommunication while acknowledging its ineffectiveness (Ingram, *Church Courts*, pp. 341–2).
14 Aklundh, 'Church Courts', pp. 16, 115, 178.
15 Houlbrooke, *Church Courts*, p. 49; Houlbrooke, 'Decline of Ecclesiastical Jurisdiction', p. 245; Jenkins, *Archdeacon of Taunton*, pp. 32–3; Jones, 'Oxford and Peterborough', pp. 115, 118, 236; Marchant, *Church under Law*, pp. 227–8; Potter, 'Canterbury', p. 77; Price, 'Excommunication', pp. 109–14; Spaeth, *Church in Danger*, pp. 59, 62, 63; Spurr, *Restoration Church*, pp. 214, 215, 217; Stieg, *Laud's Laboratory*, pp. 254–5; Tarver, 'Lichfield and Coventry', p. 54.
16 See Chapter 6 for further discussion of the reform of excommunication.
17 E.g. SHLS, D/D/ca/207, f. 217r, HRO, C1/45 (no folios), 6/12/1678 (apparitor); SHLS, D/D/ca/338 4 (no folios), 27/1/1663 (churchwarden); WRO, 802 2760, f. 299r (individual).
18 HRO, C1/35, f. 52v; SHLS, D/D/ca/207, ff. 47r, 58v, 59v, 71r, 79r, 88v, 96v.
19 HRO, C1/35, f. 57r, v.
20 Wolfe, *Leveller Manifestoes*, p. 406.
21 17 CI c.11; 13 CII c.12; Gibson, *Codex Juris*, vol. 2, pp. 1012, 1042.
22 Brooks, 'Religion and Law', pp. 339, 343.
23 Brooks, 'Religion and Law', pp. 315, 329, 332–3, 339.
24 See Manning, *Religion and Society*, p. 19: Puritan discipline was different but, if he is implying that it was more sympathetic, this may be open to challenge.
25 Brooks, 'Religion and Law', pp. 338, 341.
26 Brooks, 'Religion and Law', pp. 336–7; Marchant, *Church under Law*, p. 4; Rushton, 'Local Laws, Local Principles', p. 193; Russell, *Crisis of Parliaments*, pp. 238–40.
27 See Cavill, 'Perjury', pp. 204–5 for ability to clarify charge(s) and examples of further questioning.
28 Marchant, *Church under Law*, p. 4.
29 HRO, C1/34, f. 13v.
30 HRO, C1/35, ff. 14v, 44r, 44v.
31 WRO. 802 2760, ff. 146v, 206v, 272r, 272v.

32 See the section '*Ex officio* procedures' in Chapter 1.
33 Appendix 4, Tables 4–6.
34 Ingram, *Church Courts*, pp. 249, 332; Houlbrooke, *Church Courts*, p. 45.
35 HRO, C1/35, ff. 14v, 52v.
36 WRO, 802 2760, f. 218r (Shrieve); SHLS, D/D/ca/207, f. 280r (Devonsheere).
37 WRO, 802 2760, f. 188r (Bauke); SHLS, D/D/ca/243, f. 104r (St Alban).
38 17 CI c.11; Firth and Rait, *Acts and Ordinances*, vol. 1, p. 879 (abolition of bishops and 'Episcopal Jurisdiction' 1646).
39 13 CII c.12.
40 Gibson, *Codex Juris*, p. 1042, implies abolition and laments its passing; other 'abolitionists' are Chapman, *Ecclesiastical Courts*, p. 51; Hockaday, 'Gloucester', p. 224; Marchant, *Church under Law*, p. 225; Tarver, *Church Court Records*, p. 2; Till, *Church Courts*, p. 20 (although he admits the procedure continued in practice).
41 For Winchester e.g. HRO, C1/37 (no folios), 5/10/1663 (Aldridge); Wells, SHLS, D/D/ca/350 (no folios), 7/11/1671 and 28/11/1671 (Balch), 10/11/1675 (Shattock); Worcester, WRO, 794 011 2722 2, Book 32, f. 165r, 4/11/1680 (Francklin); both Till and Potter give examples of its use in the 1660s (Till, *Church Courts*, p. 20; Potter, 'Canterbury', p. 194).
42 D/D/ca/350 (no folios), 7/11/1671, 28/11/1671 (Balch); 10/11/1675 (Shattock); in both entries the judge ordered compurgation – '*d(omi)nus junxit*' and '*D(omi)nus monuit*' – but both cases end inconclusively and without any definite statement concerning oaths by the accused or compurgators.
43 HRO, C1/37 (no folios), 5/10/1663 '(Aldridge) *obtulit*', i.e. offered.
44 WRO, 794 011 2722 2, Book 32 – Francklin '*peti(v)it se ad purgat(i)onem suam Canonicam admitti Jus*' (he himself sought the law to be followed/observed for his canonic purgation), f. 163r; he '*obtulit ... ad p(ur)gandum se iuxta assig(natio)nem Dom(ini) Judican(tis)*' (offered to purge himself according to the direction of the judge), f. 165r; the entry does not say Francklin took an oath but the three compurgators '*praestiterunt juramentum*' (swore on oath).
45 For a range of views see Carlson, *Marriage*, pp. 148–9; Hill, *Society and Puritanism*, pp. 299–300; Houlbrooke, *Church Courts*, p. 46; Ingram, *Church Courts*, pp. 332–4; Ingram, *Carnal Knowledge*, pp. 107, 126, 168; Quaife, *Wanton Wenches*, p. 191.
46 Hill, *Society and Puritanism*, pp. 299–300; Houlbrooke, *Church Courts*, p. 46; Quaife, *Wanton Wenches*, p. 191; Potter, 'Canterbury', p. 102.
47 Champion, 'Recourse to Law', pp. 187, 192–6.
48 Ingram, *Church Courts*, p. 372.
49 See Appendix 4, Tables 7–9.
50 See Appendix 4, Table 10.
51 HRO, C1/35, f. 3r (Andrewes), f. 3v (Batt), f. 1r (Symes).
52 SHLS, D/D/ca/207, f. 289r (Carpenter, Tomkins); WRO, 794 011 2722 2, Book 32, f. 166v (Beauchampes).
53 SHLS, D/D/ca/207, f. 289r; HRO, C1/35, f. 3v.
54 See Appendix 4, Table 11.
55 SHLS, D/D/ca/207, f. 280r (Morse, Dible); HRO, C1/35, f. 13r (Hayes).
56 SHLS, D/D/ca/207, f. 288v (Aishe); HRO, C1/35, f. 24r (Watt); f. 6v (Marshall).
57 SHLS, D/D/ca/207, f. 247r (Farthing); HRO, C1/35, f. 8r (Wayte); f. 53v (Cawte).
58 SHLS, D/D/ca/243, f. 104r.
59 SHLS, D/D/ca/207, f. 284r (Stoddey); HRO, C1/35, f. 16v (Brickleton).
60 WRO, 794 011 2722 2, Book 32, ff. 162r, 165v (the Turtons); f. 211v (Gray); f. 220v (Peale); f. 210v (Patrick).
61 See Appendix 4, Table 12.
62 HRO, C1/35, ff. 8v, 31v (Cooper); ff. 7v, 30v (Lipscomb); f. 54v (Dastyn).
63 HRO, C1/35, f. 9r.
64 HRO, C1/35, ff. 13r, 42v.
65 WRO, 802 2760, f. 218v (Evesham); HRO, C1/34, f. 25v (Chilworth); C1/35, f. 54r (Hambledon); SHLS, D/D/ca/354 (no folios), 14/12/1675 (Fivehead).
66 SHLS, D/D/ca/354 (no folios), 2/10/1673.
67 WRO, 794 011 2722 2, Book 32, f. 132r.
68 HRO, C1/35, f. 31r.
69 HRO, C1/45 (no folios), 15/10/1680.
70 HRO, C1/33 (no folios), 12/11/1619.

71 E.g. SHLS, D/D/ca/207, f. 267v (Cheepewrighte).

72 WRO, 794 011 2722 2, Book 32, f. 158v.

73 HRO, C1/35, f. 29v (Fuller); f. 57r (Charlock); WRO, 802 2760, f. 172r (Whittall).

74 SHLS, D/D/ca/331, f. 153v.

75 Postles, 'Penance and the Market Place', p. 446; Quaife, *Wanton Wenches*, pp. 192–5 (for some graphic examples); Ingram, *Carnal Knowledge*, p. 282 (likewise).

76 Carlson, *Marriage*, pp. 149–50; Ingram, *Church Courts*, p. 54; Ingram, *Carnal Knowledge*, pp. 110, 208, 352, 396, 416; Postles, 'Penance and the Market Place', pp. 441, 448.

77 Postles, 'Penance in the Market Place', p. 460; HRO, C1/37, f. 1r.

78 HRO, C1/35, f. 1r.

79 For examples of severity and commutation in the sixteenth century see Ingram, *Carnal Knowledge*, pp. 111–14, 315.

80 HRO, C1/35, f. 25v (Holbrooke); WRO, 802 2760, f. 422v (Bane).

81 HRO, C1/35, f. 25v (Orchard); f. 3v (Batt); f. 14v (White).

82 HRO, C1/35, f. 13r and ff. 42v–43r.

83 SHLS, D/D/ca/207, f. 245r (Bowden); f. 237r (Ward); f. 289v (Tucker).

84 HRO, C1/35, f. 21r.

85 WRO, 802 2760, f. 219r (White); f. 390r (Marten).

86 HRO, C1/35, f. 25v (Orchard); SHLS, D/D/ca/207, f. 240r (Jellett); f. 237r (Ward); f. 284r (Stoddey); D/D/ca 243, f. 49v (Mondai).

87 HRO, C1/35, f. 16v.

88 HRO, C1/35, f. 1r.

89 WRO, 794 011 2722 2, Book 32, f. 224r (Taylor); f. 166v (Beauchampes); SHLS, D/D/ca/338 4 (no folios), 11/3/1663 (Cox); D/D/ca/350 (no folios), 30/10/1671 (Bagg); HRO, C1/37 (no folios), 7/9/1663 (Wither).

90 SHLS, D/D/ca/207, 224, 243.

91 The word 'humiliation' appears over and over again in the literature: Carlson, *Marriage*, pp. 149–50; Postles, 'Penance and the Market Place', *passim*; Ingram, *Church Courts*, pp. 3, 258, 335; Ingram, *Carnal Knowledge*, e.g. pp. 209, 313; Jones, 'Oxford and Peterborough', p. 110; Outhwaite, *Ecclesiastical Courts*, p. 11.

92 Ingram, 'Judicial Folklore', pp. 62, 68–74.

93 WRO, 802 2760, ff. 81v, 204r.

94 Ingram, 'Judicial Folklore', pp. 81–2.

95 Ingram, 'Judicial Folklore', pp. 81–2; Ingram, *Carnal Knowledge*, pp. 111, 396; Ingram, *Church Courts*, p. 335.

96 Hill, *World Turned Upside Down*, *passim* and, in particular, pp. 12, 308–10, 312; Cressy, *Birth, Marriage, Death*, e.g. pp. 182, 185 (baptism), 332, 334 (marriage), 418 (burial).

97 Henry Attwood armiger and William Copley gent, churchwardens of Claines (WRO, 794 011 2722 1, Book 30, f. 258r); records for six Michaelmas terms – 1675, 1678, 1680 ('regular') and 1676, 1679, 1682 ('visitation') – have been examined.

98 E.g. HRO, C1/37 (no folios), 1/10, 19/10, 2/11, 5/12, all 1663.

99 E.g. WRO, 802 2884, f. 118v (3/1612); 802 2760, f. 25v (11/1613); 807 093 2724, Book 38, f. 70r (11/1693).

100 Hill, *Society and Puritanism*, p. 300; Ingram, *Church Courts*, p. 331; Ingram, *Carnal Knowledge*, p. 106; Marchant, *Church under Law*, pp. 145, 217; Houlbrooke, *Church Courts*, p. 79; Stieg, *Laud's Laboratory*, p. 271; McIntosh, *Havering*, p. 251; Wrightson and Levine, *Terling*, pp. 120, 136, 140, 156, 164; Jones, 'Oxford and Peterborough', p. 14; Gowing, *Domestic Dangers*, pp. 48–9; Dabhoiwala, *Origins of Sex*, pp. 22, 66–7 (but see p. 42).

101 Potter, 'Canterbury', pp. 210–11.

102 Ingram, *Church Courts*, p. 331.

103 See Ingram, *Church Courts*, pp. 325–7; Jones, 'Oxford and Peterborough', pp. 14, 217; Litzenberger, *Tewkesbury Churchwardens' Accounts*, p. ix; Marchant, *Church under Law*, p. 138; Wrightson and Levine, *Terling*, pp. 138, 139.

104 McIntosh, *Havering*, p. 251.

105 See Thomson, 'Diocese of Winchester', pp. 59, 61, 65; for Worcester, WRO, 712.1 716 093 3965 (also Barratt, 'Condition of the Clergy', p. 352); for Wells, Stieg, *Laud's Laboratory*, p. 96.

106 Dabhoiwala, *Origins of Sex*, pp. 66–7.

107 See e.g. Postles, 'Penance and the Market Place', p. 465.

108 Marchant, *Church under Law*, p. 138.

109 WRO, 794 011 2722 2 Book 32, f. 224v.

110 SHLS, D/D/ca/295, f. 163v (12/1633); WRO, 794 011 2722 2, Book 32, f. 158v (9/1680), f. 166r (11/1680); WRO, 807 093 2724, Book 38, f. 109r (2/1694), f. 120r (9/1695), f. 120v (6/1696).

111 The Dean and Chapter of Worcester were summoned over chancel problems (WRO, 802 2760, ff. 233r, 247v).

112 See Houlbrooke, *Church Courts*, p. 52; Price, 'Thomas Powell', p. 106; Till, *Church Courts*, pp. 31–2.

113 SHLS, D/D/ca/295, f. 156r.

114 See Bodl, Clarendon MS 92, f. 95r (I owe this reference to Miller, *After the Civil Wars*, p. 138); Houlbrooke, *Church Courts*, p. 51; Ingram, *Church Courts*, pp. 57–8; Jones, 'Oxford and Peterborough', pp. 88–9; Marchant, *Church under Law*, p. 145; Spurr, *Restoration Church*, p. 217.

115 Bowden, *Economic Change*, pp. 19, 29, 166, 192, 193, 369.

116 Houlbrooke, *Church Courts*, p. 271; Ingram, *Church Courts*, p. 10; Marchant, *Church under Law*, pp. 141, 243; Brinkworth, *Archdeacon's Court*, vol. 1, p. xv.

117 HRO, C1/45, 27/1/1683 (no folios); WRO, 802 2760, f. 242v (Hopkins); SHLS, D/D/ca/243, ff. 59r (Salte), 68v (Lane), 69r (Coate), 71r (Tucker and Warren), 101r (Snow).

118 Houlbrooke, *Church Courts*, p. 52; Price, 'Excommunication', p. 106; Price, 'Thomas Powell', pp. 94–112; Till, *Church Courts*, pp. 30–1.

119 1 EI c.2; 23 EI c.1; 29 EI c.6; 35 EI c.1; 35 EI c.2 (religion); 18 EI c.3; 39 EI c.4; 43 EI c.2 (poor laws).

120 Hindle, *State and Social Change*, p. 181.

121 Bradford, 'Social and Economic History', pp. 312, 314 (her dates are imprecise and she ranges over 'the 17th century', 'the Commonwealth', 'the Restoration' and 'the 18th century' all in one paragraph).

122 Hindle, *State and Social Change*, p. 186.

123 Dunning, 'Economic and Social History', pp. 504–14.

124 Willis Bund, 'Ecclesiastical History', pp. 56–7; Locke, 'Social and Economic History', pp. 456–7.

125 See, for numbers and scale, 'Church and people: the impact of its courts on society' in Chapter 3; specific references to the Lord Chief Justice etc. can be found e.g. in TNA, E 377/70 and E 377/71 (Hampshire 1675–6).

126 17 CI c.11 ('abolition' of the courts, 1641).

127 Firth and Rait, *Acts and Ordinances*, vol. 1, p. 879 (abolition of bishops and 'Episcopal Jurisdiction' 1646); Potter, quoting Shaw, gives 1643 but this was just a bill and Outhwaite is right to link the courts to the fate of the bishops but wrong to state that bishops were abolished in 1643; both Jones and Outhwaite are imprecise in implying the specific abolition of consistory courts in 1646 (Potter, 'Canterbury', p. 174; Shaw, *English Church*, vol. 1, pp. 120–1; Outhwaite, *Ecclesiastical Courts*, p. 78; Jones, 'Oxford and Peterborough', pp. 29–31).

128 For Hampshire quarter sessions see Coleby, *Central Government and the Localities*, pp. 6–7; for Oxford etc., see Jones, 'Oxford and Peterborough', p. 34; for Winchester (and Worcester and Wells), there would appear to be little or nothing in their archives, especially for 1653–60: by then everything seems to have been done by the 'Judges for Probate of Wills' … 'att London' or 'Westminster' and whether any 'local' machinery existed as well is not at all clear.

129 Firth and Rait, *Acts and Ordinances*, vol. 2, pp. 702–3; Green, *Re-establishment*, p. 132.

130 Firth and Rait, *Acts and Ordinances*, vol. 2, pp. 715–18.

131 Brooks, 'Law and Revolution', pp. 350, 351.

132 Capp, 'Stability and Flux', p. 9; Coleby, *Central Government and the Localities*, pp. 52, 55, 59 (major generals).

133 See the section 'Explaining the shifting balance of charges' in Chapter 2.

134 See the section 'Church and people: the impact of its courts on society' in Chapter 3; and, in particular, TNA, E 377/36; Coleby, *Central Government and the Localities*, pp. 54, 61, 62–3; Foster, 'English and Welsh Parishes', p. 26; McCall, 'Breaking the Law of God and Man', pp. 140, 143, 155–6, 165–7.

135 Cressy, *Birth, Marriage, Death*, p. 12.

136 Hill, *World Turned Upside Down*, pp. 19, 79, 127, 252; Cressy, *Birth, Marriage, Death*, e.g. pp. 174; Brooks, 'Law and Revolution', p. 320.

137 Coleby, *Central Government and the Localities*, p. 52.

138 Hill, *World Turned Upside Down*, pp. 282, 288.

139 14 CII c.12.

140 17 CII c.2; 22 CII c.1.

141 13 CII c.12.

142 Bradford, 'Social and Economic History', p. 314.

143 Willis Bund, 'Ecclesiastical History', pp. 56–7, 74–5; Willis Bund, 'Political History', p. 227; Allison and Dunning, 'Nonconformity', pp. 536–8; Haydon, 'Kineton', pp. 163, 168.

144 Mildon, 'Hampshire and the Isle of Wight', pp. 413, 417–20; Coleby, *Central Government and the Localities*, pp. 4, 5, 134–8, 200–3.

145 See the section 'Church and people: the impact of its courts on society' in Chapter 3; specific references to the Lord Chief Justice etc. can be found e.g. in TNA, E 377/70 and E 377/71 (Hampshire 1675–6).

146 See *ODNB* for these bishops, of whom only Lake (Bishop of Bath and Wells 1616–26) 'regularly heard disciplinary cases', but these were 'usually in his palace at Wells' and must have been private sessions as there is no evidence of personal direction of regular *ex officio* sittings of the consistory court by him or any of the others (the key source is the preambles in the court books, for which see the Bibliography).

147 SHLS, D/D/ca, e.g. 313, f. 33r (15/11/1636); Bishop Thomas of Worcester 1683–9 sat in court on several occasions in the 1680s but for instance business (WRO, 794 011 2722 2 Book 32, ff. 163v, 168r, 281v); developments were much the same at Salisbury under Bishop Seth Ward 1667–89 (Whiteman, 'Seth Ward', pp. 171, 179).

148 *ODNB*.

149 Bodl, Tanner 42, f. 5 (or f. 7?), 7/4/1673.

150 Underdown, *Fire from Heaven*, pp. 68–9, 70–1, 83–4, 95, 107, 248 (morals), pp. 75–6, 95, 106, 248, 262 (religion), p. 100 (neighbours, etc.), p. 250 (decline); see also Hindle, *State and Social Change*, pp. 179–80.

151 LMA, PR95/TR/1/1/1 (Clapham); SLSL, 787 (St George's Southwark); HRO, 27M79/PR 3 (Heckfield), 39M69/PR3 (Hursley).

152 Ingram, *Church Courts*, p. 398.

5
The case of Worcester

This survey has so far compared the consistory courts in three archdeaconries within the dioceses of Winchester, Worcester and Wells with one another and, more importantly, their operation before and after the Wars and Interregnum.[1] The conclusions are, essentially, that, while the focus of prosecutions moved in somewhat different ways in the respective dioceses between the 1610s and the 1670s, the trajectory of ecclesiastical justice in all three archdeaconries was only in one – downward – direction.

Critics may focus on the limitations of this analysis: three terms, three years, three archdeaconries. *Ex officio* court books for Winchester and Wells disappear after the 1680s. They continue for Worcester, however, into the 1690s and beyond and it is therefore possible to compare, for this diocese, operations at the beginning with those at the end of the century. Worcester's records for three out of eight of its deaneries – Evesham, Kidderminster and Pershore – will be interrogated for both the 1610s and the 1690s: seven whole years apiece, all four law terms, from 1611 to 1618 and from 1690 to 1697.

As with the earlier analyses, the same basic pattern will be followed but the survey will be confined to the truly critical factors, the detail will be much sparser and the presentation will be much leaner. Charges will be discussed and compared to establish the nature of church discipline within the three deaneries and how it changed by the turn of the century; numbers summoned, numbers attending and 'completion' rates will be used to determine the extent of church control. Concluding sections will attempt to set the consistory courts in context – to measure and explain their diminishing role in society by the early eighteenth century.

The nature of church discipline

Charges against the laity

There was very little change of importance in the prosecution of clergy and churchwardens over the century.[2] There were always negligent churchwardens, and complaints about structure of buildings, fittings within them and presentments were problems 'for ever'. When a clergyman was brought to court it was most commonly for a clandestine marriage in the 1610s or a problem with a licence in the 1690s. More exceptionally but occurring in both periods were multiple charges against an incumbent, 'Magister' Balamy running up five offences on his charge sheet in 1615 and Thomas Haughton appearing in four of the seven years of the 1690s.[3] One of their company excelled himself even more uniquely in the 1610s by indulging in 'divers suits, informacons and quarrels' with the Fellows of several Oxford colleges, causing his absence from his parish, 'to the great scandale' of his parishioners.[4] This was truly 'out of the ordinary' and, overall, change was slight.

Nor did the pattern of offences change much, at first glance, with the laity. The same three categories – morals, religion and finance – applied at both times. The chief moral offences were incontinence (adultery and fornication), bastardy, clandestine marriage and sex before marriage. In the 1610s incontinence was top of the list; by the 1690s it had been replaced by bastardy, but incontinence remained a close second. Clandestine marriage and sex before marriage, whether in the 1610s or the 1690s, were the only other charges with any significance. Financial issues to do with church rate, Easter offerings and the like remained minute in both the 1610s and the 1690s. There was an exceptional year at both those times, however: 18 people were charged with a church rate offence in 1616–17 and 15 in 1694–5. Without these exceptional years the numbers of financial offenders would hardly have registered.

Religion saw the greatest change. Work and play during service time on the Sabbath formed the largest categories of 'religious' prosecutions within the three deaneries during the 1610s. Failure to attend church or to receive communion came next, at about half the levels of work and play, while standing excommunicate and abusive behaviour in church or churchyard seem to have been small but persistent problems. Recusancy and dissent were important issues, raising questions of support for the Church of England and the size and strength of the opposition, but prosecutions in the consistory court of Worcester reveal little. The summoning of 29 recusants (presumably Catholics) from the deaneries of Pershore and Kidderminster in 1612–13 was quite exceptional and, without them, prosecutions in this category would have been virtually zero.

The pattern of prosecutions was very different in the 1690s. Brawling remained an occasional – and the only other notable – problem in the category. Precisely four people were so charged, among them the wife of Thomas Mills of Abberton (Pershore) for 'rayling, brawling and assaulting the Minister in performance of his Ministerial Office in the Church and other enormous Crimes', which case presumably remained unresolved, like so many, as the entry concludes with the comment that she had 'run away to London'.[5] Two men were charged with 'publick neglect of God's worship' and, after failing to appear, were condemned to excommunication – two men, over seven years, in a population of at least 40,000 – but it does show that attempts to enforce Sunday worship were still 'live'.[6] There were no prosecutions specifically for recusancy or dissent in the three deaneries and prosecutions in all the other categories of religious offence seem to have shrunk almost to nothing.

The balance of charges

The shifting balance of the charges within the three deaneries over the century is the most striking change.[7] Church rate rose from 3 per cent of charges in the 1610s to 14 per cent in the 1690s but numbers of accused remained minute and it was the steep fall in religious prosecutions which changed the proportions among the three categories. This fall had implications for the key balance between religious and moral charges. 'Moral' charges had outweighed 'religious' charges somewhat in the 1610s but the difference – 55 per cent moral, 42 or 43 per cent religious – was not so great. By the 1690s, however, while moral charges had dropped on average to 23 per year, 'religious' charges had shrunk to two, which left proportions at 80 per cent (moral) and 7 per cent (religious). The nature of ecclesiastical policing in Worcestershire, more moral than religious from the beginning, had swung almost wholly over the course of the century in the direction of morals.

Explaining the shifting balance from 1690

The church courts were struck, as if by lightning, by the Glorious Revolution of 1688–9. The Revolution produced the Toleration Act and the movement known as the Reformation of Manners. Both statute and movement stemmed from the Revolution. Toleration came as a recognition that religious uniformity had failed and as a reward to the dissenters for their support of William of Orange and the overthrow of the Catholic James II. The Reformation of Manners took root as supporters of the new regime felt the need to show that they had higher standards than their predecessors of the Restoration. The war against Louis XIV and the need for a greater measure of national unity brought greater urgency to these issues.[8] Both had consequences for the consistory courts.

The Toleration Act of 1689 removed or, at least, made it impractical to proceed with most 'religious' prosecutions . While 'all' were required to attend 'some Congregation or Assembly of Religious Worship', Protestant dissenters, at least, could now claim exemption from the rubrics and canons of the Church of England and enjoy, instead, legitimate but separate existence under the new dispensation.[9] The Reformation of Manners comprised groups of volunteers who sought to uphold moral standards by detecting 'sin' and enforcing punishment in the courts (secular or religious).[10] Their pressure and campaigns at the end of the seventeenth century and in the early years of the eighteenth were bound to increase the volume of prosecutions on moral grounds in the consistory (as well as the secular) courts.

The Revolution of 1688–9 had, thus, important consequences for the *ex officio* proceedings of consistory courts, not just in the three deaneries but in the other five deaneries of Worcester and, no doubt, nationwide. The focus of *ex officio* prosecutions during the years of the Restoration, certainly at Worcester and Winchester, if not Wells, had been the prosecution of 'religious' infractions. The Revolution meant a huge shift in the balance of prosecutions. Toleration, one child of the Revolution, spelt the death of most religious prosecutions and, at the same time, another child, the Manners Movement, spurred a campaign to raise moral standards.

This near elimination of 'religious' prosecutions and the boost (albeit temporary) to 'moral' matters occurred just as a new man took charge at Worcester. Edward Stillingfleet, Bishop of Worcester 1689–9,[11] brought new force to these trends in his consistory court. He was conscientious, taking much greater interest than his predecessors in the proceedings of his consistory court, and he took personal charge, apparently sitting as a judge, on numerous occasions in the 1690s.[12] He was sympathetic towards Protestant dissenters and his interest in schemes of comprehension can be traced to the 1670s when, as a prebendary of St Paul's, he had been one of the leading figures in an attempt at *rapprochement* between the 'Baxterite' dissenters and the Church of England.[13] Stillingfleet arrived at Worcester in the new climate of toleration and his 'Charge', delivered to his clergy in his primary visitation in 1690, urged them to avoid both provocation and excessive friendliness towards dissenters but to be respecters of conscience.[14] This was a neutral stance but probably sympathetic to dissenters and generally conciliatory. The Church would have to abandon prosecutions and rely instead on example and such evangelistic powers as it could command.

Stillingfleet was also an advocate of the Reformation of Manners and in this he enjoyed the support of the two Archbishops of Canterbury, Tillotson and Tenison, in the 1690s.[15] He preached of his wish for 'Vigorous and Impartial Execution of the Laws against Looseness and Debauchery',[16] and he came to Worcester with a clear imperative to raise morals standards. There was an inevitable tilt away from religious prosecution and towards morals in light of the Revolution and Toleration, and it is true that morality was the only work of any importance left, church rate apart, to the consistory courts. The change of emphasis arose in part out of political necessities of the times but was also very much driven by the new bishop. Stillingfleet's moral vision may well have been tempered by sympathies with the poor and he was doubtless moved by the plight of vagrants and bastards but, possessed of a strong moral purpose, he brought a new – moral – urgency to the work of his court.

This was inevitably the direction of travel followed elsewhere, though perhaps with more faltering steps, and probably lacking the drive of Stillingfleet, as the eighteenth century unrolled. While there are differences of emphasis between them and their methodology is not always clear, Anne Tarver and William Jacob agree on the decline of 'religious' prosecutions and the greater focus on morality in their accounts of consistory courts in the eighteenth century. The tilt towards morals, so evident at Evesham, Kidderminster and Perhsore by the 1690s, prevailed also, according to Tarver, Jacobs and several other researchers, in the neighbouring deanery of Warwick and in an area stretching from London to Lancashire and Northumberland, from Norwich to Oxford and Hereford, and from Devon to Lichfield, Coventry and Carlisle.[17] Donald Spaeth takes a slightly different view and claims there were more 'religious' than 'moral' cases, but his largest number of 'religious' prosecutions is for fabric and fittings – practical rather than spiritual issues – and his sample is small, based on presentments, not prosecutions or convictions, and makes no distinction between decades before and decades after 1689.[18]

The roots of these developments – religious toleration and pursuit of moral standards – can be traced ultimately to the turbulent history of the years of the Restoration. The struggles for dominance by the Anglicans and for survival by the dissenters, the failure to reach a settlement and the threat to both posed by James II and his Catholic policies forced politicians and Protestants to accept toleration. At least one social problem – bastardy – was growing somewhat, at the same time, from 1.2 per cent of births in the 1670s to 1.8 per cent in the 1690s. Illegitimacy was not yet back to the levels of the 1610s but reformers and ecclesiastics such as Stillingfleet and his colleagues may have been aware of a growing problem even if they did not have the benefit of Laslett's statistics.[19]

The chief point arising from all this is that the balance, already more moral than religious in the 1610s, had tilted drastically in the consistory court at Worcester by the 1690s and prosecutions shifted, almost exclusively, from religious to moral matters. That was, in essence, the pattern, the changing nature of control sought by or forced upon the ecclesiastical authorities in the Diocese of Worcester, to judge from trends at Evesham, Kidderminster and Pershore, over the course of the seventeenth century.

The extent of church discipline

Indicators

Extent is best determined, as with the comparison of the 1610s and the 1670s, by examining numbers of sessions and summons and response, together with completion of business and the scale of guilt.

There was a dramatic fall in the number of sessions of the consistory court at Worcester in the course of the seventeenth century. The average number of plenary sessions per year fell from 41 to 16 – that is, from something a little under one a week to fewer than one every three weeks, or a decrease of more than three-fifths over the century. This was accompanied by a corresponding fall of *in camera* sessions by half. A glance at the relevant tables is instructive: it is a simple yet telling illustration of the trajectory of decline at Worcester in the space of 90 or so years.[20]

Two hundred and thirteen people were summoned from the Deanery of Pershore to the consistory court at Worcester in the four law terms of 1612–13.[21] Over one hundred people were summoned from Pershore in three more of the seven years from 1611 to 1618, and likewise from Evesham in one of the specimen years. Otherwise numbers of people from these three deaneries always remained below one hundred. One hundred turns out, however, to have been more than twice as high as numbers in any of the seven years of the 1690s. The largest number

THE CASE OF WORCESTER **165**

during that time was 43, again from Pershore, in 1693–4, and numbers in single figures were quite common.

The consistory court at Worcester suffered a severe decline in total numbers summoned from the three deaneries over the course of the seventeenth century: from 1,850 or so to just over 350. Such numbers would suggest averages of just over 260 a year between 1611 and 1618, some 50 in the corresponding period of the 1690s, and would amount to a drop of more than four-fifths over the course of the century.

While numbers summoned changed – dramatically downwards – during the course of the seventeenth century, there was very little change in the proportions who came to court.[22] The response of about 10 per cent of the summoned cannot be determined for either decade but, at both times, 40 per cent or so came to court and 50 per cent failed to put in an appearance. These response levels had damaging implications, of course, for the completion of business. Cases where the outcome cannot be established or where people emerged as innocent from the proceedings in court remained much the same in both periods but there was a rise – progress – in the proportions of guilty verdicts of about 6 per cent, which appears largely to account for a corresponding drop from 48 per cent to 40 per cent – an improvement – in unresolved business.[23] It still meant, however, that at the end of the century a substantial proportion of the court's work – two-fifths – was paralysed.

Actual numbers of people pronounced guilty were, moreover, minute.[24] Clergy numbers were the only ones to increase, from ten at most to 14, over the respective timescales. Churchwardens fell, in round figures, from over 200 to 60. Nearly 550 laymen and women in the three deaneries were found guilty of a religious, moral or rate offence over the seven years in the 1610s, fewer than 80 in the 1690s. These figures represent falls among churchwardens of some 70 per cent and among the laity of 85 per cent.

It would seem that on all the measures – sessions, summonses, attendance and convictions – the grasp of the consistory courts at Worcester was weakening. The one exception concerned numbers of clergy hauled before the court, reflecting, no doubt, the infusion of discipline by Stillingfleet. Falling numbers of churchwardens might, logically, suggest the opposite unless deterrence played a part and churchwardens were chastened by the fate of the clergy.

The impact of the Church on the diocese, *c.* 1690–*c.* 1740

It remains to consider the effect of the Church on society at the turn of the seventeenth century. The question is the extent to which the Church, through its judicial machinery, exercised effective control in the communities, and more particularly its impact on religious life and on moral behaviour as the nation moved into a new age after a century of revolution.

Protestant dissenting groups were undoubtedly stronger in the Diocese and Archdeaconry of Worcester at the end than at the beginning of the seventeenth century. The Puritans had been growing in strength in the early years of the century, capturing the magistracy and lectureships, and when the lid came off repression with the momentary amnesty of 1672–3 and when the results of the census of 1676 were revealed, substantial numbers of dissenting ministers and congregations were shown to exist in the diocese.[25] It was the Glorious Revolution of 1688–9, however, which transformed matters permanently. The Toleration Act allowed freedom of worship in public to dissenting congregations. Dissenters (Presbyterian, Independent, Baptist and Quaker) could seek a licence under the terms of the Act and by the early years of George I's reign there were probably some 20 meeting houses of one dissenting group or another in the archdeaconry and diocese. Some housed large congregations: Presbyterians numbered 300 at Stratford, for example, and 200–250 at Warwick, where Joseph Carpenter enjoyed a ministry of over 40 years, while some 700 Baptists took part in meetings at Pershore.[26] Evidence from composite sources suggests, moreover, that the total numbers of centres and 'hearers' from all dissenting denominations at this time in Worcestershire came to at least 30 and 5,500 respectively.[27] Nor were these developments exceptional and, to put matters in a wider context, there were, again, some large congregations in the other archdeaconries: 1,000 Independents meeting at Gosport (Winchester), for example, and more than 800 Baptists at Taunton (Wells). Dissenters met in 50 or 60 licensed meeting houses in Hampshire (the Archdeaconry of Winchester) and nearly 100 in Somerset, accommodating nearly 9,000 and more than 17,000 from a range of denominations in the two dioceses respectively. Figures supplied by Michael Watts suggest there were some 360,000 dissenters, who would have formed about 6 per cent of the total population of England and Wales.[28]

At the same time, Catholic recusant families continued to survive and prosper. The Throckmortons, Talbots and Blounts were as strong as ever in Worcestershire; the Bishops, Cannings and Sheldons thrived in neighbouring Warwickshire (part of which lay in the Worcester Diocese); while the Tichbornes retained their position in the Winchester diocese.

Catholics formed a 'small but significant ... community', meanwhile, in Warwick.[29] Catholic numbers, though smaller, were probably more stable than those of their dissenting counterparts, which seem to have peaked in the 1720s but thereafter suffered a measure of decline by the 1730s and 1740s.[30] With all these religious groups, Catholic and Protestant, some sense of perspective must be borne in mind as well and, for all their congregations, meeting places and families, they were far outnumbered by Anglican worshippers and county (or diocesan) populations.

A complete set of statistics is equally difficult to establish for moral and social matters. That leaves the way open for speculation, and there are even suggestions that the campaign for 'conformity' with higher standards was largely 'successful' in the early eighteenth century: that public morals improved and that the church courts were, at least in part, responsible. This would fly in the face of 'normal' behaviour through the ages and a more tenable view is that vice remained much the same in the 1740s as in the 1690s – that is, there was no improvement – in spite the efforts of the courts, spiritual and secular.[31] Much immoral behaviour is clandestine and it is difficult to discover statistics, but this is less so with bastardy. The claim of the 'manners' movements to have brought more than a thousand cases a year to court in the first decade of the eighteenth century could signal success or, alternatively, the scale of the problem.[32]

Bastardy, at least, had more public results and was the cause of much concern among some on principle and among the wider public because of its implications, as has been said more than once in this account, in terms of costs and the poor rate. The statisticians of bastardy calculate that illegitimacy rose from 1.2 or 1.3 per cent in the 1670s to 1.8 per cent in the 1690s. While these percentages may seem tiny fractions of the total numbers of births, they could represent one hundred illegitimate births a year in every diocese if spread evenly over the 26 dioceses in the 1670s and 175 or more in the 1690s. Illegitimacy rates continued to rise in the eighteenth century to 2, 3 and 4 per cent of all births. By the 1780s they had passed 5 per cent, which could have meant some 750 births per year per diocese.[33] The consistory court at Worcester, meanwhile, managed 16 convictions for bastardy over seven years in the three deaneries.

The mismatches overall between conditions in the diocese and convictions in the consistory court are striking: from the three deaneries over seven years, one conviction for a religious offence (abusive behaviour in church) as against 5,000 Protestant dissenters and perhaps one or two thousand Catholics in the diocese as a whole; 60 for moral misdemeanours as against, at a conservative estimate, eight or nine hundred illegitimacies in the diocese; and all this in a diocesan population of some 100,000.[34]

Nothing could illustrate more starkly the failure of the ecclesiastical authorities and their legal machine. The Church had failed to maintain its monopoly of worship and it was evidently failing with its moral mission. Thirty years after the last Act of Uniformity, it was necessary, in a new age and a changing climate, to tolerate diversity, to live side by side with different religions and to rely on such evangelistic skills as it could summon – not the compulsion of its courts – to preserve its identity. The Church still tried in the 1690s and beyond to impose moral standards on its flock but the rising levels of illegitimacy, the refusal of the accused to respond to a summons to attend and the minute conviction rates are sure signs of a losing battle.

This was not the failure of the consistory courts alone. Archdeacons' courts, peculiar jurisdiction courts as at Warwick (part of Worcester Diocese), and the less formal but no doubt frequent interventions of churchwardens and counselling of incumbents were other means through which the Church had sought to exercise control of the religious and moral standards of the people, not to overlook the secular courts of magistrates and the heads of families. These all played a part, together with the consistory courts, in attempting to impose controls within the communities, and the failure to do so was as much theirs as it was the consistory courts'.

Explaining the decline of the courts

The church courts of the seventeenth century were operating in a time of change. It was a world of upheavals and political, religious and social attitudes were changing with them. The courts books do not reveal much about these developments, only the result – contraction – but they continue to show some of the inherent problems of the ecclesiastical judicial machine. Among these were excommunication, compurgation, penance and class. These continued to weaken the courts, making defence more difficult, and were contributory factors in the decline of the system. Each of them will be examined briefly in turn, after which examination of the wider societal developments which really undermined the church courts will be resumed.

Excommunication

One hundred and forty-seven excommunication orders were issued by the consistory court against absentee inhabitants of the three deaneries in the one year 1611–12; numbers rose above one hundred in three more years in the 1610s, and they averaged 102 a year – 700 and more in total – over the seven years in question. There were no excommunications of offenders from the three deaneries in 1694–5 and the average had shrunk to 13 a year over the seven years, but this was still over 90 altogether (38 of them in 1693–4). 'Closure' was achieved in one case, at least, in the 1690s – that of Thomas Wood – including absolution, performance of penance and certifying of the fact to the court.[35] The books are too deficient to give a complete picture and whether Wood's was the only case of compliance or whether it was more general is difficult to say, but the silence is ominous.

The reduction in excommunications was an improvement on the earlier decade of the century. The flow had decreased because of Stillingfleet, no doubt, but even under his apparently more moderate approach excommunications were, at times, being issued on far too liberal a scale. Nothing truly reforming, such as abolition, came of this, however, and overuse of excommunication continued to be a problem. Its effects, both spiritually and in terms of livelihoods, could be harsh, though frequency deadened its impact. It continued to produce an underswell of exclusion and discontent in the communities while, at the same time, advertising the impotence of the court.[36]

Compurgation

The court books for Worcester are singularly sparse about how judgments were reached for between two-thirds and three-quarters of cases.[37] Confession – just below 20 per cent in the 1610s, just above in the 1690s – was the still the main way in which the cases of those who appeared in court from the three deaneries were determined. Compurgation came next in the 1610s, with reliance on documentary evidence somewhat lower. Methods were much the same in the 1690s except that compurgation and documents had changed places.

While the exchange was good news, it should be remembered that since 1661 compurgation had in effect been illegal.[38] It was the oath involved in compurgation, reminiscent of the *ex officio* oath, which was, no doubt, the cause of concern in 1661; but there were sounder objections to the procedure, in particular the expense involved in bringing friends and neighbours to court and the evident bias of the proceeding. The fact was that the consistory courts at Worcester and elsewhere were continuing, in the face of the law, to rely on an outdated and outmoded system to arrive at a verdict.

It would be interesting to know why this was so in the 1690s, five hundred years after the jury system had first been conceived for the secular courts. It would be interesting, furthermore, to know how often it was the defendant who volunteered to undergo the procedure and how often it was the judge who 'advised' it, but the clerk's notes are too ambivalent for certainty. There is no real evidence of volunteering by the accused in the records: the judge may have ordered Edward Yate to undergo compurgation in December 1693, and phrasing such as the accused 'has to perform compurgation' in several other cases in the 1690s sounds like a direction from the judge but does not clarify for certain whether he or the accused took the initiative.[39] An oath was sworn on most of these occasions but this, again, is not always explicit in the record. William Lloyd arrived at court in June 1693 with 'many' compurgators, clearly prepared, it would seem, for the ordeal. He was certainly cooperating but whether voluntarily or under earlier orders is not certain. His 'volunteer' compurgators asserted as true their belief in his integrity but whether under oath is, again, not clear.[40]

Proper methods of determining cases were critical to the sound administration of justice, to the fate of the individuals concerned in a case and to the respect and standing of the court in general. Compurgation, in particular, was obviously a flawed instrument, as has been discussed earlier, and the decline in its use, from 96 occasions in the 1610s to 41 in the 1690s, may reflect doubts about its value as much as a simple reduction in the volume of business.

Penance

The fate of huge numbers of people from Evesham, Kidderminster and Pershore – nearly 1,000 in the 1610s and over 160 in the 1690s – remained, as usual, unresolved and, if verdicts had been reached in those cases, more would have been found guilty and more would have suffered penance.[41] The cases of a third or so of the accused in fact reached the stage of sentencing. This took the form of penance in most cases in the earlier period (the 1610s) but, by the later period (the 1690s), warnings and orders had, between them, increased enough to overtake penance even if the margin was rather narrow.

This was, again, good news. For failure to pay church rate and allied problems such as Easter offerings, an order to pay seems to have been 'automatic' in both the 1610s and the 1690s. It is difficult to generalise about treatment of religious offenders in the 1690s as there was only one guilty verdict in the three deaneries over the seven years in question.[42] They usually received warnings (against working on Sundays for example) and orders (to attend church or to receive communion) in the 1610s but some suffered penance, and penance was 'standard' treatment of lay offenders against morality at both times.

Treatment of guilty clergy is of some interest in this respect. Guilty clergy in the 1610s and the 1690s usually received an order to reside in the parish, to conduct services or to obtain a licence, but there were some spectacular examples of clergy facing penance, or something very like it, in the earlier period. Richard Farr, rector of Evenlode, guilty of vexatious litigation, was required in 1615 to acknowledge his fault before the masters of several Oxford colleges, to 'reside upon his churche' and to adopt 'a paynefull carriadge' while there.[43] Two clerics, Richard Gosling, rector of Comberton, and Richard Gosling, vicar of Eckington, father and son, were both in the dock in 1618. Gosling senior was found guilty of conducting the clandestine marriage (no banns or licence) of his son and received an order to perform penance, but whether he did so or not is not clear. Gosling junior, meanwhile, was found guilty of incontinence and ultimately faced sequestration and deprivation.[44] William Dummer, vicar of Halesowen, who had apparently been overzealous with citations of his parishioners to the consistory court, had a narrow escape from suspension a little earlier, in 1611, when the judge revised the sentence and ordered him to deliver an apology every Sunday for one year.[45] Suspension was temporary and deferred a final decision, but that is where such cases stood at the end of the seven years under review and final outcomes are difficult to trace.

Altogether 292 penances were issued in the three deaneries in the 1610s, while 51 were issued in the 1690s under Stillingfleet. Although this was a decrease of more than four-fifths, 51 was a substantial number; furthermore, the court of Lloyd and Hough (his episcopal successors) continued to pursue, or allowed others to pursue, the immoral with some vigour, and the torment of penance hung over the heads of the accused well into the eighteenth century. John Price, chancellor to Stillingfleet and Lloyd, giving sentence in one case of incontinence in the early 1700s, praised the 'exemplary discipline of former times' and said he would not attempt to revive it, before imposing penance on the person found guilty with a white sheet and confessions in front of the whole congregation in the cathedral and in the offender's own parish. The court was apparently still operating in the same mode under Hough in the 1730s, when the presiding judge ordered a female sinner to wear a white sheet and to confess before the congregation in her local parish church.[46]

Stillingfleet, a key proponent of the Reformation of Manners, had repurposed his consistory court towards moral issues and his successors, Lloyd and Hough, took the same course. They were apparently willing to use penance in their drive against adultery, bastardy and incest. The purpose of penance was to heap shame and embarrassment on its victims.

How much support – and *schadenfreude* – or how much distaste it caused among the public in the 1690s and the early eighteenth century is difficult to say. While such vigour breathed new life into dying embers, it may have spelt the death of church discipline in the long run.

Class

The statistics for class and occupation require very little, though damning, comment. The class or occupation of most of the accused is never mentioned in the court books, but it is abundantly clear that hardly any of the upper classes were summoned to the consistory court in the 1610s and this was still the case in the 1690s. The consistory court continued to train its firepower overwhelmingly on the lower – working – classes of trade and agriculture in this and other dioceses, whether at the beginning or the end of the seventeenth century. It should be said, however, that the perpetrator of incontinence who suffered the excoriation of John Price was, quite exceptionally, a baronet, no less.

Wider reasons for decline

This brief survey of consistory court activity in the deaneries of Evesham, Kidderminster and Pershore in the 1610s and the 1690s has broadly confirmed the findings of the preceding analyses of the three archdeaconries of Winchester, Worcester and Wells. It reveals, most strikingly on this occasion, the changing nature of the concerns of the Church from a balance between moral and religious prosecutions to concentration almost exclusively on moral cases. Nor can there be much doubt about the withering and receding extent of its control and its consequent decline as a force in society. Numbers of sessions and accused fell in the course of the century, attendance remained a problem and business was stalled. Everything turned on attendance at court but instead of cooperation there was defiance, and progressing business and pronouncing verdicts suffered in consequence.

All was not uniformly bad and worsening. Comparison of the 1690s with the 1610s shows there was some improvement to the dispatch of business. There were also reductions in excommunication, compurgation and penance, which suggest awareness of the unpopularity and pointlessness of some of the methods and sanctions on which the court relied. The role of Edward Stillingfleet may be important here. He was probably responsible for the improvements – unless Timothy Baldwyn, chancellor from 1661 to 1696, had a belated attack of reforming zeal

– and, if so, the bishop may have rescued his court and postponed its complete collapse. He, together with his successor, Lloyd, and a new chancellor, John Price, kept the court alive (though the course they chose – pursuit of morals – went against the grain and, in the long run, undermined the prospects of the court).[47] In contrast with Winchester and Wells, where *ex officio* business appears to have suffered extinction by the 1690s, the consistory court at Worcester did at least survive, if in considerably weakened form.

Nor should the existence of 'alternative' forms of control be overlooked. Consistory courts were not the totality of ecclesiastical justice. The reach of the Church was extended somewhat by archdeacons' courts and by the less formal but, no doubt frequent, interventions of churchwardens, incumbents and heads of families as much in the 1690s as in the 1610s and 1620s. These mechanisms – other ecclesiastical agencies and people 'inspired' by them – still played a part, together with the consistory courts, in controlling moral and religious behaviour within the communities.

Decline, if not collapse, is, nonetheless, the most striking feature of *ex officio* operations of the consistory court at Worcester over the course of the seventeenth century. Excommunication, compurgation, penance and class bias, even fees and corruption, did not destroy the courts – in fact there were some improvements – but their persistence could only weaken the legal structure. The decisive blow was struck by the Glorious Revolution of 1688–9 which, as already described, spawned Toleration and the Reformation of Manners. Both did more than change the balance between religious and moral cases. Both had consequences – terminal consequences – for the church courts. The Toleration Act was forced on the Church in the first place by politics but it led to a change of attitude. It accustomed people, perforce, to accept the existence of different religions side by side. Toleration marked the end of consistory persecution of Protestant groups and sects.[48] Even persecution of Catholics died down and by the 1730s fanaticism seemed 'inappropriate to the age ... religious persecution was over'.[49] The Church was forced to come to terms with a new age in which uniformity was dead. It was necessary to tolerate diversity and in future to rely on such evangelistic skills as it could summon – not the compulsion of its courts – to preserve and extend its identity.

The impact of the Reformation of Manners is more complex. The movement, again initially propelled by political considerations, at first encouraged the pursuit of moral business in the courts but it undermined them in the long run. Underlying currents may be difficult to identify and quantify but were no doubt crucial for the future of ecclesiastical justice. Undoubtedly, 'the great overturning' of the 1650s, with the overthrow of the church courts and an explosion of extremist sects, let loose new attitudes and a rejection of moral as well as religious norms.[50] It would seem that 'social values' were changing and, by the eighteenth century, 'a major social cultural shift – the decline of legal regulation of consensual activity between men and women' was emerging. The existence of 'moral police', spiritual or secular, bred 'resentment' and minute control of personal morals was no longer acceptable. People became less willing to accept intrusiveness and regulation of their personal lives. The public turned hostile to the Reformation of Manners – some of the hostility was even 'muscular' – and by the 1720s and 1730s the movement was dead and pursuit of moral causes in the courts (secular and religious) was in decline.[51]

The two developments – toleration and changing social attitudes – may well be linked: 'sexual toleration grew out of religious toleration' and religious change, by elevating conscience above external laws, may well have helped to loosen social controls in the long run.[52] Conditions in the three deaneries and in the other archdeaconries by the eighteenth century – the existence of Protestant groups side by side with the Anglican Church and the increase in bastardy and fornication – may well reflect these new attitudes. It would be a mistake, however, to imagine the change was drastic or complete. There were limits to religious toleration. There was none is the legislation of 1689 for Unitarians and Catholics and their exclusion from education and politics continued into the nineteenth century. There were also limits to progress in public thinking about vagrancy and bastardy. Whipping may have gone but forcible removal of 'outsiders' to their original parish, exemplified by the appointment of an official for the purpose at Warwick in the 1620s, had not.[53] This became the governing principle, exemplified in the Act of Settlement of 1662, for treatment of vagrants.[54] Punishment and work were seen as solutions and as best done in a house of correction (a workhouse) as early as the 1570s at Worcester and Winchester.[55] More 'holding centres' of this kind followed in the city of Worcester (1703), the town of Warwick (1717) and at places such as Odiham and Gosport in the Diocese of Winchester in the eighteenth century.[56] When a hospital was set up at Winchester in the 1730s it was claimed, in order to attract donations, that 'it reduces the numbers of vagrants by depriving them of their most plausible reasons for begging – i.e. sick relations'.[57] Much of this was by voluntary initiative but true benevolence is questionable. The regimes were harsh and the motives were largely fear of revolt and fear of the costs of disorder and bastardy.

Otherwise, Toleration and Reformation of Manners apart, the spiritual courts continued to suffer attrition from the ever-growing remit of the secular magistrate. Groups of 'recusants' were still being hauled before the quarter sessions at Warwick, for example, after 1689 and into the early eighteenth century, although persecution died down thereafter.[58] King and Parliament continued, as before, to prefer recourse to the secular courts because they had greater powers than their spiritual counterparts. In the 1690s they passed laws protecting the Sabbath, constraining swearing and blasphemy, and thereby increasing the role of the magistracy over morals and behaviour.[59] By the 1730s hostility produced a sufficient head of steam for some MPs to propose another bill which would have placed limits, if it had come into law, on church court fees and the powers of excommunication. Dismantling continued and in the course of the eighteenth and nineteenth centuries further categories – incontinence, sex before marriage and misbehaviour in church or churchyard – were in effect removed from ecclesiastical jurisdiction.[60]

In some ways, as in the earlier periods, the Church connived, doubtless unwittingly, in the transfer of business from church to secular courts. A number of bishops – not just Stillingfleet but Burnet, Patrick, Kennett, Wake – and Archbishop Tenison were supporters of the Reformation of Manners and condoned or encouraged its use of the secular arm just as Morley had done at Surrey in the 1670s. There were exceptions, such as Sharpe, Gibson and Trelawny, who tried to keep church business within the church courts, but significant numbers of 'prominent ecclesiastics' declared their support for and preached on behalf of the Movement.[61] Lloyd, continuing the practice of his predecessors, Babington and Thornborough, served as a magistrate in the county.[62] Leading figures in the Church may in this way have helped to undermine their own disciplinary machinery.

The thrust of the work of Anne Tarver and William Jacob on ecclesiastical justice in the eighteenth century is the 'busyness' of the courts, but even they record a decline in *ex officio* prosecutions towards the end of the century.[63] It would seem the good ship 'Worcester Consistory Court' remained afloat under Captain Stillingfleet and his successors, Lloyd and Hough, its religious cargo gone, its moral cargo sliding off the deck, as it steered a disastrous course into a sea of troubles.

Notes

1 The subject matter of Chapter 5 is discussed in a separate article (Thomson, 'Church Discipline') more fully but under the limitations of the COVID-19 pandemic and related problems of access to libraries, and here it is both summarised and revised.

2 Appendix 5, Tables 1–3.

3 WRO, 802 2760, ff. 109r, 113r, 115r (Haughton); f. 236v (Balamy – he lacks a first name in the relevant court book).

4   WRO, 802 2760, f. 230r.
5   WRO, 807 093 2724, Book 38, f. 116v.
6   WRO, 807 093 2724, Book 38, f. 114v: four cases in the tables were in fact two people whose cases fell in August and September 1693 and so straddled two of the seven years of this study.
7   Appendix 5, Table 4.
8   Dabhoiwala, *Origins of Sex*, pp. 52, 85.
9   1 W+M c.18; see e.g. Houlbrooke, *Church Courts*, p. 270; Ingram, *Church Courts*, pp. 372–3.
10 Dabhoiwala, *Origins of Sex*, p. 52; Gowing, *Common Bodies*, p. 180; Isaacs, 'Anglican Hierarchy', p. 393; Smith, *Pastoral Discipline*, p. 9.
11 Prebendary of St Paul's 1667–89, Dean 1678–89, Horn, *Fasti 1541–1857*, vol. 1, pp. 6, 8, 40, 47; Bishop of Worcester 1689–99, Horn, *Fasti 1541–1857*, vol. 7, p. 108.
12 WRO, 807 093 2724, Book 38, back pages; see the section 'Bishops as presiding officers' in Chapter 1; see also entry in *ODNB* (but the figures for sittings do not distinguish between *ex officio* and instance sessions).
13 Keeble and Nuttall, *Correspondence of Richard Baxter*, item 937; Baxter, *Reliquiae Baxterianae*, Part 3, p. 156; Thomson, 'Dissenters and Recusants', p. 97; Thomson, *Bishop Morley*, p. 56; for the 1670s and much more see *ODNB* (Stillingfleet).
14 Stillingfleet, *Bishop of Worcester's Charge*, p. 24.
15 See e.g. *ODNB* for these bishops; for interest in 'Manners', see Dabhoiwala, *Origins of Sex*, p. 56; Smith, *Pastoral Discipline*, p. 9.
16 Stillingfleet, *Reformation of Manners* (date of publication is 1700, after his death; date of delivery of the sermon is not known), pp. 27, 28 (Dr Colin Haydon drew my attention to this source); Stillingfleet, *Bishop of Worcester's Charge*, pp. 41, 42.
17 Dabhoiwala, *Origins of Sex*, pp. 52, 59; Haydon, 'Kineton', pp. 160–1, 168–9; Jacob, 'Love and Charity', pp. 207–8; Jacob, *Lay People*, p. 142; Marshall, 'Hereford and Oxford', pp. 78–85; Smith, *Pastoral Discipline*, pp. 26–31; Tarver, 'Lichfield and Coventry', pp. 98–9, 105, 437.
18 Spaeth, *Church in Danger*, p. 114; this illustrates problems of classification and comparison – Spaeth includes prosecutions against churchwardens under 'religion', whereas my 'religious' category concerns prosecutions against ordinary parishioners (e.g. church attendance), and charges against churchwardens (e.g. fabric or fittings) are treated separately.
19 Laslett, 'Comparing Illegitimacy', p. 14.
20 Appendix 5, Tables 5–7.
21 Appendix 5, Table 8.
22 Appendix 5, Table 9.
23 Appendix 5, Table 10.
24 Appendix 5, Tables 11–14.
25 See the section 'Church and people: the impact of its courts on society' in Chapter 3.
26 Allison and Dunning, 'Non-Conformity', pp. 536–8; Evans, *Baptist Interest under George I*, pp. 95–109.
27 Watts, *Dissenters*, p. 509 (men, women and children).
28 Johnson, 'Dissenters in Hampshire', p. 305 (Gosport); Evans, *Baptist Interest under George I*, pp. 95–109 (Taunton); Watts, *Dissenters*, pp. 507–10.
29 Willis Bund, 'Ecclesiastical History', pp. 51, 53, 54, 87; Haydon, 'Kineton', p. 167; Haydon, 'Mouth of Hell', pp. 23, 24, 25; Allison and Dunning, 'Non-Conformity', pp. 536–8.
30 Watts, *Dissenters*, pp. 382–93; Johnson, 'Dissenters in Hampshire', pp. 161–3.
31 Rushton, 'Local Laws, Local Principles', p. 195; Dabhoiwala, *Origins of Sex*, p. 61; Isaacs, 'Anglican Hierarchy', p. 404.
32 Dabhoiwala, *Origins of Sex*, p. 59; Isaacs, 'Anglican Hierarchy', p. 404 (even higher figures).
33 Laslett, 'Comparing Illegitimacy', p. 14.
34 See the section 'Populations' in Chapter 1.
35 WRO, 807 093 2724, Book 38, f. 159r.
36 See *ODNB* for a more generous but vaguer assessment.
37 Appendix 5, Table 15.
38 13 CII c.12; see, for discussion of compurgation after 1660, the sections '*Ex officio* procedures' in Chapter 1 and 'Compurgation' in Chapter 4.
39 WRO, 807 093 2724, Book 38, f. 70r, Yate, '*D(ominu)s ass(ignavi)t eum ad purgand(um)*', i.e. the judge assigned him to purgation; f. 110r, Dilworth; f. 114r, Brookes; f. 159r, Grove – all three say '*habet ad purgand(u)m se*', i.e. he has to purge himself; f. 157r, Loyd.

40 Silence (about oaths) obtains (Brookes); for Yate, Dilworth and Grove, compurgators took an oath ('*juram(en)tu(m)*'); Loyd '*introduxit in Compurgatores suos multos Inhabitan(tes) Eccl(es) i(a)e su(a)e p(ar)o(chia)lis qui in eorum conscien(tia) affirmaver(un)t...*' i.e. Loyd produced as his compurgators many parishioners ... who from their knowledge confirmed (their belief in his innocence).

41 Appendix 5, Table 16.

42 One of these, with a penance, is shown in the relevant table; the other, guilty of a religious offence, suffered likewise but his case falls outside the selected years.

43 WRO, 802 2760, f. 230r.

44 WRO, 802 2760, ff. 320v–323v (both Goslings).

45 WRO, 802 2884, f. 116r.

46 Robertson, *Diary of Francis Evans*, p. xvii; Haydon, *Kineton*, p. 161.

47 For Stillingfleet, WRO, 807 093 2724, Book 38, back pages; for Lloyd, Robertson, *Diary of Francis Evans*, pp. xvi and e.g. 32, 103 133.

48 E.g. Houlbrooke, *Church Courts*, p. 270; Ingram, *Church Courts*, p. 372.

49 Haydon, 'Kineton', p. 169; Haydon, 'Mouth of Hell', p. 25.

50 Cressy, *Birth, Marriage, Death, passim*, especially pp. 174, 182, 332–4, 416–18; Hill, *Society and Puritanism*, p. 331; Hill, *World Turned Upside Down*, pp. 12, 308–10, 312.

51 Dabhoiwala, *Origins of Sex*, pp. 52, 55, 59, 64, 67, 72; Ingram, 'Juridical Folklore', p. 81; Ingram, *Church Courts*, pp. 371–2; Ingram, *Carnal Knowledge*, p. 424; Stone, *Road to Divorce*, p. 41; Isaacs, 'Anglican Hierarchy', p. 404.

52 Dabhoiwala, *Origins of Sex*, pp. 80–7.

53 Dunning, 'Economic and Social History', pp. 504–14.

54 14 CII c.12.

55 Shillington, 'Social and Economic History', p. 424; Locke, 'Social and Economic History', p. 454.

56 Locke, 'Social and Economic History', p. 457; Dunning, 'Economic and Social History', pp. 504–14; Shillington, 'Social and Economic History', p. 429.

57 Shillington, 'Social and Economic History', pp. 424, 429.

58 Allison and Dunning, 'Non-Conformity', pp. 536–8; Haydon, 'Kineton', p. 169.

59 E.g. 6+7 W+M c.11; 9 WIII c.35; see also Issacs, 'Anglican Hierarchy', p. 403.

60 27 Geo III c.44; 23+24 Vic c.32; I owe this information to Anne Tarver ('Lichfield and Coventry', pp. 3, 123).

61 Dabhoiwala, *Origins of Sex*, pp. 52, 61–2; Isaacs, 'Anglican Hierarchy', pp. 403, 407, 399, 402, 406; Smith, *Pastoral Discipline*, p. 10; for Morley and magistrates, see Bodl, Tanner 42, f. 7 (7/4/1673) and discussion in the section 'Wider reasons for decline by the 1670s' in Chapter 4.

62 Babington was bishop 1597–1610, Thornborough was bishop 1617–1641; for Lloyd, bishop 1699–1717, see Robertson, *Diary of Francis Evans*, e.g. pp. 11, 32, 102, 112, 132, although there are ambiguities about some of these entries, e.g. 'My Lord went to Worcester being quarter Sessions week' and the even sparer entry, 'Quarter Sessions at Worcester'.

63 For 'busyness', Jacob, 'Love and Charity', p. 205; Jacob, *Lay People*, pp. 135–7; Tarver, 'Lichfield and Coventry', pp. 9, 412; for admission of decline, Jacob, 'Love and Charity', pp. 205, 212; Tarver, 'Lichfield and Coventry', pp. 129, 131, 134, 154, 437–8.

6
The failure of reform

The return of the monarch in 1660 could have been more than straightforward restoration. Several modern authorities lament the lost opportunity; it was, in their view, the optimum moment, while the institutions of church and state were centre stage, not merely to restore but to reform.[1] Contemporary politicians and churchmen certainly saw the opportunity even if they failed to fulfil promise. There were in fact frequent attempts in the 1660s and 1670s – some of them, such as Worcester House and Savoy, prodigious – to achieve church unity, or 'comprehension', in 1660–2, together with numerous subsequent bills with the same objective in the 1660s and 1670s.

Nor, more specifically, did overhaul of the courts lack advocates in the late seventeenth and early eighteenth centuries. Criticisms had been voiced in the Millenary Petition of 1603 and a few gestures towards reform were 'flagged' in the Canons of 1604. These were supposed to cap fees, restrain the behaviour of apparitors and improve the proceedings of registrars in order to limit corruption and intrusion.[2] It was one thing to legislate, another to enforce. The new canons proved tentative and, ultimately, meaningless as far as the church courts were concerned, and there were more calls for reform in the Root and Branch Petition during the revolution of 1640–1.[3] To leave aside the peripheral – and wilder – comments of John Milton and Edmund Hickeringill,[4] the cause gained powerful advocacy from such secular figures as Sir Henry Vane and Sir Edward Dering in 1641;[5] from Sir Leoline Jenkins and Sir Matthew Hale in the 1660s;[6] and from a succession of ecclesiastics, including Sheldon and Sancroft, in the 1660s and 1670s,[7] and Stillingfleet and Tillotson in the 1690s.[8] Francis Atterbury, Bishop of Rochester, revived the campaign in the last years of Queen Anne's reign.[9]

Vane and Dering both proposed schemes to modify episcopal government through regional or county commissions, Dering's each with a 'bishop', 'overseer' or 'moderator' as president, Vane's, more radically, with lay and clerical membership.[10] Numerous proposals from the years of the Restoration to the early eighteenth century are characterised by many overlaps and some inconsistencies but boil down to four proposals worth reporting. One of them, designed, possibly, to improve the quality of officials, was restriction of judicial appointments to no more than one life, presumably removing reversions of offices to families or descendants but, by leaving life appointments, a rather marginal proposal.[11] Another, to tackle corruption by public display of fees, was hardly original – it had been a requirement since at least 1604 – and was somewhat naïve at best, at worst suspiciously disingenuous.[12] Yet another, to speed proceedings, put forward a limit of four terms for completing a case but, lacking any means to achieve the target, the proposal was destined to remained an aspiration.[13]

Excommunication, the fourth issue, arose most frequently in the documents. The proposal from Jenkins, that excommunication should be made in writing, was purely administrative.[14] Jenkins and Sheldon, more positively, expressed concerns in an identical phrase about the use of excommunication 'upon slight matters' and Hale, venturing the possibility of 'some other penalty ... for smaller offences', continued in this more moderate, if vague, tone.[15] Another proposal, from Jenkins, Sancroft, Stillingfleet and Atterbury, *mutatis mutandis*, concerned people who refused to pay church rate or court fees. They were no longer to face the procedure *de excommunicato capiendo* but instead a writ *de contumaci capiendo*. They would, thus, escape excommunication and be pronounced in contempt, which meant the penalties were less severe (they could still expect a church burial, for example); but the distinction appears technical, the ultimate destination – prison – was the same and the list of other offences which could trigger an excommunication remained as fearsome as ever.[16] It is difficult to see how such proposals would have 'revolutionised the church courts',[17] while it is only too clear that they had fired all round the target but missed the bullseye.

It would be anachronistic to expect machinery on 'advisory, conciliation and arbitration' lines in the seventeenth century but the Litany, for example, with its pleas for mercy and the parable of the prodigal son, with its stress on forgiveness, were as much a part of the Christian message in the seventeenth century as in the twentieth. There seems to have been a stark mismatch, however, between prayers and sermons in church services, on the one hand, and excommunication in the church courts, on the other, in the earlier century. The disjunction was recognised by at least one seventeenth-century thinker and writer, Richard Baxter, and though he was *parti pris*, having lost a parish and having suffered imprisonment, he challenged excommunication and put the stress on repentance and forgiveness when he wrote, for example, 'true Excommunication ... supposeth due means to convince the Person that his words and deeds are sin ... and that he be heard ... admonished and earnestly persuaded to repent; and not Excommunicated till after all this he continue impenitent'.[18]

The men in the 'command module' were often past their best. It took a long time, inevitably, to reach such heights. The Restoration is noticeable for 'leadership' by ageing bishops in the dioceses of this study, and Duppa, Fleetwood and Creighton were all in their 70s when they took charge respectively of Winchester, Worcester and Wells. Others, in an age without church commissioners or pension plans, clung to office and income – Thornborough of Worcester and Morley of Winchester into their 80s and Peirs of Wells until he was 90.[19] Atterbury, at the other extreme, seems to have had too much aggression to make headway with reform. Numerous church court personnel, to compound the problem, enjoyed appointments for life and had a vested interest in the *ancien régime*. Some of these latter attitudes were clearly exposed in the largely blocking response of 'judges and advocates' – one of whom was Dean of the Court of Arches, no less – to the remit they had received from Sheldon in 1668 to consider a gamut of reforms.[20] In this sense, the Interregnum had been not long enough to allow these men to retire or die and make way for new, reforming officials, and greed and sloth – standard obstacles to change – were allowed free rein to abort and strangle any threat to their interests.[21]

Two other developments at this time may have helped to undermine the reform programme. The first was the surrender of separate clerical taxation in 1664.[22] Convocation had been automatic when Parliament met but was henceforth redundant politically – it never met from 1664 to 1689 – and the clergy had lost not only opportunities for contact and debate but also their necessary (financial) bargaining power to move the wheels of King and Parliament and get things done. The other factor lay in the attempts at a religious settlement between Anglicans and Presbyterians during the reign of Charles II.[23] Conferences and bills about church unity, at the very least, turned attention away from 'lesser matters' such as church courts and, worse, by provoking fierce arguments and generating an atmosphere of distrust and bitterness, they dashed all hope of cooperation and reform.[24]

The reform programme failed, whatever the reasons, and the church courts were left with all their inherent and systemic failings, among them excommunication, compurgation, penance, class and fees, which have all been identified by other historians and fully discussed in relation to the archdeaconries and deaneries of this study. It must be acknowledged that the ecclesiastical system had suffered these afflictions for centuries and, if they had weakened the courts, they had not killed them. Failure to complete business often arose for good reason, such as the need to wait for further inquiry, testimony from ministers and churchwardens, transfer from summary *ex officio mero* to the more detailed *ex officio promoto* proceedings and, of course, illness and even death.[25] The courts of the three archdeaconries could be relenting and merciful on occasion. Relaxing compurgation, permitting arbitration, allowing private penance, commuting penance and waiving fees can all be found in the court books of Winchester, Worcester and Wells,[26] and elsewhere.[27] Finally, some of the work of the courts, in particular punishment of bastardy, enjoyed widespread support among ratepayers.[28]

Many of these failings were, no doubt, as bad – or worse – in the secular courts, yet the latter survived while the church courts declined. It is possible that higher standards were applied by 'the general public' to courts overseen by bishops and their officials than to the secular courts. Both the spiritual and the secular courts were more probably, in truth, disliked in equal measure; but at least the secular courts dealt with theft and murder, for example, fulfilling acceptable and necessary functions, whereas the church courts focused on personal behaviour – adultery and fornication – and were bound to appear intrusive and cause resentment.

It was a slightly different story with instance business. Reputation and standing in the community lay at the heart of defamation actions while finance, livelihoods and inheritance were critical in disputes about marriage, tithe and wills. These were the staples of instance business in the consistory courts. People at large – laymen and women – brought these actions, not the Church, because the outcome mattered to them. This is why the legal records were usually much larger for instance than for *ex officio* business: at Worcester, for example, in the 1610s *ex officio* business for five years covered 880 pages, while instance business for two of those years devoured 1,080.[29] This further explains why the church courts of the three dioceses, and elsewhere, no doubt, continued to deliberate into the eighteenth and nineteenth centuries. Instance business, not *ex officio* work, kept the consistory courts alive.

Two decisive blows struck the whole apparatus of church courts in the seventeenth century: the upheavals of the 1640s which abolished the bishops and, with them, their consistory courts; and the Toleration Act of 1689. After 14 years of absence, the church courts were restored but without the *ex officio* oath and, on paper, at least, without compurgation, and they never truly regained their authority at the Restoration. Toleration had the immediate effect of depriving them of much of their work and, in the long run, the emergence of ideas of conscience as the basis for religion began to encourage similar views about social freedoms.

The Church suffered, otherwise, a long war of attrition which proved more deadly than the many failings of the system. The Reformation brought religious divisions and, at the same time, population growth and harvest failure intensified the social problems of bastardy and vagrancy. These were matters of conviction and conscience to some, but the common denominator and central concern of the 'establishment' – King, Parliament, gentry and merchants – was security. Act after Act from Elizabethan Uniformity to the Clarendon Code transferred enforcement of church attendance, recusants, dissenters, licences and conventicles to secular magistrates. A string of poor laws did the same for misbehaviour, drunkenness, vagrancy and bastardy. These had been very much the business of the church courts but the preference of government, politicians and lawyers for magistrates and judges, with their greater powers, increased the role of the secular judicial system at the expense of ecclesiastical justice, and the process continued into Georgian and Victorian times.

Evan Davies, Anne Tarver and William Jacob are three historians who take a more optimistic view, insisting on the vitality of the courts they have examined, but all three suffer from considerable limitations. The optimism of Davies about the courts of Worcester and Chichester applies only to the 1660s, 1670s and 1680s and not beyond.[30] Tarver claims business was 'buoyant' at Lichfield, but the number of *ex officio* cases appears to have been minute in an adult population of at least 140,000.[31] Jacob asserts similarly, the 'busyness' of the ecclesiastical courts, but this turns out to be confined to a handful of locations during the first half of the eighteenth century.[32] None of the three is able to deny decline in the end and all three acknowledge the collapse of *ex officio* business: Davies, whether religious or moral, whether at Chichester or Worcester, from 1689; Tarver and Jacob by the late eighteenth and early nineteenth centuries.[33] What is lacking, more importantly, in all three cases, however, is perspective. They all begin their studies after the Restoration of 1660 or the Revolution of 1688–9 and their conclusions essentially lack the wider – and more telling – perspective which would have come from comparisons with court activity before the upheavals of the 1640s and 1650s. The last two, Tarver and Jacob, must leave historians wondering, moreover, why, if the church courts were so effective and popular in the eighteenth century, their role was to be truncated, their golden age terminated, so shortly afterwards.[34]

Very little doubt can remain, in light of the foregoing analysis, about the state of *ex officio* proceedings in the consistory courts of the three dioceses of Winchester, Worcester and Wells by the end of the seventeenth century. There is nothing particularly new or astonishing about the argument. Several voices expressed concerns on the floor of the House of Commons in 1668, for example, according to the reports of John Milward MP and John Nicholas, Clerk to the Privy Council.[35] The damning comments of Gilbert Burnet about the state of the church courts – 'oppressing the people', 'dilatory', 'fraudulent', as well as their 'expense' and 'corruption' – were quoted earlier, and he appears to despair of reform.[36] A string of historians – Ralph Houlbrooke, Martin Ingram, Martin Jones, William Marshall, Brian Outhwaite, Donald Spaeth, Barry Till and Anne Whiteman – all believe the church courts were eclipsed during the seventeenth and eighteenth centuries.[37] This study, concentrating on the seventeenth century as a whole and its aftermath, merely confirms – and gives more force to – their view. By the late seventeenth century decline was steep in *ex officio* cases and similarly in instance business but, while *ex officio* prosecutions all but disappear at Winchester and Wells by the 1680s and were clearly waning at Worcester by the 1690s, instance work continued, albeit in shrunken form, into the eighteenth century in all three dioceses and, certainly at Winchester, even into the nineteenth century.[38] Nor were the church courts alone in their decline: civil actions in the secular courts, from London to Newcastle and from Bristol to Kings Lynn, suffered a parallel fate between 1650 and 1750.[39]

The consistory courts of the three archdeaconries were hardly flourishing at the beginning of the seventeenth century and the courts of Winchester and Wells seem to have ceased to operate, at least in *ex officio* terms, after the 1670s and 1680s. Court books for the two dioceses may simply be missing, but the trends in surviving documents are clearly – and steeply – downwards. There was still apparently some *ex officio* life in the court at Worcester in the late seventeenth and early eighteenth centuries, but, again, comparison with the 1610s is striking and there can be no doubt that the scale of its work was considerably reduced overall by the 1690s. Its business was narrowing, largely confined to moral cases, and even with these business was shrinking and nowhere near the scale of the 1610s.

This can only mean that the role of the Church in society, certainly the extent and nature of its control over morals and religious belief and practice, was retreating as well. The archidiaconal courts would have strengthened the impact of the Church somewhat, a point made several times in the course of this analysis, and there were other agents of control – quarter sessions and 'internal' mechanisms – which would have 'regulated' the morals and religion of the communities. These 'alternatives' and the overall condition of society are enormous subjects in themselves and this study cannot hope to provide a truly comprehensive survey of the state of society and who or what was responsible for it. It can only contribute to a final tally to be made in light of future research. It is enough here to say that considerable change had been wrought over politics and society in the course of the hundred years or so in question. Both were very different from the 1610s and 1620s by the end of the seventeenth century and these developments had a massive – damaging – effect on the church courts, their nature and their extent.

As it was, the role of the church courts, certainly their *ex officio* disciplinary work, was contracting drastically in the later seventeenth and early eighteenth centuries and by the 1830s a Royal Commission on the Ecclesiastical Courts revealed that the total number of *ex officio* cases nationally was 50. There were no such cases at Winchester, Worcester or Wells.[40]

Notes

1   E.g. Jones, 'Oxford and Peterborough', p. 246; Outhwaite, *Ecclesiastical Courts*, p. 85; Sykes, *Sheldon to Secker*, pp. ix, x, 19, 188; Till, *Church Courts*, pp. 7–8; Whiteman, 'Re-establishment', pp. 112, 130 (general), 117, 119 (courts).
2   Canons 134, 136 and 138 (1604); see e.g. Bray, *Anglican Canons*.
3   Tanner, *Constitutional Documents*, p. 56; Gardiner, *Constitutional Documents*, p. 137.
4   Milton, 'Of Reformation'; Hickeringill, 'Test or Tryal'.
5   Shaw, *English Church*, vol. 1, p. 92.
6   For Jenkins, Bodl, Tanner 315, ff. 66 ('postilld with Sir L. Jenkins his own Hand and endorst with the Bps Hand'), 102 ('postilld with Sir L. Jenkins's hand'), 109 ('Sir L.J.' – his work? his hand?). For Hale, Bodl, B. 14. 15. Linc., pp. 11, 13 ('contrived and formed by Math. Hale', p. 8).
7   Bodl, Addit. MS c. 308, f. 114 (Sheldon – no name – but 'Lambeth House'); Sykes credits Sancroft and quotes Tanner 300, f. 143 (Sykes, *Sheldon to Secker*, pp. 188–9); but Jones relegates him to annotations of Sheldon's efforts (Jones, 'Oxford and Peterborough', p. 247).
8   LPL, MS 1743, pp. 111–8 (Stillingfleet), pp. 151–4 (Tillotson); there are no dates but both are given their titles ('Bishop' and 'Archbishop'), which implies the 1690s.
9   LPL, MS 929, no. 107; the index gives the date '1713' and Gareth Bennett links the bill to Atterbury (Bennett, 'Convocation of 1710', p. 316).
10 Shaw, *English Church*, vol. 1, p. 92.
11 Bodl, Tanner 300, f. 143; Tanner 315, ff. 98, 102.
12 Bodl, Tanner 315, ff. 66, 88.
13 Bodl, Tanner 315, f. 75.
14 Bodl, Tanner 315, f. 66.
15 Bodl, Tanner 315, f. 88 (Jenkins); Bodl, Addit. MS c. 308, f. 114 (Sheldon? from 'Lambeth House'); Bodl, B. 14. 15. Linc., p. 13 (Hale).
16 Bodl, Tanner 280, f. 189; Tanner 300, f. 143; Tanner 315, ff. 98, 102, 109; LPL, MS 929, documents 107, 119; Bennett implies the change was an improvement but Outhwaite condemns its introduction in 1813 (Bennett, 'Convocation of 1710', p. 316; Outhwaite, *Ecclesiastical Courts*,

pp. 103, 128); see also Jones's comment that reforms, producing more robust courts, might have precipitated an earlier downfall (Jones, 'Oxford and Peterborough', p. 250).

17 Entry on Stillingfleet *ODNB*.
18 Baxter, 'English Nonconformity', p. 106.
19 For all these bishops, see e.g. Foster, *Alumni Oxonienses*; Venn, *Alumni Cantagrigienses*, *ODNB*.
20 Bodl, Tanner 315, f. 88.
21 Whiteman, 'Re-establishment', pp. 120, 129–30; Jones, 'Oxford and Peterborough', p. 246.
22 For conflicting views on the surrender see Sykes, *Sheldon to Secker*, pp. 41–3; Hutton, *Restoration*, p. 213; Outhwaite, *Ecclesiastical Courts*, p. 85.
23 See e.g. Thomson, *Bishop Morley*, pp. 13, 50, 54, 55, 56, 60, 90 (bills); 41–5, 46–7 (conferences).
24 See e.g. Thomson, 'Dissenters and Recusants', pp. 86, 88, 89, 95, 106; Thomson, *Bishop Morley*, pp. 42, 46–7; Keeble and Nuttall, *Correspondence of Richard Baxter*, items 1034, 1093.
25 E.g. WRO, 802 2760 (1610s), f. 211v (Allames/inquiry); f. 227r (Fitter/evidence); f. 277v. (Rowson/testimony of a minister); f. 288r (Cooke/testimony of churchwardens); f. 273v (Steward/to hear the will of the court); f. 160r (Weaver/to observe further proceedings); f. 227r (Andros/*aegrotat*); f. 320r (Perks/death); SHLS, D/D/ca/224 (1621), f. 113v (Harvie/*promoto*).
26 E.g. HRO, C1/35, f. 14v (compurgation), f. 17v (arbitration); f. 14v (private penance), f. 1r (commuting penance); f. 3v (sentencing); f. 7r (fees).
27 For Sabbath working and marriage problems, Carlson, *Marriage*, pp. 146, 152; for compurgation, Ingram, *Church Courts*, p. 33; for arbitration, Houlbrooke, *Church Courts*, p. 271; for commutation, Houlbrooke, *Church Courts*, pp. 47, 278; Ingram, *Church Courts*, p. 57; Marchant, *Church under Law*, pp. 138, 139; for fees, Houlbrooke, *Church Courts*, p. 51; Marchant, *Church under Law*, pp. 142, 228, 231, 235; Potter, 'Canterbury', p. 115.
28 Houlbrooke, *Church Courts*, pp. 47, 263; Ingram, *Church Courts*, pp. 10, 17, 31, 83.
29 WRO, 802 2760 (1613–18); 790 011 2513 9 (1614–16).
30 Davies, 'Religious Uniformity', Abstract I, p. 1; Abstract II, pp. 3–4.
31 Tarver, 'Lichfield and Coventry', pp. 9, 412, ('buoyant'), 129, 154, 437–8 (decline of *ex officio* cases); this information illustrates, again, the difficulty of ensuring exact comparability: her figures exclude church rate and churchwardens' accounts but include perjury and *promoto* cases, while mine are the opposite in all four respects; Whiteman, *Compton Census*, Appendix A, p. lxxxiii.
32 Jacob, *Lay People*, pp. 135–7; Jacob, 'Love and Charity', pp. 205 ('busyness'), 207–8 (handful).
33 Davies, 'Religious Uniformity', Abstract II, pp. 3, 4; his 'methodology' – different years, lengths of time and classifications of charges, inclusion or not of *promoto* cases, the way of calculating percentages – produces different figures from mine but they agree, in the main, about the trend; Jacob, 'Love and Charity', pp. 205, 212; Tarver, 'Lichfield and Coventry', p. 154 (*ex officio* 1810–29).
34 Instance business underwent statutory abolition in the nineteenth century, e.g. 6 + 7 W IV c.71; 18 + 19 Vic c.41; 20 + 21 Vic c.77; 20 + 21 Vic c.85; this was in addition to demolitions of *ex officio* business.
35 Robbins, *Diary of John Milward*, pp. 191, 215, 218, 222; BL, Egerton MS 2539, f. 168r (Nicholas).
36 See the section 'Attendance' in Chapter 1; Foxcroft, *Supplement to Burnet's History*, pp. 331, 503.
37 Houlbrooke, *Church Courts*, pp. 262, 263, 266, 267, 269, 270; Ingram, *Church Courts*, pp. 368–73; Jones, 'Oxford and Peterborough', pp. 65, 83, 91–8, 234–6; Marshall, 'Hereford and Oxford', pp. 74–7; Outhwaite, *Ecclesiastical Courts*, p. 83; Spaeth, *Church in Danger*, pp. 59–64; Till, *Church Courts*, p. 30; Whiteman, 'Re-establishment', p. 120.
38 A study of the consistory court books shows that instance business at Winchester fell by more than four-fifths in the period 1620–80 (HRO, C2/44; C2/85).
39 Champion, 'Recourse to Law', p. 179.
40 Outhwaite, *Ecclesiastical Courts*, p. 84.

Appendix 1
Diocesan chancellors

Table 1. Winchester

Name	Dates	Documentation
RIDLEY Thomas	9/1596–by 4/1628	Start
		HRO, 11M59/A3/1/2, f. 19r Note: Joint appointment of Ridley LLD+Saye LLB VG 'con et div' 9/1596; but mistaken? see e.g. HRO, 21M65/C2/29, p. 1, Ridley LLD VG OP + Saye LLB Surrogate 4/1596.
		End: Ridley's terminal date rests on the date of Mason's appointment
MASON Robert	4/1628–by 7/1662	Start
		HRO, 11M59/A3/1/2, f. 19r, Mason LLD VG OP 4/1628, a reference to him
		HRO, DC/B5/8, f. 10r, Mason LLD VG 4/1628, endorsement of his appointment
		End
		HRO, 21M65 C2/72, Mason LLD VG, 31/5/1662, no folios, last reference
		HRO, 21M65/A1/32, f. 37r, Mason LLD predecessor of Bramston 7/1662, patent, last reference
BRAMSTON Mondeford	7/1662–by 10/1679	Start
		HRO, 21M65/A1/32, f. 37r, Bramston LLD VG OP, 7/1662, patent
		End
		HRO, 21M65/C2/84, Bramston LLD, 3/10/1679, no folios, last reference

MORLEY Charles	10/1679–by 8/1698	Start
		HRO, DC/B5/11, f. 60v, Morley LLB Chancellor VG 10/1679, endorsement
		End
		HRO, 11M59/A3/1/2, f. 18r, Peter Mews LLB VG OP 8/1698, first reference

Notes:

Dates: these are the dates of starting and ending in office; 'by' = evidence for a precise date is missing.

Putative chancellors of Winchester:

William Saye: J. Foster claims, without evidence, that Saye was chancellor but whether of the cathedral or the consistory court is not clear (Foster, *Alumni Oxonienses*; a reference in the patent (HRO, 11M59/A3/1/2, ff. 18–19) for Mews mentions the appointment of Ridley and Saye jointly and severally; and Saye appears as VG+OP (HRO, C1/28). Saye was, on the other hand, only LLB (but then so were Morley and Mews); joint appointment is exceptional; he appears as surrogate of Ridley in other books (e.g. HRO, C1/26, p. 23); the note in the patent for Mews was written 100 years later.

William Meyricke: Levack, *Civil Lawyers*, p. 255 suggests his appointment 'perhaps' in 1632; but he was described as 'commissary' in 1631 and 1633 (LMA, DW/VB1, HRO, B1/32); Mason was still described as Chancellor in HRO, B1/33 (1636).

William Turner: Foster and Wood both claim he was chancellor (Foster, *Alumni Oxonienses*; Wood, *Athenae Oxonienses*, vol. 1, Fasti, column 270); but the only reference in the court books gives him as surrogate (HRO, C1/29/1, f. 11v).

Table 2. Worcester

Name	Dates	Documentation
GORCHE Barnaby	*c.* 2/1611–*c.*2/1618	Start
		WRO, 794 011 2513 7 (instance book), p. 320, Gorche LLD VG OP 2/1611, first reference
		End
		WRO, 794 011 2513 10, p. 509, Gorche LLD VG OP 2/1618, last reference
HELME Christopher	2–3/1618–1628?	Start
		WRO, 794 011 2513 10, p. 527, Helme 'Offilis', later LLD VG OP 3/1618, first reference
		End
		WRO, 794 011 2513 12, p. 935 7/1626, Helme LLD, previously LLD VG OP, last reference
LITTLETON James	by 5/1628–1646?	Start
		WRO, 794 011 2513 13 p. 25, Littleton LLB VG OP 5/1628, first reference
		End
		WRO, 794 011 2513 17, p. 458, Littleton LLD VG OP 6?/1646, last reference
BALDWYN Timothy	1/1661–by 7/1696	Start
		WRO, 716 093 2648 10 iii, p. 10 or f. 5v, Baldwyn LLD VG OP 1/1661, patent
		End: see Price below
PRICE John	7/1696–6/1705	Start
		WRO, 716 093 2648 10 iii, p. 122 or f. 61v, John Price LLB VG OP 7/1696, patent
		End
		Robertson, *Diary of Francis Evans*, p. 110, death, 12/6/1705; Worcester Cathedral Library, A 77, f. 11r, appointment of successor, 27/6/1705

APPENDICES 189

Table 3. Wells

Name	Dates	Documentation
DUCK Arthur	by 7/1616–1640s?	Start
		SHLS, D/D/ca/199, f. 268r, Duck LLD VG OP 16/07/1616, first reference
		End
		SHLS, D/D/ca/334, f. 138v, Duck LLD VG OP 03/07/1641, last reference; death 1648 e.g. *ODNB*
PEIRCE Edmund	by 11/1662–1667 or 1668	Start
		SHLS, D/D/ca/337, no folios, Peirce milit LLD VG OP 11/11/1662, first reference
		End
		SHLS, D/D/ca/346, no folios, Peirce milit LLD VG OP 30/07/1667, last reference
DEANE Henry	by 1/1668–12/1672	Start
		SHLS, D/D/ca/346, no folios, Deane LLD VG OP 28/01/1668, first reference
		End
		SHC, D/D/ca/351, no folios, Deane LLD VG OP ??/03/1672, last reference
BAYLIE John	by 4/1673–?/1689?	Start
		SHLS, D/D/ca/353, no folios, Baylie LLB VG OP 08/04/1673, first reference
		End
		SHLS, D/D/ca/363, no folios, 7/11/1688, last appearance (in the archdeacon's court)
		SHLS, D/D/ca/365, no folios, William Hughes VG OP 20/10/1690 (other references include LLB), first appearance

Note:

To illustrate the traps – or, at least, the potentials for misunderstanding – Thomas Holt is referred to as chancellor several times in 1663–4 (SHLS, D/D/ca/337, 341); the confusion is clarified, for once, in Ken's register (D/D/B Reg 23, f. 9r) where Holt is identified as cathedral chancellor not consistory court chancellor – and see Horn, *Fasti 1541–1857*, vol. 5, p. 13.

Appendix 2
The nature of Church discipline

Table 1. Charges against the laity: Winchester: morals

	Sbm	Marriage	Incont	Bastardy	Harbour	Incest
1619	4	9	27	42	1	2
1621	2	0	38	18	1	0
1623	8	2	26	20	3	0
Total	14	11	91	80	5	2
Average	5	4	30	27	2	1
%	2%	1%	12%	11%	1%	0%
1663	4	1	5	4	0	0
%	7%	2%	9%	7%	0%	0%
1678	0	0	0	0	0	0
1680	0	0	0	0	0	0
1681	0	0	0	0	0	0
Total	0	0	0	0	0	0
Average	0	0	0	0	0	0
%	0%	0%	0%	0%	0%	0%

Notes:

Abbreviations: 'Sbm' = sex before marriage; 'Marriage' = any irregularities to do with marriage; 'Incont' = sexual incontinence (fornication and adultery); 'Harbour' = harbouring or giving shelter and succour to unmarried pregnant women

Numbers: these are of charges laid against the laity – not precise numbers of men and women, some of whom faced several charges.

Percentages: these are of all charges (moral, religious and church rate) against the laity.

Table 2. Charges against the laity: Worcester: morals

	Sbm	Marriage	Incont	Bastardy	Harbour	Incest
1613	7	47	28	27	6	1
1614	3	31	64	20	6	1
1615	6	19	64	50	5	5
Total	16	97	156	97	17	7
Average	5	32	52	32	6	2
%	2%	12%	20%	12%	2%	1%
1661	8	2	21	24	1	13
%	9%	2%	22%	26%	1%	14%
1675	0	5	5	7	0	0
1678	4	2	5	1	0	0
1680	4	12	3	2	0	0
Total	8	19	13	10	0	0
Average	3	6	4	3	0	0
%	9%	22%	15%	11%	0%	0%

Table 3. Charges against the laity: Wells: morals

	Sbm	Marriage	Incont	Bastardy	Harbour	Incest
1618	6	9	52	42	3	0
1621	10	5	58	29	2	0
1624	24	6	84	48	2	0
Total	40	20	194	119	7	0
Average	13	7	65	40	2	0
%	7%	3%	33%	20%	1%	0%
1633	11	12	52	8	2	1
1637	2	0	18	20	0	0
1640	8	3	30	29	0	0
Total	21	15	100	57	2	1
Average	7	5	33	19	1	0
%	6%	5%	31%	18%	1%	0%
1663	0	8	1	1	0	3
%	0%	53%	7%	7%	0%	20%
1671	1	6	3	5	0	1
1673	0	6	0	0	0	0
1675	0	2	0	3	0	0
Total	1	14	3	8	0	1
Average	0	5	1	3	0	0
%	0%	50%	10%	30%	0%	0%

Table 4. Charges against the laity: Winchester: religion

	Ch attend	Work	Play	Comm	Bapt	Rec	Dissent	St excom	Abuse
1619	17	14	5	114	0	1	5	17	17
1621	17	7	0	19	1	1	0	14	6
1623	22	21	19	81	0	0	0	23	6
Total	56	42	24	214	1	2	5	54	29
Average	19	14	8	71	0	1	2	18	10
%	7%	6%	3%	28%	0%	0%	1%	7%	4%
1663	35	0	0	4	2	0	0	0	0
%	63%	0%	0%	7%	4%	0%	0%	0%	0%
1678	3	0	0	1	0	0	7	0	0
1680	8	0	0	8	0	0	5	0	0
1681	2	0	0	0	0	16	0	0	0
Total	13	0	0	9	0	16	12	0	0
Average	4	0	0	3	0	5	4	0	0
%	25%	0%	0%	18%	0%	31%	24%	0%	0%

Notes:

Abbreviations: 'Ch attend' = church attendance; 'Work/Play' = on the Sabbath; 'Comm' = communion; 'Bapt' = baptism; 'Rec' = recusant, usually Catholic; 'Dissent' = Protestant non-conformists (e.g. Anabaptists, Quakers, sectaries, separatists); 'St excom' = standing excommunicate; Abuse – e.g. misbehaviour in church or churchyard.

Numbers and percentages: see note under Table 1. Charges against the laity: Winchester: morals.

Table 5. Charges against the laity: Worcester: religion

	Ch attend	Work	Play	Comm	Bapt	Rec	Dissent	St excom	Abuse
1613	4	47	22	6	0	1	0	9	19
1614	9	67	20	17	3	2	0	3	4
1615	13	54	25	18	0	0	0	21	20
Total	26	168	67	41	3	3	0	33	43
Average	9	56	22	14	1	1	0	11	14
%	3%	22%	9%	5%	0%	0%	0%	4%	5%
1661	0	9	4	0	0	0	0	0	0
%	0%	10%	4%	0%	0%	0%	0%	0%	0%
1675	9	0	0	0	0	0	0	4	2
1678	0	0	0	0	0	0	1	0	0
1680	2	1	0	5	0	0	4	1	2
Total	11	1	0	5	0	0	5	5	4
Average	4	0	0	2	0	0	2	2	1
%	13%	0%	0%	6%	0%	0%	6%	6%	5%

Table 6. Charges against the laity: Wells: religion

	Ch attend	Work	Play	Comm	Bapt	Rec	Dissent	St excom	Abuse
1618	10	24	13	1	0	0	0	1	17
1621	6	9	11	0	0	0	0	0	12
1624	17	17	41	2	0	0	0	0	19
Total	33	50	65	3	0	0	0	1	48
Average	11	17	22	1	0	0	0	0	16
%	6%	9%	11%	1%	0%	0%	0%	0%	8%
1633	5	3	12	1	0	0	0	9	9
1637	4	21	10	0	0	0	0	11	7
1640	2	5	3	0	0	0	0	0	2
Total	11	29	25	1	0	0	0	20	18
Average	4	10	8	0	0	0	0	7	6
%	3%	9%	8%	0%	0%	0%	0%	6%	6%
1663	1	0	0	0	0	0	0	0	0
%	7%	0%	0%	0%	0%	0%	0%	0%	0%
1671	0	0	0	0	0	0	0	3	1
1673	0	0	0	0	0	0	0	0	0
1675	0	0	0	0	0	0	0	0	0
Total	0	0	0	0	0	0	0	3	1
Average	0	0	0	0	0	0	0	1	0
%	0%	0%	0%	0%	0%	0%	0%	10%	0%

Table 7. Comparison of communion charges

	MT	E+T terms
Winchester		
1623–4	81	16
1680–1	8	8
Worcester		
1614–15	17	8
1678–9	0	0
Wells		
1624–5	2	1
1674–5	43	0

Notes:

Abbreviations: MT = Michaelmas term; E+T terms = Easter and Trinity terms.

Sources: Winchester, HRO, C1/35, C1/45; Worcester, WRO, 807 2760, 7940 011 2722 2 Book 32; Wells, SHLS D/D/ca/ 243, 254.

Uncertain 'provenance': Worcester, 807 2760 'Extract 1614' appears twice in the middle of proceedings for 1615 (ff. 276v, 403r) but, because the meaning of 'Extract' is not clear and the dates conflict, communion charges in these sections have been ignored.

Overlapping accused people: particularly a problem at Winchester 1623–4 where 11 of the 16 accused of 1624 were among the 81 of 1623, their cases presumably still unresolved by 1624, and therefore only five were new cases.

Large numbers: at Winchester Easter and Trinity terms 1681 a further 14 were named, without specific charge, but all were from the Catholic household of the Tichborne family and likely to have been communion offenders – not counted, as all figures in this study are 'actual' and not 'speculative'; at Wells the 43 of Michaelmas term 1674 represent, apparently, a massive purge at Broadway in Taunton Archdeaconry.

Types of communion offence: Excluded: at Winchester Easter and Trinity terms 1624, three (an incumbent and two churchwardens) for failing to arrange a communion service at Christmas 1623; at Wells, likewise, in Easter and Trinity terms 1625 the churchwarden of Huish Champflower was accused of failing to provide wine.

Included: at Worcester Michaelmas term 1614 numerous of the 17 for sitting or standing to receive or going to the wrong church.

Table 8. Charges against the laity: church rate

Winchester		Worcester		Wells	
1619	12	1613	0	1618	3
1621	44	1614	3	1621	0
1623	69	1615	4	1624	0
Average	42	Average	2	Average	1
%	17%	%	1%	%	1%
				1633	15
				1637	6
				1640	3
				Average	8
				%	7%
1663	1	1661	0	1663	1
%	2%	%	0%	%	6%
1678	0	1675	7	1671	0
1680	1	1678	0	1673	0
1681	0	1680	0	1675	0
Average	0	Average	2	Average	0
%	2%	%	8%	%	0%

Notes:

Percentages are of all lay charges in a particular year.

Vagueness of some of the charges: e.g. 'deteyning monie from the Church'; 'deteyning 24 shillings due to the church' (HRO, C1/33, 3/12/1619; 12/11/1619 no folios).

Inclusion, for convenience, of one or two charges about money but not church rate: e.g. 'for not paying the clerk his dueties' (WRO, 802 2760, f. 329r); 'for deteyning a bull and 4 sheepe from martyrworthy church' (HRO, C1/35, f. 9v).

Table 9. Changing balance of charges

	Winchester	Worcester	Wells
1610s/20s			
Moral	27%	50%	64%
Religious	56%	49%	34%
1670s/80s			
Moral	0%	56%	89%
Religious	98%	35%	11%

Appendix 3
The extent of Church discipline

Table 1. Sessions: Winchester

Plenary				Camera			
1619	1621	1623	Average	1619	1621	1623	Average
6	8	6	7	1	4	8	4
1663				1663			
10			10	14			14
1678	1680	1681		1678	1680	1681	
3	6	1	3	0	0	0	0

Table 2. Sessions: Worcester

Plenary				Camera			
1613	1614	1615	Average	1613	1614	1615	Average
26 (8)	20 (11)	18 (7)	21 (9)	3	1	0	1
1661				1661			
6			6	3			3
1675	1678	1680		1675	1678	1680	
6	7	8	7	0	0	4	1

Notes:

Figures in brackets are the numbers of occasions when a date is a heading – the larger figures, without brackets, are drawn from extra notes attached to many cases. *Camera*: for 1680, four (sessions) is an estimate – three cases appear to have been on one day and the other two may have occurred on separate occasions, making three sessions – all at the bishop's palace – plus one other in the chambers of one of the surrogates (WRO, 794 011 2722 2 Book 32, ff. 158v, 165v, 166r).

Table 3. Sessions: Wells

Plenary				Camera			
1618	1621	1624	Average	1618	1621	1624	Average
13	14	13	13	0	1	8	3
1633	1637	1640		1633	1637	1640	
14	11	13	13	2	3	0	2
1663				1663			
6			6	2			2
1671	1673	1675		1671	1673	1675	
13	3	9	8	2	1	1	1

Table 4. Summons: lay clergy churchwardens: Winchester

1619	1621	1623	Average
406	296	357	353
1663			
683			683
1678	1680	1681	
34	55	16	35

Note:

The numbers in Tables 4–6 are the total numbers summoned to court in each Michaelmas term – each person (lay, churchwarden and clergyman) has been counted once.

Table 5. Summons: lay clergy churchwardens: Worcester

1613	1614	1615	Average
264	275	368	302
1661			
86			86
1675	1678	1680	
63	20	43	42

Table 6. Summons: lay clergy churchwardens: Wells

1618	1621	1624	Average
251	227	307	262
1633	1637	1640	
315	223	159	232
1663			
47			47
1671	1673	1675	
29	10	9	16

Table 7. Response: Winchester

	Present	Absent	?	Total
1619	159	268	108	535
1621	123	309	42	474
1623	184	387	16	587
Average	**155**	**321**	**56**	**532**
%	**29%**	**61%**	**10%**	**100%**
1663	63	1538	34	1635
%	4%	94%	2%	100%
1678	5	42	7	54
1680	11	72	7	90
1681	0	16	0	16
Average	**5**	**43**	**5**	**53**
%	**10%**	**81%**	**9%**	**100%**

Table 8. Response: Worcester

	Present	Absent	?	Total
1613	151	162	23	336
1614	131	217	24	372
1615	142	223	61	426
Average	**141**	**201**	**36**	**378**
%	37%	53%	10%	100%
1661	42	58	10	110
%	38%	53%	9%	100%
1675	18	118	19	155
1678	3	63	2	68
1680	22	94	10	126
Average	**14**	**92**	**10**	**116**
%	**12%**	**79%**	**9%**	**100%**

Table 9. Response: Wells

	Present	Absent	?	Total
1618	107	333	61	501
1621	59	326	48	433
1624	140	411	72	623
Average	102	357	60	519
%	20%	69%	11%	100%
1633	94	669	44	807
1637	69	375	42	486
1640	34	291	36	361
Average	66	445	41	551
%	12%	81%	7%	100%
1663	47	2	0	49
%	96%	4%	0%	100%
1671	10	25	4	39
1673	1	6	3	10
1675	6	7	0	13
Average	6	13	2	21
%	27%	61%	12%	100%

Notes:

Numbers are the totals of people – lay, clerical and churchwardens – summoned.

The mismatch between Tables 4–6 and Tables 7–9 arises because Tables 4–6 enumerate the total numbers of accused people in a particular term while Tables 7–9 record their attendances and absences during the term. In Tables 4–6 each person is counted once and Tables 7–9 record their attendances and absences: e.g. at Winchester, in Michaelmas term 1619, the 'cohort' of people accused was 406 but some were summoned to court two, three and four times, hence the total of 535 in this table.

Attendance *in camera* is included in these figures.

Table 10. Completion of business: Winchester

	Unresolved	Innocence	Guilt	Guilt or Innocence?	Total
1619	248	49	84	25	406
1621	211	19	60	6	296
1623	210	8	115	24	357
Total	669	76	259	55	1,059
Average	223	25	86	18	353
%	63%	7%	24%	5%	100%
1663	647	9	27	0	683
%	95%	1%	4%	0%	100%
1678	24	0	10	0	34
1680	40	0	11	4	55
1681	16	0	0	0	16
Total	80	0	21	4	105
Average	27	0	7	1	35
%	76%	0%	20%	4%	100%

Notes:

Scope: laymen and women, churchwardens and clergymen.

Numbers are of people or outcomes – one outcome (unresolved, innocent, guilty) per person by the end of the Michaelmas term in question – and the few who were guilty of more than one offence have been counted once.

Guilt or Innocence?: these are cases where a conclusion was reached, usually shown by '*dimiss*', but the outcome, or 'verdict', is left unclear – no statement at the end and no indication of guilt or innocence in the account of the proceedings.

Table 11. Completion of business: Worcester

	Unresolved	Innocence	Guilt	Guilt or Innocence?	Total
1613	113	15	119	17	264
1614	147	7	96	25	275
1615	213	19	120	16	368
Total	473	41	335	58	907
Average	158	14	112	19	302
%	52%	5%	37%	6%	100%
1661	52	12	19	3	86
%	60%	14%	22%	3%	100%
1675	52	0	5	6	63
1678	15	0	5	0	20
1680	31	1	10	1	43
Total	98	1	20	7	126
Average	33	0	7	2	42
%	78%	1%	16%	6%	100%

Table 12. Completion of business: Wells

	Unresolved	Innocence	Guilt	Guilt or Innocence?	Total
1618	183	11	52	5	251
1621	148	4	74	1	227
1624	219	14	71	3	307
Total	**550**	**29**	**197**	**9**	**785**
Average	**183**	**10**	**66**	**3**	**262**
%	**70%**	**4%**	**25%**	**1%**	**100%**
1633	268	5	37	5	315
1637	171	1	48	3	223
1640	127	0	31	1	159
Total	566	6	116	9	697
Average	189	2	39	3	232
%	81%	1%	17%	1%	100%
1663	10	2	35	0	47
	21%	4%	74%	0%	100%
1671	21	0	8	0	29
1673	4	0	6	0	10
1675	4	0	5	0	9
Total	29	**0**	19	**0**	48
Average	10	**0**	**6**	**0**	**16**
%	60%	0%	40%	0%	100%

Table 13. Lay guilt: changing balance of verdicts

		Morals	Religion	Rate
1610/20s				
Winchester	Guilty verdicts	10	27	13
	%	21%	53%	26%
Worcester	Guilty verdicts	26	51	0
	%	34%	66%	0%
Wells	Guilty verdicts	14	18	0
	%	44%	56%	0%
1670/80s				
Winchester	Guilty verdicts	0	8	0
	%	0%	100%	0%
Worcester	Guilty verdicts	1	2	0
	%	33%	67%	0%
Wells	Guilty verdicts	3	0	0
	%	100%	0%	0%

Notes:

Scope: laymen and women and not clergy or churchwardens.

Numbers are averages for the three sample Michaelmas terms of each diocese.

Numbers of guilty verdicts and people: there is a fairly close correlation but a few people were found guilty of more than one charge.

Table 14. Lay guilty verdicts: morals

	Sbm	Marriage	Incont	Bastardy
1610/20s				
Winchester	4	1	1	4
	8%	2%	2%	8%
Worcester	2	6	5	11
	2%	8%	7%	14%
Wells	3	2	4	5
	10%	6%	13%	16%
1670s/80s				
Winchester	0	0	0	0
	0%	0%	0%	0%
Worcester	0	1	0	0
	0%	33%	0%	0%
Wells	0	2	0	1
	0%	67%	0%	33%

Notes:

Dates: these are for the three sample Michaelmas terms of the respective dioceses.

Crimes: convictions rates for some crimes are too small or non-existent (e.g. incest or standing excommunicate) and have been omitted.

Numbers: these are averages for the three terms and are of guilty verdicts, not people, which, though much the same, are not identical because a few people were guilty of more than one offence.

Percentages: these reflect the proportions of all convictions including e.g. incest and standing excommunicate and not just the crimes listed in the table.

Abbreviations: Sbm = sex before marriage; Marriage = any irregularities to do with marriage; Incont = sexual incontinence.

Table 15. Lay guilty verdicts: religion

	Ch attend	Work	Play	Comm	Bapt	Rec	Dissent	Abuse
1610s/20s								
Winchester	5	7	5	8	0	0	0	2
	9%	14%	9%	16%	0%	0%	0%	3%
Worcester	3	21	10	7	0	1	0	6
	4%	27%	13%	9%	0%	1%	0%	7%
Wells	3	5	7	1	0	0	0	2
	10%	16%	23%	3%	0%	0%	0%	6%
1670s/80s								
Winchester	3	0	0	2	0	0	3	0
	37%	0%	0%	25%	0%	0%	37%	0%
Worcester	0	0	0	0	0	0	1	1
	0%	0%	0%	0%	0%	0%	33%	33%
Wells	0	0	0	0	0	0	0	0
	0%	0%	0%	0%	0%	0%	0%	0%

Notes:

Date, Crimes, Numbers and Percentages: see Table 14.

Abbreviations: Ch = church; Work/Play = on the Sabbath; Comm = failure to take communion; Bapt = baptism; Rec = recusant, usually Catholic; Dissent = Protestant nonconformists; Abuse = e.g. misbehaviour in church or churchyard.

Table 16. Lay guilty verdicts: church rate

Before 1640	
Winchester 1610s/20s	13
	26%
Worcester 1610s	0
	0%
Wells1610s/20s	0
	0%
After 1660	
Winchester 1670s/80s	0
	0%
Worcester 1670s/80s	0
	0%
Wells 1670s	0
	0%

Appendix 4
Explaining the decline of the courts

Table 1. Sanctions: Winchester

	V et M	Adj	Excomm	Total
1619	0	171	97	268
1621	0	236	73	309
1623	0	261	126	387
Average	0	222	99	321
%	0%	69%	31%	100%
1663	884	525	129	1,538
%	57%	34%	8%	100%
1678	6	22	14	42
1680	17	40	15	72
1681	12	0	4	16
Average	12	21	11	43
%	27%	48%	25%	100%

Notes:

Abbreviations: 'V *et* M' = *viis et modis*; 'Adj' = adjournment; 'Excomm' = excommunication.

Numbers are of orders – *viis et modis*, adjournment or excommunication – issued by the judge in response to absence, not of people (some of whom received more than one *viis*, adjournment or excommunication order).

Table 2. Sanctions: Worcester

	V et M	Adj	Excomm	Total
1613	23	26	113	162
1614	21	86	110	217
1615	18	101	104	223
Average	21	71	109	201
%	10%	35%	55%	100%
1661	18	32	8	58
%	31%	55%	14%	100%
1675	42	50	26	118
1678	2	51	10	63
1680	33	47	14	94
Average	26	49	17	92
%	28%	54%	18%	100%

Table 3. Sanctions: Wells

	V et M	Adj	Excomm	Total
1618	22	216	95	333
1621	29	171	126	326
1624	5	286	120	411
Average	19	224	114	357
%	5%	63%	32%	100%
1633	104	434	131	669
1637	14	296	65	375
1640	8	190	93	291
Average	42	307	96	445
%	9%	69%	22%	100%
1663	0	1	1	2
	0%	50%	50%	100%
1671	9	3	13	25
1673	3	3	0	6
1675	2	5	0	7
Average	5	4	4	13
%	38%	31%	31%	100%

Table 4. Evidence: Winchester

	Confess	Compurg	Inquiry	Arbitration	Testimony	Doc	Nil	Total
1619	16	10	1	0	27	61	291	406
1621	24	12	14	0	6	13	227	296
1623	61	12	11	4	24	8	237	357
Total	101	34	26	4	57	82	755	1,059
Average	**34**	**11**	**9**	**1**	**19**	**27**	**252**	**353**
%	**10%**	**3%**	**2%**	**0%**	**5%**	**8%**	**71%**	**100%**
1663	16	3	0	0	23	2	639	683
	2%	0%	0%	0%	3%	0%	94%	100%
1678	1	0	0	0	0	0	33	34
1680	0	0	0	0	0	0	55	55
1681	0	0	0	0	0	0	16	16
Total	1	0	0	0	0	0	104	105
Average	**0**	**0**	**0**	**0**	**0**	**0**	**35**	**35**
%	**1%**	**0%**	**0%**	**0%**	**0%**	**0%**	**99%**	**100%**

Notes:

Abbreviations: 'Confess' = confession; 'Compurg' = compurgation; 'Doc' = documentary evidence; 'Nil' = no information.
Numbers are of accused people: laymen and women, churchwardens and clergymen.

Table 5. Evidence: Worcester

	Confess	Compurg	Inquiry	Arbitration	Testimony	Doc	Nil	Total
1613	65	10	1	0	2	3	183	264
1614	51	9	0	0	8	9	198	275
1615	73	17	0	0	2	2	274	368
Total	189	36	1	0	12	14	653	907
Average	63	12	0	0	4	5	218	302
%	21%	4%	0%	0%	1%	2%	72%	100%
1661	19	0	3	0	10	3	51	86
%	22%	0%	3%	0%	12%	3%	59%	100%
1675	2	0	0	0	0	4	57	63
1678	0	0	0	0	0	0	20	20
1680	6	1	0	0	5	0	31	43
Total	8	1	0	0	5	4	108	126
Average	3	0	0	0	2	1	36	42
%	6%	1%	0%	0%	4%	3%	86%	100%

Table 6. Evidence: Wells

	Confess	Compurg	Inquiry	Arbitration	Testimony	Doc	Nil	Total
1618	12	4	8	0	15	21	191	251
1621	2	4	18	0	2	27	174	227
1624	14	8	20	0	11	34	220	307
Total	28	16	46	0	28	82	585	785
Average	**9**	**5**	**15**	**0**	**9**	**27**	**195**	**262**
%	4%	2%	6%	0%	4%	10%	75%	100%
1633	5	4	10	0	34	21	241	315
1637	18	5	10	0	4	21	165	223
1640	3	2	8	0	0	10	136	159
Total	26	11	28	0	38	52	542	697
Average	9	4	9	0	13	17	181	232
%	4%	2%	4%	0%	5%	7%	78%	100%
1663	21	0	0	0	9	14	3	47
%	45%	0%	0%	0%	19%	30%	6%	100%
1671	5	1	0	0	0	0	23	29
1673	1	0	0	0	0	0	9	10
1675	3	1	0	0	0	2	3	9
Total	9	2	0	0	0	2	35	48
Average	**3**	**1**	**0**	**0**	**0**	**1**	**12**	**16**
%	**19%**	**4%**	**0%**	**0%**	**0%**	**4%**	**73%**	**100%**

Table 7. Outcome: Winchester

	Warning	Order	Penance	Dismissal	Unresolved	Total
1619	5	44	2	111	244	406
1621	6	24	10	44	212	296
1623	11	44	32	46	224	357
Total	22	112	44	201	680	1,059
Average	7	37	15	67	227	353
%	2%	11%	4%	19%	64%	100%
1663	8	19	8	13	635	683
%	1%	3%	1%	2%	93%	100%
1678	0	11	0	0	23	34
1680	0	9	0	5	41	55
1681	0	0	0	0	16	16
Total	0	20	0	5	80	105
Average	0	7	0	2	27	35
%	0%	19%	0%	5%	76%	100%

Notes:

Groups: the table covers the fates all three groups – laymen and women, churchwardens and clergymen – included in this study.

Numbers are of people or outcomes – one outcome per person.

Distinction between warning and order: warnings, in this study, were prohibitions and therefore negative – not to do something – while orders were positive and required action; the distinction is not always clear, however, and decisions about the category are sometimes arbitrary.

Table 8. Outcome: Worcester

	Warning	Order	Penance	Dismissal	Unresolved	Total
1613	21	18	53	52	120	264
1614	29	23	30	28	165	275
1615	24	21	38	37	248	368
Total	74	62	121	117	533	907
Average	**25**	**21**	**40**	**39**	**178**	**302**
%	**8%**	**7%**	**13%**	**13%**	**59%**	**100%**
1661	10	3	9	7	57	86
%	12%	3%	10%	8%	66%	100%
1675	2	0	3	8	50	63
1678	0	0	1	2	17	19
1680	2	5	2	5	29	43
Total	4	5	6	15	96	125
Average	**1**	**2**	**2**	**5**	**32**	**42**
%	**3%**	**4%**	**5%**	**12%**	**76%**	**100%**

Table 9. Outcome: Wells

	Warning	Order	Penance	Dismissal	Unresolved	Total
1618	0	1	21	39	190	251
1621	5	1	7	30	184	227
1624	0	0	53	59	195	307
Total	5	2	81	128	569	785
Average	2	1	27	43	190	262
%	1%	0%	10%	16%	73%	100%
1633	0	0	10	29	276	315
1637	4	0	40	11	168	223
1640	0	1	25	7	126	159
Total	4	1	75	47	570	697
Average	1	0	25	16	190	232
%	1%	0%	11%	7%	82%	100%
1663	1	12	10	21	3	47
%	2%	26%	21%	45%	6%	100%
1671	0	2	2	2	23	29
1673	0	0	1	0	9	10
1675	0	3	2	0	4	9
Total	0	5	5	2	36	48
Average	0	2	2	1	12	16
%	0%	10%	10%	5%	75%	100%

Appendix 5
The case of Worcester

Table 1. Charges against the laity: morals

	Sbm	Marriage	Incont	Bastardy	Harbour	Incest
1611–12 EKP	7	25	56	46	10	1
1612–13 EKP	20	23	74	45	10	0
1613–14EKP	11	38	35	32	4	0
1614–15 EKP	10	39	39	19	2	0
1615–16 EKP	16	11	42	37	5	3
1616–17 EKP	13	12	57	47	12	3
1617–18 EKP	8	10	35	14	6	0
Total	85	158	338	240	49	7
Average p.a.	12	22	48	34	7	1
%	5%	10%	21%	15%	3%	0%
1690–1 EKP	0	2	0	1	0	0
1691–2 EKP	0	2	6	3	0	2
1692–3 EKP	10	3	12	12	0	4
1693–4 EKP	2	6	16	21	0	1
1694–5 EKP	6	6	1	4	0	0
1695–6 EKP	6	0	0	4	0	2
1696–7 EKP	14	3	15	5	0	1
Total	38	22	50	50	0	10
Average p.a.	5	3	7	7	0	1
%	18%	10%	23%	24%	0%	5%

Notes:

Abbreviations: 'EKP' = Evesham, Kidderminster, Pershore; 'Sbm' = sex before marriage; 'Marriage' = any irregularities to do with marriage; 'Incont' = sexual incontinence (fornication and adultery); 'Harbour' = harbouring (giving shelter and succour to unmarried pregnant women).

Charges/people: these are numbers of charges laid against the laity but not precise numbers of men and women (though nearly so), some of whom faced several charges.

Deaneries and charges: these are the total numbers of charges p.a. for the three deaneries combined.

Percentages: these are out of all charges (moral, religious and church rate) against the laity.

Table 2. Charges against the laity: religion

	Ch attend	Work	Play	Comm	Bapt	Recus	Dissent	St excom	Abuse
1611–12	6	5	57	6	1	0	0	0	9
1612–13	20	22	15	14	9	29	0	44	16
1613–14	11	16	16	18	0	1	0	10	15
1614–15	25	20	6	12	0	2	0	1	2
1615–16	16	45	9	21	0	0	0	16	12
1616–17	7	27	32	8	1	0	0	16	12
1617–18	5	5	19	0	0	0	0	1	5
Total	90	140	154	79	11	32	0	88	71
Average p.a.	13	20	22	11	2	5	0	13	10
%	6%	9%	10%	5%	1%	2%	0%	6%	4%
1690–1	0	0	5	0	0	0	0	0	1
1691–2	0	0	0	0	0	0	0	0	1
1692–3	2	0	0	0	0	0	0	0	0
1693–4	2	0	0	0	0	0	0	0	1
1694–5	0	0	0	0	0	0	0	0	0
1695–6	0	0	0	0	0	0	0	0	0
1696–7	0	0	0	0	0	0	0	0	1
Total	4	0	5	0	0	0	0	0	4
Average p.a.	1	0	1	0	0	0	0	0	1
%	2%	0%	2%	0%	0%	0%	0%	0%	2%

Notes:

Abbreviations: 'Ch attend' = church attendance; 'Work/Play' = on the Sabbath; 'Comm' = communion; 'Bapt' = baptism; 'Rec' = recusant, usually Catholic; 'Dissent' = Protestant nonconformists; 'St excomm' = standing excommunicate.

Charges/people, deaneries, percentages: see notes under Appendix 5, Table 1. Charges against the laity: morals.

Table 3. Charges against the laity: church rate

1611 -12	1612 -13	1613 -14	1614 -15	1615 -16	1616 -17	1617 -18	Total	Av p.a.	%
13	6	6	1	5	18	1	50	7	3

1690 -1	1691 -2	1692 -3	1693 -4	1694 -5	1695 -6	1696 -7	Total	Av p.a.	%
0	1	1	5	15	4	5	31	4	14

Charges/people, deaneries, percentages: see notes under Appendix 5, Table 1. Charges against the laity: morals.

Table 4. Balance of charges

		Morals	Religion	Rate	Total
1610s	Average no. of charges p.a.	125	95	7	227
		55%	42%	3%	100%
1690s	Average no. of charges p.a.	24	2	4	30
		80%	7%	13%	100%

Table 5. Plenary sessions

1611 -12	1612 -13	1613 -14	1614 -15	1615 -16	1616 -17	1617 -18	Average p.a.
37	53	41	47	41	44	41	43

1690 -1	1691 -2	1692 -3	1693 -4	1694 -5	1695 -6	1696 -7	Average p.a.
15	17	16	17	16	14	17	16

Table 6. *In camera*

1611 -12	1612 -13	1613 -14	1614 -15	1615 -16	1616 -17	1617 -18	Average p.a.
3	12	4	2	3	2	0	4

1690 -1	1691 -2	1692 -3	1693 -4	1694 -5	1695 -6	1696 -7	Average p.a.
0	2	3	4	1	2	1	2

Table 7. Balance of sessions 1610s/1690s

	Plenary
1611–18	43
1690–7	16
% Change	63%
	In camera
1611–18	4
1690–7	2
% Change	50%

Notes:

Sources: plenary sessions for the 1690s are laid out at the back of court book WRO, 807 093 2724, Book 38; the remainder – plenary sessions for the 1610s and *in camera* sessions for both periods – are 'reconstructions' from dates in the proceedings (when dates are given) in books 802 2884, 802 2760 and 807 093 2724, Book 38.

Table 8. Summons

	E	K	P	
1611–12	122	50	112	
1612–13	68	94	213	
1613–14	62	101	90	
1614–15	73	80	86	
1615–16	88	60	124	
1616–17	77	76	146	
1617–18	18	18	98	
Total	508	479	869	1,856
1690–1	6	13	15	
1691–2	21	4	14	
1692–3	7	15	40	
1693–4	9	22	43	
1694–5	15	2	23	
1695–6	4	5	16	
1696–7	13	28	39	
Total	75	89	190	354
% Fall				81%

Table 9. Response

	Present	Absent	?	Total
1611–18				
Total	1,071	1,290	174	2,535
Average p.a.	153	184	25	362
% p.a.	42%	51%	7%	100%
1690–7				
Total	218	274	62	554
Average p.a.	31	39	9	79
% p.a.	39%	50%	11%	100%

Table 10. Completion of business

	Unresolved	Innocent	Guilt	G or I?	Total
E 1611–18	33	2	34	4	73
K 1611–18	41	4	20	3	68
P 1611–18	53	11	50	9	124
Total	127	17	104	16	265
%	48%	6%	39%	6%	100%
E 1690–7	4	1	5	1	11
K 1690–7	6	1	4	2	13
P 1690–7	10	1	14	1	26
Total	20	3	23	4	50
%	41%	5%	47%	9%	100%

Notes:

Scope: laymen and women, churchwardens and clergymen.

Numbers are the averages for each of the three deaneries (Evesham, Kidderminster and Pershore) over the seven years of the 1610s and the 1690s; they represent one verdict (unresolved, innocent, guilty) per person in question and the few who were guilty of more than one offence have been counted once for simplicity.

Abbreviations: 'G or I?' = guilt or innocence; the question mark means the case was settled (usually with the word '*dimiss*') but it is not clear whether the person emerged as guilty or innocent from the proceedings.

Table 11. Lay guilt: morals

	Sbm	Marriage	Incont	Bastardy	Harbour	Incest	Total
1611–18							
E 1610s	9	5	6	20	3	1	44
K 1610s	4	20	12	19	2	0	57
P 1610s	31	21	42	46	11	2	153
Total	**44**	**46**	**60**	**85**	**16**	**3**	**254**
%	**8%**	**8%**	**11%**	**16%**	**3%**	**1%**	**46%**
1690–7							
E 1690s	6	8	3	4	0	0	21
K 1690s	7	0	3	6	0	1	17
P 1690s	2	2	8	6	0	4	23
Total	**15**	**10**	**14**	**16**	**0**	**5**	**60**
%	**19%**	**13%**	**18%**	**21%**	**0%**	**6%**	**77%**

Notes:

Abbreviations: 'Sbm' = sex before marriage; 'Marriage' = any irregularities to do with marriage ; 'Incont' = incontinence; 'Harbour' = harbouring (giving shelter and succour to unmarried pregnant women).

Numbers: these are of individual verdicts per offence (a few people were guilty of more than one transgression) for the seven years in each deanery.

Discrepancies arise because of 'whole number' problems.

Percentages are out of all convictions (moral, religious and church rate) against the laity.

Table 12. Lay guilt: religion

	Ch attend	Work	Play	Comm	Bapt	Rec	Dissent	St excom	Abuse	Total
1611–18										
E 1610s	20	18	28	28	1	0	0	7	17	119
K 1610s	2	8	7	2	0	0	0	0	2	21
P 1610s	9	48	32	4	0	2	0	18	22	135
Total	31	74	67	34	1	2	0	25	41	275
%	6%	14%	12%	6%	0%	0%	0%	5%	7%	50%
1690–7										
E 1690s	0	0	0	0	0	0	0	0	0	0
K 1690s	0	0	0	0	0	0	0	0	0	0
P 1690s	0	0	0	0	0	0	0	0	1	1
Total	0	0	0	0	0	0	0	0	1	1
%	0%	0%	0%	0%	0%	0%	0%	0%	1%	1%

Notes:

Abbreviations: 'Ch attend' = church attendance; 'Work' and 'Play' = work and play on the Sabbath; 'Comm' = communion; 'Bapt' = baptism; 'Rec' = recusant, usually Catholic; 'Dissent' = Protestant nonconformists; 'St excom' = standing excommunicate; 'Abuse' = e.g. misbehaviour in church or churchyard.

Numbers, discrepancies, percentages: see Table 11. Lay guilt: morals.

Table 13. Lay guilt: church rate

	E	K	P	Total	%
1610s	12	1	5	18	3%
1690s	1	0	15	16	21%

Table 14. Proportions of lay guilt

	Morality	Religion	Rate	Total
1611–18				
EKP average no. p.a.	254	275	18	547
%	46%	50%	3%	100%
1690–7				
EKP average no. p.a.	60	1	16	77
%	77%	1%	21%	100%

Table 15. Evidence

	Confess	Compurg	Inquiry	Arbit	Test	Doc	Nil info	Total
1611–18								
E	80	13	4	0	9	9	393	508
K	55	19	2	0	16	12	375	479
P	154	64	8	0	54	20	569	869
Total	**289**	**96**	**14**	**0**	**79**	**41**	**1,337**	**1,856**
%	**16%**	**5%**	**1%**	**0%**	**4%**	**2%**	**72%**	**100%**
1690–7								
E	26	2	0	0	0	3	44	75
K	10	2	0	0	10	7	60	89
P	39	3	0	0	5	8	135	190
Total	**75**	**7**	**0**	**0**	**15**	**18**	**239**	**354**
%	**21%**	**2%**	**0%**	**0%**	**4%**	**5%**	**68%**	**100%**

Notes:

Abbreviations: 'Confess' = confession; 'Compurg' = compurgation; 'Arbit' = arbitration; 'Test' = testimony either personal or of a neighbour/friend; 'Doc' = documentary evidence; 'Nil info' = no information.

Numbers are of accused people, laymen and women, churchwardens and clergymen.

Table 16. Outcome

	Warning	Order	Penance	Dismissal	Unresolved	Total
E 1611–18	47	71	71	69	250	508
K 1611–18	11	49	44	55	320	479
P 1611–18	72	67	177	132	421	869
Total	130	187	292	256	991	1856
Average	43	62	97	85	330	619
%	**7%**	**10%**	**16%**	**14%**	**53%**	**100%**
E 1690–7	2	18	16	4	35	75
K 1690–7	0	7	16	19	47	89
P 1690–7	4	38	19	49	80	190
Total	6	63	51	72	162	354
Average	**2**	**22**	**17**	**23**	**54**	**118**
%	**2%**	**18%**	**15%**	**20%**	**45%**	**100%**

Notes:

Scope: the chart covers the fates of all three groups – laymen and women, churchwardens and clergymen – included in this study.

Numbers are of people or outcomes – one outcome per person.

Bibliography

Original documents

British Library
Egerton MS 3329
Harley MSS 280; 595; 7377

Exeter Cathedral Library
D+C 3553

Hampshire Record Office
3M82W/PW 1; 27M79/PR3; 75M72/PW 1, 2
11M59/E2/155656
21M65/A1/30; /32; /33
21M65/B1/28; /32; /35; /37; /41; /44; /53
*21M65/C1/33; /34; /35; /37; /45
21M65/C2/
DC/B5/6, /8, /11

Herefordshire Archive and Record Centre
AA20/57/05/15

Kent History and Library Centre
DRb/Ar/1/17

Lambeth Palace Library
Abbot's Register
MSS 639; 929; 1743

London Metropolitan Archives
DW/VB 1/ etc.
P95/ALLI/45; P95/TR/1/1/1

The National Archives
E 377/ etc.

Oxford Bodleian Library
Additional MSS
B. 14. 15. Linc
Clarendon MSS
Tanner MSS

Somerset History and Library Service
D/D/B Reg 23
*D/D/ca/207, 224, 243, 295, 313, 331, 338 (bundles 2 + 4), 350, 354
DD/SAS/C795/TN/26
D/D/vc 48, 79, 86

Southwark Local Studies Library
MS 787

Worcestershire Record Office
712.1 716 093 3965
716 093 2648 10 iii
*794 011 2513 18, Book 20
*794 011 2722 1, Book 30
* 794 011 2722 2, Book 32
794 011 2722 4, Book 39
*802 2760
*802 2884
802 2951 box 1 (1661, 1664); 802 2951 box 2 (1679)
*807 093 2724, Book 38
*these are the documents – consistory court books – fundamental to this study.

Printed documents

Andrewes, L. *Articles to be Inquired of … in the Primary Visitation of … Lancelot Lord Bishop of Winchester … Anno 1619*. London: B. Norton, J. Bill, 1619.

Baxter, R. *English Nonconformity as under King Charles II and King James II*. London: T. Parkhurst, 1689.

Hickeringill, E. *Test or Tryal of the Goodness and Value of Spiritual Courts*, 2nd edition. London: G. Larkin, 1683.

Lake, A. *Articles to be Enquired of in the Triennial Visitation of the Diocese of Bath and Wells holden anno 1626*. London: W. Stansby, 1626.

Mews, P. *Articles of Visitation and Enquiry Concerning Matters Ecclesiastical .....of the Diocese of Bath and Wells at the Triennial Visitation of ... Peter, Lord Bishop of that Diocese ... 1679*. Oxford: L. Lichfield, 1679.

Milton, J. *Of Reformation touching Church Discipline in England and the Causes that hitherto have hindered it*. London: T. Underhill, 1641.

Morley, G. *Articles of Visitation and Enquiry*. London: J. Collins, 1674.

Stillingfleet, E. *Reformation of Manners, the true way of honouring God: with the necessity of putting the laws in execution against Vice and Profaneness*. London: H. Hills, 1700.

Stillingfleet, E. *Bishop of Worcester's Charge to the Clergy of his Diocese in his Primary Visitation Sept. 11 1690*. London: H. Mortlock, 1991.

Thornborough, J. *Articles to be Enquired of ... in the Visitation of the Right Reverend Father in God, John, Lord Bishop of Worcester*. London: J. Grismand, 1626.

Secondary books

Baxter, R. *Reliquiae Baxterianae*. Edited by M. Sylvester. London: Parkhouse et al., 1697.

Bowden, P.J. *Economic Change: Wages, profits and rents 1500–1750*. Cambridge: Cambridge University Press, 1990.

Bowler, H. *Recusant Roll No. 2 1593–1594*, vol. 57. London: CRS, 1965.

Bray, G. *Anglican Canons 1529–1947*. Woodbridge: Boydell and Brewer, 1998.

Brinkworth, E.R. *Act Book of the Archdeacon's Court: Liber Actorum 1584*, vol. 1, XXIII. Oxford: ORS, 1942.

Browning, A. *English Constitutional Documents vol. 8 1660–1714*. Oxford: Oxford University Press, 1953.

Burn, J.S. *High Commission: Notices of the court and its proceedings*. London: Russell Smith, 1865.

Burn, R. *Ecclesiastical Law*, 2 vols. London: Strahan, 1824.

Carlson, E.J. *Marriage and the English Reformation*. Oxford: Blackwell, 1994.

Chapman, C.R. *Ecclesiastical Courts, Officials and Records*. Dursley: Lochin, 1997.

Cheney, C.R. *Medieval Texts and Studies*. Oxford: Oxford University Press, 1973.

Coleby, A. *Central Government and the Localities: Hampshire 1649–1689*. Cambridge: Cambridge University Press, 1987.

Cressy, D. *Birth, Marriage and Death: Ritual religion and life cycle in Tudor and Stuart England*. Oxford: Oxford University Press, 1997.

Cross, F.L. and Livingstone, E.A. *Oxford Dictionary of the Christian Church*. Oxford: Oxford University Press, 1997.

Curtis, M.H. *Oxford and Cambridge in Transition 1558–1642*. Oxford: Clarendon Press, 1959.

Dabhoiwala, F. *The Origins of Sex: A history of the first sexual revolution*. Oxford: Oxford University Press, 2012.

Dictionary of National Biography (Compact Edition), 2 vols. Oxford: Oxford University Press, 1975.

Elton, G.R. *England 1200–1640*. Cambridge: Cambridge University Press, 1969.

Evans, J. *The Baptist Interest under George I (TBHS, 2.2)*. London: TBHS, 1911.

Fincham, K.C. *Visitation Articles and Injunctions of the Early Stuart Church*, 2 vols. Woodbridge: Boydell and Brewer, 1994, 1998.

Firth, C.H. and Rait, R.S. *Acts and Ordinances of the Interregnum 1642–1660*, 2 vols. London: HMSO, 1911.

Foster, J. *Alumni Oxonienses*, 4 vols. Oxford: Parker, 1891–2.

Foxcroft, H.C. *Supplement to Burnet's History of My Own Time*. Oxford: Clarendon Press, 1902.

Gardiner, S.R. *Reports of Cases in the Courts of Star Chamber and High Commission*, Series V, 39. London: Camden Society, 1886.

Gardiner, S.R. *Constitutional Documents of the Puritan Revolution 1625–1660*. Oxford: Clarendon Press, 1906.

Gibson, E. *Codex Juris Ecclesiastici Anglicani*, 2 vols. Oxford: Clarendon Press, 1761.

Gowing, L. *Domestic Dangers: Women, words and sex in Early Modern London*. Oxford: Clarendon Press, 1996.

Gowing, L. *Common Bodies: Women, touch and power in seventeenth century England*. New Haven, CT: Yale University Press, 2003.

Greaves, R.L. *Deliver Us from Evil*. New York: Oxford University Press, 1986.

Green, I.M. *Re-establishment of the Church of England*. Oxford: Oxford University Press, 1978.

Haller, W. *Liberty and Reformation in the Puritan Revolution*. New York: Columbia University Press, 1955.

Hasler, P.W. *House of Commons 1558–1603*, vol. 3. London: HMSO, 1981.

Henning, B.D. *House of Commons 1660–1690*, 3 vols. London: Secker and Warburg, 1983.

Hill, C. *Society and Puritanism in Pre-Revolutionary England*. London: Panther, 1969.

Hill, C. *The World Turned Upside Down*. London: Temple Smith, 1972.

Hindle, S. *The State and Social Change in Early Modern England 1550–1640*. Basingstoke: Macmillan, 2002.

Horn, J.M. *Fasti Ecclesiae Anglicanae 1300–1541*, 12 vols. London: Athlone Press, 1962–7.

Horn, J.M. *Fasti Ecclesiae Anglicanae 1541–1857*, 12 vols. London: Athlone Press, 1969–2004.

Houlbrooke, R.A. *Church Courts and the People during the Reformation 1520–1570*. Oxford: Oxford University Press, 1979.

Humphery-Smith, C.R. *Phillimore Atlas and Index of Parish Registers*. Chichester: Phillimore, 1984.

Hutton, R. *Restoration*. Oxford: Clarendon Press, 1985.

Ingram, M. *Church Courts, Sex and Marriage*. Cambridge: Cambridge University Press, 1987.

Ingram, M. *Carnal Knowledge: Regulating sex in England 1470–1600*. Cambridge: Cambridge University Press, 2015.

Jacob, W.M. *Lay People and Religion in the Early Eighteenth Century*. Cambridge: Cambridge University Press, 1997.

Jenkins, C. *Act Book of the Archdeacon of Taunton 1623–1624*, vol. 43. Somerset: SRS, 1928.

Journal of the House of Lords, vol. 11. London: HMSO, 1767–1803.

Keeble, N.H. and Nuttall, G.F. *Calendar of the Correspondence of Richard Baxter*. Oxford: Clarendon Press, 1991.

Kenyon, J. *The Popish Plot*. London: Heinemann, 1972.

LeNeve, J. and Hardy, T.D. *Fasti Ecclesiae Anglicanae*. Oxford: Oxford University Press, 1854.

Levack, B.P. *Civil Lawyers in England 1603–1641*. New York: Oxford University Press, 1973.

Litzenburger, C.J. *Tewkesbury Churchwardens' Accounts 1563–1624*, vol. 7. Stroud: TBGAS, 1994.

Lyon Turner, G. *Original Records of Early Non Conformity under Persecution and Indulgence*, 3 vols. London: Fisher Unwin, 1911–14.

Manning, R.B. *Religion and Society in Elizabethan Sussex*. Leicester: Leicester University Press, 1969.

Marchant, R.A. *Puritans and the Church Courts in the Diocese of York 1560–1642*. London: Longman, 1960.

Marchant, R.A. *Church under the Law: Justice, administration and discipline in the Diocese of York 1560–1640*. Cambridge: Cambridge University Press, 1969.

McIntosh, M.K. *A Community Transformed: The manor and liberty of Havering 1500–1620*. Cambridge: Cambridge University Press, 1991.

Miller, J. *Popery and Politics in England 1660–1688*. Cambridge: Cambridge University Press, 1973.

Miller, J. *After the Civil Wars: English politics and government in the reign of Charles II*. Harlow: Longman, 2000.

Nelson, W. *Rights of the Clergy*. London: Harper, 1709.

Outhwaite, R.B. *Rise and Fall of the English Ecclesiastical Courts 1500–1860*. Cambridge: Cambridge University Press, 2006.

Owen, D.M. *Records of the Established Church of England*. London: British Records Association, 1970.

Oxford Dictionary of National Biography, 60 vols. Oxford: Oxford University Press.

Paley, R. *House of Lords 1660–1715*. Cambridge: Cambridge University Press, 2016.

Peters, R. *Oculus Episcopi: Administration in the Archdeaconry of St Albans 1580–1625*. Manchester: Manchester University Press, 1963.

Pruett, J.H. *The Parish Clergy under the Later Stuarts: The Leicestershire experience.* Champaign: Illinois University Press, 1978.

Purvis, J. *Dictionary of Ecclesiastical Terms.* London: Nelson, 1962.

Quaife, G.R. *Wanton Wenches and Wayward Wives.* London: Croome Helm, 1979.

Robbins, C. *Diary of John Milward.* Cambridge: Cambridge University Press, 1938.

Robertson, D. *Diary of Francis Evans Secretary to Bishop Lloyd 1699–1706.* Oxford: Parker, 1903.

Rogers, F.N. *Practical Arrangement of Ecclesiastical Law.* London: Benning, 1849.

Russell, C. *Crisis of Parliaments: English history 1509–1660.* Oxford: Oxford University Press, 1971.

Shaw, W.A. *History of the English Church 1640–1660*, 2 vols. London: Longman, 1900.

Simon, R.G. *Restoration Episcopate.* New York: Bookman, 1965.

Smith, M.G. *Pastoral Discipline in the Church Courts: Hexham 1680–1730.* Borthwick Paper, 62. York: Borthwick Institute, 1982.

Spaeth, D.A. *Church in an Age of Danger: Parsons and parishioners 1660–1740.* Cambridge: Cambridge University Press, 2000.

Spurr, J. *Restoration Church of England 1646–1689.* New Haven, CT: Yale University Press, 1991.

Stieg, M. *Laud's Laboratory: The Diocese of Bath and Wells in the early seventeenth century.* Lewisburg, PA: Bucknell University Press, 1982.

Stone, L. *Road to Divorce: England 1530–1978.* Oxford: Clarendon Press, 1990.

Sykes, N. *From Sheldon to Secker.* Cambridge: Cambridge University Press, 1959.

Tanner, J.R. *Constitutional Documents of the Reign of James I 1603–1625.* Cambridge: Cambridge University Press, 1930.

Tarver, A. *Church Court Records.* Chichester: Phillimore, 1995.

Thomson, A. *The Clergy of Winchester England 1615–1698: A ministry in crisis.* Lewiston, NY: Mellen, 2011.

Thomson, A. *Bishop Morley: Politician, benefactor, pragmatist.* Winchester: Winchester University Press, 2019.

Thrush, A. and Ferris, J.P. *House of Commons 1604–1629.* Cambridge: Cambridge University Press, 2010.

Till, B.D. *Church Courts 1660–1720: Revival of procedure.* Borthwick Paper, 109. York: Borthwick Institute, 2006.

Tyacke, N. *History of the University of Oxford*, vol. 4. Oxford: Clarendon Press, 1997.

Underdown, D. *Fire from Heaven: Life in an English town in the seventeenth century.* London: HarperCollins, 1992.

Usher, R.G. *Rise and Fall of High Commission.* Oxford: Clarendon Press, 1914.

Venn, J. and Venn, J.A. *Alumni Cantabrigienses*, 4 vols. Cambridge: Cambridge University Press, 1922–7.

Watts, M. *The Dissenters from the Reformation to the French Revolution.* Oxford: Clarendon Press, 1978.

Whiteman, A. *Compton Census of 1676: A critical edition*. Oxford: British Academy, 1987.

Wolfe, D.M. *Leveller Manifestoes of the Puritan Revolution*. New York: Nelson, 1944.

Wood, A. *Athenae Oxonienses*, 2 vols. London: Knaplock, 1721.

Wrightson, K. and Levine, D. *Poverty and Piety in an English Village: Terling 1525–1700*. London: Academic Press, 1981.

Articles and chapters

Allison, K.J. and Dunning, R.W. 'Borough of Warwick: Non-conformity'. In *VCH: History of the County of Warwick,* vol. 8, edited by W.B. Stephens, 536–8. London: Oxford University Press, 1969.

Bennett, G.V. 'Convocation of 1710: An Anglican attempt at counter revolution'. In *Studies in Church History*, vol. 7, edited by G.J. Cuming and D. Baker, 311–19. Cambridge: Cambridge University Press, 1971.

Bradford, G. 'Social and Economic History'. In *VCH: History of the County of Somerset*, vol. 2, edited by W. Page, 267–352. London: Constable, 1911.

Brooks, C.W. 'Law and Revolution: The seventeenth century English example'. In *Law, Lawyers and Litigants in Early Modern England*, edited by M. Lobban, J. Begiato and A. Green, 292–326. Cambridge: Cambridge University Press, 2019.

Brooks, C.W. 'Religion and Law in Early Modern England'. In *Law, Lawyers and Litigants in Early Modern England*, edited by M. Lobban, J. Begiato and A. Green, 327–35. Cambridge: Cambridge University Press, 2019.

Capp, B. 'The Double Standard Revisited: Plebian women and male sexual reputation in Early Modern England', *P+P* 162 (1999): 70–100.

Capp, B. 'Introduction: Stability and Flux'. In *Church and People in Interregnum Britain*, edited by F. McCall, 1–16. London: London University Press, 2021.

Cavill, P. 'Heresy, Law and the State', *EHR* 129, 537 (2014): 270–90.

Cavill, P. 'Perjury in Early Tudor England'. In *Studies in Church History*, vol. 56, edited by R. McKitterick, C. Methuen and A. Spicer, 182–209. Cambridge: Cambridge University Press, 2020.

Champion, W.A. 'Recourse to Law and the Meaning of the Great Decline 1650–1750: Some clues from the Shrewsbury local courts'. In *Communities and Courts in Britain 1100–1900*, edited by C.W. Brooks and M. Lobban, 179–98. London: Hambledon Press, 1997.

Coningsby, T. 'Chancellor, Vicar General, Official Principal – a Bundle of Offices', *ELJ* 2, 10 (1992): 273–85.

Cox, J.C. 'Ecclesiastical History'. In *VCH: History of the County of Hampshire and the Isle of Wight*, vol. 2, edited by H.A. Doubleday and W. Page, 1–103. London: Constable, 1903.

Dunning, R.W. 'Borough of Warwick: Economic and social history'. In *VCH: History of the County of Warwick*, vol. 8, edited by W.B. Stephens, 504–14. London: Oxford University Press, 1969.

Foster, A. 'What Happened to English and Welsh Parishes 1642–1662?' In *Church and People in Interregnum Britain*, edited by F. McCall, 19–40. London: London University Press, 2021.

Haydon, C. 'The Mouth of Hell: Religious discord at Brailes Warwickshire c.1660–1800', *Historian* 68 (2000): 23–7.

Haydon, C. 'The Church in the Kineton Deanery of the Diocese of Worcester 1660–1800'. In *National Church in Local Perspective: The Church of England and the regions 1600–1800*, edited by J. Gregory and J. Chamberlain, 145–73. Woodbridge: Boydell, 2003.

Hockaday, S.F. 'The Consistory Court of the Diocese of Gloucester', *TBGAS* 46 (1924): 195–287.

Houlbrooke, R.A. 'Decline of Ecclesiastical Jurisdiction under the Tudors'. In *Continuity and Change: Personnel and Administration of the Church of England 1500–1642*, edited by R. O'Day and F. Heal, 239–57. Leicester: Leicester University Press, 1976.

Ingram, M. 'Juridical Folklore in England Illustrated by Rough Music'. In *Communities and Courts in Britain 1100–1900*, edited by C.W. Brooks and M. Lobban, 61–82. London: Hambledon Press, 1997.

Isaacs, T. 'The Anglican Hierarchy and the Reformation of Manners 1688–1738', *JEH* 33, 3 (1982): 391–411.

Jacob, W.M. 'In Love and Charity with Your Neighbour: Ecclesiastical courts and justices of the peace in England in the eighteenth century'. In *Studies in Church History*, vol. 40, edited by K. Cooper and J. Gregory, 205–18. Cambridge: Cambridge University Press, 2004.

Laslett, P. 'Introduction: Comparing illegitimacy over time and between cultures'. In *Bastardy and Its Comparative History*, edited by P. Laslett, K. Oosterveen and R.M. Smith, 1–64. London: Arnold, 1980.

Locke, A. 'Social and Economic History'. In *VCH: History of the County of Worcester*, vol. 4, edited by J.W. Willis Bund and W. Page, 447–63. London: Constable, 1924.

McCall, F. 'Breaking the Law of God and Man: Secular prosecutions of religious offences 1645–1660'. In *Church and People in Interregnum Britain*, edited by F. McCall, 137–70. London: London University Press, 2021.

Mercer, K. 'Ecclesiastical Discipline and the Crisis of the 1680s: Prosecuting Protestant dissent in the English church courts', *JEH* 72, 2 (2021): 352–71.

Muldrew, C. 'Rural Credit, Market Areas and Legal Institutions in the Countryside in England 1550–1700'. In *Communities and Courts in Britain 1100–1900*, edited by C.W. Brooks and M. Lobban, 155–78. London: Hambledon Press, 1997.

Postles, D. 'Penance and the Market Place: A Reformation dialogue with the medieval church c.1250–1600', *JEH* 54 (2003): 441–68.

Price, F.D. 'An Elizabethan Church Official – Thomas Powell Chancellor of Gloucester Diocese', *CQR* 255, 128 (1939): 94–112.

Price, F.D. 'Gloucester Diocese under Bishop Hooper 1551–1553', *TBGAS* 60 (1939): 51–151.

Price, F.D. 'Abuses of Excommunication and the Decline of Ecclesiastical Discipline under Elizabeth I', *EHR* 57 (1942): 106–15.

Rushton, P. 'Local Laws, Local Principles: The paradoxes of local legal processes in Early Modern England'. In *Law, Lawyers and Litigants in Early Modern England*, edited by M. Lobban, J. Begiato and A. Green, 185–206. Cambridge: Cambridge University Press, 2019.

Scott Holmes, T. 'Ecclesiastical History'. In *VCH: History of the County of Somerset*, vol. 2, edited by W. Page, 1–67. London: Constable, 1911.

Shillington, V. 'Social and Economic History'. In *VCH: History of the County of Hampshire and the Isle of Wight*, vol. 5, edited by W. Page, 409–34. London: Constable, 1912.

Spaeth, D.A. 'Common Prayer? Popular observance of the Anglican Liturgy in Restoration Wiltshire'. In *Parish Church and People*, edited by S.J. Wright, 125–46. London: Hutchinson, 1988.

Thomson, A. 'Church Discipline: The operation of the Winchester consistory court in the seventeenth century', *History* 91, 303 (2006): 337–59.

Thomson, A. 'Restorer or Reformer? George Morley's spiritual jurisdiction over the Diocese of Winchester 1662–1684', *SH* 34 (2012): 73–100.

Thomson, A. 'George Morley, Dissenters and Recusants: National and diocesan perspectives 1660–48', *SH* 36 (2014): 84–108.

Thomson, A. 'Revival of a Diocese: The role of Bishop Morley at Worcester 1660–1662', *MH* 44, 1 (2019): 56–70.

Thomson, A. 'Church Discipline in Seventeenth Century England: Flourishing or floundering? The Worcestershire experience', *MH* 45, 3 (2020): 292–308.

Whiteman, A. 'Re-establishment of the Church of England 1660–1663', *TRHS* 5 (1955): 111–31.

Willis Bund, J.W. 'Ecclesiastical History'. In *VCH: History of the County of Worcester*, vol. 2, edited by J.W. Willis Bund and W. Page, 1–90. London: Constable, 1906.

Willis Bund, J.W. 'Political History'. In *VCH: History of the County of Worcester*, vol. 2, edited by J.W. Willis Bund and W. Page, 197–233. London: Constable, 1906.

Theses

Aklundh, J. 'Church Courts in Restoration England 1660–1689', Ph.D., University of Cambridge, 2018.

Barratt, D.M. 'The Condition of the Clergy between the Reformation and 1660', D.Phil., University of Oxford, 1949.

Davies, C.E. 'The Enforcement of Religious Uniformity in England 1668–1700 with special reference to the Dioceses of Chichester and Worcester', D.Phil., University of Oxford, 1982.

Johnson, R.N. 'Protestant Dissenters in Hampshire 1640–1740', Ph.D., University of Winchester, 2013.

Jones, M.D.W. 'Ecclesiastical Courts Before and After the English Civil War: Office jurisdiction in the dioceses of Oxford and Peterborough 1630–1675', B.Litt., University of Oxford, 1977.

Marshall, W.M. 'Administration of the Dioceses of Hereford and Oxford 1660–1760', Ph.D., University of Bristol, 1977.

Mildon, W.H. 'Puritanism in Hampshire and the Isle of Wight from the Reign of Elizabeth I to the Restoration', Ph.D., University of London, 1934.

Potter, J.M. 'Ecclesiastical Courts in the Diocese of Canterbury 1603–1665', M.Phil., University of London, 1973.

Tarver, A. 'The Consistory Court of the Diocese of Lichfield and Coventry and Its Work 1680–1830', Ph.D., University of Warwick, 1998.

Thomson, A. 'The Diocese of Winchester Before and After the English Civil Wars: A study of the character and performance of its clergy', Ph.D., University of London, 2004.

Whiteman, A. 'The Episcopate of Seth Ward Bishop of Exeter 1660–1667 and Salisbury 1667–1689', D.Phil., University of Oxford, 1951.

Index

Abberton, 162
absolution, 7, 34, 119–21, 122, 148, 170
abuse (misbehaviour, disturbance)
    in church or churchyard, 52, 61–2, 96, 102, 161, 162, 176
    against clergy, 61
Acts of Parliament *see* church attendance; church courts; Clarendon Code; Test Acts; poor law
Acts of the Commonwealth (1650s), 74, 76, 151
adultery
    Act (1650), 74, 76, 151
    definition, 47, 48
    executions, 75
    intrusiveness, 182
    see also fornication; incontinence
adjournment (reservation), 21, 118–19, 121, 123
Aishe, Thomas, 132
Aisholt, 96, 136
Aklundh, Jens, 36, 120–1
Alan, John, 62
Alcester, 52
Aldridge, George, 96, 127
Alexander, Francis (surrogate), 35, 36
Allercott, John and William, 97
amnesty (1672–3), 167
Alton, 52, 59, 143
Alverstoke, 99
Amport, 131, 137
Anabaptists, 60, 74, 153
Andover, 152, 153
Andrewes, Lancelot, Bishop of Winchester, 39, 55, 78, 153
Andrewes, Richard, 131
Anne, Queen of Great Britain, 179
apparitors (agents of the court)
    corruption, 147, 179
    proxy system, 147
    viis et modis, 21
    work, 17, 25
arbitration, 26, 121, 125, 129, 180, 182
Archbold, John (surrogate), 34, 35, 36
archdeacons' courts, 12, 16–17, 19, 26, 112, 184
assizes

action against recusants (prosecutions), 58, 75, 109
encroachment on the church courts, 149, 150, 151, 153, 154
judges (Lord Chief Justice, Common Pleas, King's Bench), 150
see also secular courts
attendance at church
    Acts, 149, 151, 152, 163
    cases, 52, 64, 97
    charges (prosecutions), 52–3, 55
    convictions (guilt), 96, 102
    recusancy (refusal to attend church), 109
    requirement for office, 76
    sentencing, orders, 97, 132
    significance for dissent and recusancy, 58
attendance at church courts
    aedibus (*in camera*), 84
    diocesan comparisons, 94
    importance of attendance, 93, 166, 173
    regular sessions, 4
    sanctions (*viis* and excommunication) to compel attendance, 31, 103, 107, 118
    statistics, 98–9, 166
Atterbury, Francis, Bishop of Rochester, 179, 180, 181
Ayling, Robert, 136

Babington, Gervase, Bishop of Worcester, 153, 176
Badsey, 105
Bagg, John, 138
Baker, Thomas, 52
Balamy, curate of St Lawrence, Evesham, 70, 105, 135, 161
Balchilde, Thomas, 97
Baldwyn, Thomas, 145
Baldwyn, Timothy, Chancellor of Worcester,
    appointment for life, 31
    attendance, 31, 33, 37–8
    corruption, 145, 146, 147
    experience, 29
    pluralism, 30
    qualifications, 28
    reform, 173
    surrogates, 34

240   CHURCH COURTS AND THE PEOPLE IN SEVENTEENTH-CENTURY ENGLAND

training by, 37–8
the Baleers, 48
Ballie, Thomas, 49
Bane, Richard, 136–7
Bangse, George, 95
baptism
  charges, 57
  excommunication, 21, 119
  recusancy and dissent, 57, 58, 107
  sacrament, 155n6
Baptists, 153, 167
Barley, Peter, 48
Barling, Elizabeth, 19, 131, 136
Basing, 69, 109
Basingstoke, 69
bastardy
  Acts, Bills, 27, 51, 77, 149, 152, 175
  cases, 95, 96
  charges (summonings, prosecutions)
    in the church courts, 49–50, 75, 161
    in secular courts, 149
  convictions (guilt), 75, 102, 103, 113, 168
  punishments (sentencing)
    by the Church, penance, 131, 171
    by magistrates (deportation, whipping,
      workhouse), 149, 175
  secular expansion of prosecutions, 12, 27,
    51, 149, 152
  statistics of bastardy, 76, 110–11, 113, 168
  support for persecution
    costs, 51, 74, 168, 172
    moral concerns of the Church, 17, 73, 169
    numbers rising, 175
    Reformation of Manners, 162–3, 168
    Stillingfleet, 164–5, 172
  see also church courts; charges;
    convictions; penance
Batt, Joanna, 131, 137
Batt, John, 50, 131
Bauke, Roger, 126
Baxter, Richard, 108, 181
Baylie, John, Chancellor of Wells, 28, 30, 32, 94
Beauchampes, 131, 138
Bedhampton, 109
Belbroughton, 99
Belling, John, 95
Bengeworth, 53, 61, 99
Bennett, Henry, 136
Bennett, John, 96, 97
Bennett, Nicholas, 146
Berrie, Richard, 48
bestiality, 49
Bicknoller, 97
Bilson, Thomas, Bishop of Winchester, 39, 153
Binstead, 61, 71, 72
bishops
  abolition, 1, 127, 150
  blame for decline of the church courts
    apathy, 39
    bias with statistics, 110
    compromising with upper classes, 64,
      77, 144
    feebleness, 39, 87, 181
    ignorance, 39
    nepotism, 28
    support for secular courts, 153–4, 176

motivation
  religion, 55, 76
  social concerns, 76, 164, 176
  security, 77, 154
private sessions, 71, 84, 104, 112, 145
sitting in the church court, 39–40, 94, 153,
  163
structure of church courts, 11, 16
reform of the courts, 121, 181
surveys (Whitgift, Compton, bias with
  statistics) 107, 58, 76, 108, 110
vicar general's role, 25
visitation articles, 18, 20, 78
Bishops Waltham, 69
Bissell, John, 62, 140
Blake, Thomas, 64
Blandford, Walter, Bishop of Worcester, 39,
  153
Blockley, 61, 137
the Blounts, 108, 167
Book of Common Prayer, 18, 51, 56, 146
Botley, 19, 69, 105
Bowden, Francis, 137
Bowden, William, 62
Brading, 66, 103, 105, 122, 123
Bramston, George (deputy), 35
Bramston, Mondeford, Chancellor of
  Winchester
  appointment for life, 31
  attendance, 32, 34–5
  experience, 29
  pluralism, 30
  qualifications, 28
  surrogates, 35
Bredicot, 99
Brent, Nathaniel, 150
Bretforton, 65
Brickleton, Gilbert, 132, 138
Bride, Michael, 21
Bridgwater, 108
Bright, Nicholas, 49, 80n17
Brinkworth, E.R., 12, 147
Bristol, 184
Brixey, Thomas, 97
Broadway, 197
Bromsgrove, 62
Brooke, William, 50
Brooks, C.W., 151
Broom, 99
Brown Candover, 109, 133
Brunsdon, Thomas, 96, 97
Bulford, Elinor, 95–6
Bulpane, Richard, 48
burials, 21, 22, 74, 96, 119, 120, 180
Burnet, Gilbert, Bishop of Salisbury, 31, 176,
  184
Burrow, Alexander, 96
Butler, Samuel, 99
the Butlers, 97
Bye, Jethro, 57
Byrn, Walter, 49

Calbourne, 53
Cambridgeshire, 3, 73, 112
Campe, George, 131

INDEX   **241**

the Cannings, 108, 167
canons of the church
   Canon Law, x, xi, 18, 19, 55, 179
   concerning churchwardens, 64
   concerning the clergy, 68
   conflicts, canon and common law, 123
   individual canons, 13n21, 19, 20, 27,
      41n13, 51
Canterbury, diocesan court
   charges, 73
   class, 143
Capp, Bernard, 74
Carlson, Eric, 3, 112
Carpenter, Joseph, 167
Carpenter, Robert, 131
Carlisle, 164
Catherington, 70
Catholics
   Acts, 58, 59, 77, 174, 175
   cases, 59, 60
   causes of persecution
      Elizabethan plots, 58
      Gunpowder Plot, 107–8
      Popish Plot, 76, 152
      Louis XIV, 163
   charges (prosecutions) in church courts,
      59, 60, 149, 161, 162
   charges in secular courts, 75, 109, 149, 153
   charges in High Commission, 91, 149
   convictions (guilt)
      in church courts, 102, 113
      in secular courts, 109
   definition (of recusant), 58–9
   families, 108, 167
   Instrument of Government/Humble
      Petition and Advice, 75
   statistics, 76, 109, 110, 111, 167–8
   Tichborne bond, 24
Cawte, William, 132
Census (1676, Compton Census), 15, 76, 108,
   110, 167
Chaddesley Corbett, 70
Challicombe, James, 48
chancellors
   appointments for life, 31
   attendance at court, 34
   conflict with bishop, 36
   corruption, 143, 147
   deputies, 34–6
   effectiveness, 37–8
   experience, 28–30
   inadequacies, 38
   post and responsibilities of chancellors, 16,
      25–6
   qualifications of chancellors and deputies
      28, 35
   scholarship of chancellors, 34
Chappell, Thomas, 54
Chard, 54, 97, 134
charges, *see* church courts; churchwardens;
      clergy; lay people; individual crimes
      (e.g. bastardy, communion, dissent)
Charles II, King of England, Ireland and
      Scotland, 10, 151, 153, 242
Charlock, Thomas, 69, 105, 122, 123, 135–6
Chartrain, William, 99

Cheepewrighte, Edward, 105
Cheltnam, Ellis, 62
Chester, 34, 73, 119
Cheyny, Thomas (deputy), 35
Chichester, 2, 183
Chilbolton, 103
Chilworth, 134
Christchurch, 109
church courts (the main items, many of which
      have separate and more detailed entries
      elsewhere in the index)
   abolition (1640s), 1, 12n3, 150, 151,
      158n127
   adjournments (reservation), 21, 118–19,
      121
   attendance, 93–4, 166
   charges (citations, prosecutions)
      against lay people, 46–64, 161–2
      against churchwardens, 64–8, 145, 161
      against clergy, 68–72, 145–6, 161
      balance or proportions of charges, 72–3,
         162–5
      distinguishing charges from guilt, 5
   completion of business, 100, 166
   confession, 23–4, 26, 125, 129, 170
   convictions (guilt), 102–5, 166
   decline, *see* completion of business;
      sessions; summoning
   evidence or ways of determining a case,
      23–4, 26, 125, 129, 170
      documents, 24, 29, 51, 99, 170
      pregnancy, 47
      witnesses, 48, 49
      see also arbitration; confession;
         compurgation; *ex officio* oath;
         inquiry; rumour
   extinction of the courts
      at Wells, 184
      at Winchester, 4, 7, 32, 184
   failings of the courts
      class, 141–4, 173
      compurgation, 125–30, 170
      excommunication, 118–22, 169
      ex officio oath, 122–5
      fees, 147
      penance, 136–41, 171–3
   impact on society
      religious impact, 106–10, 167–8
      social impact, 110, 168–9
   inquiry, 24, 26, 125, 129
   law and the church courts, 17–19
   location
      bishop's palace, 39, 71, 92, 104, 112, 145
      cathedral, 86
      in aedibus (or *in camera*), 21, 32–3, 86,
         87, 94, 165
      other private hearings, 112
   officials, 24–6
   opponents
      reformers, 179–82
      critics, 184
   orders (judgements)
      against churchwardens, 133–4
      against clergy, 135–6
      against lay people, 24, 132–3
   penance, 136–41, 171–3

procedures (in outline), 19–24
reasons for decline by the 1670s
    Cavalier Parliament, 152
    encroachment of the secular courts, 149, 151–4
    legacy of the 1650s, 150–1
    role of bishops in secular encroachment, 153–4
    wish for security, 148–9, 152
reasons for decline by the 1690s
    Glorious Revolution, 174
    Reformation of Manners, 174–5
    role of bishops in secular encroachment, 176
    security, 175
    social attitudes, 174–5
    Toleration Act, 174
reduction in the scope of the church courts in the eighteenth and nineteenth centuries, 176
restoration of the courts (1661), 1, 12n4, 127, 152, 182–3
scholarship, 2–4, 183
sentencing, *see* orders; procedures; penance
sessions, 85–6, 87, 165
strength of the courts, mercy, 4, 100, 134, 180, 182
structure or system, 16–17
summoning statistics, 89–91, 165–6
Church Lench, 97, 98
church rate
    cases, 97
    charges, 2, 63–4
    convictions (guilt), 98, 102–3
    sentence, 133
    guilt at Worcester, 161, 162, 164, 166, 171
churchwardens
    cases, 65, 66, 67, 96, 97, 98, 99, 103–4, 134
    charges, prosecutions, citations, 64–8, 72, 161
    church court, churchwarden role in, 24
    convictions (guilt), 103–4, 133, 166
    importance of churchwardens, 64–5
    informal corrections of shortcomings, 112
    oaths, 122
    penance, the role of churchwardens, 24, 136–8
    composition, 18, 20
    delivery to visitations, 17, 112
    discrepancy between presentments and charges, 60
    distinction, accusations and not guilt, 61, 101
    restraints on, 144
    sentencing, 93, 133–4
    secular involvement in law enforcement, 154
    visitations, 17, 18, 20
citations, *see* charges
Civil Wars (1640s), 5, 8, 74, 144, 148, 150
clandestine marriage
    cases
        clergy, 105, 122, 172
        lay, 51, 72
    charges, 23, 51, 69, 70, 161
    convictions (guilt), 102

definition, 51, 151
excommunication, 105, 123
penance, 131, 172
suspension of clergy, 135–6
Clapham, 154
Clarendon Code (1660s), 26–7, 77, 152, 183
Clarendon Constitutions (1164), 128
class, 3, 141–6
    class conflict, 148
    class imbalance and decline of church courts, 4, 117, 143–6, 148, 173
    omission in court books, 141–3, 145, 173
    punishment of the poor to shame the rich, 144
    upper classes and church officials, 145–6, 173
clergy
    abuse, assault on, 61, 162
    cases, (of clergy in court) over
        chancel, 69, 105
        clandestine marriage, 69, 105, 122, 135, 172
        communion, 70, 135
        dissent, 69, 72
        drink, 135
        fighting, 71
        incontinence, 71, 106, 172
        licences, 19, 69, 105, 122, 132
        oaths, 69, 70, 105, 135
        pluralism, 69, 135
        services, 19, 69, 105, 135, 172
        surplice, 19, 69, 70, 105, 135
        vexatious behaviour, 161, 172
    charges, 18, 26, 68–72, 161
    convictions (guilt), 104–6, 134–5, 166
    counselling, 112, 121, 169
    sanction against, excommunication, 105
    sentencing
        deprivation or defrocking, 172
        orders, 19, 33, 111, 135–6
        penance, 136, 172
        suspension, 106, 122, 135–6, 172
    taxation of, 181
Coke, Edward, 123, 154
Cole, Ellis, 47
Cole, Richard, 71
Colebard, John, 64
Coleby, Andrew, 11, 12, 75, 153
Colenett, Thomas (surrogate), 32, 35, 36
Colinge, John, 51
Comberton, 172
commissaries, 16, 25, 29, 30
Commonwealth (1650s), 55, 75, 106, 111, 152
communion
    canonic requirement, 55
    cases, contrast of the 1610s with the 1690s, 107, 161–2
    clergy, 70
    churchwardens, 63, 65, 66
    convictions (guilt), 102, 103
    excommunication, 21, 22, 119
    Michaelmas term, 10, 56
    offence, sitting, standing, 56, 70, 105, 135
    prosecutions, numbers, 55–6, 107
    refusal a signal of discontent, 58, 105, 107
    requirement for office, 26, 77 *see also* Clarendon Code

INDEX   **243**

sacramental status, 55, 155n6
sentencing (orders, penance), 97, 132, 161, 169, 171
Tichborne's bond and communion, 147
completion of business by the church courts, 95–101, 121, 166, 173, 182, *see also* church courts
compurgation, 125–30
applications of the oath, 96, 126, 127–8, 171
decline of use, 129, 130
illegal, 127, 128, 129, 152, 170
Compton, Henry, Bishop of London, Census, 15, 76, 108, 110, 167
Compton, Thomas (wife of), 125, 127
confession (in court)
cases, 33, 96, 98, 125
as a determinant in a court case, 23–4, 26, 125, 129
intimidation, 125, 127
statistics, 125, 170
see also church courts; evidence
Congregationalists, 74
constables, 11, 153, 154
Conventicle Acts (1664, 1670), 77, 152, *see also* Clarendon Code
conventicles, 27, 59, 60, 77, 132, 145, 183
convictions (guilt), *see* church courts
Cooke, Joanna, 97
Cooke, Joshua (deputy), 35
Cookes, Edward, 105
Cooper, Thomas, 133
corruption, 179
apparitors, 147, 179
chancellors, 31, 40, 146, 147
church courts, 31, 144–5, 147, 148, 176, 184
compurgation, 128, 244
Cosyer, Christopher, 70
Court of Arches
appeals, 16
chancellors, 29–30
hostile to reform, 181
Court of High Commission, 1, 37
abolition (1641), 1, 91, 150
fines and imprisonment, 24, 125
Coventry, 164
Cowp, Jane, 99
Cox, Joanna, 138
Creech St Mary, 97
Creighton, Robert, Bishop of Wells, 39, 108, 110, 153, 181
Creighton, Robert, deputy, 35, 36
Cressy, David, 5, 74, 75–6, 151
Crewkerne, 61, 96
Criddle, Thomas, 96
Cromwell, Oliver, 76, 106, 150
Cullumbyne, John, 20
Curle, Samuel, 48
Curry Rivel, 137

Dabhoiwala, Faramerz, 3, 5, 144
Danby, Thomas, 77, 108
Darrell, Nicholas (surrogate), 35, 36
Dastyn, Richard, 133
Davie, Tomasina, 48

Davies, Evan, 2, 4, 10, 12n8, 37, 94, 100, 112, 183, 186n33
Davies, John, 97
Daylesford, 137
Dean and Chapter, Worcester, 145
Deane, Henry, Chancellor of Wells
attendance at court, 32
improvement of the court, 35, 87, 94
no pluralism, 30
qualifications, 28
death penalty, 24
adultery, 74, 75, 151
incest, 74, 151
secular courts, 148, 149
Declaration of Indulgence (1672), 108, 153
decline of church courts, *see* church courts
Devon, 164
Devonsheere, Michael, 126
Dewes, Richard, 88
Dible, Thomas, 132
Dicks, William, 64
dissent
Acts, 58, 77, 152, 162–3, 167
cases, 59, 97, 152
causes of persecution, 76
charges (citations, prosecutions, summonings)
by the church courts, 59, 60, 73, 113, 161, 162
in the secular courts, 149, 153, 176
conviction (guilt), 102–3, 113
definition, 58–9
Morley and, 77, 153
numbers, 108, 111, 113, 167
Compton Census (1676), 108, 110, 167
Indulgence (1672), 108
Whitgift (1603), 110
secular prosecutions, 152, 153, 183
sentencing, orders (to conform), 132
documentary evidence in court, 24, 99, 125, 128, 170, *see also* church courts; evidence
Dodderhill, 67
Dorchester, 112
Dowdinge, Thomas, 88
Droxford, 103
Duck, Arthur, Chancellor of Wells,
absence, 32, 33
education, 28
experience, 28
pluralism, 29, 30
scholarship, 32, 37, 40
surrogates, 40
Dudley, 99, 108
Dummer, William, 172
Duppa, Brian, Bishop of Winchester, 87, 181
Durley, 133

Eckington, 172
Edward I, King of England, 18
Edward VI, King of England and Ireland, 18
Egglesfeild, John (surrogate), 34–5
Elizabeth I, Queen of England and Ireland, 18, 107, 108, 109, 152, 183
Elms, William, 96, 97

Elton, Geoffrey, 6
Essex, 73, 112, 143
Evenlode, 172
Evesham
  deanery, 11, chapter 5, *passim*
  town, 55, 66, 70, 99, 103, 105, 108, 134, 135
evidence (forensic, used in court)
  absence of, 126, 128, 148
  certifying, 24, 99
  defective, 102, 128, 148
  importance (relative), 170
  ways of determining cases, 23–4, 26, 47, 48–9, 125, 129, 170
  see also arbitration; church courts; compurgation; confession; *ex officio* oath; inquiry
Exclusion crisis (1679), 74
excommunication, 21, 118–22, 169–70
  absolutions, 119–20, 170
  association with an excommunicate, 62
  cases, 56, 105, 107, 123, 125, 140, 162
  criticism, 121, 181
  lesser and greater excommunication, 21–2
  decline of church courts, cause of, 121, 148, 170, 174
  defence of excommunication, 120–1, 174
  reform, failure of, 176, 180
  sanction/punishment distinction, 22–3, 107, 108
  statistics, 119, 169–70
  standing excommunicate, 62
  see also baptism; church courts; clandestine marriage; clergy; court attendance
Exeter, 34
exhibitionism, 49
ex officio oath, 122–5
  abolition and confirmation, 1, 23, 26, 123, 127
  criticism, 123, 124, 129–30
  defence, 124, 148
ex officio proceedings (office business), *see* church courts

Fareham, 61
Farr, Richard, 172
Farthing, James, 132
fees
  church courts, 147, 148, 176, 179, 180, 182
  marriage ceremony fees, 46
  secular court fees, 148
Feilde, John, 52
Fifth Monarchy Men, 74, 108, 116n88, 153
finance, *see* church rate
the Fitters, 99
Five Mile Act (1665), 77, 152, *see also* Clarendon Code
Fivehead, 65, 134
Fleetwood, James, Bishop of Worcester, 39, 78, 108, 110, 153, 181
fornication
  Act (1650), 74, 76, 151
  definition, 47, 48
  evidence, 128
  intrusiveness, 182

see also adultery; incontinence
Foster, Andrew, xiv, 13n17
Fox, George, 108
the Framptons, 51, 122, 123
Francklin, John, 127–8
Fuller, Thomas, 19, 105, 135

Gate, John, 98, 100
George I, King of Great Britain and Ireland, 167
Gibson, E., *Codex Juris*, 22–3
Glorious Revolution (1688–9), 1, 5, 10, 155, 167
  decline of church courts and, 162, 163, 174
  see also Reformation of Manners; Toleration Act
Gloucester, 146, 147
the Goddards, 48
Goodaker, Timothy, 70, 72, 105–6, 115n67, 135
Goodlad, James, 71, 72
Goodland, Frances, 21
Gorche, Barnaby, Chancellor of Worcester
  attendance at court, 31, 33
  experience, 29
  pluralism, 30
  qualifications, 28
  surrogates, 34
Gosling, Richard Jr, 172
Gosling, Richard Sr, 172
Gosport, 167, 175
Gosse, Joanna, 96, 97
gossip, 3, 47, 84, 112
Gough, Francis, 96
Gowing, Laura, 3
Gray, Mary, 132
Great Malvern, 103
Green, Richard, 17
Greene, Isotta, 49
Grigg, Humphrey, 48
guilt
  churchwardens, 103–4
  clergy, 104–5
  comparative statistics, 98, 166
  degrees of guilt, 96, 97–8, 98–9
  lay, 102–3
  see also church courts

Haines, Robert, 53
Hale, Edward, 56
Hale, Sir Matthew, 151, 179, 180
Halesowen, 64, 99, 172
Hall, Joseph (surrogate), 34, 35, 36
Hall, William, 99
the Halls, 53
Hambledon, 134
Hampshire, 14, 15, 16, 75, 107–9, 153, 167
Hanley Castle, 67, 97, 98, 109, 132, 134
harbouring (giving shelter to pregnant women), 18, 47, 50, 57, 131
Harding, John, 96, 97
Harding, Simon, 133
Harewell, William (surrogate), 34, 35
Harris, John (deputy), 35

INDEX　　245

Hastings, Joanna, 48
Haughton, Thomas, 19, 161
Havant, 66, 69, 105
Hawkins, Alice, 131
Hawkins, William (surrogate), 34, 35
Hawkins, William, of Alton, 52
Hay, Joyce, 52
Haydon, Colin, xiv, 177n16
Hayes, Robert, 132
Hayling Southwood, 97
Haywards, Thomas, 60
heads of families, 169, 174
Hearst, Christopher (surrogate), 35
Heckley, Richard, 59
Helme, Christopher, Chancellor of Worcester, 28, 29–30, 31
Heming, John, 95
Henry VIII, King of England, 18
Herbert, Benjamin, 71
Hereford, 164
Hickeringill, Edmund, 179
Higgins, John, 58, 59
Highclere, 96
Hilary, William, 6, 9, 10, 90, 111
Hill, Christopher, 4, 5, 74, 75–6, 143, 151
Hite, Richard and Martha, 47–8
the Holbrookes, 136
Holt, Thomas (surrogate), 35, 36
Hooper, John, Bishop of Gloucester, 39
Hough, John, Bishop of Worcester, 172, 176
Houghton, 96
Houlbrooke, Ralph, 2, 4, 17, 22, 114n8, 143, 147, 184
Huish, Richard, 52
Humble Petition and Advice (1657), 75, 77, 151
Hunt, Mary, 48
Hunt, Rebecca, 60
Hunt, William (surrogate), 34–5, 86
Hutchins, William, 62
Hyde, Edward, Earl of Clarendon, 151

illegitimacy, *see* bastardy
imprisonment
    bastardy, 75
    fornication, 74, 75, 151
    High Commission, 24, 125
    secular courts, 24, 27, 149
    significavit, 24, 62, 120, 125
    Wolvesey, 24
incest
    Act (1650), 74, 151
    charges, 2, 46, 51–2
    death penalty, 74, 151
    definition, 51–2
    penance, 172
    see also church courts
incontinence (sexual)
    cases, 48–9, 161
    clergy, 106, 172
    convictions (guilt), 95–6, 97, 172
    definition, 47–8
    evidence
        compurgation, 96, 124–5, 126
        confession, 31, 124–5

rumour, 49
penance, 123–5, 131, 172
removal of prosecutions from the church courts, 176
statistics, 49
incumbents, *see* clergy
Independents, 74, 153, 167
Ingram, Martin, 2, 4, 22, 94, 143, 147, 184
inheritance, 46
Inkberrow, 108
innocence, 24, 95, 96, 100, 130
inquiry by the church courts
    cases, 33, 95, 97, 124
    ex officio oath, 124
    inquiry, use of, by the courts, 24, 26, 125, 129
    see also church courts; evidence
instance business
    abolition, 184, 186n34
    chancellors and, 33–4
    Coke and, 123
    distinction, office and instance, 1–2
    importance of, 79n3, 123, 182
    proceedings, lengthy, 23
    secular courts and, 123, 151
Instrument of Government (1653), 75, 77, 131

Jacob, William, 3, 164, 176, 183–4
James I, King of England, Ireland, Scotland, 108, 152
James II, King of England, Ireland, Scotland, 1, 10, 163, 165
Jellett, Francis, 137
Jenkins, Sir Leoline, 121, 179, 180
Jephcott, John (surrogate), 34, 35, 36
Johnson, Richard, 99
Jones, Martin, 2, 4, 12n3, 12n8, 73, 90, 94, 100, 158n127, 184

Kenyon, J., 76
Kidderminster
    deanery, 11, chapter 5, *passim*
    town, 20, 108, 138
Kilton, 71, 106
Kineton, 52
King, Stephen, 63
Kings Lynn, 184
Kings Norton, 66
Kings Somborne, 97, 99, 132, 137
Kings Worthy, 19, 47, 52, 132
Knight, Ralph, 96
Knight, Thomas, 64

Lake, Arthur, Bishop of Bath and Wells, 18, 39, 78, 153, 159n146
Lake, Thomas, 69–70
Lancashire, 164
Lasher, Joshua (deputy), 35, 36
Laslett, Peter, 3, 11, 12, 73, 76, 165
Latemore, Edward, 62
Laud, William, Archbishop of Canterbury, 9, 86, 94, 100, 113n3, 114n27, 119
Lawnder, Abraham, 55

lay people, treatment by the church courts
attendance at court, 93–5, 166
charges
church rate, 63–4
moral charges, 47–52
relative importance or balance of the charges, 72–3
religious charges, 52–62
at Worcester, 161–2
'class' and the courts, 141–6, 173
compurgation, 125, 127, 170
excommunication, 119, 169–70
guilt of, 102–3, 166
numbers summoned to court, 89–90, 165–6
orders from the court, numbers of, 130, 131–2, 133, 171
penance, numbers, 130–2, 171
lay people, their condition in society
bastardy, 76, 110–11, 165, 168
religious diversity, 74, 76, 108–9, 110–11, 167
lectureships, 108, 167, *see also* Puritans
Lee, Originale, 54
Leicestershire, 92
Levine, David, 3, 112, 143
licences
clergy, 19, 69, 70, 72, 105, 106, 122, 132, 135, 161, 172
indulgences, 108
marriage, 17, 21, 51, 151, 172
professions, 19, 142
toleration, 167
Lichfield, 3, 164, 183
Lincoln, 34
Lipscomb, Richard, 133
Liss, 96
Little Witley, 137
Littleton, James, Chancellor of Worcester, 28, 30, 31, 34
Lloyd, William, Bishop of Worcester, 40, 172, 174, 176
Loyd, William, 171
London, 73, 143, 150, 184
Longstock, 137
Louis XIV, King of France, 163
Loy, William, 61
Lyndhurst, 69, 111
Lyndwood, William, Provinciale, 18, 26, 36
Lyon Turner, G., 11, 12

McCall, Fiona, 11, 12, 75
McIntosh, Marjorie, 3, 143
Madeley, widow, 50, 57
Mager, William, 61
Magna Carta (1215), 123, 128
magistrates, *see* church courts; secular/church court relations; decline of church courts/transfer of prosecutions; secular courts; quarter sessions
Mallard, Mathew, 54
Marchant, Ronald, 2, 94, 119, 124, 143, 144–5, 147
marriage
ex officio and instance procedures, 1–2, 150–1, 182

civil marriages (Act 1653), 151
see also clandestine marriage; incest; sex before marriage
Marshall, Thomas, 132
Marshall, William, 3, 4, 184
Marshatt, Samuel, 19, 69, 105
Marten, John, 137
Martin Hussingtree, 59, 66
Mason, Robert, Chancellor of Winchester, 28, 29, 30, 31, 32, 41n7
masturbation, 46, 49
Mathews, Lancelot, 62, 139–40
Mathon, 52
Maunder, Christopher, 96, 126–7
Mercer, Kit, 73
methodology, 8–12, 160
Methwin, Anthony (surrogate), 34, 35, 36
Mews, Peter, Bishop of Winchester, 39, 78, 153
Mews, Peter, Chancellor of Winchester, 31
Michelmersh, 71
Mildon, Wilfred, 153
Millenary Petition (1603), 179
Miller, John, 76, 158n114
Mills, Robert, 71, 106
Milton, John, 179
Milward, John, 184
Minchin, Thomas, 55
Minehead, 132
Minstead, 69
Mitchell, Alexander, 50
Mondai, Arthur, 137
Moore, John, 63–4
moral issues
bastardy, 49–51
charges, 46–52, 161
clandestine marriage, 51
incest, 51–2
incontinence, 48–9
sex before marriage, 47–8
shift from religious to moral prosecutions, 72–3, 162,
Worcester (all charges), 161–2
see also adultery; bastardy; fornication; incontinence; sex before marriage church courts (charges)
More, John, 63
More, Thomas, 59
Morehall, John, 51
Morley, Charles, Chancellor of Winchester, 19, 28, 30, 31, 32, 35, 38, 40
Morley, George, Bishop of Worcester and Winchester
age, 181
Articles, 18, 78
avoidance of court, 39, 153
Compton Census, 108, 110
decline of church courts/trust in secular courts, 87, 153, 176
nepotism, 30, 40
sectaries, 58–9, 77
Morley, John (surrogate), 35, 86
Morse, John, 132

Naunton Beauchamp, 67
nepotism, 30, 40

Newcastle, 184
Newport, 69, 105, 122, 135, 153
Newton, George, 71
Newton, Isaac, 11
Nicholas, John, 184
North Petherton, 53, 61
North, Richard, 122, 123
Northcote, Elias, 61
Northumberland, 164
Norton Fitzwarren, 61, 105
Norwich, 2, 73, 94, 119, 143, 146, 147, 164
notary public, 21, 25, 146
the Nowells, 48

Oake, Maria, 48–9
oaths, 95, 122
    Catholics and recusants, 58
    chancellors, 27
    rural dean oaths, 69, 70, 105, 135
    see also compurgation; churchwardens;
        clergy; *ex officio* oath
occupations, 54, 142–3
Odiham, 175
offences, *see* church courts; charges
Offenham, 135
officials principal, *see* chancellors
Oldbury, 108
Old Swinford, 62
Ombersley, 97, 98, 132
Orchard, Mary, 137
orders or warnings (sentence) of the court
    case (or example), 111
    churchwardens, 133–4
    clergy, 135
    distinction between orders and warnings, 130
    lay people, 24, 132–3
    see also church courts
Otterbourne, 109
Outhwaite, Brian, 3, 4, 12n3, 158n127, 184
Overton, 61
Ovington, 97, 134
Owslebury, 59
Owsley, Elizabeth, 96
Oxford
    absolution, 120
    archdeacon's court, 12
    attendance at court, 94
    charges, 73
    class imbalance, 143
    completion of business, 100
    decline, 49
    excommunications, 119
    numbers summoned to the court, 90–2
    probates in the 1650s, 150
    prosecutions numbers, 91–2

Parliament
    Cavalier, 75, 76, 77, 129, 152
    Exclusion of Catholics, 77
    Long, 9, 74, 129, 130, 146, 150
    Rump, 76, 106, 150
    and the secular courts, 12, 176
    and security, 5, 75, 76, 77, 79, 106, 149,
        152, 183

transfer of powers to the Church 1974, xi
    see also Acts
Parry, Henry, Bishop of Worcester, 39, 153
Patricke, John, 97, 98, 132
Payne, William (deputy), 35, 36
Peale, William, 132
Peirce, Edmund, Chancellor of Wells, 28, 29,
    30, 35, 43n62
Peirs, William, Bishop of Bath and Wells, 39,
    71, 87, 94, 100, 153, 181
penance
    cases, 97, 124–5, 126, 127, 131, 132, 138,
        170, 172
    clergy, 136, 172
    commutation, 24, 132, 136, 138, 139, 182
    crimes (bastardy, church attendance,
        clandestine marriage, communion,
        incontinence, misbehaviour, morals,
        Sabbath), 131–2, 171
    critics, 139, 140
    decline, 130–1, 140, 172
    humiliation, 24, 136, 137, 139, 141, 148,
        172
    numbers, 130–1, 172
    proceedings (choreography), 24, 136–7
    supporters, 139–41, 148, 173
    see also church courts
Pence, Benjamin, 33
Penne, John, 60
Peopleton, 96
perjury, 124–5, 129, 186n31
Pershore
    deanery, 11, chapter 5, *passim*
    town, 55, 137
Peterborough
    absolution, 120
    attendance at court, 94
    charges, 73
    class imbalance, 143
    completion of business, 100
    decline, 49
    excommunications, 119
    numbers summoned to the court, 90–2
    probates in the 1650s, 150
    prosecutions numbers, 91, 92
Peters, Robert, 88
Petersfield, 137
Phillipps, Edward, 71
Phillips, Thomas, 19
Pippen, Jane, 59
Pistor, Robert, 69, 105
play on the Sabbath, *see* Sabbath
Poor, William, 48, 124, 127
poor law
    Acts (1576, 1598, 1601, 1610, 1662, 1685,
        1692), 51, 74, 149, 152
    encroachment on the church courts, 27, 51,
        149, 175, 183
Popham, Thomas, 49
Popish Plot, 76, 152
population, 15–16, 85–6, 90, 103, 168–9
Portsmouth, 153
Potter, Jean, 2, 4, 73, 143
Prerogative Court of Canterbury, 150
Presbyterians, 74, 75, 77, 115n74, 116n88,
    167, 181

presentments
  accusations or preliminary charges and not
    guilt, 61, 101
  churchwardens and presentments, 17, 20,
    67, 112, 134, 161
  definition of presentments, 20
  disjunction between presentments and
    cases in court, 60
Price, John, Chancellor of Worcester, 31, 172,
  173, 174
Proctor, Mary, 71, 106
prosecutions, *see* charges; citations; moral
    charges; religious charges; church rate
    charges; churchwardens; clergy;
    Quakers; Catholics; secular courts
Prosser, Henry, 19
Protectorate, 5, 55, 75, 76, 106, 111, 148, 152
Protestants, *see* dissent
Prynne, William, 123
  punishment, 96, 97, 113
  excommunication of, 22–3, 118
punishment, *see* death penalty;
    excommunication as a punishment;
    fines; imprisonment; penance
Puritans
  freedom (1650s), 75
  offices (magistrates, lectureships), 108, 167
  opposition to church courts, 123
  persecution of (1590s/1600s), 39, 58
  Sabbath, 57, 107

Quaife, Geoffrey, 3, 73, 83n130, 88, 114n27
Quakers, 74
  numbers, 108
  prosecutions (secular), 60, 75, 153
  prosecutions (visitations), 60
  quarter sessions, 75, 108, 149, 150, 153,
    176, 178n62, 185
  see also secular courts
quarter sessions
  capture of the sessions by Puritans, 108
  collapse of borough courts in the 1640s,
    150
  encouragement by bishops of quarter
    sessions, 153–4, 176
  encroachment on church courts, 149, 151,
    152, 153, 154
  prosecutions against dissenters and
    recusants, 75, 108, 149, 153, 175–6

Ranters, 74
Reason, Robert, 20
rector, *see* clergy
recusancy, *see* Catholics
recusancy rolls, 109–10, 150
reform, church courts
  1604 Canon Law, 179
  1660s, 179–81
  nineteenth-century reform, x
Reformation, x, 55, 148, 183
Reformation of Manners, 163, 168, 174–5,
  176
registrars, 25, 34, 146, 179
religious issues

baptism, 57
charges or prosecutions against
    lay people, 52–62, 161
  church attendance, 52–3
  communion, 55–6
  dissent and recusancy, 57–61
  misbehaviour in churches/churchyards, 61–2
  Sabbath, work and play on, 53–5
  shifting balance of charges, 72–3, 162
  standing excommunicate, 62
  Worcester (all charges), 161–2
  see also church courts (charges)
religious divergence, *see* Catholics; dissent
Restoration (1660)
  ageing bishops, 181
  charges against
    churchwardens, 66–7
    clergy, 69
    laity, 47–54
    shift of charges to religion, 55, 73, 132,
      163
  church court attendance, 93–4
  completion of business, 100
  compurgation, 23, 26, 127–8, 129
  convictions (guilt), balance and decline in
    the 1660s, 103
  ex officio oath, 26, 123, 127, 181
  legacies of the 1650s
    missed opportunity, 179
    security concerns, 75–152
  orders from court, 132
  penance, 131, 138
  recovery of the sittings 1661, 87
  reform of the courts, 180
  summonings to church courts, 90, 91
Richards, Joan, 60
Ridley, Thomas, Chancellor of Winchester
  attendance at court, 32, 33
  experience, 29
  pluralism, 30
  qualifications, 28
  scholarship, 34
  surrogates, 35, 40
Ringwood, 137
Ripple, 59
Rivett, Timothy (surrogate), 35, 36
Robertson, George, 64
Robinson, Francis, 147
Rocke, Philip, 135
Romsey, 63, 103, 107
Ropley, 133
Rood, Edward, 105
Root and Branch Petition (1640–1), 179
Rowe, Elizabeth, 61
Rowington, 99
Rowley Regis, 132, 140
Royal Commission on the Ecclesiastical Courts,
  185
rumour, 47, 49, 112 *see also* evidence; church
    courts
Rye House plot, 76, 152
Sabbath (breaking), work and play
  Acts, 1690s, 176
  cases, 53, 54
  charges (prosecutions)

INDEX   **249**

in church courts, 46, 53, 54, 55, 95, 154, 161
in secular courts, 75, 149, 176
convictions (guilt), 96, 97, 102, 103
dissent, recusancy and their relationship to breaches, 57, 107
types of work and play, 53, 54
sacraments, x, 119, 155n6, *see also* baptism; communion
St Alban, John, 97, 126
St Mary Bourne, 92, 96
Salisbury, 73, 143, 159n147
Salkelite, John, 20
Sancroft, William, Archbishop of Canterbury, 179, 180
Sands, Emanuel, 49
Saunders, Jane, 56, 99
Searle, John, 96, 126–7
Searle, Richard, 53
sects, *see* dissent
secular courts
  encroachment on church courts, 5, 26–7, 51, 149–54, 175–6, 183
  strengths of, 128–30, 139
  failings, 182
  see also assizes; quarter sessions; church courts/encroachment
security concerns, 5, 74, 75, 76, 77, 79, 106, 144, 149, 152, 183
Seekers, 74
Selden, John, 151
sentencing, *see* orders; penance; church courts
Settlement Act (1662), *see* poor law
Severn Stoke, 132
sex before marriage
  charges, 1, 47–8, 161
  evidence
    gossip, 47, 49
    pregnancy, 47–8
  penance, 131
  see also charges; church courts
Shalfleet, 99, 132
Shallett, Joseph (deputy), 35, 36
Sharrock, Robert
  pluralism, 36
  position (surrogate), 35, 36
  qualifications, 35
  scholarship, 18, 36, 40
Sheldon, Gilbert, Archbishop of Canterbury
  inquiry, Compton Census, 58, 76, 108
  reform of the church courts 121, 179, 180, 181
the Sheldons, 108, 167
Sherier, Edward, 97
Sherman, John, 52
Shrieve, Richard, 126
Shrawley, 137
significavit, 24, 62, 120, 125
simony, 18, 71
skimmingtons, 139–40
Slaie, John, 61
Slape, James, 49
Smith, Bartholomew, 19
Smith, Thomas, 133
Sneade, Richard, 99
Snow, Bennetta, 48, 124–5

social, change in attitude, 5, 130, 140–1, 175, 183, 185
Somerset, 14, 15–16, 16–17, 55–6, 73, 109, 149, 153, 167
Southampton, 56, 65, 107, 132, 138, 153
South Warnborough, 132
Spaeth, Donald, 3, 4, 164, 184
Sparsholt, 66, 131, 136, 138
Standish, David, 35, 36
Steeven, Hugh, 54
Stieg, Margaret, 143
Stillingfleet, Edward, Bishop of Worcester,
  charge (his episcopal), 164
  disciplining clergy, 166
  dissenters 163
  law and the courts, 19
  morals (and Reformation of Manners) 164, 165, 172
  reform of the courts, 179, 180
  rescue of the courts, 173–4
  restraint of the court, 170, 172
  sittings in court, 39–40, 163
  toleration, 164
Stoddey, William, 61, 132, 137
Stogursey, 61, 104, 132, 137
Stone, Hugh, 61
Stourbridge, 52
Stradling, John, 47
Stratford, 167
Stuckie, George, 49
Studley, 139
Suckley, 71
summoning to court
  churchwardens, 91
  clergy, 92
  decline of, 90–1, 113, 119
  excommunicates, 62
  lay people, 89–91
surplice, *see* clergy; church court charges
Surrey, 6, 9, 14, 15, 16, 26, 29, 30, 153, 176
Sweete, Nichola, 122, 123
Symes, Richard, 19, 48, 131, 136, 138
Symond, Edward, 53–4

the Talbots, 108, 167
Tangley, 135
Tardebigge, 105
Tarver, Anne, 3, 164, 176, 183–4, 186n31
Taunton
  town, 71, 86, 108, 131, 132, 167
  for archdeaconry, *passim*
taxation, clerical, 181
Taylor, Anne, 98, 138
Taylor, William, 60
Tenison, Thomas, Archbishop of Canterbury, 164, 176
Test Acts (1673, 1678), 59, 77
Thirlby, Charles (deputy), 35, 36
Thistlewaite, Peregrine (deputy), 35
Thomas, William, Bishop of Worcester, 159n147
Thornborough, John, Bishop of Worcester, 39, 78, 153, 176, 181
Thorne, George, 53
the Throckmortons, 107–8, 167

Thruxton, 98
the Tichbornes, 24, 60, 108, 141–2, 143, 147, 167, 197
Till, Barry, 3, 4, 184
Tillotson, John, Archbishop of Canterbury, 164, 179
Timsbury, 70, 106, 135
Titchfield, 97, 109
toleration (religious toleration)
    in the 1650s, *see* Instrument of Government, Humble Petition and Advice
    Act 1689, 163, 165
    effect on church courts, xi, 163–4, 167, 174, 175, 182–3
Tomkins, John, 131
Traske, Mary, 97
Trebeck, Andrew (surrogate), 34
Trussell, William (surrogate), 35, 36
Tucker, Welch, 137
Turton, John, 132
Turton, William, 132
Tutball, John, 61
Twyford, 66, 109

Underdown, David, 112, 154
Underhill, Richard, 105
Unitarians, 175
Upham, 132
Upper Clatford, 99
Upton Grey, 19, 105, 135
Upton on Severn, 66, 67

vagrancy
    Acts, 51, 74, 149, 152, 175
    causes of, 148, 183
    encroachment of the secular courts, 27, 149, 152, 153
    numbers of vagrants, 110
    security (motive for persecution), 5, 74, 76, 77, 78, 79, 106, 144, 149, 153, 183
    treatment of vagrants, 149, 154, 175
Vane, Sir Henry, 179–80
verdicts in the church courts, *see* guilt
vicar, *see* clergy
vicars general, *see* chancellors
viis et modis, 21, 25, 37, 118
visitations
    system, 10, 16–17, 19–20
    articles, 18–19, 20, 78
    churchwardens and presentments, 17, 20, 67, 104, 112, 133
    at Worcester, 3–4, 7, 39, 53, 56, 57, 60, 67, 72, 79, 90, 97, 100, 102, 111, 120, 132

Wakelie, William, 61
Walker, Robert, 49
Ward, Joanna, 137
Ward, Seth, Bishop of Salisbury, 159n147
Wardall, John, 132
Warmestry, Thomas (surrogate), 34, 35, 36
warnings, *see* orders; church courts
Warwick, 108, 149, 153, 164, 167–8, 169, 175, 176

Watt, James, 53–4, 132
Watts, Michael, 11, 12, 41n3, 167
Wayte, John, 132
Wayte, Thomas, 19, 52
Webb, Ambrose, 69
Webb, John, 61
Weild, 92
Wellington, 67
Wells, Alice, 50, 131
Wells
    St Cuthbert, 109
    for Taunton archdeaconry proceedings, *passim*
West Buckland, 96, 135
Wherwell, 96
Whitchurch, 106
White, Henry, 125, 137
White, Richard, 137
Whiteman, Anne, 11, 15, 73, 184
Whitgift, John, Archbishop of Canterbury, 107, 110
Whitestaunton, 61
Whittall, William, 135–6
Wickham, Edward (surrogate), 35, 36
Wilkins, John, 49
Willett, Ralph (surrogate), 34
William the Conqueror, x
William of Orange, 109, 163
Wilton, 61
Winchester
    parishes and city, 69, 97, 136, 138
    quarter sessions, 150
    workhouse or hospital, 175
    for archdeaconry, diocese and court, *passim*
Wither, George, 138
Withers, Robert (surrogate), 34
Withycombe, 97
Withypool, 137
Wixford, 76
Wonston, 97
Wood, Thomas, 170
Woodhouse, William (surrogate), 35, 36
Worcester
    city, 70, 175
    for archdeaconry, diocese and court, *passim*; *see also* dean and chapter; church courts; population; visitations
Worcestershire, 14, 15–16, 16–17, 108, 109, 149, 162, 167–8
work on the Sabbath, *see* Sabbath
Wrightson, Keith, 3, 112, 143

Yacron, Anthony, 95
Yardley, 62
Yate, Edward, 171
York, 2, 16, 34, 73, 94, 119, 143, 146, 147, 150

Printed in the USA
CPSIA information can be obtained
at www.ICGtesting.com
LVHW042218151223
766085LV00003B/11